Complex Systems and Applied Linguistics

Published in this series

Complex Systems
and Applied Linguistics

DIANE LARSEN-FREEMAN
LYNNE CAMERON

To: Heekyeong,

Happy Teaching

and Learning!

Diane Larsen Freeman

OXFORD
UNIVERSITY PRESS

OXFORD
UNIVERSITY PRESS

Great Clarendon Street, Oxford OX2 6DP

Oxford University Press is a department of the University of Oxford.
It furthers the University's objective of excellence in research, scholarship,
and education by publishing worldwide in

Oxford New York

Auckland Cape Town Dar es Salaam Hong Kong Karachi
Kuala Lumpur Madrid Melbourne Mexico City Nairobi
New Delhi Shanghai Taipei Toronto

With offices in

Argentina Austria Brazil Chile Czech Republic France Greece
Guatemala Hungary Italy Japan Poland Portugal Singapore
South Korea Switzerland Thailand Turkey Ukraine Vietnam

OXFORD and OXFORD ENGLISH are registered trade marks of
Oxford University Press in the UK and in certain other countries

© Oxford University Press 2008

The moral rights of the author have been asserted

Database right Oxford University Press (maker)

First published 2008

2012 2011 2010 2009 2008

10 9 8 7 6 5 4 3 2 1

ISBN: 978 0 19 442244 4

Printed and bound by Eigal S.A. in Portugal

Contents

Acknowledgments

We gratefully acknowledge the many scholars who have contributed to this book by either reading the entire manuscript and offering comments (Paul Meara, Leo van Lier, Henry Widdowson) or by doing the same with a portion of the manuscript. In alphabetical order they are Lyle Bachman, Nick Cameron, Nick Ellis, John Holland, Jin Yun Ke, John Schumann, Ari Sherris, John Swales, Elka Todeva. The usual caveat applies, in that it is we who bear full responsibility for what we have written. In addition, we are grateful to Mickey Bonin for getting us together. Diane Larsen-Freeman would also like to extend her gratitude to the students in her course, 'Chaos/Complexity Theory', offered at the Applied Linguistics Summer Institute at Pennsylvania State University during the summer of 2005 for their many helpful questions and comments.

We also need to acknowledge the patience and guidance of Cristina Whitecross of Oxford University Press and of our editor, Simon Murison-Bowie. We appreciate Gad Lim's assistance with the preparation of the index. We are grateful to all these people, plus, of course, our families and friends for their continuing support during the long gestation of this project.

We are grateful to the following for permission to reproduce figures:

Anthony S. Kroch. 1990. 'Reflexes of grammar in patterns of language change'. Language Variation and Change. Cambridge University Press. One figure from page 223 (adapted from A. Ellegard 'The auxiliary do: The establishment and regulation of its use in English' in F. Behre (ed.). Gothenburg Studies in English. Almqvist and Wiksell, Acta Universitatis Gothoburgensis, Stockholm).

Paul Meara. 1998. 'Towards a new approach to modelling vocabulary acquisition' in N. Schmitt and M. McCarthy (eds.). Vocabulary, Description, Acquisition, Pedagogy. Cambridge University Press.

Michael Muchisky, Lisa Gershkoff-Stowe, Emily Cole, and Esther Thelen. 1996. 'The epigenetic landscape revisited: A dynamic interpretation' in C. Rovee-Collier, L. P. Lipsitt, and H. Hayne (eds.). Advances in Infancy Research, Vol. 10. Ablex Publishing Corporation.

Esther Thelen and Linda B.Smith. 1994. A Dynamic Systems Approach to the Development of Cognition and Action, figures 3.8 and 3.10. © 1994 Massachusetts Institute of Technology, by permission of the MIT Press.

Preface

Many of the ideas in this book—'complexity' and 'chaos,' for example—excite the imagination. Such terms are certainly evocative. Nevertheless, the terms, and importantly, the concepts underlying them, do not mean the same within the theory we present here as they do in everyday language. 'Chaos' does not mean complete disorder, and 'complexity' does not mean complicated. The complex systems approach we adopt in this book originated in the physical and biological sciences, and these terms have precise meanings within these disciplines. As the complexity approach has moved out from physics and biology to the human sciences, and even to the humanities, these terms and associated concepts have been used in an extended way that springs from analogical and more general applications. Indeed, here, we do not use the approach to calculate equations or to model systems; instead, we use the approach for a complexity description of topics of concern to applied linguistics. However, even when describing, we think it is essential to stay as true as possible to the original meaning of the terms. For this reason, following the introductory chapter in which we attempt to situate a complexity approach both within its originating fields and within fields closer to applied linguistics, we have included two chapters that introduce the terms as they are used in their source disciplines in order to create understandings that we extend and apply more descriptively in subsequent chapters.

Complexity theory is a perspective that we encountered independently—one that we both concluded helped us make sense out of, and bring coherence to, our experience in applied linguistics and to ask questions we might not have otherwise asked. It is a way that we have found both challenging and exhilarating. The challenges have come, first of all, in grappling with literature from outside of our field—research reports and theoretical discussions in mathematics, physics, and biology. One of us has some knowledge of mathematics, and that has helped a little, but our reading of the complexity theory literature has, out of necessity, been selective. A second challenge has been in 'translating' our understanding into applied linguistics. This has been somewhat easier to do, as we are both applied linguists, and although we have different areas of primary interest, we are well steeped in the issues in our focal areas. Often, attributes of complex systems in one field, such as ecology, have much in common with characteristics of other fields such as immunology or economics. As a result, the complex systems approach is inherently interdisciplinary; insights and results can be translated across fields. Nevertheless, a challenge remains, and that is to avoid making superficial comparisons across disciplines.

As complexity theory originated in the physical sciences, we are also sensitive to accusations of being overly enamored with the physical sciences. Applied linguistics research investigates language—its learning and its use— and thus it is an endeavor that seeks to understand fundamentally human phenomena. Nevertheless, science, at its best, in its openness to exploration and discovery and in its commitment to empirical rigor, has qualities that we value. As educators, the 'attitude of inquiry' of science (Larsen-Freeman 2000a) is one that we find laudable and worthy of emulation. Further, since the present century has been characterized as the century of biology, it should not be surprising, being alive at this point in time, that we should find attractive and illuminating a theory whose roots lie in biology.

However, we admit to a more nettlesome problem. In writing this book, we have faced the dilemma of how to talk about matters of complexity theory. This is because our ways of knowing are so bound up with the language we use to discuss them. For this reason, developing a new perspective is also a language challenge—one that we have not always found straightforward ourselves. It is easy to fall back into old ways of thinking, and requires continual monitoring to ensure that ways of talking (or writing) reflect complex dynamic ways of thinking.

We are also fully aware of the risks of importing theories from outside our discipline. It is quite natural to analogize; indeed, that is precisely one way new meaning is made, a theme on which we elaborate below. However, there is a risk in analogizing if it does not come from a deep understanding, and that is why the following chapters contain the detail they do. Clearly, from the fact that we have chosen to write this book, we believe that the benefits promise to outweigh the risks. The final challenge, then, and perhaps the most demanding one of all, is the need to address the question that any applied scholar must—the 'so what?' question.

So what does this promised new way of looking at issues deliver? How has our understanding and practice as researchers and teachers been altered? Are we, as a result, closer to solutions to real-world problems involving language, its learning, and its use? Are we better practitioners? These have proven to be daunting questions, around which we will have much to say in subsequent chapters. Given the nascent research in complex systems and applied linguistics, the tentative nature of our claims is quite natural, and we hope easily understood. In any case, it seemed sufficiently important to share the insights that this new view has afforded us at this point in time, in order that we might encourage others to join in the quest for making sense out of the 'new science' of complexity, as it is often referred to.

The science we make use of has been called the 'new science' even within its source disciplines. It is certainly new to applied linguistics, although there are signs to suggest that interest is growing within our field. Some indication of this growing interest is provided by the colloquia organized by Ellis and Larsen-Freeman on emergentism at AILA 2005 in Madison, Wisconsin; de Bot on methodology of dynamic systems theory at the joint American and

Canadian Associations for Applied Linguistics Conference in Montreal, 2006; and by Schumann and his students on the interactional instinct and Atkinson on sociocognitive dimensions of second language acquisition at the American Association for Applied Linguistics Conference 2007 in Costa Mesa, California. We are certainly not the only ones to be exploring a complexity approach to see what it has to offer applied linguistics, and we will be drawing on the work of colleagues as well as our own here. Nevertheless, it is still very early on in the development of the approach and certainly in its application to topics of concern in applied linguistics. For this reason, there will be questions that readers will have that will remain unanswered, and no doubt some of our ideas are inchoate. This book opens a conversation and invites collaboration with others. It is not the last word.

I

Complexity theory: what's it all about?

In our daily lives, complexity and constant change can be difficult to live with. One way we cope is to seek the comfort of routines. Another way is to downplay the continual change that we experience by turning the living, dynamic world into named objects and thinking about them as fixed entities, as river, tree, city, or person. We turn our life experiences into stories, and our continually changing selves into sets of more or less fixed attributes, attitudes, and identities.

The same preference for an artifice of simplicity and synchronicity appears in our scholarly work. Change is inherent to most of our concerns as applied linguists, and yet in our theories we everywhere find processes converted into objects. A post-modern response to over-simplification of the world through a focus on entities is to fragment and disperse, to deny wholeness by making it multiple, hybrid, and difficult to grasp. Complexity theory, in contrast, embraces complexity, interconnectedness, and dynamism, and makes change central to theory and method.

Complexity theory aims to account for how the interacting parts of a complex system give rise to the system's collective behavior and how such a system simultaneously interacts with its environment. The field of complex systems intersects traditional disciplines of physical, biological and social sciences, as well as engineering, management, economics, medicine, education, literature, and others. Its power comes not only from its application to many different disciplines, but also from the fact that it can be applied to many different levels. It can, for example, be applied to neurons in the human brain, cells and microbes in the human body, and flora and fauna in an ecosystem as well as to more social activities such as the way information flows over a social or computer network, the dynamics of infectious disease transmission, and the behavior of consumers and firms in an economy. Each of these phenomena works as a 'complex system'.

It is important to note from the outset that the word 'complex' has a special meaning as used here. It does not merely mean complicated. Although the agents or components in a complex system are usually numerous, diverse, and dynamic, a defining characteristic of a complex system is that its behavior emerges from the interactions of its components.[1] The emergent behavior is often non-linear, meaning disproportionate to its causal factors. In other words, sometimes a great deal of energy may be expended with nothing to show for it; on other occasions, the slightest pressure on the system can have dramatic effects, such as the dire consequences for our ecological system from even a slight temperature rise. The agents or elements in a complex system change and adapt in response to feedback. They interact in structured ways, with interaction sometimes leading to self-organization and the emergence of new behavior. They operate in a dynamic world that is rarely in equilibrium and sometimes in chaos.

Complex systems have been referred to by a number of names depending on which dimension of their behavior is being emphasized. To emphasize the fact that they change over time, they are often referred to as 'dynamic(al) systems' and to emphasize the fact that adaptation and learning occur in these systems, they are sometimes called 'complex adaptive systems'. The complex systems in which we are interested have no distinct permanent boundaries; they are not a 'thing' themselves. They exist only through the fluxes that feed them, and they disappear or become moribund in the absence of such fluxes. For example, a tropical cyclone comes into being due to certain sea and air current conditions, and it is sustained by them. When these change, such as when a tropical cyclone hits land, it weakens and eventually dies out. Of course the overall weather system remains, and if the conditions that caused the first cyclone prevail, then a new cyclone might be spawned further up the coast; however, the particular perturbation caused by the original cyclone disappears in the absence of the fluxes that fed it.

Some antecedents of complexity theory

Complexity theory has many disciplinary progenitors; therefore we can only be selective in tracing its genealogy here.[2] In this section we point to particular key influences on the development of complexity theory; the next two chapters elaborate on them. We begin our treatment in 1940 with the work of biologist Conrad Waddington. Waddington challenged the assumption of the day, which was that genes carried the full description of an organism's form. Instead, he showed that genes are only the starting point for embryogenesis. Once embryogenesis is underway, each step in the process of development creates the conditions for the next one. In other words, 'the form of the body is literally constructed by the construction process itself—and is not specified in some pre-existing full instruction set, design or building plan ...' (van Geert 2003: 648–9).

Biologist von Bertalanffy (1950) followed in proposing 'general systems theory' to account for how complex order arises.[3] Von Bertalanffy opposed reductionism in explaining an entity as the sum of the properties of its parts, advocating instead a systems approach—understanding the relationships among the parts which connect them to the whole.

In the 1970s, chemist Ilya Prigogine (Prigogine and Stengers 1984) would contribute to this line of thinking through the study of systems that he called 'dissipative'. A dissipative system is open to energy from outside of itself, which, once taken in, leads to reactions out of which complex patterns self-organize. Self-organization is the creation of more complex order spontaneously; the resulting more complex structure is not planned or managed by an outside source. Thus, the study of dissipative systems focuses on the close interplay between structure, on the one hand, and change (or dissipation) on the other.

Also, in the 1970s, Chilean biologists Humberto Maturana and Francisco Varela (1972) came to an important awareness from their study of vision, which contributed to the evolution of complexity theory. They came to realize that vision was not received by the nervous system as a camera lens receives an image, but rather it is from light and color that our eyes construct images. Based on this insight, they proposed that living organisms are characterized by what they termed 'autopoiesis'. Autopoietic systems continually change and build new structures while maintaining their identity.

Developments in the 1980s shifted to the search to understand the increasing order and structure in open systems. Haken (1983) and Kelso (1995) worked on the relationship between components of a system which give rise to a new macroscopic order not present in any of the components, an interdisciplinary study called 'synergetics'. In 1984, the Santa Fe Institute was founded and became an important independent research center for a multidisciplinary understanding of complex adaptive systems. Many researchers were involved in this effort; here we can but cite a few of the major figures.[4] We do so along with the books they wrote for a lay audience because the titles of such works are telling: biologist Stuart Kauffman's (1993) *The Origins of Order: Self-organization and Selection in Evolution* and (1995) *At Home in the Universe: The Search for the Laws of Self-organization and Complexity*, physicist Murray Gell-Mann's (1994) *The Quark and the Jaguar: Adventures in the Simple and the Complex*, and computer scientist/psychologist John Holland's (1995) *Hidden Order: How Adaptation Builds Complexity* and (1998) *Emergence: From Chaos to Order*.

Overlapping a great deal with complexity theory is 'dynamic systems theory', whose lineage is more mathematical than biological. At the turn of the century, the French mathematician Henri Poincaré developed the study of non-linear dynamics as a mathematical discipline in its own right. However, it especially took off when the digital computer was developed after World War II. Even the early models allowed for the study of complexity and dynamism unheard of in the history of science up until that point in time. The development of the computer also led to some fundamental ideas about systems represented in new systems approaches such as 'cybernetics' (Wiener 1948; von Neumann 1958).

In the 1960s, the French mathematician René Thom (1972, 1983) began to study the properties of general systems that exhibit sudden changes, more particularly of discontinuities, which he called 'catastrophes'. 'Catastrophe theory' involves the description of the (sudden, abrupt) discontinuities induced by the continuous local perturbations of a system. The catastrophes, sometimes triggered by small changes, result in sudden and unpredictable shifts in the behavior of the entire system.[5] About this same time, using the computer to model weather systems, meteorologist Edward Lorenz also observed the sudden switches in behavior that Thom had identified. Lorenz further pointed to the fact that simulated dynamic weather systems settle into regular, but never identical patterns, called 'strange attractors'. Lorenz also found that some of these patterns are highly sensitive to initial conditions, an observation that became known as 'the butterfly effect' from the title of a paper given by him in 1972 to the American Association for the Advancement of Science in Washington, D.C. entitled 'Predictability: does the flap of a butterfly's wings in Brazil set off a tornado in Texas?'. The flapping wings of the butterfly represent a small change in the initial condition of the system, which affects a chain of events leading to a large-scale phenomenon like a tornado. Had the butterfly not flapped its wings, the path of the system might have been vastly different. These observations are more likely these days to be associated with 'chaos theory'.

Chaos theory is the study of non-linear dynamical systems, i.e. systems that do not unfold over time in a linearly predictable manner. Such study has 'revealed the chaotic nature of a wide variety of physical systems' including certain classes of neural networks (van Gelder and Port 1995: 35–6). It is important to note, however, that in this context, chaos is not complete disorder, but is rather behavior that arises unpredictably in a non-linear system. Because of their complexity and because the trajectories of chaotic systems are susceptible to even minor perturbations, at no point in time in the evolution of such systems can chaos be predicted.

Applying complexity theory

Despite their diverse origins, this research and these theories have left their mark on what we will refer to as 'complexity theory'. Complexity theory deals with the study of complex, dynamic, non-linear, self-organizing, open, emergent, sometimes chaotic, and adaptive systems (Larsen-Freeman 1997). In the last twenty or so years, complexity theory has been taken from its originating fields of biology, mathematics, and physics, and applied in other disciplines. Business management was early on the scene, adopting ideas and terms from complexity theory to understand organizations as complex systems (Battram 1998) and dynamic processes such as supply and demand chains. Economists working at the Santa Fe Institute and elsewhere developed models of economic systems as complex adaptive systems, and epidemiologists have modeled the spread of disease as a complex system.

Closer to our own field, developmental psychologists have seen the potential in applying dynamical systems theory to child motor development and other human systems (Thelen and Smith 1994; Port and van Gelder 1995) and have suggested enticing possibilities for other areas of psychology:

> A dynamics systems approach to cognition and action provides a biological ground for cultural and contextual accounts of human cognition ... mental life as emergent from the activities of everyday life. (Thelen and Smith 1994: 329)

More recently, in psychology, Spivey has developed a complex dynamic view of mind that he calls 'continuity psychology' (Spivey 2007). He aims to convince cognitive psychologists of the inadequacies of a computer metaphor of mind and of the viability of a replacement view that sees the mind in continual flux and mental processes as continuously dynamic. According to Spivey this entails dropping 'the assumption of stable symbolic internal representations ... continuing on to a fully ecological dynamical account of perception, cognition, and action' (ibid.: 332) that connects brain, body, and world.

In our own field of applied linguistics, Larsen-Freeman (1997) wrote explicitly about the value of seeing second language acquisition from a chaos/complexity theory perspective, following up in 2002 (2002a) by showing how such a perspective can help to overcome the dualism that often besets our field. Meara (1997, 2004, 2006) used dynamic modeling to describe vocabulary development or loss. More recently, de Bot, Lowie, and Verspoor (2005, 2007) have applied dynamic systems theory to second language acquisition, and Herdina and Jessner (2002) have used it to discuss changes in multilingual proficiency on an individual level and to provide a more dynamic description of multilingualism. Lee and Schumann (2003) have used the lens of complex adaptive systems to view the evolution of language. Cameron (2003a) has applied complexity theory to the dynamics of metaphor in discourse showing how language and conceptual development interact. Most recently, contributors to a special issue of the journal *Applied Linguistics* (December 2006), co-edited by Ellis and Larsen-Freeman (2006), have addressed a number of issues of concern to applied linguists, using complexity theory in an emergentist approach.

It seems that the tide of complexity is lapping at our feet as applied linguists, making it timely to consider how the assumptions and perspectives of our own field may be challenged by complexity. In the pages that follow, we suggest that complex systems can be found throughout applied linguistics. The language used by a discourse community can be described as such a system, as can the interactions of learners and their teacher in a classroom, as can the functioning of the human mind. We aim to show that reconceptualizing these and other phenomena in terms of complexity opens up the possibility for new understandings and actions.

Is anything ever new?

Again, it is right that we pause to pay homage to our forebears. Certainly, some of the propositions that we entertain in this book are not new. For instance, the ancient Greek philosopher Heraclitus viewed the world as constituted of a constant flux, a ceaseless river, an endless play of forms and figures. The Renaissance, as Widdowson (personal communication) has pointed out to us, was obsessed with 'mutabilité' and how to cope with it—religious belief was one way of imposing order on perpetual change. The Enlightenment sought rational alternatives through the philosophy of science, but there was never any denial of variation and change, nor any pretence that the underlying general laws proposed accounted for every particular.

Nevertheless, resolving the tension between the two poles of stasis and dynamism has been elusive. In more modern times, the tension has been characterized by what Bernstein (1983) called 'the Cartesian anxiety'. Varela *et al.* elaborate:

> This feeling of anxiety arises from the craving for an absolute ground. When this craving cannot be satisfied, the only possibility seems to be nihilism or anarchy. The search for a ground can take many forms, but given the basic logic of representationism, the tendency is to search either for an outer ground in the world or an inner ground in the mind. By treating mind and world as opposed subjective and objective poles, the Cartesian anxiety oscillates endlessly between the two in search of a ground.
> (Varela *et al.* 1991: 141)

The search for groundedness in the mind led linguist Chomsky (1965) to investigate mental competence rather than performance, while sociolinguists, such as Weinreich, Labov, and Herzog (1968: 99) sought to find order in the social world by creating 'a model of language which accommodates the facts of variable usage ... and leads to a more adequate description of linguistic competence'. Applied linguists have followed suit, preferring to explain the facts of language acquisition either through an appeal to a mental competence (for example, Gregg 1990), or by taking language use factors into account, showing patterns in variability (which have led them to coin and use the hybrid term 'variable competence' (R. Ellis 1985; Tarone 1990). But mental competence, when it is seen to be 'irreducibly self-contained, cannot meaningfully relate to the world "outside"' (Leather and van Dam 2003: 6)—which applied linguists must do—and the hybridity of more socially-oriented approaches have tended to treat the world (context) as an independent variable that influences linguistic form, not as a dynamic system itself. Here, perhaps, complexity theory may contribute to a resolution.

From a complexity theory perspective, there is nothing static about language. There is no need to distinguish performance from competence. Humans 'soft assemble' (Thelen and Smith 1994) their language resources in order to respond in an intentional way to the communicative pressures at hand. As they do so, patterns emerge, such as those language-using patterns that manifest in linguistic corpora. However, performance stabilities arising from the dynamics of language use are transformed with further usage (Bybee 2006). Since the patterns are variegated in form (Tomasello 2000), even the very categories of language itself are negotiable and subject to change. Moreover, the context of language use is no more pre-existing and external to the language user than are language resources. In other words, context is not a stable background variable outside the individual that affects linguistic choice. Instead, a complexity theory view sees the individual and context as coupled. Because of the coupling, the context itself can change in a process of co-adaptation between the individual and the environment.

This shift in perspective

> reflects the necessity of understanding cognitive systems not on the basis of their input and output relationships, but by their *operational closure*. A system that has operational closure is one in which the results of its processes are those processes themselves.
> (Varela *et al.* 1991: 139–40)

The advantage of this type of explanation is its 'reciprocal causality' (Thompson and Varela 2001), in which there is 'upwards' emergence of the patterns from individuals interacting, which is none the less 'downwardly' constrained due to both the historic trajectory of the system and by its present-day sociocultural norms. Thus, a complexity theory-informed view—one shared by Varela *et al.* and ourselves—rejects classical Darwinism which, like the behaviorism it spawned, viewed the environment as external to and independent of the organism (Juarrero 1999: 108).

Complexity theory goes one step further. Not only is there ongoing interaction between the sociocognitive (our preferred term) and the environment, it is also the case that humans shape their own context. As such, seeking an explanation for individual differences in cause-effect patterns and generalizable findings does not fit a complexity theory perspective either. It 'is no longer sufficient to talk about individual differences in SLA against a backdrop of a universal learner … variation becomes the primary given; categorization becomes an artificial construct of institutionalization and scientific inquiry' (Kramsch 2002: 4; Larsen-Freeman 2006b); as Kramsch says, paraphrasing Yeats: it may not be possible 'to tell the dancer from the dance'. More recently Ushioda (2007) puts it this way: 'The unique local particularities of the person as self-reflective intentional agent, inherently part of and shaping his or her own context, seem to have no place in [the earlier] kind of research'.

Although we will return to these ideas throughout this book, for now, we submit that complexity theory offers us new ways of conceptualizing and perceiving, changing our 'objects of concern' into processes, change, and continuities. While complexity-informed research is new to applied linguistics, it is growing. Not surprisingly, many of the details we discuss here remain to be worked out. None the less, applied linguistics should, at the very least, seriously consider what is on offer and how it might contribute to the development of our field.

On human agency and critical stances

Some applied linguists, having listened to us talk about complexity theory, have expressed to us their concerns about its potential to deny human agency. The self-organizing nature of complex systems may make it appear that human volition or intention has no part to play in shaping language resources. Once the system is set into motion, it 'self-organizes'. We understand this interpretation and therefore the objection. However, the concern can be dispelled, we think, with a clarification. It is not that human intentionality is ignored. We certainly accept the fact that humans make choices in the moment to employ the semiotic resources, including linguistic ones, they have at hand to realize their transactional, interpersonal, self-expressive, etc. goals and the multiple dimensions of self and identity, affective states, and social face. However, it is not contradictory to state that, at the same time that humans are operating in an agentful way, the resources of the language in the individual and in the speech community are being transformed beyond the conscious intentions of their speakers. It is not that we plan to change language; language changes. As historical linguist, Rudy Keller (1985: 211) observes: 'Language is thus a consequence of human actions, albeit actions which are only unintentionally transformative'. We return to the issue of human agency at the end of Chapter 3 and throughout the book.

Others have raised questions about the possibility of adopting a critical stance in complexity theory. Can it really deal with issues of power and control? Can it be transformative, in the sense of seeking social change? If self-organization and sensitivity of the system to initial conditions suggest inevitability, then is a system simply fated to go on reproducing itself? In the social world, such an outcome would resemble a situation where 'the rich get richer and the poor get poorer'. These are important questions, for which we can only respond in a general way at this point. While complexity theory may not show us what kind of intervention will right an unjust system, it does help us to understand the system better. As with any theory, the responsibility for how it is used lies with its users. Moreover, one of the relevant issues arising out of a complexity understanding is that in our efforts to rectify injustice in an *open* complex system, little, if anything is foreclosed. The system is always open to change.

Enlightenment, and even Marxist, understandings of causality are guided by what Osberg (2007) calls 'a logic of determinism'. This logic is based on a linear and individual conception of cause and effect, in which self-determined causes yield somewhat predictable consequences; causality is based on processes that are fully determined. As such, there is no freedom within the process for anything else to occur. However, there is an alternative to this logic available in complexity theory. Complexity theory suggests that, in complex dynamic systems, the system has the freedom to develop along alternative trajectories, what (Osberg 2007) calls 'a logic of freedom':

> This is a logic in which choice is an *operator* in the process itself—part of its internal 'mechanics'—not something that happens to a process, something applied to it from the outside. Since emergent processes are not fully determined—they contain within themselves the possibility of freedom—the logic of emergence could therefore also be characterized as a *logic of freedom* (rather than a logic of determination).
> (Osberg 2007: 10)

Thus, for complex systems, while a system's potential might be constrained by its history, it is not fully determined by it. 'Knowing how to negotiate our way through a world that is not fixed and pre-given but that is continually shaped by the types of actions in which we engage' (Varela *et al.* 1991: 144) is a challenge of being human.

What if?

In our view, the most important shift in perspective offered to applied linguists by complexity theory is the view that the world is not composed of 'things', stable objectified entities. Instead, change and adaptation is continuous in the world and the phenomena that comprise it, and any perceived stability emerges from the dynamics of the system. In what follows, we pose a series of 'What if?' questions, which follow from this shift of perspective. What if we view applied linguistic concerns from this perspective? How will we understand or do things differently?

- What if dichotomies that have been axiomatic in certain linguistic theories, such as the one between performance and competence, obscure insights into the nature of language and its learning rather than facilitate them? The fact is that language is being continually transformed by use, 'structure-process' Bohm calls it (in Nichol 2003). As such, the dualistic thinking is perhaps unnecessary (Larsen-Freeman 2002a). While this is not a new insight, of course, complexity theory forces us to contend with, not ignore, the dynamism of language and all the messiness it engenders.
- What if applied linguists should be seeking to explain how language learners increase their participation in a second language community rather than, or in addition to, how they acquire the language of the community (Sfard 1998)? Since its modern day origin, many SLA researchers have been motivated to arrive at an understanding of the language acquisition process that is essentially cognitive and individual. They seek to understand the acquisition of a mental grammar. Others have been arguing all along that the language acquisition process is a social act and cannot be accounted for

at the level of the individual cognition. What if these two positions can be united in a sociocognitive understanding of language development?

- What if the process of learning and the agents who engage in it, i.e. the learners, cannot be usefully separated (Larsen-Freeman 1985)? It has been assumed in some areas of language learning research that some day researchers will reach an understanding of the process of language acquisition, apart from learners themselves. But is it truly possible to separate the learner from learning, or is it the case that each individual achieves the success that he or she does in a unique way? What if individual routes to acquisition/participation no longer need to be idealized away (de Bot, Lowie, and Verspoor 2005)?

- What if language is viewed as an open, continually evolving, system rather than a closed one? Concepts such as 'end-state' grammars would be anomalous since open systems are constantly undergoing change, sometimes rather rapidly. If there is no end state to language, it may be unhelpful to think in terms of fossilization as an end state to second language learning (Larsen-Freeman 2005).

- What if learning another language is a matter not only of learning conventions, but also of innovation, of creation as much or more than reproduction? It would follow that teaching should not be characterized as helping students develop the same mental model of language that the teacher possesses, even if this were possible, because such a view would encourage the teaching of conformity to uniformity (Larsen-Freeman 2003). Moreover, if this is all that is achieved, should we be surprised if we leave students to contend with 'the inert knowledge problem' (Whitehead 1929), whereby they learn the rules and conventions of a language, but cannot use them in real time for their own purposes?

- What if we truly understand that teaching does not cause learning? At best, there is a non-linear relationship between the two. It follows, then, that classical experimental design in which significant differences are attributed to pedagogical 'treatments' could be more generous or more penurious than they should be when it comes to ascribing value to the 'treatment', i.e. the effects that are found could be due to teaching that occurred before the experiment; conversely, the effects of the treatment might not be visible immediately.

- What if language learning tasks are not viewed as static 'frames', but rather more variably, evolving through use by individuals (Coughlan and Duff 1994)? Furthermore, what if tasks are seen, not as providing input, which then migrates piecemeal to inside the learner's head, but instead as providing affordances (van Lier 2000)?[6] From the latter perspective, learning is construed as 'the development of increasingly effective ways of dealing with the world and its meanings' (van Lier 2000: 246).

- What if understanding through talk is achieved, not by choosing words to contain meanings and then placing meanings on the table for one's interlocutor to pick up, but rather is the result of the dynamics of the system? And what if all aspects of language use are dialogic (Bakhtin 1981), involving some construction of the other person in one's mind in order to speak in a way that caters specifically for him/her, attending to his or her response and using this as adaptive feedback?

• What if absolutist prescriptions and proscriptions about teaching are doomed to fail because they do not take into account the organic nature of change and the fact that pedagogic interventions are more valuable when they are adaptable, rather than expected to sustain standardization? If, instead, for example, we see learners and teachers as continually adapting to what others in the classroom do, then we have new ways of understanding why certain teaching interventions may fail and of developing better ones.

As descriptions of applied linguistic problem areas, the above 'what ifs' may not be new—what is new is the application of complexity theory to link across them. We think that complexity theory offers greater coherence in explaining what we already know. Further, as we have already indicated, it offers new methods of research, and it opens new fields of enquiry that we would not otherwise have noticed and new ways of intervening in applied linguistic problem areas.

Complexity theory: metaphor or more?

Sometimes when we have talked or written about using ideas from complexity theory, we have been challenged as to whether we are 'just' being metaphorical. There are two ways to answer this question: firstly, to reject the 'just' and to assert the importance of metaphor; and secondly, to discuss what it would mean to say that the comparison between systems in applied linguistics and complex systems is more than metaphor. Our contention, to be supported throughout this book, is that complexity theory offers applied linguistics at least an important new metaphor that brings with it new ways of thinking about issues in the field, and, maximally, may push the field towards radical theoretical change.

The necessity of metaphor

Metaphors are not just literary tools for ornamenting language; they are indispensable to the human mind. Whenever we have to contemplate the abstract, voice the difficult, or make sense of the complicated, we turn to metaphor. Metaphor enables us to 'see' or understand one thing in terms of another, through analogies[7] or mappings between two conceptual domains[8] (Cameron 1999). Consider two metaphorical statements:

1 The brain is the body's control center.
2 The brain is a computer.

The 'target domain' i.e. the topic of the metaphor, in each of the statements is *the brain*. In statement 1 the metaphor 'source domain' is 'the body's control center', and in statement 2 it is 'a computer'. The transformation brought about through the metaphorical mapping of source to target domains is much more than a substitution of one lexical item with another; it includes processes of interaction (Black 1979) and/or blending (Fauconnier and Turner 1998) of the constructs, values, and affect connected to the lexical items, processes that may produce new understandings and perspectives not just in the target domain but in the source too.

Importantly, the domains linked by a metaphorical mapping are distinct or different in some ways. The more poetic the metaphor, the wider the 'distance' between the domains. Statement 1 above, 'the brain is the body's control center', comes from a children's science text where it was used to explain how the brain moves the limbs. A picture was used to illustrate and encapsulate the metaphor, with a cross-section of the head showing a control center such as might be found in an airport or railway. The brain was divided into rooms, labeled 'legs' or 'arms', full of machines with levers and switches, and manned by operatives whose task was to coordinate the actions of the rest of the body. This metaphor helps convey some of the workings of the brain, but it is limited in its explanatory power because, in essential ways, the brain is *not* like a concrete control center with separate functions.

Statement 2 above, 'the brain is a computer', bears some resemblances to the control center metaphor, but, in the form of 'information processing' or 'the computational mind' metaphor, it has had a huge impact on cognitive science and linguistics over the last decades. Metaphors, in mapping from one domain to another, carry not just single ideas, but networks of connected ideas. When a metaphorical idea is developed into a collection of linked metaphors that are used to talk and think about some aspect of the world, it starts to function as a model or theory. Boyd (1993) calls these productive analogies 'theory-constitutive metaphors'. This is what happened with the theory of the brain as information-processor. From the analogy between the brain and the computer, scientists and linguists developed computational models of the brain, which used concepts from computing to understand brain functioning and suggested further lines of research and theory development. What began as a metaphor became a useful tool for investigation and theorizing, and underpinned the cognitive paradigm across a range of disciplines.

Over time, the metaphorical nature of analogies can gradually get lost, as awareness of domain differences fade and similarities strengthen. Metaphors can become so familiar that we forget they are metaphorical and start to see them as 'the truth'. This may be what happened to the 'computational mind' metaphor in linguistics (as suggested by Lantolf 2002: 94). In the field of language teaching, for example, terms such as 'input' and 'output' became just the 'normal' way to talk about listening and speaking. In downplaying or disregarding differences between the domains of the analogy, there is a risk of building too high on metaphorical foundations. When speaking becomes 'output', for example, we can lose sight of how humans construct meaning through social interaction.

The limits of the 'brain as computer' metaphor are currently being more and more widely discussed, and new metaphors and theories are being introduced by socioculturalists, cognitive linguists, and by those of us who find our inspiration in complexity theory. The minimal claim that we are making for complexity theory is that it adds another way of understanding phenomena in our applied linguistic problem space. A much stronger claim would be that complexity can push the field into a paradigm shift, a radical change of theory-constitutive metaphors (Kuhn 1970). Spivey (2007), for example, makes exactly this claim for the field of cognitive psychology. Our stance is that the next years may indeed see a paradigm shift into complexity-inspired theories in applied linguistics, but there is much work to be done in order to evaluate the wisdom of such a move; this book aims to provide some of the background needed to make such judgments.

In the history of ideas, metaphor has often been responsible for provoking shifts in thinking across and within disciplines. The source domains of metaphors are affected by the 'zeitgeist', and it is no coincidence that a move away from machine and computer metaphors to ecological or complexity metaphors seems to be happening at this point in our history, when the negative impact of technology on climate is becoming increasingly salient, and when globalization and local, everyday life are becoming ever more connected. The computer metaphor of mind took hold of the shared consciousness of psychologists and others at a point when computers appeared full of promise and excitement, opening up new possibilities through their speed and accuracy. It is perhaps not surprising that metaphors of complexity, dynamics, and emergent wholeness appear particularly seductive just now. Maasen and Weingart (2000) examine the spread of metaphors in 'the dynamics of knowledge', and pay particular attention to the use of metaphors from the field of 'chaos theory', which is nowadays seen as part of complexity theory but which attracted a great deal of interest in its own right around the early 1990s. They describe the stages in which metaphor shifts between everyday language and scientific disciplines: firstly, lexis is borrowed from everyday language into science (for example, 'memory', 'chaos', 'complexity') where it is assigned specific, technical meanings; then the ideas are metaphorically transferred across into other disciplines (for example, from physics to biology, brain science, or organization theory); finally, the theoretical ideas become the source domain for metaphors back into everyday language, carrying with them a sense of scientific authoritativeness (for example, 'evolution' and 'survival of the fittest' applied to social life). With the complexity metaphor or analogy, we find ourselves in the middle stages, where ideas are transitioning across disciplines and also beginning to seep back into everyday language with their newer technical senses attached.

There are various dangers attached to metaphor that it is useful to be aware of. A first problem can arise when an idea like 'chaos' has both a scientific and an everyday sense. The use of terms can evoke resonances and meanings simultaneously from both arenas, which may lead to muddy thinking or 'intellectual impostures' (Sokal and Bricmont 1998). Technical or mathematical terms may be used in ways that are actually wrong or meaningless but sound impressive and authoritative.

Secondly, it has long been acknowledged that the bringing together of source and target domains in metaphor both 'hides and highlights' aspects of the domains (Lakoff and Johnson 1980). Aspects of the target domain that are connected easily and vividly to the source domain will be highlighted; while other aspects of the target domain may be hidden, because there is no corresponding aspect of the source domain to be applied. If we compare Juliet to the sun (as in the oft-quoted Shakespearean metaphor), we highlight her beauty and importance, but hide other aspects that may be important, such as her family background. N. Ellis (2007) addresses this danger in his response to de Bot *et al.*'s (2007) application of dynamic systems theory to second language acquisition. He warns that, in highlighting individual variability, the dynamic systems analogy plays down, or hides, well attested regularities in language development across individuals. In this chapter we have already addressed the issue that a systems metaphor may background human agency. As with any use of metaphor or analogy, we need to be alert to what is being hidden by our choice of metaphor, as well as what is being highlighted, and take seriously the need to explain the limits of mappings—what cannot be claimed from a complex systems perspective, as well as what can.

A third risk lies in assuming that a single metaphor, even one that taps into an extensive network of concepts, will suffice to underpin theory. Because of the domain differences that lie at the heart of metaphorical mappings, no single metaphor can ever serve as a complete mapping from one idea to another. To build better theory or understanding we need to bring in additional metaphors (Spiro *et al.* 1989). Complexity theory may offer a very rich analogy to applied linguistics, but it is unlikely to be sufficient, and will need to be complemented with other theories and/or other metaphors, in turn raising the question of compatibility.

The fourth potential problem with using metaphor is that, if a metaphor is to be employed effectively and validly, users need a certain level of knowledge of the source domain. Cameron (2003a) showed some of the problems that arise in understanding metaphors when either or both of the two domains involved in a metaphor are unfamiliar. In these instances, restricted knowledge can lead to the cross-domain mappings shifting from their intended meanings. To prevent mis-mappings, and inaccurate use of the complexity metaphor, a good understanding of the basics of the theory is vital, and we will attempt to provide that in this book. We will explain the concepts of complexity theory and examine how they can be mapped in a justified and consistent manner on to applied linguistic domains.

Despite the risks associated with reasoning through metaphor and analogy, these tools are indispensable. Every attempt to understand the world builds on previous understandings in some way, and metaphor offers a particularly imaginative and far-reaching building method.

More than metaphor

Complexity theory will serve applied linguistics as more than metaphor if it works as a bridge that takes us into a new way of thinking or theoretical framework, that is then rigorously developed within the field. The metaphor serves as 'a temporary aid to thinking' (Baake 2003: 82) and is eventually literalized into field-specific theory, research, and practice.

As an idea like complexity spreads to fields outside its origins in mathematics and science, and as it is used more widely, there is a broadening and loosening of theoretical commitments such as defining criteria for categories (Maasen and Weingart 2000; Baake 2003). For example, classification criteria for complex systems in originating fields are very explicit, whereas, for applications outside these originating fields, criteria seem to be 'deliberately vague' (Baake 2003: 197). Holland (1995) presents an explicit definition, in which a complex system must show evidence of seven basic properties and mechanisms, but also offers a broader, vaguer definition, in which complex adaptive systems are systems that exhibit 'coherence in the face of change' (1995: 4). Given this slippage in the nature of criteria, it becomes more and more difficult to distinguish claims of classification from claims of metaphorical similarity. If we claim, for example, that 'interlanguage is a complex system', do we mean that interlanguage fulfils the criteria for being a complex system or that interlanguage is metaphorically like a complex system? What we need to be able to do, if complexity theory is to move past its metaphorical and bridging role, is to develop a field-specific classification: i.e. we need to be able to answer that question using criteria defined for the field of applied linguistics. Categorization is just one aspect of theory-building alongside others, including: the relationship to other theories and existing work; clarification of the nature of hypotheses; what counts as data and evidence; the role of description, explanation, and prediction; and the development of empirical methods. We return to these issues in Chapter 8.

In this book, we aim to present complexity theory as a metaphorical bridge for readers and to contribute to the development of a complexity theoretic framework for applied linguistics.

Complexity in relation to existing theories

When reading the 'What if?' section, the reader might have thought about one or more theories that address the same issues. As complexity theory is appropriated across the social sciences for its 'multidisciplinary power' (Wilson 2000: 4), it may not replace existing theories, but rather work at a supra-disciplinary, more abstract, level than current theoretical frameworks, offering a general set of patterns, outcomes, and descriptions that can be applied to many different sorts of systems (Baake 2003). We propose that applied linguistics has much to gain from looking to complexity. What might this involve for theory?

A theory or theoretical framework is used to describe and explain (and, in some paradigms, also to predict) empirical phenomena. Theory and theorizing are as essential to responsible work in the human and social sciences, as they are in the natural sciences. It is actually impossible to work, or live, without theorizing. Every minute of the day we are categorizing and making assumptions, predicting and explaining. In order to do something as simple as catching the bus to work, we use and construct theories about how heavy the traffic will be at different times of day, how various streets connect with each other, or the expected procedures for buying tickets. This informal and intuitive theory-building is part of our cognitive capability as human beings. Formal theory-building builds on this capacity, making assumptions explicit, labeling categories precisely, and testing explanations for logical consistency and congruence with what is observed in the real world.

The theory that we choose to work with, explicitly as researchers and perhaps implicitly as teachers, will dictate how we describe and investigate the world. It controls how we select, out of all that is possible, what to investigate or explain, what types of questions we ask, how data are collected, and what kinds of explanations of the data are considered valid.

In deciding which type of data to collect, a complexity theory approach with its central focus on dynamics, requires us to look for change and for processes that lead to change, rather than for static, unchanging entities. Furthermore, data are not cleaned up before analysis to get rid of inconvenient 'noise' (de Bot, Lowie, and Verspoor 2007). We expect data to be noisy and messy because the dynamics of complex systems produce variability. In addition, a key feature of complexity theory is that context is seen as an intrinsic part of a system, not as a background against which action takes place. When data are collected about a complex system, information about context is thus automatically included as part of the data.

A complexity approach requires new ways of explaining language-related phenomena that do not rely on reductionism and that move away from simple cause-effect explanations to explanations that involve processes of self-organization and emergence. For example, complex systems approaches to language acquisition do not require innate knowledge of language rules, but explain the development of language through self-organization in the mind of individuals engaged in social interaction and through self-organization at levels higher than the individual. In addition, complexity theory requires us to revisit the idea of predicting behavior. Whereas positivist research is based on the assumption that there are universal laws and thus sets predictability as a goal of the research process, from this complexity theory perspective, no two situations can be similar enough to produce the same behavior; thus predictability becomes impossible. We do know, though, at a more general level the types of behavior likely to occur in complex systems and can map from the specific system we are concerned with to possible and probable patterns.

Conceptual tools for a complexity theory approach

The central focus in a complexity approach is the study of the behavior of complex systems. The next two chapters describe in detail the key characteristics of these dynamic, open, non-linear systems. The understanding of complex systems provides the core of theoretical frameworks for the applied linguistic concerns of language use, first and second language development, and language classrooms. It needs to be complemented with other, compatible, theories that together cover all that needs to be described and explained about the phenomena of interest. For example, to theorize about language classrooms, we need a theory of instructed learning and social interaction, as well as a theory of language. In what follows, we discuss briefly what conceptual tools and theories we have drawn on in building our complexity theory approach.

We have taken much from applications of *dynamic systems theory* to human development (Smith and Thelen 1993; Thelen and Smith 1994; Kelso 1995; Port and van Gelder 1995). Dynamic systems theory does away with the distinction between competence and performance (de Bot, Lowie, and Verspoor 2005). Dynamic system researchers feel no need to invoke an underlying mental competence to explain human behavior in context. Instead, an organism's ongoing activity continuously changes its neural states, just as growth changes the physical dimensions of the body.

Emergentist approaches to language (MacWhinney 1998, 1999) have been offered as an alternative to grammars which specify a fixed set of rules to account for grammatical sentences, and, as such, can serve a complexity approach in accounting for certain aspects of language development. Emergentism in first language acquisition (for example, Bates and MacWhinney's 1989 Competition Model) and in second language acquisition (N. Ellis 1998, 2005; Ellis and Larsen-Freeman 2006; Larsen-Freeman 2006b; Mellow 2006) are closely aligned with a complexity theory approach to language development.

Connectionism features models that usefully describe the dynamics of some aspects of language use and development (Gasser 1990; Spivey 2007). Connectionists use computers to model neural networks in the brain, and these networks are complex dynamic systems. Certain nodes in connectionist networks modeling language are strengthened as language data are taken in; others are weakened. Language can thus be seen as a 'statistical ensemble' of interacting elements (Cooper 1999: ix), constantly changing. Because of their dynamic nature, connectionist models combine language representation with language development, obviating the need for two different theories (Mellow and Stanley 2001). Thus, 'Connectionism provides a conceptual vehicle for studying the conditions under which emergent form arises and the ways in which emergence can be constrained' (Elman *et al.* 1996: 359). However, connectionism treats time in a particular way that is not always compatible with the complexity approach we are developing. Furthermore, because forgetting in most connectionist learning is 'catastrophic', whereby the learning of something later replaces the learning of something earlier and makes the earlier learning irretrievable, connectionist models of a certain sort—those that operate with a back propagation algorithm—do not lend themselves to models of second language acquisition (Nelson 2007). In the end, connectionism still lies within a computational metaphor of brain/mind. It is useful, but there are limits to its usefulness.

When it comes to seeing language in complexity terms, several existing linguistic theories share with our complexity perspective the assumption that language forms emerge from language use. *Usage-based grammar* (for example, Bybee 2006), *emergent grammar* (for example, Hopper 1988, 1998), *cognitive linguistics* (for example, Langacker 1987, 1991; Barlow and Kemmer 2000; Croft and Cruse 2004), and *construction grammar* (Goldberg 1999) take grammar to be the result of one's experience with using language. *Corpus linguistics* (for example, Sinclair 1991), *conversation analysis* (for example, Schegloff 2001), and *computational linguistics* (for example, Jurafsky *et al.* 2001) have given applied linguists access to the nature and range of experience an average speaker has with language, which increases our understanding of language as an emergent system.

Probabilistic linguistics, unlike traditional linguistics, embraces the variability of linguistic behavior and sees linguistic regularity as an endpoint, not a means (Pierrehumbert 2001; Bod, Hay, and Jannedy 2003). Probabilistic linguists treat linguistic phenomena non-categorically, i.e. they seek to account for the gradience of linguistic behavior manifest, for example, in judgments of well-formedness that are not absolute, but rather display properties of continua. Probabilistic linguistics assumes not only that language changes over time, but also that it is inherently variable, making it compatible with a complexity approach.

Although, as with complexity theory, functional linguistic theories do not abstract language from its context in an attempt to get at its essence, unlike complexity theory, many do not construe language use as a dynamic process. Perhaps Halliday's *systemic-functional linguistics* (for example, 1973), which sees language as a social process that contributes to the realization of different social contexts, comes closest. Halliday's grammar is functional 'in the sense that it is designed to account for how language is used' (Halliday 1994: xii), offering a principled basis for describing how and why language varies in relation to both who is using it and the purposes for which it is used (Halliday and Hasan 1989). The importance systemic-functional linguistics accords aspects of social context in the way that influences speakers' use of available language resources for making meaning is compatible with ideas presented in this book.

Harris' *integrationist linguistics* presents another theory that overlaps some of our premises. Integrationist linguistics see linguistic signs not as 'autonomous objects of any kind, either social or psychological', but as 'contextualized products of the integration of various activities by individuals in particular communication situations' (Harris 1993: 311). This type of linguistics is situated or contextualized, that is, the roles of language in social activity are the core of the definition of language (van Lier 2004: 20). Further, integrationism declines to accept that text and context, language and world are distinct and stable categories (Toolan 1996).

When we consider learning and interaction, Vygotskyan *sociocultural theory* (for example, Lantolf and Pavlenko 1995; Lantolf 2006a) can helpfully be part of a complexity theoretic framework that erases the boundary between language learning and language using (Cameron 2003a; Larsen-Freeman 2003). Van Geert (1994) argues that Vygotsky's zone of proximal development (ZPD)[9] can be cast in the form of a dynamic systems model, which produces a variety of non-linear growth patterns. Most importantly, with its central precept that language using and learning are social processes, sociocultural theory (for example, Lantolf 2006a) shares with complexity theory the idea that learning and language can emerge from the interactions of individuals.

Sealey and Carter's (2004) *social realist approach* also sees human agency in relation to social phenomena, and as such, can provide a complexity approach with many concepts around the interconnection of structure and agency.

Ecological approaches in applied linguistics take a specific complex system, an ecological system, to use as a base metaphor to account for how language users and learners interact with their environment or context. Ecological approaches (see, for example, the contributions in Kramsch 2002; Leather and van Dam 2003; van Lier 2004), which focus on an understanding of relationships, can thus contribute to a complexity framework in many ways. Ecological approaches force an awareness of the interconnectedness of individuals, pairs of individuals, communities, etc., or as Clarke (2007) puts it, of 'systems within systems within systems'.

As the book proceeds we draw in these approaches and theories to build up a complexity approach to applied linguistic issues.

This book

We begin Chapter 2 by exploring the concepts comprising complex systems. Concepts are introduced throughout the chapter, beginning with the idea that a 'system' is an ensemble of components and that relations among the components give it some identity as a whole. We then contrast simple systems, in which the relations among components do not change, and complex systems, in which relations do change, often in a non-linear way. The central properties of complex systems are introduced, exemplified, and discussed in relation to applied linguistic systems: dynamism, complexity, openness, non-linearity, self-organization, adaptation, and emergence. The chapter then moves to a discussion of recent advances in understanding the nature of change in complex systems, brought about by increased computer power and new mathematical modeling techniques. These advances mean that complex systems no longer have to be idealized into simpler systems, but can be understood in their own right.

In Chapter 3, we explore the consequences of two contrasting types of change that can occur in a complex system: steady change and sudden change. The reader is introduced to the topological images and constructs that are used to describe system dynamics, in which system change is seen as movement in a trajectory across a 'state space' or 'phase space'. We explain how non-linearity can lead to sudden and dramatic change, called a 'phase shift', and how this is described in terms of 'attractors'. In a summary of the complex systems background, a procedure for exploring applied linguistics systems in terms of complexity is laid out. We go on to explore the relation of theory and world. We explain what, from a complexity theory perspective, is seen to be in need of empirical investigation. We examine the nature of hypotheses and theories, discussing what counts as data, how they are collected, the role of context, what counts as evidence, and the nature of descriptions and explanations, particularly causality. The issue of human agency and intentionality is discussed and linked to ethical responsibility.

Having laid the ground work and, having promised not only challenges but also exhilaration, we proceed in the following four chapters to show how complex systems theory can lead to new awareness in applied linguistics. In this chapter, we have previewed some of these in our 'what if' statements.

In Chapter 4, on language and its evolution, we point out that distinctions such as competence versus performance that underpin certain linguistic theories give rise to a convenient, but problematic, assumption that language structure is independent of language use. However, this longstanding view is now being challenged by functional, cognitive, and probabilistic linguists and by connectionists, emergentists, and developmental psychologists, who hold that linguistic representations are the product of speakers' experience of language. These usage-based approaches to language and language development view grammar, phonology, and lexis alike as dynamic systems that emerge from frequently-occurring patterns of language use rather than as fixed, autonomous, closed, and synchronic systems. This is because complexity theory connects real-time processing and all its variability to change over time. The value of this perspective is that language is no longer perceived as an idealized, objectified, atemporal, mechanistic 'thing'. The value to applied linguists is that they have access to a conceptualization of language that is much more appropriate for dealing with developmental issues, for connecting language use and language learning.

In Chapter 5, we look at first and second language acquisition (SLA) from the perspective of complexity theory. Everyone who has studied language acquisition knows that it is both systematic and variable. Much effort in SLA has gone into addressing such questions as 'What does systematic mean?' and 'How can a learner's interlanguage be termed "systematic" when in most researchers' data, there appears to be such variability?' This issue is aggravated by the fact that so much of the variability appears to be random—sometimes a target form is supplied in an obligatory context, other times it is not—leading to characterizations of learner performance as unsystematic, even 'volatile' (Long 2003). Faced with such volatility, it is reasonable to ask if learner language is systematic at all. While from a complexity theory perspective it would be hard to sustain the notion of an interlanguage representing discrete linear stages between two points of competence, as we shall see in Chapter 5, instability and variability of performance need not be seen as a threat to the notion of systematicity in (inter)language. Thus, if we view interlanguages as complex dynamic systems, then the question of whether an interlanguage is systematic or variable no longer arises, and we can concentrate on how to find the systematic patterns in variability.

In Chapter 6, we use the constructs of complex systems to describe discourse, and begin by reinterpreting face-to-face talk as a trajectory of a coupled system. This framework is applied to show how various discourse phenomena, from adjacency pairs to genres and idioms, can be described in complexity terms. We find an intriguing way of seeing language use as a property of the discourse and not of individuals, with individuals only having latent potential for language use until they realize this in a discourse environment. Traditional theories of language as system have no space for the figurative, and yet it is a pervasive and inherent feature of language use, and, as such, needs to be accounted for. Premature rejection of aspects of language in use, as imposed by Saussurean and Chomskyan approaches to linguistic theory, seems particularly risky for applied linguistics—we need theories about real-world language use to inform research into real-world language use.

In Chapter 7, we will see how complexity theory gives us a means to account for emergent phenomena in collective ways that reflect interaction between people, minds, and language in language classrooms. While resisting the idea of a 'complexity method' as inappropriate, we offer four essentials of a complexity approach to the language classroom and illustrate them through reinterpreted data from second and foreign language situations. Every class of students and teacher shows different patterns of interaction and behavior. Seeing how teacher–student language use co-adapts into stable patterns can help to diagnose problems and to devise suitable interventions in order to better manage the dynamics of learning.

Of course, it is also important to ask about the 'empirical directives' coming out of a complexity theory approach (Candlin, comment in Kramsch 2002: 91), which make it distinctive from other approaches. We therefore conclude this book with a discussion in Chapter 8 of what a research agenda for applied linguistics from a complex systems perspective would look like. In this last chapter we review the 'empirical directives' of a complexity approach, examining adaptations of existing methods alongside new methods such as mathematical modeling, formative experiments, and design studies.

Conclusion

The surge of interest in our field in chaos and complexity metaphors over the last few years suggests that it has a particular and timely appeal. The focus on connectedness, change, and dynamics fits with what people see happening to their lives with the drive towards globalization, increases in computing power, the speed and pressure of a postmodern life, the apparent unpredictability of world events, and the recognition of joint responsibility for ensuring survival on planet Earth. However, we believe that complexity theory, as metaphor or as over-arching approach, offers much more than merely a fit to the zeitgeist and can make a valuable contribution to the development of applied linguistics, to its ontology, and to its epistemology. Some, such as the complexity scientist Kauffman (1995: 303–4) would go further

> If the theories of emergence we have discussed here have merit perhaps we are at home in the universe in ways we have not known since we knew too little to doubt. I do not know if the stories of emergence ... will prove to be correct. But these stories are not evidently foolish. They are bits and pieces of a new arena of science, a science that will grow in coming decades toward some new view of emergence and order in this far-from-equilibrium universe that is our home.

Notes

1 Notice that this is different from saying that the whole is greater than the sum of its parts.

2 We draw on van Gelder and Port (1995) and van Geert (2003) for some of this discussion.

3 Among others who worked with this theory were anthropologists Margaret Mead and Gregory Bateson and economist Kenneth Boulding.

4 Waldrop (1992) gives a historical review of the scholars associated with the Santa Fe Institute in his book *Complexity: The Emerging Science at the Edge of Order and Chaos.*

5 The importance of catastrophe theory to linguistics and semiotics—an issue Thom himself has expounded—comes from the fact that it is most directly concerned with a dynamical conception of syntactic structures, a proposition developed by the school of 'morphodynamics'. The theory has essentially to do with the effect of local (quantitative, micro-) variations on global (qualitative, macro-) structure.

6 An affordance is an opportunity for use or interaction presented by some object or state of affairs to an agent. For example, to a human being, a chair

affords sitting, but to a woodpecker it may afford something quite different (Clark 1997: 172), just as a hole in a tree is an affordance for a woodpecker, but not for a sparrow.

7 There is no clear boundary between metaphor and analogy, especially when metaphor is seen as conceptual as well as linguistic. Many metaphors rely on analogy (although some metaphors seem to connect domains imagistically) and some analogies are metaphorical, because they make connections between very different domains.

8 The concept of 'domain' is problematic and has been discussed at length within cognitive linguistics (for example, Croft and Cruse 2004). It is used here as a convenient shorthand for the concepts or ideas attached to a lexical item.

9 The ZPD is defined as the difference between what a person can do on his or her own and what the person can do when working with others or a more knowledgeable other.

2

Complex systems

This chapter begins the process of explaining the nature of complex systems. As we saw in Chapter 1, we need to understand complexity, and thus complex systems, as the source domain of our metaphor/analogy in order to create meaningful and valid mappings on to problem spaces in applied linguistics, and for the further purpose of developing complexity-inspired theory and tools for our field.

In this chapter, we take a close look at the characteristics of complex systems and at what distinguishes them from other sorts of systems. We will see that an important feature, perhaps the most important feature, of complex systems is *change*. These systems are in flux all the time; there is no stopping them. Therein lies their basic appeal to applied linguists, and their intrinsic similarity to the kinds of systems that we deal with: language, discourse, classrooms, learning—these are also dynamic. To take just one of these as an example, the learners in a language classroom are dynamic as a group; the group that the teacher meets one day will be different when she meets them the next day. Friendships flourish and decline; health problems come and go; windy weather makes students more lively, while hot humid weather may make them less responsive; lesson activities may motivate or disappoint. In all sorts of ways, the group is never the same two days running, or even from one minute to the next. This is what we mean by 'dynamic'.

Existing theory often removes the dynamism from the systems by, as it were, stopping the changing system at one point in time. This stalled system, now static and fixed, becomes the object of study and analysis. Complexity theory offers theory and methods for understanding systems in change. By putting time and change back into our applied linguistic systems, we suggest we can reach better understandings of the processes of using and learning language.

As we meet complex systems and their characteristics in this chapter and the next, we explain them and illustrate them with examples from the natural world and from applied linguistics. These chapters reflect something of the processes of our own encounters with the theory, as the new ideas we encountered in complexity theory resonated with the applied linguistic problems we tussle with on a daily basis. Our aim though is to go beyond a feeling of resonance, in which a description from complexity theory strikes one as importantly parallel to some aspect of applied linguistics. We aim to establish understandings of these, sometimes difficult, concepts so that we can develop, in Chapters 4–7, a more closely argued case for using complexity theory to build a new framework, in which descriptions and explanations of patterns of behavior derive from 'robust and typical properties of the systems, not [from] ... details of structure and function' (Kauffman 1995: 19).

What is a system?

In the abstract and as a broad definition, a system is produced by a set of components that interact in particular ways to produce some overall state or form at a particular point in time. Systems differ from sets, aggregates, or collections, in that belonging to the system affects the properties of the components. For example, the experience of belonging to a secondary school system affects students: they may wear uniforms, be influenced by school values, or be inspired by their teachers. We might take the 'earth-moon duo' as another example of the system effect (Juarrero 1999: 109). Certain properties of the earth, such as its ocean tides, only exist because of the moon; the moon's orbit results from the gravitational pull of the earth. The earth and moon, or school students and their teachers, belong to systems, not just to collections.

The connections among components create a kind of unity or wholeness about the system. Each of the following are systems, some simple, some complex:

- a traffic light system
- a transport system
- the solar system
- a living cell
- an ecological system
- a grammatical system
- a speech community
- a city
- a domestic heating system.

A system has elements that interact to form a connected whole.

Not all the exemplar systems listed above are 'complex'. Traffic lights and a domestic heating system are not complex but simple systems, since they have just a small number of elements of a single type, together with predictable patterns of behavior. A complex system has different types of elements, usually in large numbers, which connect and inter-

A complex system is a system with different types of elements, usually in large numbers, which connect and interact in different and changing ways.

act in different and changing ways. The technical term 'element' is non-specific, encompassing animate and non-animate entities, people and animals, as well as 'objects' like planets and trees. In complexity theory, system elements are sometimes called 'agents', a term used to refer to individual humans and other animate beings, as well as aspects and combinations of them: an agent might be an individual, a household, a nerve cell, a species.

The rest of the chapter elaborates this initial description of complex systems, beginning with the system components, and using a very simple system as a starting point.

The components of complex systems

In so-called 'simple' systems, a small set of similar components are connected in predictable and unchanging ways. In the system that is a week, the component elements are days that follow each other in a strict order. In the system that is the (UK) traffic lights, there are three lights that appear in a fixed sequence: red; red and amber; green; amber; red—and then again, and again. Figure 2.1 shows the successive states of this simple system. The three different colored lights are the elements of the system; their different combinations produce four permutations that are made use of in stopping and starting traffic. The system works successfully to organize traffic because the sequence of the lights is predictable to road users, and because each state of the system has a meaning; for example, drivers know that an amber light means that the traffic will shortly have to stop.

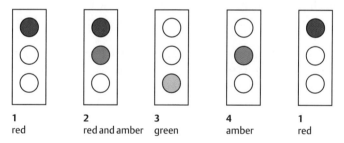

Figure 2.1 The (UK) traffic light system

The traffic light system moves through the four stages, repeatedly and predictably. It is a simple system, largely unaffected by the actions of drivers or other aspects of the environment. An alternative visualization of the system moving through these stages, or states, is shown in Figure 2.2.

A domestic heating system is another 'simple' system, in that it has a small number of components, radiators perhaps, or convector heaters that are connected through timers, thermostat, and switches. The interactions between the heaters lead to the house being heated to various levels during the day or night. The different levels of heating that are produced as the timers and

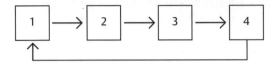

Figure 2.2 The traffic light system moving through its four states

thermostat switch the heaters on and off are the successive states of the heating system. The behavior of this simple system is completely predictable (Battram 1998).

With simple systems, if we know the 'rules' that elements follow in their interactions, the future state of the system can be predicted. So if we see a red and amber light, we can confidently predict that green will follow; if it is the middle of an autumn afternoon, and we know that the timer on the heating system has been set to start at four, we can predict that the house will soon be warmed up.

One way in which complex systems often differ from simple systems is in having many different types of elements or agents; i.e. they are 'hetero-geneous'. If we take a town's transport system as an example of a complex system, the agents in the system include citizens, drivers, and policy makers, while other elements will include roads, vehicles of various sorts, and traffic laws. The ecosystem of a forest would include as component agents: animals, birds, insects, and people, while component elements would include trees, winds, rainfall, sunshine, air quality, soil, rivers. Not only are there many components, but, in these complex systems, they are of different kinds or types.

> Heterogeneity: the elements, agents, and/or processes in a complex system are of many different types.

The components of a system may be processes, rather than entities. An alternative way to see the forest ecosystem, for example, would be as a set of interconnected processes: processes of growth and decay, of feeding and digestion, of mating and breeding. Cognitive systems are process systems rather than concrete systems like the earth and moon (Juarrero 1999:112). Language-using systems may also be seen as process systems.

The components of complex systems may them-selves be complex systems, and thus 'subsystems' of the bigger system. If we take the city as a complex system (Wilson 2000), it can be seen as having many interacting subsystems: the road system is a subsystem, city planning is a subsystem, the school system could be taken as a subsystem, and so on.

> The elements, agents, and/or processes in a complex system may themselves be complex systems.

Applied linguistic complex systems are likely to contain many subsystems. For example, if we see the speech community as a complex system, then it will also have within it sociocultural groups that themselves function as complex systems; individuals within these sub-groups can be seen as complex systems, as can their individual brain/mind systems. There are complex systems 'all the way down' from the social to the neurological levels. The complexity of a complex system arises from components and subsystems being interdependent and interacting with each other in a variety of different ways.

The dynamics of complex systems

A dynamic (or, more accurately, dynamical[1]) system is, quite straightforwardly, one that changes with time, and whose future state depends in some way on its present state. As humans we are aware of being dynamic; we live in the dimension of time. We mark its passing with festivals and celebrations. We notice the signs of our bodies' change over time, with excitement in youth and with regret as we get older. At some levels, however, we think and operate as if time did not matter. In our daily lives and at a human level, the constant motion of subatomic particles is irrelevant. We give people and things names, conflating dynamism and permanence. A tree is labeled with the noun 'tree', as if trees were static entities that did not change, like tables. Sometimes we suddenly become aware of dynamism that we previously ignored, as happened in 2006–2007 when warm, dry summers, storms and floods were seen, not just as isolated phenomena, but as connected into a larger, dynamic picture called 'climate change' or 'global warming'.

In the type of complex systems that we are concerned with, everything is dynamic: not only do the component elements and agents change with time, giving rise to changing states of the system, but the ways in which components interact with each other also change with time. If components are themselves complex systems, then the dynamism goes 'all the way down' too, in that all subsystems nested inside the bigger system are in flux. A system of human activity or development will be dynamic at each level of social or human organization, from the sociocultural, through the individual and down to the neural and cellular.

> Dynamism: in a complex dynamic system, everything changes, all the time.

The mathematics of 'dynamical systems' caters for both discrete and continuous change in systems, although most of the systems we are concerned with are continuously dynamic. Discrete change is change that occurs in steps or stages, from one state to another different state; the traffic light system has four discrete states and moves from one to the next, with no intervening stage. There is no state that is midway between amber and red when the system is on its way to 'stop'. Continuous change, on the other hand, does not proceed in steps but never stops. Take any plant in nature: it grows continuously. It may slow down if the weather is cold, but growth continues; it may go through cycles of flowering and dying back, but growth of some sort still continues. We will suggest that language, language use, and language development are continuously in action.

Levels and scales

We should here distinguish between 'levels' and 'scales' as two different ways of approaching and describing the activity of a system. A dynamic system can be examined on several timescales. For instance, in the city example, the overall system may develop on a timescale of months and years, or on an historical dimension of decades and centuries. Within these timescales are activities proceeding on other scales: supply systems to shops operate on a scale of days and weeks; traffic on city streets may change over hours within a day, as traffic jams form and dissolve.

A different kind of scale is that of size, and features in the human and social systems we are interested in. To try to avoid confusion, we here use 'level' to refer to this dimension. We may want to examine the city system at the overall level of the 'city', which is connected into larger level systems such as 'region' or 'nation'. Within the city, activity at a range of levels will contribute to the whole system: at the levels of neighbourhoods, streets, and individuals. We may want to think about the individual involved in language processing as not only connected to various levels of social organization, but also to think about language processing as arising from nested, smaller levels of human organization, such as brain, neural, or cellular activity.

In a complex system, there is connection across activity at different timescales and at different levels of social and human organization. The different levels and scales do not stand in a hierarchical relation to each other, in which those at the top influence those lower down. The influence of one level or scale on another can work in any direction, and we may be better to think of them as 'nested' (Bronfenbrenner 1989; Lemke 2000b; Byrne 2002). We come back to this point about the direction of influence when we consider emergence in the next chapter.

The non-linearity of complex systems

Non-linearity results from the dynamics of the interactions among elements and agents. To explain non-linearity, we start from what it is not. Imagine a <u>linear</u> transport system that contains roads, cars, buses, and the people who use them. In this linear system, the relations among the elements and agents remain fixed, and change in the system is constant and proportionate. So, if the people use more cars,

> Non-linearity: the interactions among elements and agents in a complex system change over time. This makes for non-linearity.

the roads will be proportionately busier; if more people take the bus, the buses will be fuller and there will be proportionately fewer cars on the road. If more roads are built for the same number of cars, the roads will be proportionately less busy. The future of this linear system is completely predictable. Of course, real life is not so linear! For example in the transport system that includes London, planners of the huge orbital motorway failed to take account of the fact that a new road doesn't just spread out the same number of cars across a bigger space, but actually encourages people who live near the new road to use it for short local journeys. It wasn't long before the new road was blocked with unexpected traffic jams. The linear scenario doesn't work because we are dealing not with proportional change arising from linear relations among elements and agents, but with non-linear change.

Non-linearity is a mathematical term, referring to change that is not proportional to input. While we have on the whole avoided the mathematical world in this book, mathematics, and its limits, is integral to complexity theory, so we do sometimes make reference to these influences. Here, it is relevant to note that continuous and non-linear change presents challenges to mathematics (Norton 1995). There are alternative ways to work with dynamical systems, which avoid mathematical problems. These include using computers to find numerical solutions to equations, and avoiding the equation-solving problem altogether by constructing simulated models of the systems that explore their behavior over time. We return to these avenues at later points in this and other chapters because they can each contribute to an understanding of the nature of change in non-linear dynamical systems. That understanding becomes part of the metaphorical application of complex dynamic systems we are constructing for applied linguistics.

Complexity arises from the non-linear nature of the connections or interactions between the components of a dynamic system. In a non-linear system, the elements or agents are not independent, and relations or interactions between elements are not fixed but may themselves change. This is what happened with the building of the London ring road—people's driving habits and road usage changed as a result of the new road.

We know that aspects of language development are non-linear. For example, measures of vocabulary learning in a second language (Laufer 1991; Meara 1997) show that learning begins quite slowly; once a certain number of words are mastered, learning increases in rate until vocabulary size reaches some level that seems to serve the student well enough, and then the rate of learning slows down. Vocabulary size does not increase linearly over time. On a graph, the rate of vocabulary growth with proficiency appears as an *S*-shaped curve like that in Figure 2.3.

Open systems

Many of the examples of systems we have used so far are 'open' systems, in that energy and matter can come into the system from outside. In the case of the motorway around London, the system was open to use by people who lived in areas close to the new road, not just those making long-distance journeys who had been included in the plan.

An open system can continue to maintain an ordered state[2] if it is 'fed' by energy coming into the system, whereas a closed system will reduce to a stable state or equilibrium. A mug of coffee spilled on a carpet will spread out until

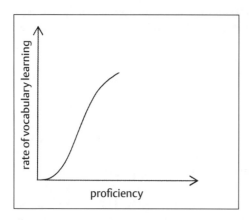

Figure 2.3 Non-linear growth of vocabulary
(adapted from Meara 1997: 115)

absorbed and then stop; like a closed system, it reaches a state of equilibrium in which the coffee stops spreading across the carpet. When there is not too much traffic in a road system, a state of order will be maintained where the traffic flows freely from starting point to destination. If the system is open to more and more traffic, it will eventually reach equilibrium in the form of gridlock. If it is also 'open' in the sense that more roads are constructed to provide for the increasing traffic, free-flowing order may be maintained, but it may be costly and demanding to keep the system in this non-equilibrium but ordered state.

Most biological systems, and some physical and chemical ones, are open. Energy, in the form of food, supports human systems and replaces what has been dispersed through action. The most interesting systems are those that are open and 'far-from-equilibrium', and yet remain stable, by using energy from outside the system (Prigogine and Stengers 1984; Thelen and Smith 1994: 53). Kauffman (1995: 20) gives a nice example of an open, far-from-equilibrium system that remains ordered: when a bath full of water is emptying, a whirlpool can be created as the water goes down the plughole. The system of water flowing through the bath can be maintained in an ordered or stable state, in which the whirlpool continues whirling, by adjusting the taps so that water comes into the bathtub at the same rate as it leaves it.

> **Openness:**
> open systems allow energy or matter to enter from outside the system. Being open can enable a 'far-from-equilibrium' system to keep adapting and maintain stability.

We should stress here that the kind of order or stability we are discussing is 'stability in motion' or a 'dynamic stability', not a stability that is static or fixed. A further example of this kind of dynamic stability might be the financial stability which an individual maintains over a period of months as money flows in and out of bank accounts. Readers may find resonance here with the dynamics of a language: English, for example, is open to all sorts of influences, and is continually changing, yet somehow maintains an identity as the 'same' language, a dynamic equilibrium. These types of systems that stabilize through continuous change are sometimes called 'non-equilibrium dissipative structures', because of the energy or matter that is dissipated as they continuously adapt to remain stable (Prigogine and Stengers 1984).

Adaptation in complex open systems

Another watery example of an ordered, non-equilibrium state being maintained by a flow of energy is the system that is a swimmer floating in the sea or in a swimming pool. The water is not by itself able to support a floating human body,[3] but if the swimmer makes small movements of hands or feet, he or she can stay floating on the surface of the water indefinitely. The floating swimmer and pool system is not in equilibrium because, without the extra input of energy produced by waggling hands or feet, floating would cease. The small movements act as energy brought into the system that is sufficient to keep the swimmer afloat. The swimmer has to continually adapt to the (lack of) buoyancy of the water in order to keep afloat.

> Adaptive: in adaptive systems, change in one area of the system leads to change in the system as a whole.

The process in which a system adjusts itself in response to changes in its environment is adaptation, and systems that work in this way are called 'complex adaptive systems', an important class of complex systems. In the above example, the movements of the swimmer are adaptations made in response to the environment—to the need to prevent sinking. This activity to maintain order through adaptation is characteristic of living systems.

The school—a complex adaptive system that includes teachers, students, curriculum, and learning environment—is clearly an open system, and may also be a non-equilibrium dissipative structure, in which the order or dynamic stability is, hopefully, the experiencing by learners of meaningful and life-affirming education. The nature of 'meaningful and life-affirming education'—and the activity that produces it—will need to continually adapt in order to respond to changes in the learners, in other aspects of the educational system, and in society. Factors outside of school may influence students and their learning, including, for example, conflicts far away that bring refugees to the area, improvements or decline in local economic conditions, and increases or decreases in parental aspirations. An educational system which can adapt to the influences of these changing external factors will maintain the dynamic stability of effective learning in the face of continuing change. Once again, stability does not mean stagnation and stasis, but represents a dynamic system that maintains its overall identity, without being subject to wild fluctuations or chaotic change.

The interconnectedness of system and context

An open system cannot be independent of its context since there is a flow of energy or matter between system and environment; the context is part of the system and its complexity. Systems in equilibrium are continually adapting to contextual changes,

> Context is not separate from the system but part of it and of its complexity.

and may change internally as a result of adapting to external change. This relationship between system and context is quite different from that proposed by behaviorists, for example. As Juarrero (1999: 74) succinctly puts it, 'They just plunked the organism in the environment and assumed that when the appropriate stimulus occurred, boom! the organism would automatically respond'. Open systems, in contrast, not only adapt to their contexts but also initiate change in those contexts; these systems are not just dependent on context but also influence context. It is this that makes the behavior of complex open systems unique and unpredictable (Juarrero 1999).

We need to flesh out the relationship between system and context to resolve the apparent contradiction that, to understand a system we need to understand the context in which it operates, while at the same time system and context are inseparable.

First, what do we mean by 'context'? Context is the 'here-and-now' in which a system is active (Thelen and Smith 1994: 217). It is the 'field of action within which an event is embedded' (Duranti and Goodwin 1992: 3).[4] Every change in a system is influenced by context. Thus, when a person walks across a field, every moment of walking involves adaptation by the body to the context, in the form of the ground surface and all that is seen or noticed. The action of walking changes if there are stones on the path, if the ground becomes wet or muddy, if the path becomes steeper or bends around a corner. Continual adaptation of the body as system enables the walker to cross the field successfully and transforms the field in the process. Likewise, in a language-using situation—for example, if someone on holiday is trying to use the local language to buy bread—language use is continuously adapted to take account of contextual factors, such as other people in the shop, their relationship and history, the position of the desired bread on a shelf, the attitude of the shopkeeper, or hearing language used by other customers. These adaptations, in turn, affect the context of use.

A complexity perspective on context in human systems, including language-related systems, insists on the connectedness of the social, physical, and cognitive. Complex systems are open and not separated from context, but interact with contextual factors as they change over time. We therefore need an embodied view of mental activity, including language use and processing, in which mind is seen as developing as part of a physical body constantly in interaction with the physical and sociocultural environment,[5] with this interaction contributing to the emergent nature of the mind (Gibbs 2006). In this perspective, we should not speak of 'cognition' as if it were separable from the social, cultural, and physical. The interconnectedness of the cognitive, social, physical, and cultural is formalized in complexity models by incorporating relevant factors as system parameters or dimensions. (See next chapter.)

Writing about a dynamic systems theory approach to second language acquisition, de Bot *et al.* (2007) describe the language learner as a 'dynamic subsystem within a social system' (p. 14), making a distinction between the learner's 'cognitive ecosystem' and the 'social ecosystem'. This separation of systems may not be the most useful direction for a complexity perspective to take, since it appears to over-simplify the complex inter-relations among cognitive, physical, and sociocultural factors. Some simplification is of course needed in order to investigate systems of interest, and the recognition of inseparable interconnectedness does not entail that all contextual factors are to be taken as equally important. It requires empirical work to decide on the relative importance of contextual factors to a particular system and on how they are to be incorporated into a description or model of the system. The interconnectedness of a complex open system and its context makes an ecological perspective particularly relevant as complementary to a complexity perspective on applied linguistics (Kramsch 2002; Spivey 2007).

Sociocultural theory also makes a strong connection between mind and sociocultural context, described as 'the organic unity of mental and social processes' (Lantolf 2006b: 31). Although not much mentioned explicitly, physical factors and processes are included in Vygotsky's theory of psychological development, evidenced in his studies of deaf-mute and aphasic language use (Kozulin 1990). Sociocultural theory in applied linguistics, however, seems to place a somewhat different emphasis on the interaction of environment and system than do either dynamic systems theory or complexity theory. Sociocultural theory appears often to emphasize the influence of sociocultural environment over the adaptive activity of human mental systems. (See discussion between de Bot *et al.* 2007 and Lantolf 2007.) This difference may be a matter of terminology and highlighting, or it may come from somewhere deeper in the ontologies of the theories; further detailed work in both frameworks and further open-minded discussion are needed to clarify the issue.

However, like complexity and dynamic systems approaches, sociocultural theory implies that the individual cannot be seen as autonomous and bounded, but instead sees boundaries between individual and context as blurred and changing. By incorporating various environmental or contextual factors as system parameters, complexity theory offers a methodological device to describe the blurring of these boundaries.

The importance of context for complex systems cannot be underestimated. The notion of context-dependency takes on a different sense within the complexity framework. It becomes more than a separable 'frame' surrounding a system that is needed to interpret its behavior (Goffman 1974). The 'here-

and-now' of context shapes the system, orders the system, and adapts the system.

Summary: features of complex systems

It should be clear that complex systems are *complicated*, in that they have many different types of elements and agents connected in multiple ways. It should also be clear that *complexity* is a technical term that refers to something quite distinct from being complicated. In this chapter so far, we have looked at the key features of complex systems:

- heterogeneity of elements or agents
- dynamics
- non-linearity
- openness
- adaptation.

Complex systems often show fascinating types of change, and in the next chapter we focus on the processes of change, adaptation, self-organization, and emergence in complex systems. Because these processes are at the heart of what makes complexity interesting, suggestive, and theoretically tempting, readers will find that they are sometimes differently emphasized in writers' choice of labels for these systems. The various labels used, including complex systems/dynamical systems/dynamic systems/complex dynamic systems/complex adaptive systems, often refer to the same particularly interesting set of complex systems—those open systems that are far-from-equilibrium yet maintain stability through continuous change and adaptation. Hereafter, we use the term 'complex systems' to refer to systems that are heterogeneous, dynamic, non-linear, adaptive, and open.

> The term 'complex systems' as used here refers to systems that are heterogeneous, dynamic, non-linear, adaptive and open.

The Center for the Study of Complex Systems at the University of Michigan produces a useful grid (Table 2.1) that summarizes the nature of complex systems from a range of fields using these key features, together with examples of 'emergent behavior' that we discuss in the following chapter but that at this point can be taken as referring to phenomena observed at the level of the whole system.

Table 2.2 uses these same features to describe, in a preliminary and very generalized manner, aspects of two complex systems in applied linguistics that we explore in detail in later chapters.

An ecological example

The following summarizing example of a complex system in nature may help reinforce the key features of being heterogeneous, dynamic, non-linear,

Field	Economics	Finance	Ecology	Population epidemiology
Agent	consumers	investors	individual animals	susceptibles
Heterogeneity	tastes, incomes	risk preferences, information	eating, nesting, breeding, habits	risk factors
Organization (system)	families, firms	mutual funds, market makers	schools, herds, food chains	social groups
Adaptation	effect of advertising, education	learning	hunting, mating, security	infection avoidance or spread
Dynamics	price adjustment	stock price movements	predator-prey interactions, competition	disease spread
Emergent behavior	inflation, unemployment	market movements	extinction, niches	epidemics

Table 2.1 Complex systems models in the social, life, and decision sciences (adapted from http://www.pscs.umich.edu/complexity-eg.html)

Field	Spoken interaction	Classroom language learning
Agents	speakers, their language resources	students, teachers, languages
Heterogeneity	speaker backgrounds, styles, discourse topics	abilities, personalities, learning demands
Organization	dyads, speech communities	class, groups, curricula, grammars
Adaptation	shared semantics, pragmatics	imitation, memorizing, classroom behaviors
Dynamics	conversation dynamics, negotiation of understanding	classroom discourse, tasks, participation patterns
Emergent behavior	discourse events, idiom, specific languages e.g. 'English'	language learning, class/group behavior, linguae francae

Table 2.2 Examples of complex systems in applied linguistics

adaptive, and open, and show how an awareness of system interconnectedness can change thinking. It concerns the evolving pattern of mule deer herds in the Grand Canyon National Park in America. Here we see a complex system that was pushed by external forces away from its previous stability and how it adapted to these contextual forces.[6] Decisions made in the early twentieth century that impacted on the system failed to take account of the interconnectedness of all the subsystems, and produced unexpected results.

The deer ecology as complex system with mixed elements and agents: deer, predators, people, forest.

Throughout centuries, mule deer have lived on the North Rim of the Grand Canyon and, before Europeans arrived, were hunted as part of the subsistence lifestyle of native peoples.

The dynamics include hunting by people and by predators.

The system is open to outside influence.

In 1906, President Roosevelt designated the region as a Game Preserve to protect the 4,000 deer. Attitudes at the time were that deer were 'good' animals and anything that killed the deer was 'bad' and should be shot. In the following 25 years, 781 mountain lions, 554 bobcats, 4,889 coyotes and all 30 of the wolves were killed. The deer, not surprisingly, thrived, with nearly 20 per cent increase in numbers each year. But such growth caused problems. The increasing numbers competed with each other, and with farmed cattle and sheep, for the available food. By 1921 there were estimated to be 100,000 deer and the grass, shrubs, and small trees were eaten, with 80–90 per cent of the available food in the forest used up. In two years, almost two thirds of the deer died, mostly of starvation. The deer continued to die of starvation and some were shot, and by 1939, the numbers were reduced, literally decimated, to 10,000.

Non-linear change in hunting by human predators leads to change in system.

Change in one part of the system leads to change in another.

The dynamics lead to adaptation in the system as a whole.

Changes in the numbers of deer have been attributed over the years to development, logging, fawn survival rate, and fire control policies leading to changing habitat. The numbers of deer fluctuate but have never again reached the really high levels of the 1920s.

The elements of the system are interdependent.

Initial implications of a complexity perspective

How does taking a complexity view of applied linguistics begin to change our perspectives as researchers or as practitioners?

It's all connected

A first shift in understanding from adopting a complexity approach to language issues in the real world is an increased awareness of the *intercon-*

nectedness of the components of a system in producing the whole, and of the system and its context. We cannot properly understand a system and how it behaves without understanding how the different parts of the system interact with each other; it is not enough to understand the parts just in themselves. Furthermore, once we start thinking of how a system as a whole can only be understood by knowing about the interactions of its components, different aspects of a situation stand out as being important and in need of our attention.

> Understanding a system and how it behaves requires understanding of how the different parts of the system interact with each other, and of how the system interacts with its context.

An example of how systems thinking can radically change the face of research can be found in the evolving history of discipline boundaries faced with complexity thinking applied to planet Earth in the idea of 'Gaia'. Gaia is the name given to the earth seen as an organism, a large complex system. When James Lovelock developed his idea that the earth can be seen to be functioning as a single system, he faced the disdain of many conventional scientists working within distinct disciplines such as chemistry and biology, who had interests in maintaining the separation of fields. Thirty or so years later, the systems view has gained respect in academia, and, the new supra-discipline of 'Earth Systems Science' is making a major impact on our understanding of whole system phenomena such as global warming. Researchers have come to realize that they need to understand the interconnectedness of the Earth's biological, chemical, geological, and other processes if they are to make sense of whole system phenomena.

Working with complexity

Adopting a complexity perspective requires us to take seriously the interconnectedness of system components within and across levels and scales, as well as how they interconnect with the system's context. Until fairly recently the only way to work with complexity was through simplifying the system in some way, in a process of 'idealization'. The non-linearity of complex systems can be idealized away by taking the system to be linear; this simplification makes cause and effect directly proportional one to the other, and in a ratio that is unchanging over time. A different sort of idealization occurs when some of the components of a system are removed from the picture altogether or are reduced to a more simplified form. Newton's laws of motion and gravity, for example, work to predict the movement of the planets by adopting the idealization that planets are perfect spheres (Cohen and Stewart 1994: 406–7). In experimental psychology, theories and experiments have often proceeded by idealization of context: separating system from context, or replacing the usual context with a laboratory context. Some areas of applied linguistics have inherited this procedure, for example, studies of task-based learning that take learners into the laboratory to talk on tasks and analyze the data without attending to effects of the context of learning. Idealization of complex systems has often involved the removing of 'noise' from data: for example, removing individual variation by averaging across samples. However, it may be precisely this variability that holds the key to how learning happens (Thelen and Smith 1994).

Complexity theory stresses the importance of all these inconvenient aspects of real-world activity. When we idealize away aspects of a complex system, we may be losing some essential interacting element that contributes to adaptation. If we can find ways to work with complex systems *in all their complexity*, we may produce better (i.e. more accurate and more useful) descriptions and explanations.

How then do we work with complexity and dynamics in exploring applied linguistic systems? Firstly, it will be necessary to have data collected over all relevant timescales that are of interest, and in sufficient detail. We would then need to find a way to describe the data that fits the data and explains it, and that contributes to expectations about future system activity. In applied linguistics, this fitting together of data and explanation would tend to be a 'theory'. In dynamic systems theory, this is done through a set of equations that describe the system mathematically, and that could be used to build a computer model. 'Quantitative modeling' that uses accurate and complete data would be able to produce testable predictions (van Gelder and Port 1995: 15). However, precise quantitative models are unlikely to be possible for human cognitive and social systems, such is their diversity, subtlety, and interactivity, leaving two further possibilities for working with complexity. The first is 'qualitative modeling' and the second 'dynamical description' (ibid.: 16–17).

In qualitative modeling, a complex dynamic model is used as an analogical model for the system under investigation. The model produces sufficiently similar outcomes to those observed in the real-world system for it to be a useful tool for exploring the real-world system. Computer modelers simulate a complex system by putting in numerical values to describe the state of the system. The output of one iteration of the model becomes the input for the next. This process is repeated with new values, over and over again. The multiple iterations then show the dynamics or 'evolution' of the model system as the values change. Connectionist network models work in this analogical way in modeling neural or cognitive activity. Connectionist networks differ from real-world systems in being discretely dynamic, whereas cognitive activity is continuously dynamic. However, at certain timescales they work sufficiently well to be useful tools as qualitative models (Spivey 2007; van Gelder and Port 1995). Computer modeling allows systems to be described and explored without the need to idealize, or at least without such radical idealizations as those described above. Qualitative models still use reduced and idealized versions of the complexity of the real-world system. Computer modelers have to decide what to include and what to exclude in their models.

In fact what happens is more of a process of finding a 'best fit', in that various models are developed and tested to find the one that produces outcomes over time that are convincingly similar to the outcomes of the real-world system. In Chapter 8 we will outline some of the various types of computer models and simulations that have been used to investigate real-world complex systems, and discuss issues of validity. The point to be made here is that even the best models are still simplifications and thus serve as approximations and metaphors for the complex systems.

Dynamic description is what we have called 'adopting a complexity perspective', and is described by van Gelder and Port (1995: 17) as the use of 'a general apparatus for understanding the way systems—including, in particular, non-linear systems—change over time'. In this way of working with complexity, we may not attempt to build models but rather use concepts and ideas from complexity theory as a perspective from which to approach particular problems in applied linguistics.

Complexity thought modeling

Exploring a problem from a complexity perspective can be approached by engaging in 'complexity thought modeling', where, in a parallel with 'thought experiments' in more positivist approaches, aspects of a particular problem are described in terms of complex, dynamic systems in order to develop hypotheses for research or plans for action, or even actual computer models.

From this chapter, we have seen how one might start the process of thought modeling a complex dynamic system by:

- identifying the different components of the system, including agents, processes and subsystems
- for each component, identifying the timescales and levels of social and human organization on which it operates
- describing the relations between and among components
- describing how the system and context adapt to each other
- describing the dynamics of the system
  - how the components change over time, and
  - how the relations among components change over time.

In the next chapter we focus on system dynamics and go more deeply into the various ways in which change manifests itself in complex systems.

Notes

1 The word 'dynamical' is the form used in the area of mathematics known as 'dynamical systems theory'. In non-mathematical treatments, some writers keep the original form, while others drop the '–al' and use the more everyday form.

2 The idea of the 'state' of a system is explained in more detail in the next chapter. Here it is only necessary to note that the state of a system is the way it is behaving at any particular moment.

3 Other than the Dead Sea, of course.

4 A complexity perspective on Duranti and Goodwin's anthropological view of context will extend what it means to be 'embedded'.

5 The term 'environment' is sometimes used, both in this book and more widely in the dynamic-systems literature, to refer metonymically to 'context'. In work adopting an ecological perspective, 'ecology' is used as an alternative to 'environment', further emphasizing the mutual connectedness of system and context. Systems are then sometimes referred to as 'ecosystems' to emphasize their embeddedness in this ecology or context.

6 Thanks are due to the National Park Ranger who provided the example.

3
Change in complex systems

Having established the nature of complex systems, in this chapter we explore the different types of change that can occur in a complex system, and the consequences of such change. We use a variety of different sorts of systems to exemplify and explain the ideas: people riding horses; traffic jams; infants learning to reach out and grasp toys; the spread of English language teaching. In developing the ideas of change in complex systems, we pay particular attention to the kind of sudden, radical change which can occur as a result of self-organization in a complex dynamic system. The reader is introduced to the geometrical images and constructs that are used to describe system dynamics, in which system change is seen as movement in a trajectory across a 'state space' or 'phase space'. We explain how non-linearity can lead to sudden and dramatic change, called a 'phase shift', and how this is described in terms of the emergence of 'attractors' in state space. Stability and variation around attractors are key constructs in applications of complexity to applied linguistics, resonating with individual language development, with language use, and with language evolution. The key constructs of complex dynamic systems are summarized and presented as a way of thinking through the nature of the complex systems at play in our applied linguistic domains of interest.

The chapter concludes with further discussion of implications for theorizing and researching complex systems which sets the foundation for the next part of the book, and we return to the question of human agency in complexity theory.

Types of change in complex systems

As we saw in the last chapter, dynamics and change are at the heart of complexity theory. Because of their non-linearity, complex systems evolve and adapt in several different ways, internally and through external connections to their environment. Internal self-organizing changes alter the structure of a system, while response to energy and matter coming from outside, leads to adaptive change that maintains order or stability. We now look in more detail at these types of change in complex systems.

The first key point to note is that complex systems can change smoothly and continuously for periods of time but may then go through more dramatic types of change when they alter their nature radically, sometimes entering a period of turbulence, or 'chaos', where the system keeps on changing dramatically.

Recall from the previous chapter that a complex dynamic system moves through a sequence of states, either discretely from one state to the next, or continuously as states evolve seamlessly one from another. Human systems, and thus those of most interest to applied linguistics, have continuous rather than discrete dynamics; change never stops. At any specific moment, the system can be said to be in a particular state. What we mean by 'the state of a system' at the particular time is its current behavior, the patterns of activity of its component elements and agents. This use of the word 'state' differs from its everyday use, which implies lack of dynamics, and the reader is encouraged to think of the 'state' of a dynamic system in terms of movement or activity. If we were to consider the state of a school as a complex dynamic system at a particular time, we would think of how the agents (students, teachers, administrators, etc.) and elements (curriculum, resources, etc.) are interrelating (through many different processes that might for example include teaching literacy or holding parents' meetings), and how they connect to form the whole system.

> A complex system can change smoothly, or it can shift suddenly and radically.

> The state of a system is the (dynamic) behavior of elements or agents at a particular point in time.

When a complex system changes from one state to another, what changes is the nature of the activity of the system or its patterns of behavior. The school system, like any continuous dynamic system, changes state all the time: each thought that passes through a student's mind changes the system, each point in a lesson builds on and differs from the previous moment, and, on a longer timescale of months and years, each new intake of students alters the system. In the ecological example of the mule deer in the National Park, developed in the previous chapter, it might be appropriate for authorities to monitor the continuously changing state of the system at yearly or half-yearly intervals. They would have two measures of the state of the system, but change would still be taking place continuously between the monitoring points. A description of the state of the system made at a monitoring point would include, not just the numbers of animals, but also the patterns of interaction between predators, deer, humans, and environment, such as the frequency of deer shooting by humans or the patterns of hunting by lions. In the years after 1921 that saw two-thirds of the deer starving to death, it would be clear from the huge change in numbers and patterns, from a state in which numbers nearer to 100,000 thrived to the state in which the deteriorating environment could support only 20,000, that something more dramatic than steady continuous change had occurred; the system is showing a different type of change that is one of the hallmarks of complex dynamic systems, and that we therefore need to consider in some detail.

A further example of a dynamic system changing is the movement of a horse and its rider (Thelen and Smith 1994: 62–3). Because of its anatomy, a horse has four, distinctly different, ways of moving, or 'gaits', described in English by specific verbs: 'walk', 'trot', 'canter', 'gallop'. Not only do these different gaits appear at different speeds, from the slowest 'walking' to the fastest 'galloping', but there is a significant shift in the manner of movement when the horse and rider change from one gait to the next. A conventional collocation exists in English that describes such a shift to a faster type of movement as 'break into', which captures something of its radical nature: 'the horse *broke into* a trot/canter/gallop'. These different ways of moving are not just faster versions of walking, but are distinctly different one from another, with a change in how the pairs of back and front legs move relative to each other. A rider on the back of a horse learns to adjust his or her movement with each shift in gait. As the horse trots, the rider rises up and down in the saddle. At a gallop, the rider crouches lower and does not move vertically as much. As the gait changes, so the rider adapts to the change in type of motion.

In terms of complex systems, the moving horse and rider form a complex dynamic system connected into the context or environment through such factors as the surface and weather conditions. The rider usually acts to control the speed of the horse, encouraging it to increase speed and then to shift from its first state 'walking' into a different gait, 'trotting'. If there is nothing to change the system, horse and rider can continue to trot. Within the trotting gait, speed can decrease or increase to a certain, limited extent, but at some point the change in speed is sufficient to prompt a further shift in movement, either back to a 'walk' or faster into a 'canter'.

The horse-and-rider system displays both types of change that can occur in complex systems. On the one hand, the state of the system can change steadily within a gait, as when the horse trots faster or more slowly. On the other hand, the system changes dramatically when the horse reaches particular speeds that prompt a shift to a new gait. Dramatic and sudden changes of this kind are called *phase shifts* or *bifurcations*. The states of the system before and after a phase shift are very different.

> A system undergoes a phase shift when its behavior changes suddenly to a new and radically different mode.

The state space landscapes of complex systems

Work in complex systems, and related areas, has developed tools for understanding system change that use spatial and topographical images to describe how a system changes over time. In a vivid spatial metaphor, a complex dynamic system is visualized as wandering across a landscape, up hills and down through valleys, occasionally coming to a halt when a valley is too deep to get out of easily but resuming its journey if it gathers enough energy to escape. The landscape includes areas where the system hovers on the edge of various, very different possibilities. Ridges between very different valleys reflect sudden changes in the state of the system. Figure 3.1 shows this kind of landscape and gives the reader an idea of this spatial metaphor before we proceed to explain more precisely how it can represent change in a complex dynamic system.

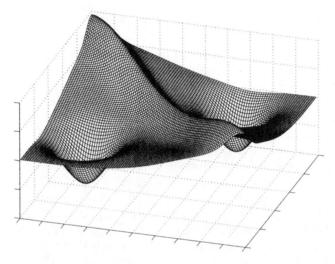

Figure 3.1 A topological state space landscape (from Spivey 2007: 18)

Landscapes such as Figure 3.1 represent the 'state space' of a system. A state space is a collection of all possible states of a system; each point in the landscape represents a state of the system. If Figure 3.1 were not metaphorical but were a real landscape, the path of a person walking through the landscape could be fully described through four parameters. Three of these would be physical: height above sea level, longitude, and latitude; the fourth would be temporal, describing the time at which the walker passed through each physical point. To see the landscape as a state space, the walker becomes a complex dynamic system. As he or she moves across the landscape, the system moves through successive states. The path of the walker is the path of the system, called its trajectory. The four parameters of the walker's landscape become the parameters which describe the complex system and the dimensions of the system's state space. This basic idea of visualizations of the behavior of complex systems will be explained in several different ways to help readers' understanding.

The term 'phase space' is often used interchangeably with 'state space', although as Port and van Gelder (1995), Juarrero (1999), and Spivey (2007) point out, the use of 'phase space' should be restricted to spaces with at least one dimension that reflects change over time.

Moving through state space

The state space of a system is constructed by putting together all the possible states of a system, and each point in the state space is described by a particular set of values of the system's parameters. (How we know what these are will be discussed later.) We

A phase space is a state space with at least one dimension relating to change over time.

return to the very simple traffic light system from Chapter 2 to introduce this idea, and then increase the complexity of our example systems. The traffic light system has four states, or patterns of lights, that are conventionally employed:

- red
- amber
- green
- red and amber

and four other states that are technically possible, and which may be used somewhere in the world as traffic signals, although not as far as we know:

- amber and green
- red and green
- no lights at all
- all three lights together.

The state space of the system is the set of all possible states, i.e. the eight states that include those that are used and those that are not used. Each colored light (each giving one parameter of the system) is placed along a separate dimension, so we have a three-dimensional space with eight possible states.

Each colored light parameter has just two values, 'on' and 'off'. 'Off' is given the value zero, and 'on' is given the value 1. The states of the traffic light system can then be shown graphically as the vertices of the cube with each side 1 unit long, shown in Figure 3.2.

The 'state space' of the system comprises the eight points where the sides of the cubes intersect, the vertices of the cube, shown marked by small spheres in Figure 3.2. The bottom left vertex of the cube is the zero position, and would be the state, 'no lights at all'. The bottom right vertex would be the state where the parameter value of the red light is 1 (on) and of the green and amber lights is 0 (off).

The state space of a system is a visualization of all possible states that the system could be in. The system may not, in practice, make use of all the possibilities. In the traffic light example, the system only 'occupies'[1] four of its possible states, and never occupies the other four (as far as we know, at least). As the system changes, it moves from one point in its state space to another,

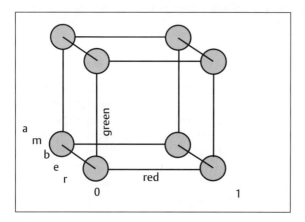

Figure 3.2 The state space of the traffic light system shown as vertices of a three-dimensional cube

and the sequence of these states can be plotted as a path or 'trajectory' in the state space, adding a fourth, temporal, parameter. In Figure 3.3, four vertices of the cube state space have been heavily shaded to indicate they are actual states of the system, while the others remain lightly shaded, as possible, but not actual, states. As the system changes, it moves through its four actual states (as in Figure 2.2) from 1 (red) to 2 (red and amber) to 3 (green) to 4 (amber); this is its trajectory through its state space.

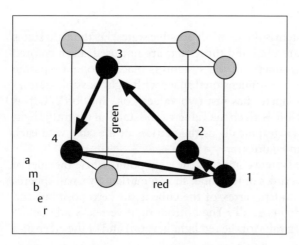

Figure 3.3 The trajectory of the traffic light system through its state space

This very simple system is dynamic, but it is not complex. It is discretely dynamic, since it occupies its four states but does not occupy the space between them. A continuously dynamic system would be continuously occupying states as it moved across the state space, not leaping from one discrete state to another as the traffic light system does. The traffic light system is of little interest to us as applied linguists but it has hopefully served its purpose in introducing the abstract but key idea that change in a system can be seen as a trajectory through the system's state space. The rest of the chapter will build from this introductory visualization.

System parameters

Each aspect needed to describe a system contributes a parameter, and thus a dimension, to the state or phase space of that system. In a simplified example of the phase space of a human system, given by Thelen and Smith (1994: 56–8), a person's physical fitness is hypothetically, and simplistically, described by two parameters or 'observables': heart rate and body temperature. All possible values of these can then be shown on a two-dimensional landscape or space as in Figure 3.4 below. The person's physical fitness is likely to occupy a small area inside the phase space of the system. It does not roam widely across the fitness phase space, since neither heart rate nor body temperature can fluctuate to extremes. There will be a small area that represents the intersection of normal values of heart rate and body temperature, and a larger area that shows places where the system might move to—for example, if the person were sick—or in another direction—if the person were to take up an exercise program and increase fitness. Either illness or training might shift the system temporarily away from the normal or preferred region, but the system would return there if the temporary changes ceased. Continuing exercise might eventually shift the preferred region in the state space, although personal experience suggests that the preferred region is fairly strongly fixed in adults despite one's best efforts. The person's fitness is what Thelen and Smith call 'dynamically stable', in other words, it is not rigidly fixed but moves in a limited way, within the preferred region (shaded dark in Figure 3.4) and sometimes into the larger region.

A state space or phase space represents the 'landscape of possibilities' of a system, and, as it changes and adapts over time, the system moves through this landscape.

Complex systems often have many parameters and thus have multidimensional phase spaces that we cannot draw, or even imagine. What happens then is a kind of metaphorical compression of dimensions; the multidimensional system is shown in three dimensions (as in Figure 3.1) and described using the three- and four-dimensional vocabulary of hills, valleys, and trajectories.

Attractors in state space

In the topological vocabulary of system landscapes, states, or particular modes of behaviors, that the system 'prefers' are called *attractors* (Thelen

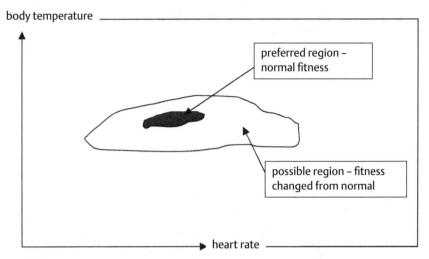

Figure 3.4 The (hypothetical) phase space of a person's fitness as measured by two parameters (based on Thelen and Smith 1994: 58)

and Smith 1994: 56). On the two-dimensional landscape in Figure 3.4, the preferred region of fitness that the system keeps returning to (shaded dark) is an attractor for the person's fitness system. Attractors are areas in the state space land-

> An attractor is a region of a system's state space into which the system tends to move.

scape of a system and are visualized in several ways that will be described in this section.

Figure 3.4 is a two-dimensional visualization, with the attractor shown as a bounded area or region.[2] In a three-dimensional landscape such as Figure 3.1, the boundaries of the region would be like geographical contours and, instead of an area, an attractor in three dimensions would look like a valley or a well, a depression in the landscape.

Figure 3.5 shows a further way to visualize the idea of attractor states in the phase or state space of a system. It is a kind of cut-through of the three-dimensional landscape with the system shown as a ball rolling over the landscape. As the system shifts into a new mode of behavior or attractor state, it is shown as rolling into a well or basin in the phase space landscape. Figure 3.5(a) represents a system like the horse-and-rider that moves between several shallow attractors. The four gaits of the moving horse-and-rider system would look like four wide and fairly deep wells in the system's state space landscape. In each attractor state, i.e. gait, the horse-and-rider behavior is stable for a while. As its speed increases, it will eventually move into a new attractor, for example, from 'trot' to 'canter'. The increase in speed enables the system to leave the basin of attraction and continue on a trajectory across the landscape to the next attractor.

If, however, the state space landscape is more like Figure 3.5 (b) with a very strong attractor, shown as a deep well with steep sides, the system may not be able to 'escape' and may come to rest at the bottom of the well. In this case, the system has moved into a fixed and stable behavioral mode and stays there. An example of such a mode might occur when a person starts a new job. After a period of time with much change (shown as movement around

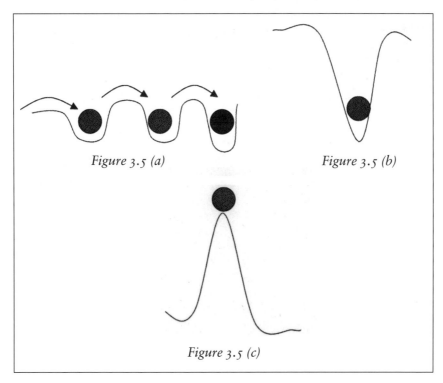

Figure 3.5 (a)   Figure 3.5 (b)

Figure 3.5 (c)

Figure 3.5 *The trajectory of a complex system across attractors in its phase space landscape (based on Thelen and Smith 1994: 60)*

the landscape), things settle down into a routine that is relatively fixed and unlikely to change again in the short term; the system of the person at work is in a deep attractor.

The third possibility shown as Figure 3.5 (c), represents a very unstable mode of behavior for a system. Perched on top of a hill, any small perturbation to the system is likely to push it off and downwards. In terms of the fitness example, the person may visit the gym every day and exercise long and hard for a period of one month. (In western Europe and North America this is likely to be January, as people act on resolutions made for the New Year.) The intensive exercise produces a new peak of fitness, which is, however, not very stable. Any change in the person's life, for example, slipping on the ice and damaging an ankle, that slows down or stops the gym work for a while, will lead to fitness quickly moving away from the peak. Steep peaks in a state space landscape represent very unstable places for the system to be, quite opposite to that of being in a well or a valley. The system cannot remain in such a state for any length of time; it will roll off the peak and continue its trajectory through its state space.

The final visualization of the state space of a complex dynamic system is shown in Figure 3.6 (from Spivey 2007: 17). Here the reader or viewer is positioned directly above a two-dimensional picture of the state space, which represents a higher dimensional space. The arrows represent the direction the system would move in; a longer arrow represents stronger attraction, which would mean faster movement of the system.

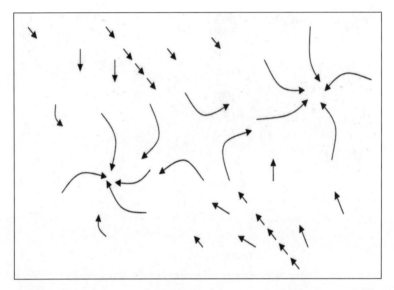

Figure 3.6 A phase space landscape for a dynamic system with two attractor basins (from Spivey 2007: 17)

By moving a finger or pencil through the landscape following the direction and strength of the arrows, the reader will replicate the trajectory of the dynamic system. There are two attractors, shown by the sets of arrows on either side of the diagram that direct movement inwards. The arrows produce a spiraling trajectory that takes the system into the attractor where it comes to a halt. The attractor lies in an 'attractor basin', a region in which the attractor exerts a force on the system. The system may orbit around the basin, or settle inside it. (See next section.)

Finally we return to the three-dimensional topographic image of a state or phase space, having established the metaphorical nature of these various displays in which high dimensional systems are reduced to two or three dimensions. Figure 3.1, reproduced below as Figure 3.7 (from Spivey 2007: 18), shows the same type of phase space as Figure 3.6 with two attractor regions. The strength of attractors is now shown by the steepness of the slopes around the sides of the basins.

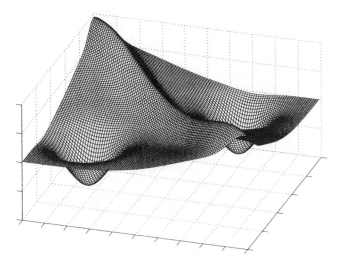

Figure 3.7 The topological state space landscape shown in Figure 3.1. Note the two attractors that appear as wells in the landscape (from Spivey 2007: 18)

Control parameters

Not all of the parameters of a complex system will affect its trajectory, but there will be some that have particular influence around phase transitions; these are called 'control parameters'. The collective behavior of the system is sensitive to the control parameters, and change in the control parameters moves the system into regions of its state space. The control parameters thus 'control' the possible states that the system can occupy.

A striking example of the role of control parameters in natural systems occurred in the very warm spring of 2007 in England. Usually the months of spring see oak trees and ash trees come into leaf at around the same time; this year, there were leaves on the oak tree while the ash tree was still bare. The unusual warmth had revealed what was normally not apparent: that the two trees respond to different control parameters. The ash tree responds primarily to light; as the days get longer, so the sap rises and the buds burst. The oak tree, on the other hand, responds to temperature, and its leaves appear as the days get warmer. For the ash tree, spring proceeded as normal, and its control parameter—daylight—increased with each day that passed until it moved into its new state with leaves. The control parameter of the oak tree—temperature—increased abnormally early and so the leaves appeared early, and well ahead of the ash.

In the language learning situation, motivation[3] might seem a candidate control parameter in that it will help keep the learning system moving across its state space, avoiding attractors such as preference for watching television over doing homework. In classrooms, the action and intentions of the teacher may work as control parameters that take the system of learners and teacher forward to new learning experiences.

Control parameters are the key to understanding change in complex systems—if they can be identified, then we know what drives the system and are able to intervene.

Attractors in real-world systems

Attractors can produce order in a dynamic system by constraining the system into a small region of its state space landscape. When we look at real-world systems that have evolved to stability over time, long-term behaviors can be seen as attractors in the state space of the system (Norton 1995: 56). For example, the national examination system in England has for many years assessed students' achievement through 'A-level' examinations (standing for Advanced level). Recent moves to try to replace A-levels by a broader, more modern assessment procedure (such as the International Baccalaureate) have so far failed because of parental and other resistance. A-levels are respected as a kind of 'gold standard' by those who want to retain them, making them a deep and stable attractor in the evolving national assessment system: the system has not yet managed to achieve the impetus needed to escape this attractor.

Attractors in human sociocognitive systems would include the concepts and explanatory theories that we build about how the world works. Vygotsky (1962) uses the example of the movement of the sun to exemplify 'scientific' and 'spontaneous' concepts. People develop spontaneous concepts through their everyday experience, and these manifest themselves at group level as 'folk theories', but formal education often introduces quite different ways of understanding the same phenomena. So, our everyday experience of the sun appearing to rise over the horizon in the morning and sinking down below it in the evening, leads us to understand the sun as moving in relation to our earthly horizon. This spontaneous concept becomes an attractor in the state space of our understanding. At school, however, we learn that the sun is in fact stationary, and the movement of the earth produces an illusion of the sun rising and setting. A different attractor, the scientific concept, is introduced into the state space of understanding, which now resembles something like Figure 3.7. We are able to operate with both these ideas about the relative movement of the sun and the earth, shifting from one to the other as required by context. In other cases, early understandings need to be replaced by more advanced concepts since to maintain them as active, even for everyday contexts, may be disadvantageous; for example, young children who think that breathing in and out pushes blood around the body need to move from that understanding to a new attractor that includes differentiated functions of the circulatory and respiratory processes in the human body (Cameron 2003a).

Complexity offers a way of seeing cultural artifacts such as 'the violin' or 'the milk jug' as attractor states in the complex dynamics of human cultural development. Take the milk jug: there are many possible containers for milk (or beer or other drinks) but the jug shape, with a handle to hold and a lip to enable pouring, seems to have stabilized over time as people have tried out various possibilities and made use of those that work most effectively. We find variation in the material, size, and proportions of jugs. There are prototype jugs and less jug-like jugs, but the jug exists as a stabilized form-function object. Just as the milk jug has evolved out of interaction between people and the physical world, so too the violin (or any other musical instrument) seems to have stabilized in a particular form, albeit with some variation, that particularly suits the shape and scale of the human body, the human auditory system, and the properties of wood and other materials. The dynamic system that is humans-and-violins will continue to change, and may, in the future, shift to some new attractor form, but for the time being seems to be in a stable attractor in its phase space landscape.

Stability and variability

The examples of jug and violin illustrate the interplay of stability and variation in complex dynamic systems. The forms that exist currently are stabilized but with variability around the stability. The potential for future development lies in this variability around the relatively fixed stability. From some variation on current forms, a new form may develop that people come to prefer, as the piano forte developed from the forte piano which in turn developed from the harpsichord. Historical change on a long timescale arises from small local changes made possible by variability around current stabilities.

We have seen that stability in a complex dynamic system can be represented by the system moving into an attractor basin in its state space. The steepness of the sides of the attractor basin, a valley or well in a landscape, reflects how easy or difficult it is for the system to shift its behavior, i.e. to move on, once it has entered an attractor. Steepness thus reflects the stability of a mode of system behavior. The four gaits of a moving horse-and-rider system would look like four distinct wells or valleys in the system's state space landscape, but these would not be shaped like the extreme crevasse of Figure 3.5 (b); rather they would appear more like basins or bowls, each distinct but with sides that are not particularly steep. In each of these attractor basins, the horse-and-rider use one of the four gaits. However, the attractor gait does not occur at just one single speed; the horse can walk or trot at a

> The strength of an attractor is represented by its depth and the steepness of its sides.

range of speeds within the limits of walking or trotting. This is the variability within the stability of the gait, shown topographically by the shape of the basin around the attractor. The attractor basin or well is not very deep or steep in this case, since an increase in speed will be sufficient to shift the system out of that gait and into the next attractor gait.

Stability and variability around and within system attractors are key constructs in complexity theory. Dynamic stability is different from stasis because it includes local variation and is open to future change. The degree of variability around an attractor becomes an important measure of system stability; it becomes data rather than 'noise' around an ideal performance to be dismissed (Thelen and Smith 1994).

The depth of a well and the steepness of its walls can visually represent the strength of an attractor. A stable mode of behavior in a system occurs when the system is 'in' a strong attractor. We can thus think of the stability of the system at that point in terms of how resistant the system is to being pushed out of the attractor by perturbations from outside. A stable mode of behavior will not be disrupted by being pushed—think of the system as a ball rolling around the inside a bowl-shaped well but not leaving the well because it does not move fast enough or with enough energy to escape up and over the sides. The strength of the 'push' needed to send the system out of the attractor is one way of measuring the strength of the attractor and the stability of the system's behavior inside it.

If we are seeking an explanation of how 'order' (a concept, an artifact, a structure) comes to be in complex adaptive systems, then we may find it in thinking of a complex system that is flexible enough to maintain its stability through continuous adaptation. A stability that we observe—a language form, a testing system, language ability, a community—is not stasis, but rather is the system maintaining relative stability for a period, through continuous adaptation. In these open systems, energy or forces from outside the system may act to disrupt the system trajectory, but the system responds and maintains stability.

> Some complex systems maintain stability by adapting to change.

If the system, even in its stable states, is not fixed but shows some variability, it has the potential for further change and development. In applied linguistic systems, we will want to identify variability around stable modes of behavior, in order to know the possibilities for future change. Local variability around stabilized ways of using language contains the potential for future change.

Three types of attractors

Complexity theory has shown that three types of attractors can occur in the state space of complex dynamic systems: fixed point attractors, cyclic attractors, and chaotic attractors.

Fixed point attractors are the simplest type, representing a system moving into a stable, preferred state and remaining there. Using the metaphor of a ball rolling into a well or valley in the landscape of state space (Figure 3.5(b) or 3.7), when the system enters a fixed point attractor, it eventually settles into a single mode of behavior or stops altogether. The example often given is of a pendulum that swings backwards and forwards, its swing progressively dampened by friction, until it finally comes to rest. If the pendulum is given extra energy such as a push, it will again swing for a bit and then stop.

In a *cyclic* or *closed loop attractor*, the system moves periodically between several different attractor states, as with the pendulum. This model also fits the dynamics of predator-prey systems, like the story of the deer in the previous chapter. The populations of prey and of their predators tend to settle into periodic movement between two or more states (Cohen and Stewart 1994: 187).

A *chaotic* or *strange attractor* is a region of state space in which the system's behavior becomes quite wild and unstable, as even the smallest perturbation causes it to move from one state to another. In visual terms, this would look like a large attractor basin that is itself full of hills and valleys of different shapes and sizes around which the system moves fast and unpredictably. This kind of behavior is called 'chaos' and the attractor is labeled a chaotic attractor. We should resist the poetic imagery of the label—'chaos' as used here is a mathematical term to describe certain modes of behavior that are not predictable but are also not random.

Systems in chaotic attractors are sensitive to minute changes in conditions, as in the previously quoted example of the 'butterfly effect', in which a tiny motion such as the flap of a butterfly's wings is sufficient to generate changes that amplify to produce a tornado on the other side of the world. In a chaotic attractor, very small changes can have a large impact on the system's trajectory, sending it zooming around inside the attractor basin. It is the sensitivity to small changes that makes the behavior of chaotic systems unpredictable. To be able to predict behavior, we would need to know absolutely accurately every small detail of the starting state, called its 'initial conditions'. Any small error in describing the initial conditions will be multiplied and amplified as the system changes, leading to large variations in actual behavior. The behavior of a system in a chaotic attractor is unpredictable, although it is still technically deterministic, in that its current state determines its future states. The problem is that we cannot ever know the current state sufficiently accurately to be able to predict future behavior (Cohen and Stewart 1994: 189).

Chaos theory is the study of systems that move through chaotic attractors. Complexity theory incorporates chaotic systems and chaos theory alongside the study of non-chaotic systems.

The edge of chaos

Although human systems seem for the most part unlikely to move into chaotic attractors, since human systems are generally fairly robust (Byrne

2002), they do sometimes approach such regions of their state space. Systems near to chaotic attractors have particularly interesting behaviors—at least in the restricted kinds of complex systems whose behavior has been so far investigated—and the idea

> At the edge of chaos, a system changes with optimum balance of stability and flexibility.

of systems at or near 'the edge of chaos' creates powerful and poetic resonances (Kauffman 1995). While we need (again, and as always) to be cautious of the suggestive power of metaphors, the edge of chaos is an appealing and suggestive idea.

Kauffman and colleagues explored computer simulations of evolving network systems. They found that the networks could adapt and evolve to an 'ordered regime, not too far from the edge of chaos ... [which] affords the best mixture of stability and flexibility' (1995: 91). A system at or near the edge of chaos changes adaptively to maintain stability, demonstrating a high level of flexibility and responsiveness.

Goodwin (1995) ponders the idea that the play, or what appears to us as play, of young animals is edge of chaos behavior. He sees, in this kind of activity, 'the richest, most varied and unpredictable set of motions of which an animal is capable' (Goodwin 1995: 179). When play ceases and animals 'cool down', they revert to more ordered behavior. Repeated cycles of disordered play and return to order can produce new types of behavior.

Thus encouraged, we may think of play in language use as edge of chaos behavior (Cook 2000). An example of edge of chaos language behavior might be found in adolescents using English, playing with the vocabulary and grammar in group 'street' talk, within and across community languages (Rampton 1995). This language use displays the kind of flexibility and responsiveness that might signal edge of chaos behavior. Lexical items are invented and abbreviated, and new forms spread rapidly, through music and media, computer technology, and peer-group interaction. When the young person is engaged in the most highly variable talk, he or she is occupying a region of his or her language resource state space near the edge of chaos. When talking with people outside of the peer group, language resources come from a more stable region of the state space; they move away from the edge through various social and pragmatic pressures. While innovation is of course found in adult language use, it usually displays much less variability around stabilized norms.

Self-organization and emergence

Self-organization and emergence are alternative ways of talking about the source of phase shifts in the behavior of complex systems. After a phase shift into a new attractor in its state space, a system is said to have self-organized into a new pattern of behavior. The shift is self-organized (rather than 'other organized') because it is the dynamic properties of the system that lead it to happen, not some external organizing force. A phase shift is a major transition for the system; what the system does after the phase shift is qualitatively different from what it did before. The horse-and-rider system self-organizes and shifts from a canter to a gallop. The predator-prey system self-organizes through periodic population shifts. Self-organization can happen because the system can 'adapt' in response to changes—it can move to another region of its state or phase space.

Sometimes self-organization leads to new phenomena on a different scale or level, a process called 'emergence'. What emerges as a result of a phase shift is something different from before: a whole that is more than the sum of its parts and that cannot be explained reductively through the activity of the component parts. A traffic jam is a phenomenon on a different level from the cars involved in it. A queue on a particular road may remain for hours, although individual drivers have moved through and passed it. The traffic jam is not

> Emergence is the appearance in a complex system of a new state at a level of organization higher than the previous one. The emergent behavior or phenomenon has some recognizable 'wholeness'.

reducible to the individual cars it is generated from. Emergent phenomena in complex dynamic systems are new stabilities of behavior (sometimes emerging from previous disorder), which remain open to further change and which have different degrees of variability or flexibility around them.

A more complex type of emergence occurs when there is connection, not just upwards from lower to higher levels of the system as with the traffic jam, but in both directions, as when the simple activities of termites produces the emergent phenomenon of the termite nest (Clark 1997: 75). There is an upwards effect across levels, in which the termites produce the nest, but there is also a downwards effect, in which the changing shape of the nest results in lower level activity by termites. The nest-building system as a whole, and termite activity as components of the system, are locked in a process that has been called 'reciprocal causality' (Clark 1997; Thompson and Varela 2001).

> In reciprocal causality, there are effects across the system from lower to higher levels, and higher level activity constrains lower level activity.

Examples of emergence through self-organization abound in the complex systems we have been using as illustrations:

- Test preparation centers set up to train children to pass language exams are an emergent phenomenon in the co-adaptation of teaching provision and assessment. Once centers are established they influence the decisions of parents and children.
- Biological evolution takes place through a series of emergent new species.
- Emergence in learning occurs when new ideas fall into place in an 'a-ha moment'. Once understood, the new knowledge influences other ideas.
- A child learns to walk or to read and at some point the emergent behavior is stable enough to be labeled 'walking' or 'reading'. The act of walking

emerges from the actions of the legs and other muscles. Reciprocally, being able to walk influences how the legs and other muscles are used.

- A language, for example, French or Thai, emerges from the multiple inter-actions of its speakers. Once a language is labeled, in a socio-political act, its use is influenced by its status.
- Learning a language is not a single process of emergence but a succession of cycles of emergence. Although working with an information-processing perspective and restricted to grammar, the idea of successive 'restructurings' (McLaughlin 1990) of different aspects of the language seems to be similar to the idea of phase shifts leading to new, emergent behavior.
- Social structure emerging from and influencing individual agency and ac-tion. For example, the relation between 'habitus' and 'practice' in the work of Bourdieu would fit into a complexity, emergentist scenario (Bourdieu 1989; Sealey and Carter 2004). Habitus, as people's 'mental structures through which they apprehend the social world, ... [are] essentially the product of the internalization of the structures of that (social) world' (Bourdieu 1989: 18), but those social structures are also emergent from action in the social world.[4]

Each of these emergent properties of human and social systems operates at a higher level of organization of the system than the interacting elements or agents that produced the new phenomenon. The behavior at this higher level entrains lower level behavior. Through self-organization and emergence, systems with simple agents and rules for their interaction can produce com-plicated behaviors, processes, or phenomena: 'much coming from little' (Holland 1998: 2). However, because the system shifts up a level to produce a recognizable 'whole', often labeled as such in the lexis of a language, there is also a sense in which emergence produces simplicity from complexity (Cohen and Stewart 1994). The ant colony is a larger scale simplicity emerging from the complexity of the many ants at a lower level and scale. A painting, as a whole, is in some sense 'simpler' than the multiple interactions of color and form that it emerges from. The higher level, emergent phenomena have an identity as wholes and can be labeled as such: 'an anthill', 'Monet's Waterlilies', or 'human rights'.

Complex systems often demonstrate this movement from complexity to simplicity and then to further complexity as they evolve or change over time (Casti 1994; Cohen and Stewart 1994). Complexity thus offers a way of thinking about inter-relations across levels of social and human organization and across timescales that can reconnect simplifying dualisms such as those mentioned in Chapter 1. The reciprocal causality through which emergent phenomena or processes entrain the lower levels or scales of activity that have produced them in the first place provides an alternative to cause-effect relations in which a prior cause produces a consequent effect.

Collective variables

A complex dynamic system can be described by its 'collective variables' that bring together elements of the system that work together. At the moment of a phase shift, the collective variable does not just change continuously but jumps into a new configuration. The gait of the horse, used in an earlier example, would be a collective variable. In the traffic jam example, a collective variable might be the length of the jam—this measure can only be made for the collectivity of the traffic jam and does not apply to individual elements (cars); it only comes into being as a result of the system dynamics. When two people talk together, or when a class of students and teacher interact, their discourse might be better described by collective rather than individual variables, and in Chapters 6 and 7, we explore this possibility.

The collective variable offers a way of describing the relations among elements in a complex system; it condenses the degrees of freedom of the system; and its trace over time reveals points of emergence and self-organization.

The non-directedness of self-organization

We need to remember that the principles of complexity apply to the dynamics of criminality, terrorism, or disease equally as well as to systems of justice, peace-building, or health improvement. When complex systems self-organize and we speak of 'order' or 'co-operation' emerging from previous disorder or separation, we should not be misled by the positive connotations of these words in non-scientific language. In their technical use here, there is no assumption of an inherent drive towards improvement of the universe or of any automatic direction towards better, more hopeful states. The outcomes of self-organization and emergence may be negative, neutral, or positive in human terms.

Self-organized criticality

Systems that undergo a phase shift in which they move from one attractor suddenly into another sometimes display behavior that has been described as 'self-organized criticality' (Bak 1997). The classic example of a system building towards criticality is a pile of dry sand being constructed by grains of sand being slowly poured on to a flat surface from above (Kauffman 1995; Bak 1997). As grains of sand are added, the pile steadily accumulates, becoming higher and steeper until a critical point is reached. The addition of further sand leads to the pile collapsing in a large avalanche of sand. Just before the sand pile collapses, it reaches a state that is roughly stationary, with an equilibrium maintained between sand being added on to the pile and sand sliding off the pile in small avalanches. The sand pile in this equilibrium state has a particular shape and angle relative to the surface it rests on, and it remains in this critical state, until one of the grains poured on to it triggers the large avalanche that collapses the pile. The critical state before collapsing is what we saw above as 'the edge of chaos' (Kauffman 1995: 237).

Self-organizing critical systems like the sand pile are 'over-determined': the avalanche is bound to happen, and if one particular grain does not cause it, some other grain will. That the avalanche will happen can be predicted, but not which grain of sand will produce it. As we have seen throughout this chapter and the last, this unpredictability at local level is characteristic of complex systems— laws govern systems' global or general behavior but specific activities and causes are unpredictable.

> Systems with self-organized criticality 'tune' themselves to a critical state on the edge of chaos, with power-law distribution of avalanche-type events.

The size of an avalanche is not connected to the grain of sand that starts it: 'Big and little events can be triggered by the same kind of tiny cause' (Kauffman 1995: 236).

The sizes of the avalanches taking place around the critical state of a sand pile are distributed according to an 'inverse power-law' in which size is inversely related to frequency: small avalanches occur more frequently and large avalanches occur quite rarely. Figure 2.3 in the previous chapter showed the S-shape of an inverse power-law graph, in which the rate of growth of vocabulary is inversely related to proficiency. Technically, an inverse power-law expresses the relation between variables, or parameters, in which each successive state is inversely related to the logarithm of the previous state. We will meet other power-law distributions in later chapters; they are characteristic of complex dynamic systems.

Self-organized criticality is found in physical, biological, and other systems, prompting us to wonder what it might be like in applied linguistic systems. Just as events that parallel sand pile avalanches in other systems, including floods and earthquakes, show similar power-law distributions of events, with many small and few large ones, so 'language death' as a historical process shows many small languages becoming moribund and few widely-spoken languages dying out. The density of novel expressions in the fast-changing speech of adolescents must be poised at some critical point that just avoids comprehension problems on the part of interlocutors while conveying the speaker as suitably 'cool'. A similar balance must be maintained in the use of jargon in special-interest groups of all types, or in the demands made on learners by classroom tasks (Cameron 2001).

The idea of self-organized criticality has recently been popularized as 'the tipping point' (Gladwell 2000).[5] Here, the analogy is taken from health systems, in which epidemics such as measles or HIV are said to reach a tipping point just before they dramatically explode and infect large numbers of people. Gladwell applies the idea to examples from social and human systems, including the deliberate attempt to spread literacy among young children through the design of the television program 'Sesame Street'.

Self-organized criticality and fractals

In dynamic systems, fractals occur at the boundaries of attractor basins, where the system is poised in a critical state at the edge of chaos, like the sand pile just before it collapses. Here very simple processes produce highly complicated fractal outcomes for the system trajectory. The frequency distribution of sand pile avalanches around the critical point is fractal.

> Fractals are curves that are irregular all over. Moreover, they have exactly the same degree of irregularity at all scales of measurement.
> (Casti 1994: 232)

Many examples of fractal shapes are found in the natural world: clouds, ferns, coastlines, river deltas, galaxies (from Casti 1994). In each of these, the large scale entity has 'the same degree of irregularity' as when the entity is viewed closer to. When seen without an object or person to introduce scale, a view of rugged terrain can be difficult to make sense of—we can't tell whether what we see is a boulder, a pebble, or a grain of sand. Fractal shapes are 'scale-free'.

In some fractals—the simplest types—the shape at each scale or level is the same. This would be the case with a cauliflower, where a floret has the same shape as the whole cauliflower, and within a floret are even smaller florets with the same shape (Stewart 1998).

As with the size of avalanches, fractals are often expressible as inverse power-laws, with each successive state inversely related to the logarithm of the previous state. It is intriguing to wonder about fractals in dynamic systems of language and learning, and we discuss some possibilities in Chapter 4.

Intermezzo: change in complex systems applied to infant motor development

A pioneering application of complexity and dynamic systems theory to human development was the study by Thelen and colleagues of the biomechanics of infants learning to reach and grasp an object (reported in Thelen and Smith 1994: Chapter 9). This work is summarized in this section to consolidate many of the ideas introduced so far in the chapter and to demonstrate how analogical application of complexity theory can inspire new ways of understanding old problems.

During their first year, one of the most important skills that babies master is the ability to reach and grasp. This skill allows infants to bring objects of interest closer to them and thus contributes to survival and to cognitive development. An infant learning to reach out and grasp hold of food, a toy, or some other object has to employ perceptual and motor skills in a task that varies with features of each new context: the size and shape of the object, its distance from the child, the angle of the surface on which the object is placed, the lighting of the object, the health and strength of the infant. Children seem to want to reach objects, and initially to put them in their mouths. Over time they become more skilled at the task of reaching, until the fully developed skill emerges as one of many carried out apparently automatically. The central assumption of Thelen and Smith's dynamic version of the development of reaching is that it happens through 'the soft assembly of mutually interacting, equivalent, multiple-component structures and processes with a context' (ibid.: 249). What they mean by 'soft assembly' is that each reaching action is a response to the variable features of the particular task, in which movements such as the extension of the arm, the leaning of the body, the opening and closing of the fingers are co-adapting in order to get hold of the particular object.

The idea of soft assembly can be appreciated by thinking about another, more advanced, physical activity: gymnastics. The skilled gymnast does not learn a movement like somersaulting over a box and then apply the movement unchanged each time, since a change in context would probably lead to injury. Instead, the gymnast's body is able to carry out the movement under many different conditions. Each somersault is 'soft assembled' for, and in response to, the particular instance. The gymnast's skill lies in what we might call the 'somersault resources' of his or her mind and body, and in their adaptability for changing conditions. We suggest throughout this book that language use may be helpfully seen as the soft assembly of language resources for particular instances. And, further, we argue that Thelen and Smith's contention, that development emerges from use, can also apply to language.

In order to understand the on-line and developmental dynamics of reaching and grasping, Thelen and colleagues examined individual actions in multiple contexts. The same four children were studied in the process of reaching for a toy at multiple levels—from muscle patterns to success in touching the object—and at multiple timescales, covering the months needed to see development and down to the fractions of seconds involved in a single instance, beginning from three weeks old, before the child first displayed reaching behavior, and following through until the child could reach for objects, beyond 30 weeks old (ibid.). The study aimed to find out how the complex dynamic system of the infant changes to display stabilized reaching behavior.

Each child's trajectory towards reaching was different, because each child came to this from a different starting point—they were of different sizes, weights, muscle strengths, and development. These features are the 'intrinsic dynamics' of the child: 'before reaching begins, the system has a landscape with preferred attractor valleys that may be more or less deep, and that reflect both the infant's history and his or her potential for acquiring new forms' (ibid.: 250). One infant had intrinsic dynamics that featured uncontrolled flapping movements of his arms, which developed into directed and controlled reaching. Another infant started from very different intrinsic dynamics, preferring to sit still or move slowly, although she could grasp a toy when it was handed to her. Her developmental task was different, requiring her to learn new movements of lifting her arm and stretching for an object.

Both children had to develop control over their arms, but had to do this from their own starting points.

In development towards reaching, the dynamic systems of the infants passed through several phase shifts or transitions from which new behavior emerged. The researchers wanted to discover which parameters of the system contributed to the emergence of new behavior, i.e. were the control parameters of the system. One phase shift occurred when the infants learned how to control their movements sufficiently to get their hand near to the desired toy. The control parameter at this transition was 'regulation of arm stiffness' (ibid.: 267); once this was under control, the children were able to place their hands so that they could grasp the object. From this point in the systems' trajectories, i.e. the motor development of each child, the infants learned to adapt the movement to grasp hold of the toy through multiple attempts that built up a repertoire of solutions to the reaching task.

In working with complex systems, researchers also want to discover from their empirical data appropriate 'collective variables'. A collective variable describes the co-operative system dynamics and how it changes over time; it brings together several parameters into the single collective variable. Candidate collective variables for reaching included control of hand speed, and direction of hand movement towards the object to be grasped.

The infants developed dynamic stability in their reaching and grasping actions; that stability includes local variation that will support future change, as, for example, when they learn to do the same action from standing and lying as well as sitting. Because developmental changes emerge through phase shifts and the dynamic stabilities that result can sometimes be very stable indeed, they may look as if they are innate or hard-wired, rather than the outcome of changes in complex systems (ibid.).

Thelen and colleagues' ground-breaking work showed how a study to understand human behavior can be designed along complexity principles. They have also applied these ideas to infant walking and to infants learning about objects as permanent bounded entities. Their methods, later developed into a computer simulation (Thelen *et al.* 2001), demonstrate how a complexity approach to a developmental issue can shift away from conventional approaches that amalgamate and average data across children, thereby losing individual variation. In their study, each child achieved mastery of reaching and grasping, but followed his or her own trajectory to do so. The study shows how rich data, collected on multiple levels and multiple timescales covering the period of change, can be condensed through collective variables, and how development occurs through repeated activity in slightly different situations.

The co-adaptation of two or more systems

We now move from considering a single system changing over time to think about how two or more dynamic systems can affect each other. The deer and

predators in the Grand Canyon National Park scenario were seen as interacting in a complex system over a timescale of a century or two, but as species
they could each evolve in response to the other over a longer evolutionary
timescale in a process of co-adaptation. On evolutionary timescales, a species
that is preyed on by another species may adapt, developing camouflage that
makes them less easy to see and hunt, or, in the case of sea urchins or hedgehogs,
prickly spines that make them less desirable as food; predator species may
then develop better eyesight or spine-resistant mouthparts, in a process of 'co-
evolution' (Kauffman 1995: 216). Co-evolution on a shorter timescale occurs
in the co-adaptation of the HIV virus and the immune system of an infected
person, as the virus mutates rapidly in response to the antibodies produced
by the immune system. In co-evolution, an ecological niche may lead to a new
species that can thrive in that niche, and the ecology in turn is changed by
the new species. Co-evolution can be extended through analogy to describe
technical evolution, in which new products and services are created for new
niches, and then alter the technical landscape: the computerization of recorded
music produces the i-pod, which leads to podcasts (downloadable spoken
texts), which encourage ordinary people to produce spoken texts that can be
downloaded from their websites, which will probably have consequences, so
far unknown, for radio broadcasting.

Co-evolution, or co-adaptation, is change in a system that is motivated
by change in another, connected, system. It is the kind of change that will
be highly relevant to many applied linguistic concerns discussed in later
chapters: infants and care-givers co-adapt their language and communication
(Chapter 5); speakers in conversation accommodate to each other in accent
and lexis (Chapter 6); teacher and students co-adapt in classroom behavior
and discourse (Chapter 7).

When two systems interact and co-adapt, their state or phase spaces
change as a result. We can show co-adaptation in a landscape visualization
like Figure 3.1 by rendering the landscape dynamic rather than static. The
interrelated phase space and trajectory would then appear as something like
the interaction between a video game player driving a virtual car across a
changing scene on the screen in front of him or her, and in which the scene
changes in response to the player's driving decisions. The system that is moving across a dynamic landscape changes direction or speed in response to the
changing landscape around it. At the same time, the hills and valleys of the
phase space landscape evolve in response to the changing trajectory, rising or
sinking, appearing or disappearing, getting steeper or flattening out. The state
space landscape over which one system roams is in effect the other system,
and it changes in response to the trajectory of the first system. A real-world
example of systems co-adapting or co-evolving described below may help
explain this idea further.

The co-adaptation of language teaching and language assessment

The provision of language teaching can be seen as one complex dynamic system that is in interaction with another system, the assessment of language proficiency and achievement (Cameron 2001, 2003a). There are many interacting elements and agents in both systems, including policy makers, testers, schools and teaching, teachers, students, parents. The systems are open, in that they are influenced by global changes such as increased mobility, changing employment opportunities, or advances in testing. The two systems of language teaching and language testing *co-adapt*, in that changes in one may give rise to changes in the other. The well known phenomenon of 'washback' is a co-adaptive move by teachers and schools in response to changes in the assessment system. Washback is often seen as negative or dubious, as for example when teachers spend excessive amounts of time training students in techniques to pass an examination. Co-adaptation can be more positively exploited, by incorporating some desirable aspect of language learning, such as oral presentation skills, into assessment, in the expectation that this will lead to its appearance in classroom practice.

> Co-adaptation is the interaction of two or more complex systems, each changing in response to the other.

The history of language teaching and language assessment in a particular country can be seen as the trajectory of the teaching system through a landscape that is itself evolving as the assessment system changes (and vice versa). Changes in assessment produce new hills or valleys in the phase space landscape of the teaching system. Phase shifts may be brought about by perturbations to the systems, such as the introduction of a new test, or by gradual response to changing circumstances as the systems adapt and evolve. To exemplify processes of change and co-adaptation, consider the current growth in young learners of English (Cameron 2003b). In many countries across Europe and the far East, including China and Korea, the age at which children are being taught English is getting younger and younger. Parents are eager to do the best for their children and think that starting to learn English as a child or even a toddler will give their child an advantage. Parental pressure is one dynamic in the system and competition is another; parents want not just to get the best, but perhaps to get something slightly better than other people. Initially, some, perhaps particularly wealthy, parents send their children to private lessons, with the result that these children visibly succeed more in examinations. More parents save up and make sacrifices to send their children to private schools. Meanwhile in another, co-adapting, system, entrepreneurs see increasing opportunities to open private language schools in the changing market. They may aim at the new, less wealthy customers, charging less by having bigger classes. Others may exploit the 'quality' niche, charging a premium for very small classes. Others may offer classes for even younger children, finding yet another 'niche' in the ecology of the language school market.

Parents paying for English lessons want evidence of value for money, and testing organizations are also adaptive dynamic systems that both create and respond to opportunities. The growth in tests for young learners has lately led, through co-adaptation to the opening of special 'Young Learners Test Preparation Centers' in China. Once the centers exist, they influence behavior in other parts of the system, as children attend such centers instead of, or as well as, private classes for learning English. The appearance of these centers can be seen as a phase shift in the trajectory of the language teaching and testing system, as co-adaptation has produced this emergent phenomenon.

Other phase shifts may be on the horizon as the systems keep changing. We might predict a future problem in schools in countries where most children begin to take private lessons in addition to their school language classes. These classes will become more and more mixed in levels, while teachers with good language ability will be in demand in the private sector, where they may receive higher wages. As school language classes become difficult to staff, and the curriculum becomes increasingly irrelevant to students, the system may reach 'tipping point' where the problem becomes urgently in need of a critical phase transition. In England, for example, the government recently abandoned compulsory language teaching in the state sector for students older than 14 years.

More on context

In the previous chapter, we noted that context in complexity is interconnected, and this interconnection is formalized by incorporating relevant factors of context as system parameters. Now that some more of the complex systems apparatus is in place, we return to this idea.

If a contextual factor affects a complex system, it can be incorporated as one of the dimensions of the system's state space, and also into a collective variable if appropriate. By being incorporated into the state space, contextual factors will influence the trajectory of the system, will contribute to the development of attractor regions, and thus to phase shifts, self-organization, and emergence. Contextual factors are not external to the system, but become part of the system. In the visual metaphor that shows the state space of a system as a 'landscape of possibilities' (such as that in Figure 3.7), that landscape has as many dimensions as needed to include the physical, cognitive, and sociocultural. Context thus becomes the landscape over which the system moves, and the movement of the system transforms the context.

Thelen and Smith (1994) explain the 'special status' of context in complexity theory in connecting what happens in the here and now with change in the system and with the emergence of what they call 'global order' in the system over time. 'Global order' refers to emergent attractor states of the system and examples of global order in complex systems discussed so far would include: the action of reaching and grasping as eventually mastered by the infant (described earlier in this chapter), and other motor actions such as 'walking' or 'skipping'; the gaits of the horse-and-rider system; lexicogrammatical patterns in a language; cultural artifacts such as the violin or milk jug, and their uses; shopping habits of people in a city.

> Dynamic systems explains both the global order and the local details. The global order and the local variability are *the same thing*; they are inextricably tied together in a way that confers a special status on context—on the role of the immediate here and now. Context—the here and now—matters in three ways. First, context makes the global order. The global order is a history of perceiving and acting in specific contexts; it is through repeated here-and-now experiences that the global order is developed. Second, context *selects* the global order such that we can perform qualitatively different acts. For example, depending on the terrain, we can sometimes walk, sometimes slide, and sometimes stand still. Third, context *adapts* the global order; it fits the history of past here and nows to the task at hand. Context makes, selects and adapts knowledge ... since the global order is made by and made manifest in the details of the here and now, it is most fundamentally always context-dependent.
> (Thelen and Smith 1994: 217)

Applying these ideas to our field, the context-dependence of complex applied linguistic systems is also three-fold: language is developed in context, as use in context shapes language resources; language is applied in context, as context selects the language action to be performed; language is adapted for context, as the experience of past language use is fitted to the here and now.

Change in complex systems: summary

The appeal and power of complexity theory lies in the way in which very different types of systems share patterns of change and adaptation. The same vocabulary and descriptions can be used for neurons and ecologies, for language teaching provision and economies, for idioms and populations. The same general laws may be said to apply to these very different systems. The characteristics of complex dynamic systems discussed so far include:

- complex systems are always changing
- complex systems can change smoothly or radically
- complex systems can show self-organization through phase shifts that produce emergent behavior or phenomena on a higher level of organization
- complex systems in and near attractors show both stability and variability
- complex systems near the edge of chaos are very flexible and responsive
- systems in chaotic regions of their state space (chaotic systems) are extremely sensitive to small changes in the initial conditions

- some complex systems show criticality around phase transitions
- two or more complex systems can change in response to each other in a process of co-adaptation, and
- complex systems can be described with collective variables, and their phase shifts through control parameters.

In the following chapters, we consider systems of central concern for applied linguists. If these systems fit the criteria for being complex and dynamic, then we should expect to see them display the above characteristics.

Complexity thought modeling, continued

At the end of Chapter 2, we introduced the idea of 'thought modeling' in parallel to 'thought experiments' of positivist science. Thought modeling is designed to help researchers and practitioners use complexity theory to think about a problem or situation, as a lead-in to actual modeling, to data collection, or to practical intervention. Thought modeling begins with identifying the systems of interest and their dynamics, and then proceeds to examine the nature of change in the system and how system parameters contribute to change. The list in Table 3.1 below combines steps from Chapter 2 with those arising from this chapter:

Identify the different components of the system, including agents, processes, and subsystems.
For each component, identify the timescales and levels of social and human organization on which it operates.
Describe the relations between and among components.
Describe how the system and context adapt to each other.
Describe the dynamics of the system: • how do the components change over time? • how do the relations among components change over time?
Describe the kinds of change that can be observed in the system: steady change or discontinuous leaps from one state, or mode of action, to another in phase shifts or bifurcations.
Identify the contextual factors that are working as part of the system.
Identify processes of co-adaptation with other systems.
Identify candidate control parameters, i.e. the motors of change that seem to lead to phase shifts.
Identify candidate collective variables that can be used to describe the system, before and after phase shifts.

Identify possible fractals in the system.
Describe the state space landscape of the system: • Where are the attractor states in the state space (i.e. stabilities in the changing system)? • How deep and steep are they? (i.e. How stable are the attractor states?)
Describe the trajectory of the system in its state space. (i.e. What are common patterns of activity?)
Identify regions of the state space that are most used by the system, and those which are seldom visited. (i.e. What does the system do out of all it could possibly do?)
Describe what happens around attractors. (i.e. What kind of variability is there around stabilities?)
Identify possible emergence and/or self-organization across timescales and/or levels of human organization.

Table 3.1 Steps to guide 'complexity thought modeling' of systems

Following the steps above should produce further questions about the system to be answered but more importantly should allow one to imagine the system under different conditions and to pose questions such as: what might happen if certain parameters are changed? What might happen if the system operates over a long period of time?

The steps in Table 3.1. represent the complexity analogy or metaphor in action—the application of complexity theory to applied linguistic issues.

Implications of a complexity perspective

In Chapter 1, we suggested that complexity theory may offer a supra-disciplinary approach applicable across many fields, including our own, but that in some instances we may more appropriately invoke complexity as a metaphor. Now that we have explained many of the basic ideas of complexity in systems and their behavior, we can return to discuss that suggestion more thoroughly. We also return to the issue of human agency in complex systems, and ask the question: are you happy to be (seen as) a complex dynamic system?

Theorizing and researching complex systems

To say that a real-world system is a complex, dynamic, and non-linear system is to make a very precise claim. Once away from the tidy world of mathematics, systems become less precisely knowable and claims for complexity are more likely to rest on parallels between the behavior of a real-world system and the behavior of mathematical or physical systems. In the field of biology and evolution, these parallels are accepted as sufficient to warrant adopting a systems perspective and the development of computer models of complex biological systems. Real-world social and human systems involve a further step away from mathematics, and systems ideas can be invoked at various depths, from metaphorical comparison to theory. Adopting a complex systems perspective has radical implications for the principles and processes of theory-building and empirical investigation, which we introduce here. We then return to the issue of human agency and the role of ethics in applying complexity theory.

The nature of hypotheses and theories

In the classical scientific paradigm, theories are developed in order to describe, explain, and predict the real world. Hypotheses are tested empirically in order to prove or disprove theories. But in a complex world, much of this changes: we lose predictability; the nature of explanation changes; cause and effect work differently. A complexity approach, with its central notion of emergence, goes beyond a reductionist approach, in which 'complicated systems are analyzed into simpler constituents linked together by relatively simple rules—laws of nature' (Cohen and Stewart 1994: 33). Reductionism no longer operates effectively to explain the emergent and self-organizing.

In complexity theory, theory and 'laws' work at an abstract and general level, and explanation is in terms of the system's behavior not at the level of individual agents or elements. When a sand pile avalanches, theory and description is not about individual grains of sand but about the behavior of the system as a whole. We can never know which particular grain of sand will produce the avalanche, but we do know that it will happen and about the nature of patterns of avalanches.

Reductionist explanations are not possible because the behavior of every part of the system down to the atomic particle cannot be known. The 'unknowableness' in complex systems makes them unpredictable. Complex systems vary in the degree to which they are unknowable, with chaotic systems the most unpredictable. Complex systems are not random, but they are non-linear. They can be described, but non-linearity means that their behavior cannot be predicted. In conventional science, explanation produces prediction in the form of testable hypotheses. In complexity theory, once a system has changed or evolved, the process can be explained, for example through emergence or self-organization. Complexity theory thus brings about a separation of explanation and prediction.

The nature of descriptions and explanations, particularly causality

Complex systems types of explanation, which do not allow prediction, differ from what we are used to in applied linguistics. Emergent properties or phenomena cannot be explained in terms of the interacting elements combining to produce them as in classical reductionism.

Causality changes nature too: the particular sand grain that produces the avalanche is a cause but not an explanation. Explanation is found at a higher level of organization in terms of the structure and stability of the sand pile.

The nature of data and evidence

Adopting a complex systems perspective shifts our view of what is seen to be in need of empirical investigation, in particular the role of context and environment. It changes what we need to collect as data to understand a complex system, in particular our attitude to variation, as we saw with the rich multilevel and multi-timescale data in the study of infant reaching. It changes what we notice in the behavior of systems: flux and variability signal possible processes of self-organization and emergence; sudden phase shifts signal important changes and can direct attention to the conditions that lead up to them. The starting point or intrinsic dynamics of a system become an important aspect of understanding trajectories.

In a complexity perspective, context and environment are inseparably connected into the system, not background against which the system operates. Systems may be coupled, with one acting as dynamic context for the other. What is measured or observed thus also inseparably involves context. If language skills are tested in a laboratory setting very different from the classroom, the language use that we observe must be understood as a response to that setting and related to the intrinsic dynamics of the language user.

Complex systems that we want to understand and investigate will move between stability and flux. The concept of change occurring through stability lost and regained as a system moves from one attractor state to another, means that lack of stability in knowledge or performance may suggest something interesting happening in the system. The stability of a state of the system can be investigated by testing its resistance to perturbations. In fact, Vygotsky long ago suggested this in his experimental 'genetic method' (Kozulin 1990). Pushing a learner's language to the edge of its capability can reveal the stability of structures or lexis. A further implication for work in our field, also recognized by Vygotsky, is that training for experimental tasks changes the intrinsic dynamics or initial conditions of the system, and thus means that what is being investigated is different from behavior of the untrained system.

Variability in data is not noise to be discarded but is part of the behavior of the system, and to be expected around stabilities. If we smooth away variability, by averaging for example, we lose the very information that may shed light on emergence.

Complex systems are often sensitive to changes in context and adapt dynamically to them in a process of 'soft assembly'—the galloping motion of the horse-and-rider system will be different each time as the horse adapts to the weight of the rider, the firmness of the ground surface, wind speed and direction, and its own fitness and health. Similarly, children learning to reach and grasp adapt dynamically to the local conditions of each task. Longer term, global development emerges through these micro-level local activities. It follows that, if we want to investigate development or learning, we need to try to capture the processes of self-organization and emergence. This need to see the system changing in order to understand its dynamics has led to the development of microgenetic methods (Granott and Parziale 2002). This and other research implications are further discussed in Chapter 8.

Investigation through computer modeling involves the creation of idealized mathematical models of complex systems that include their non-linearity. The systems in the models are complex systems, but they are not real-world systems, merely miniature, idealized versions of them. The data produced by computer models can shed light on the nature of real-world systems, if the model has been carefully designed. Care is needed in assumptions built into the model, especially implicit assumptions. In the following quote, a mathematician and a biologist warn of the dangers:

> The hardest (errors) of all to spot are the implicit assumptions in the worldview that suggested the model. For example, suppose you're setting up a model of biological development based upon the idea of DNA as a message. You would naturally tend to focus upon such quantities as the amount of information in a creature's DNA string and the amount of information needed to describe the animal's physical form. If you then model development as a process of information transfer—lots of messages buzzing to and fro—you will implicitly have built a model in which information cannot be created. You will then be able to 'prove' that humans can't develop a brain because the amount of information needed to list every connection in the human brain is a lot more than the total amount of information in human DNA.
>
> But we do have brains. ... Impeccable mathematics can produce nonsense if it is based on nonsensical assumptions. ... Don't be impressed by mathematics just because you can't understand it.
> (Cohen and Stewart 1994: 186)

The use of computer modeling is indispensable to the investigation of complex systems, but models are only as good as the data and theory used to design them. Microgenetic studies of complex systems in the real world are also indispensable in order to design better models.

Human agency and complex systems

People vary in their responses to the idea that they themselves may be seen as systems, even if this is a metaphorical understanding. Some feel it to be dehumanizing, reducing human activity to something impersonal and mechanical, although in fact it is no less so than having one's mind seen as a computer. It may be a measure of how entrenched the computer metaphor has become, that we seldom hear complaints about its mechanizing view of human mental activity.

Human intentionality and agency appear to be one of the most severe problems in applying a complex systems metaphor or analogy to the kinds of behaviors and processes that interest applied linguists,[6] and thus merits close consideration. We suggest that agency issues can be grouped under the following themes: determinism, distancing, and deliberate decision-making. We discuss each in turn.

In the previous chapter, we noted that in dynamic systems, i.e. systems that change over time, future states depend in some way on the present state of the system. In this sense, dynamic systems are deterministic. However, this is different from being completely predictable, as in a simple system like traffic lights. When a system is open, connected into its environment, influences from outside can affect the system. Any change, however small, that is introduced into the system can have effects that spread through the system, diluting the determinism and rendering the outcome of system activity unpredictable. Weather forecasters can never feed absolutely exact data into their models and so can never predict future weather conditions with complete precision. Teachers can plan lessons very carefully but can never exactly know what learners will bring to the planned lesson, and so outcomes are unpredictable. The behavior of a complex system is not completely random, but neither is it is wholly predictable. This is an important point to bear in mind because it may sometimes feel that, in seeing human activity in terms of systems, we are adopting a mechanistic and deterministic perspective, in the negative sense of denying the possibility of free will. On the contrary, complexity theory restores the possibility of radical change, through the acknowledgement that all cannot be known, and through its conceptualization of open systems as connecting out into their environment, and adapting to it. A degree of determinism is thus perhaps compensated for by openness and unpredictability.

As with any method of modeling human life, describing problems in terms of complex systems can lead to a 'distancing' effect, but, we argue, this need not necessarily be dehumanizing. If, for example, shopping trends are modeled within the complexity of a city, the system appears to be free of human action or intention. Human decision-making, such as when to do the shopping, is converted into mathematical functions that represent the outcome at a population level of very many individual decisions. When we see this kind of human behavior in the abstract as a system, we may lose sight of the detail of the individual, whose actions or decisions become mathematical descriptions. This does not mean that it is being assumed that such decisions and intentions do not exist or are not important, just that there is sufficient patterning at a level above the individual to warrant working with 'trends'. If there is not, then the system (or a model of it) can be constructed to incorporate more variability. In a complex systems approach, there is no need to smooth away specific variability or to decide some detail is superfluous. As we have seen in this chapter, concern with specifics and variability lies at the heart of complexity theory.

The third metaphysical problem for a complexity approach is how to include people's deliberate decisions into a complexity theory or metaphor. Maasen and Weingart (2000) report strongly worded articles by Brügge (1993) lamenting inappropriate or 'illegitimate' comparisons between humans and chaotic systems. Brügge insists that similarities between social processes and physical processes are misleading, rather than helpful: 'people, in contrast to particles, learn continuously and can change collective behavior' (Maasen and Weingart 2000: 126). This is of course true, and it remains to some extent an open question as to how far complexity theory can accommodate deliberate decision-making. However, we can marshal some substantial support for a positive answer to this question.

Juarrero (1999) is a book-length argument to the effect that complexity theory not only allows for human agency, but actually offers the best contemporary framework for understanding intentionality. She claims that complexity offers new ways of understanding cause and explanation that can usefully underpin a dynamical theory of action. Her argument is that consciousness and self-consciousness emerge, as an instance of higher level order, from the local dynamics of the human brain in context. Consciousness then works 'top down' in a process of reciprocal causality to constrain and regulate human action.

The other angle to take on decision-making is that our agency may be more limited than we are aware of. As agents in multiple, nested, complex systems, the decisions that we make as individuals cannot help but be influenced by our connections into all kinds of social groupings. Take the most humdrum of human decisions, such as deciding to put the household rubbish out for collection. Every aspect of the decision reveals our interconnectedness: the kind of rubbish we have reflects our shopping and eating habits; the day of the week is a decision of the local council or equivalent, in turn affected by their financial planning and by national politics; the local wildlife will influence whether the rubbish is put out overnight and in what kind of container. If a trivial decision like taking out the garbage is not ours to make independently, there is no chance that more abstract decisions such as how to bring up our children or whether to intervene in an incident can be disconnected from the social-political-historical-moral-cultural influences of our time. The same argument applies to collective decisions.

The restricted or diminished view of individual agency is limited still further by evidence from psychology about our apparently conscious decisions. Studies in brain science have shown, somewhat puzzlingly, that decisions to make simple movements do not seem to be made in advance of the brain activity that initiates the movement, but 350–400 milliseconds afterwards (Libet 1985, discussed in Gibbs 2006). In another study (Wegner and Wheatley 1999), people were asked to move their limbs but also had their brains stimulated to induce involuntary movements; they were equally likely to believe the stimulated, involuntary movements to be the result of conscious decisions as the voluntary movements. As Gibbs says, 'Results such as these call into question the simple idea that the conscious self is always the author of one's bodily action' (2006: 23). The idea of agency seems to spring from reflection on action rather than from action itself.

From both directions then, it appears that our idea of agency and decision-making is more complicated (and indeed more complex) than is generally assumed. Complexity theory may help unravel some of these complications through helping us understand how a sense of self emerges from the interplay of brain, body, and world (Gibbs 2006).

As a final comment on the human agency issue, we would like to make a point about moral or ethical responsibility. A complexity perspective does not diminish the need for people to take responsibility for their actions; if anything, it increases the urgency of accepting that responsibility. As we noted earlier in the chapter, self-organization and the emergence of order in complex systems are ethically-neutral processes; it is people who must impose and apply ethics to these processes, recognizing how a decision in one part of a system can affect other parts and ripple outwards to other connected systems.

To summarize the agency issue, we see complexity theory as allowing more of the human into theory than theories that metaphorize the human mind as a computer. However, the incorporation of human actions into systems adds significantly to the task that we have assigned to complexity theory as analogy and as new perspective, and may push it further into metaphor, by taking it beyond what it was 'designed to explain' (Hull 1982: 275).

Bearing this possible limitation in mind, we proceed in the following chapters to explore the application of the complexity perspective in detail to areas of applied linguistics: language, language development, and language use.

Notes

1 The introduction of visual images brings with it spatial metaphors that contribute significantly to complexity vocabulary. There are now 'places' for the system to 'occupy', to 'move' between. 'Movement across landscape' metaphors offer useful ways to talk and think about dynamic systems.

2 The boundaries of regions are often fuzzy rather than solid and fixed, as they inevitably appear on a diagram.

3 The term 'motivation' is used very loosely here. For more detailed approaches to motivation that are compatible with a complex dynamics perspective, see Dörnyei (2003), Ushioda (2007), and Lamb (2004).

4 The relation between structure and agency in human social life, and the advantages of taking a complexity or emergentist perspective on this relation, are ably debated by Sealey and Carter (2004). In arguing for a complexity-based, realist approach to social theory, in which language as a social practice emerges from 'the interplay between structure and agency' (ibid.: 16), Sealey and Carter critique Giddens' structuration theory, which

might at first sight appear to be another theory compatible with complexity. In structuration theory, structure is seen as rules and resources that are instantiated in social action, but do not have a separate systematic existence. Although Giddens' view is dynamic, in taking social action as key, a fuller complexity perspective would see the rules and resources that comprise social structure as emerging through self-organization and acting as an attractor in the larger system of social action, exerting a force on the actions of individuals, and, importantly for social theory, accessible to scrutiny and intervention.

5 And in older idiomatic/folk descriptions such as 'the last straw' or 'the straw that breaks the camel's back'.

6 In fact, the issue of agency is of concern to complexity scientists in a reversal of the discussion here. Components of non-human complex systems are often personified, by calling aspects of a model created and manipulated by computers 'agents', and the random changes that they undergo 'decisions' or 'behaviors', etc. This may ascribe agency and intentionality where there is none (Baake 2003).

4

Complex systems in language and its evolution

Applied linguists need a theory of language. Having reviewed the characteristics of complex dynamic systems and change within them in the previous
two chapters, it may be easier to understand why here we make the case for
a view of language different from one to which many linguists and applied
linguists have subscribed in the past. Linguists often employ algebraic phrase
structure rules and static representations to specify the constraints that
particular languages or all languages must obey. They treat language as a
stable, even static, system. While such an approach may yield descriptive
adequacy, this pursuit provides no vocabulary or concepts for the discussion
of dynamic processes. Applied linguists, on the other hand, are centrally
concerned with processes: language development, language use, language
acquisition, language teaching, language learning. These processes call for
different theories and different methods from those associated with static
grammatical description. As we saw in the previous chapter, complex systems
are at one and the same time both stable and variable. Thus, in this chapter
we propose a complexity-inspired view of language, one that we feel serves
applied linguistics well. Before doing so, though, we should acknowledge a
certain level of discomfort in discussing language as a separate entity, apart
from its use in the world. Indeed, as we saw in Chapter 2, a system is connected
to its environment. Drawing a line around a particular system, albeit one as
complex as language, and segregating it from its use and from other systems,
is convenient, but at the same time, problematic. The problem arises in that
linguistic forms interact with non-linguistic information in the determination
of meaning.[1] While we, therefore, recognize that language cannot be usefully
segregated from its ecology, we discuss language here as a metonym for
situated language-using, returning to explore language-in-use in discourse in
Chapter 6. For now, though, we treat language as a system unto itself, albeit
an open and permeable one.

A complexity-inspired view of language

From a complexity theory perspective, a language at any point in time is the way it is because of the way it has been used.[2] Because the agents or users of the language change as individuals over the course of their lifetimes, not to mention that circumstances and individuals change over generations, so do the way that speakers use their language resources. Of course, the rate of language change may vary. For example, as was mentioned in the previous chapter, when language users enter adolescence, one way they distinguish themselves is through rapid innovations in their language use. However, the point is that change in both agents and their language resources is continuous. In fact, we would go so far as to say that every use of language changes it in some way (Larsen-Freeman 2003).

Consider a word at the level of the individual, for instance. Phoneticians have long known that the same word is pronounced differently by the same person with every use (Milroy and Milroy 1999). In addition, neuroscientists who model the brain as a complex, non-linear network (Globus 1995) suggest that every sensory input, every use of a word, simultaneously strengthens certain, and weakens other, connections in a neural network model. Such sensory inputs leave behind subtle neurochemical changes in the brain (Stevick 1996). Strengthened connections make the word more accessible in the future (Truscott 1998). Furthermore, as a word is used in making meaning, it can take on new meanings inferred from the environment in which it is used (Bybee 2006), including the meaning that others give it (Bakhtin 1981), to say nothing of the fact that a person's memory does not authentically preserve the original (Stevick 1996).

This does not mean that the changed use at an individual level is immediately taken up by all members of the speech community, for change takes place at different rates at different levels (MacWhinney 1999). Nor does it mean that there is nothing stable about language, for without a considerable degree of stability, rapid speech processing and mutual intelligibility would be difficult to accomplish (Givón 1999). As has been mentioned several times in this book thus far, and as will be argued in more detail in Chapter 6, language emerges 'upwards' in the sense that language-using patterns arise from individuals using the language interactively, adapting to one another's resources. However, there is reciprocal causality, in that the language-using patterns themselves 'downwardly' entrain emergent patterns.[3] Clearly, then, there are language-using patterns that endure—patterns which can be associated with particular speech acts or genres, for instance—recursive communication patterns that connect a variety of contexts, patterns of the type which feature prominently in much of Bateson's work (for example, 1991). There are patterns that are stable over the lifetimes of language users (MacWhinney 2006) or change so slowly that they seem to humans not to be in process at all, but a constant of life (Lemke 2000b), an observation termed 'the adiabatic principle'—see below.

The point not to be lost, however, is that from a complexity theory perspective, the language-using patterns are dynamic and their use probabilistic. These dynamic language-using patterns are everywhere, at every level of language. The patterns both inform and constrain what is subsequently produced. Although human brains are especially good at detecting these patterns, not all language in the environment gets registered. Our consciousness[4] becomes especially tuned to frequently-occurring language-using patterns.[5] In order to conserve our cognitive resources, patterns that are frequently used become conventionalized (Hopper 1988). However, even conventionalized patterns have the potential for change, especially when they exhibit variation, a harbinger of change to come (Weinreich, Labov, and Herzog 1968).

Patterns in language are therefore epiphenomena of interaction: they are emergent stabilities (Hopper 1988). Taken together, they comprise what in complexity terms would be called 'an attractor basin in a dynamic system'. As emergent language-using patterns are taken up as adaptations by members of the speech community, some become more privileged than others and endure or, at least, change at slower rates than others. Privilege might be bestowed because certain patterns are more frequent, have greater semantic or pragmatic utility or because they are associated with certain prestigious dialects or because of their specialized register or function. Of course, even though language is open to all sorts of influences and is continually changing, it still somehow maintains an identity as the 'same' language, as do other autopoietic systems, such as the human body, where cells are constantly being created and sloughed off even while a person from all outward appearances remains the same. Within a given timescale, social forces and motivation around national or community identity may play a role in establishing and maintaining a standard language. While such attempts do have some impact, any attempts to control language-using over time are inevitably unsuccessful. Standard languages are socio-political constructs that do not reflect the reality of language use, where there is movement through state space from one basin of attraction to another.

Dynamic patterns of language using

The language-using patterns that emerge are variegated, described by linguists by any one of a number of labels depending on their theoretical commitment. Of course, any attempt to name and describe the patterns of a language involves a selection process that is inevitably simplifying and idealizing. Meanwhile, the language system keeps changing so that any description can only be provisional and incomplete anyway. We will adopt the general term 'dynamic patterns of language using' (abbreviated as 'language-using patterns') in order to capture both their stability and their variability, though we acknowledge, due to the limitations of English, even this term suggests more fixity than we would like. These are not discrete, abstract symbolic representations upon which some logical operations can be performed. They do not necessarily correspond to traditional linguistic categories, but they are accepted as conventional by members of a given speech community. They may include words, idioms, partially lexically filled and fully general linguistic patterns. Construction grammarians, such as Goldberg (2003), call the patterns 'constructions' and consider them to be any form-meaning pattern whose form or function is not predictable from its component parts. Here, we adopt a broader definition and conceive of *form-meaning-use dynamic patterns of language using* (i.e. we do not eliminate use or pragmatics), and ones not only unpredictable, but ones that can be compositional as well, i.e. they can arise from motivated choices with probabilistically predictable component parts. (See also Taylor 1998.)[6] Goldberg (1995) posits the 'ditransitive' construction in English that dative verbs with two arguments enter into. The pattern is 'X causes Y to receive Z' (Goldberg 1995) as in 'Jill offered Paula a job and Paula sent Jill her reply'. Other, newer verbs, such as 'fax' or 'email' can 'inherit' the abstract semantics of this construction as they enter into it (for example, 'Paula faxed Jill her reply'). In this way, inheritance permits semantic generalizations across a construction. Inheritance allows for the creation of innovative patterns, such as 'Phyllis sneezed her answer to Bob when he asked if she had allergies', interpretable because of the semantics of the ditransitive pattern that Goldberg has identified. Since we are also concerned with use, we should point out that the pragmatics governing the dative pattern are evident in the different word orders that reflect a difference in the information status of the direct and indirect objects (cf. 'Jill offered Paula a job and Jill offered a job to Paula'), each of which would be appropriate in a different context.

According to Goldberg, constructions can also be what have traditionally been considered grammatical structures. For instance the form of the passive voice is made up of particular structural elements that have the grammatical meaning of defocusing the agent and instead thematically focusing on the receiver of the action. It is used when the agent of an action is unknown, redundant, concealed, non-thematic, etc. In addition, constructions can be embedded in other constructions, so that the passive voice construction could optionally include the 'by' + agent construction. Some constructions do not conform to syntactic rules (for example, 'by and large', a coordination between a preposition and an adjective), and some more general or conceptually schematic constructions are grammatical and highly productive, for example, the 'X by Y' construction, which designates the rate at which some process unfolds (for example, 'one by one', 'day by day', 'page by page') (Taylor 2004).

Other dynamic language-using patterns that exemplify this stability are more abstract and operate at a sentence/utterance level or discourse level, such as theme-rheme word order, so important for maintaining coherence in discourse, or the means by which language users distinguish foregrounded from backgrounded information, or the supra-sentential patterns of discourse that characterize different genre (see Chapter 6), or those that, indeed, are used to distinguish one language from another. There are certain stabilities that are fixed, such as frozen metaphors and collocates, which are always used the same way. There are other frequently-occurring semi-fixed patterned sequences that behave as single lexical units (Pawley and Syder 1983), such as 'I'm not at all sure that ...' but which are not fused, i.e. they are variable within limits.

Earlier, we mentioned the permeability of the language-using system. It is important to note that because these variegated stabilities emerge from language use, they are characterized not only by linguistic features, but sometimes accompanied by gesture, unique prosodies, and by affective, cognitive, and episodic and situational associations, experienced as they are embedded in a socio-historical context. For instance, Kay and Fillmore (1999) show how over the years the English pattern 'What is/are X doing with Y?' has come to take on a negative expression of incongruity (for example, 'What is *John* doing with that new car?'), in addition to its unmarked function as an information question ('What are you doing with the recipe you asked for?'). Episodic or situational associations arise from what Wittgenstein (1953/2001: 7) called 'language games', 'consisting of language and the actions into which it is woven'. The stabilities are also shaped by physical factors. The phonology of languages is influenced by what sounds are made possible in the human vocal tract, which once established, in turn, influence the development of mouth and muscles when infants learn a particular first language and use their articulatory mechanisms for a particular subset of the full range of linguistic articulations available. But even the meaningful sound combinations in a language exhibit emergent and perpetual novelty. For example in as little as 30 years, there have been striking sound changes in Cantonese with regards to the pronominal system, with /nei/ becoming /lei/ ('you') and /ngo/ going to /o/ ('I') (Zee 1999).

What adds to the complexity of the change process is that both elements and agents themselves are continuously changing. For example, the anatomical spacing of photoreceptors in the retina gives the neonate a very different view of the world from that of an older child. As we said in Chapter 1, our new understanding of vision suggests that this is not a trivial difference. We no longer compare our eyes to a camera lens; we now understand that we construct images from light and color. What we see is affected by a number of things, including who we are in the moment. Thus, not only are the visual experiences of young children different, but presumably also what can be learned from them. Further, since complex systems are sensitive to initial conditions, the process of development itself changes in that earlier stages shape and constrain what will happen at later stages, 'in ways that have only begun to be appreciated' (Elman 2005: 114).

Soft assembly

Appropriating Thelen and Smith's (1994) term 'soft assembly', which we introduced in Chapter 3 in conjunction with an infant's reaching, we propose that on one level and at one timescale, the immediate context, language use is 'soft-assembled' (Thelen and Smith 1994) by individuals—a real-time process, taking into account options and constraints, the intrinsic dynamics of the speaker, the individual's language-using history, the affordances of the context, and the communicative pressures at hand. Soft assembly would work when people attempt to catch a ball, for instance, by their adjusting their position, their posture, and their hands to their visual estimation of the ball's velocity and likely time and location of contact (Spencer and Schöner 2003: 395). When two individuals soft assemble using their language resources on a given occasion and then interact and adapt to each other, the state space of both their language resources changes as a result of co-adaptation. (See Chapters 5 and 6.) On a longer timescale, at another level, say within a speech community, these local interactions are what transform the state space of the language in an ongoing way. The passing on of change across a system is a kind of 'feedback', and the process in which a system adjusts itself in response to changes in its elements is a form of self-organization. As with other complex systems, language-using patterns are *heterochronous*. A language event on some local timescale may simultaneously be part of language change on longer timescales (Lemke 2002: 80).

Let us examine transitivity as an example. Transitivity is not an a priori category, permanently associated with a given verb in a static fashion, but a central property of language use (Hopper and Thompson 1980). For example, the more frequently a verb is used, the looser the relationship between a verb and its arguments. Thus, frequently-occurring 'get' is used with a variety of arguments, but uncommonly used 'elapse' only with a noun phrase. The customary transitivity status of a verb can also be altered by analogy at any one time. For instance, a real estate agent was heard to say 'This house hasn't appraised yet', and a nurse said to a patient, 'Have they sampled you yet?' (i.e. 'Have they taken a sample from you yet?'). Such creativity occurs frequently in ordinary talk (Carter 2004), though Thompson and Hopper (2001: 49) point out that the degree to which the examples just given are seen as novel varies from one person to the next. They also note that with a few such instances, even the ones thought to be novel, lose their novelty — 'Thus the dividing line between stored "argument structures" and [novel] extensions can be seen to be constantly changing under the influence of everyday language use', leading Thompson and Hopper to conclude that '"Grammar" is a name for the adaptive complex, highly interrelated, and multiply categorized sets of recurrent regularities that arise from doing the communicative work that humans do' (2001: 48).

S-curves

As we said in the previous chapter, historical change on a long timescale arises from small local changes made possible by variability around current stabilities or the recurrent regularities which Thompson and Hopper note. Historical linguist Anthony Kroch (1989) has analyzed the gradual introduction of the auxiliary 'do' in English questions and negatives between 1400 and 1700. In Middle English, questions were formed by inverting the tensed verb with the subject, and negative sentences were formed by placing the negative particle 'not' after the tensed verb. Beginning some time in the fifteenth century, the pattern began to change in the case of sentences with a tensed main verb, with 'do' (or 'doth') becoming an auxiliary. By 1700, this new form had largely replaced the original usage. Figure 4.1 traces the non-linear development of periphrastic 'do' in a variety of sentence types. It can be seen that prior to 1500, most of the sentence types increase gradually. From just before 1500 to just after 1550 there is a sharp increase, followed by a decline in some for a time, yielding an S-shaped curve. Kroch hypothesizes that during the decline a major reanalysis of the English auxiliary system was occurring.

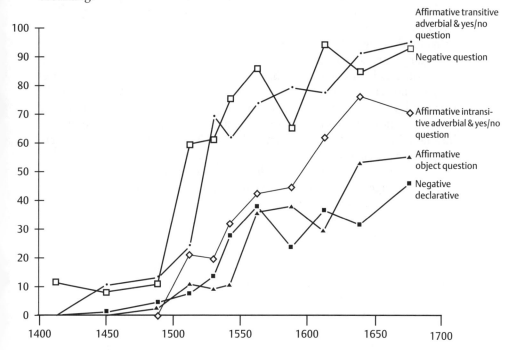

Figure 4.1 The development of periphrastic do *in English from 1400–1700 (Figure 6 from Kroch 1989). The percentage of items showing the change appears on the Y-axis and time in fifty-year intervals on the X-axis*

Interestingly, Kroch observes that population biologists have found that the S-curve also characterizes the replacement of one organism and genetic alleles that differ in Darwinian fitness with another. The replacement occurs in a context where the two species compete with differential reproductive success for the same resources. Thus, in both historical linguistics and population biology (and as we saw in Chapter 2, with the non-linear growth of vocabulary in language development), we find this S-curve relationship between two competing entities. An S-curve is produced by the logistic function or power-law, found to be characteristic of change in complex, dynamic systems.

S-curves, where there is an initial period of slow change, followed by a period of more rapid change, which, in turn, is followed by a period of slower change, have also been found for sound change over a much shorter time and even for sound change in individual speakers (Bailey 1973). Thus, at different levels and different timescales, the same pattern recurs. Not only does the overall change process not proceed at a uniform rate among the speakers of a language, but it also occurs differently from one word to the next. For example, in East Anglia and the East Midlands of England, a sound change is well established in 'must' and 'come', but the same sound change is found hardly at all in words containing the same vowel, for example, 'uncle' and 'hundred '(Chambers and Trudgill 1980: 177). While the difference in these two pairs of words may very well be due to a frequency effect (the first pair being more frequently occurring than the second), the point is that language is not a homogeneous, static entity.

Of course, historical linguists have known this for a long time. Discoveries in the nineteenth century included Grimm's Law, which showed how the Germanic languages differed systematically in consonant articulation from the other Indo-European languages and the Great Vowel Shift, which showed how later English differed systematically from its earlier forms with respect to the place of articulation of the long vowels (Brinton and Traugott 2005). They have also known for a long time that frequency of use played a significant role in language change (Fitch 2007). Indeed, recent access to large historical databases has shown convincingly that patterns of language change depend strongly on the frequency with which words are used in discourse (Lieberman *et al.* 2007, Pagel *et al.* 2007). However, with the advent of structuralism in the twentieth century, the focus shifted from tracing change in patterns over time to describing patterns in synchronic systems. (See the section in this chapter on 'The influence of linguistics'.) At least in North America, the influence of structuralism has endured to the present day. There has been an exception, however, and that is found in the work of sociolinguists.

There have been two dominant approaches to studying language variation in sociolinguistics. The first was established by William Labov (1972). It makes use of probabilistically weighted rules, called variable rules. Variable rules, unlike categorical rules, give probabilistic information, based on surveys of language use. They specify to what extent a particular linguistic form will be used by a speech community in relation to factors, such as social class, level of formality, age, sex, and race. Bailey (1973) proposed an alternative 'dynamic paradigm', called wave theory. Underlying this theory is the assumption that speech variability in a language user reflects a gradual spread of a speech pattern over time. 'As a rule moves through a speech community in waves, two forms compete with one another, even in individual speakers, but such competition is brief. The few speakers who show real variation belong to that short-lived vertical dimension of the middle part of an *S*-curve which is flat at both ends' (Preston 1996: 16).

These two approaches to variation differ in several ways. First of all, Bailey attempted to describe the variability in individual speech behavior; Labov was more concerned with group behavior (Wardhaugh 1986: 183). Second, the dynamic model suggests that all variation results from language change in progress and is short-lived, whereas Labov appears to regard variation as an inherent property of language (Wardhaugh 1986: 184), which may or may not lead to language change.

We will have more to say about these two approaches in the next chapter when we discuss second language acquisition. Let it be said for now, though, that we believe complexity theory would find merit in both approaches and would have difficulty with both as well. There is evidence in complex dynamic systems in support of the 'dynamic paradigm'. It is clear that there is flux in a complex, dynamic system at the level of the individual. This flux often takes on a bimodal pattern, as in the case of the two vowels being used in the same word by an individual speaker at different times or between the non-use and use of the auxiliary 'do' and others.[7] After a while, a point of criticality is reached (recall Bak's collapsing sandpile), followed by a phase transition in which the system self-organizes into a different state. The shift is self-organized (rather than 'other organized') because it is the dynamic properties of the system that lead it to happen within the speaker's language resources, not some external organizing force, though, of course, a language system is immanent only in its speakers. What the system does after the phase shift is qualitatively different from what it did before at the level of the individual, and perhaps at a different time, at the level of the group.

Nevertheless, complexity theory would not accept the dynamic paradigm's contention that variability is short-lived, preferring instead Labov's proposition that variability is inherent in the system, and not just the variability that leads to emergence of a new pattern. Because individuals interact and shape their own environment, each individual's experience of language is different, and each instance of that experience is different, with an individual's language resources reflecting this variability. As we saw in Chapter 3, the system maintains its stability through continuous adaptation, just as constant adjustments are required to overcome the force of gravity in order for us to stand erect on two feet. In their work applying dynamic principles to studies of how infants learn to reach, Thelen and Smith develop a view of a reach as an emergent 'dynamic ensemble' that does not exist separately from the components of the system that give rise to it (Thelen and Smith 1994: 279). With the same motivation, we see stabilized language resources as a 'dynamic ensemble' (see also Cooper 1999) that do not exist separately from embodied language use, cognition, feelings and emotions, and sociocultural influences on users. Similarly, patterns are not reducible to these (language, cognitive, affective, physical, and cultural) components, but are only explained by understanding how these components interact in real time within speakers. (See Kramsch 2007 for a discussion of the ecology of language use.)

The adiabatic principle

In many ways, the view of language we put forth in this book is inspired by our growing understanding of the dynamics of evolution. This influence should not be surprising, for after all, evolution is also a complex adaptive process. In a best-selling book *The Beak of the Finch*, Weiner (1995) reports on a longitudinal study of Darwin's finches that inhabit the Galapagos Islands.

> Most of us think of the pressures of life in the wild as being almost static. Robins sing in an oak tree year after year … . But the lives of Darwin's finches suggest that this conception of nature is false. Selection pressures may oscillate violently within the lifetimes of most animals and plants around us. Thus, the perception of stasis is really quite illusionary. Species of animals and plants look constant to us, but in reality each generation is a sort of palimpsest, a canvas that is painted over and over by the hand of natural selection, each time a little differently.
> (Weiner 1995: 106)

> [This necessitates viewing] species not as constant entities but as fluctuating things … A species looks steady when you look at it over years—but when you actually get out the magnifying glass you see that it's wobbling constantly … The world is not as stable as you think.
> (Weiner 1995: 108)

This is a key concept in complexity theory. As we indicated in Chapter 2, non-equilibrium systems maintain stability even though they are perpetually dynamic—the stability giving the appearance of no change at all. This is the adiabatic principle.

Retrospective explanations

The emergence of new species in evolutionary change and the emergence of new forms in language are not random; however, because we are dealing with contingent systems, we must be content with retrospective explanations, not predictions. As David Lightfoot (1999: 259) wrote

> Grammatical change is highly contingent—chaotic in the technical sense. Linguists can offer satisfying explanations of changes in some instances,

but there is no reason to expect to find a predictive theory of change, offering long-term linear predictions.

Einar Haugen (1980: 235) made the point many years ago that while the causes of language change are known, the results are impossible to predict. 'There are too many factors present in every human situation for us to be able to foresee all its possibilities. No sooner has one rule operated for a time than another takes over and messes it up. Such is life, and language is no different.'

Now that we have put forth our current complexity-shaped view of language, we will go back and see how this is a counterpoint to the way that language has been conceived in applied linguistics. We will return to a complexity view following this discussion.

The influence of linguistics

One influential source of ideas about language that has prevailed in applied linguistics has been the discipline of linguistics. Since applied linguists need an understanding of language, quite naturally, we have turned to linguists to fill our theoretical needs. Thus, linguists' theories of language have been enormously influential. Here we point to just three applied linguistic areas where linguists have contributed. Consider first the legacy of structural linguistics in language teaching—not only in providing the theoretical underpinning of certain language teaching methods (for example, the AudioLingual Method), but also in contributing descriptions of language to methods (for example, the Audio-Visual Method).[8] The second area is that of language acquisition. Here, we might cite the contributions of Chomsky and his followers in grappling with the issue of the (non-)learnability of language. Addressing the question of how it was possible that language acquisition could proceed so rapidly, given what was felt to be the relatively impoverished nature of the input and the absence of negative feedback, motivated claims for the existence of an innate universal grammar (UG); this would constrain the hypotheses that learners entertain as they seek to induce the rules underlying the language they are acquiring, or, in later versions of the theory, guide learners deductively. These claims have motivated a great deal of productive research in applied linguistics. The third area is that of language use in the form of discourse or text-analysis and conversation analysis, all of which have received major support from the work of functional linguists. Each of these three fundamental sub-areas of applied linguistics—language acquisition, language use, and language teaching—are treated at length in the next three chapters.

The major premise of this chapter, however, is that this impulse for wholly relying on linguists' theories of language has not been entirely successful. For their goals are different. Many linguists have set themselves the goal of explaining the 'I-language' or internal system of language—an internal component of the mind/brain—assumed to be the primary object of interest for the study of the evolution and function of the language faculty, which deals with the abstract knowledge of decontextualized linguistic properties such as subjacency and Wh-movement (Hauser, Chomsky, and Fitch 2002: 1574). Applied linguists, on the other hand, must also be concerned with what Chomsky calls the E-Language—or externalized language 'contextualized language behavior actualised in the social process' (Widdowson 2003: 22) because applied linguists must deal with culturally specific communication systems (for example, Indonesian, Spanish) and how they change. In this way, applied linguistics is more akin to the study of language change than it is to theoretical linguistics. Of course, Chomsky recognized that applied linguistics and linguistics were fundamentally different many years ago (Chomsky 1966). But failure to heed this has come at great cost to applied linguistics.

For in order to address their goal, many linguists have sought to represent the language system in idealized elegance, often stripped of the disorderliness of what had been called the noisy 'remainder' (Leclerc 1990). To do so, they have had to make certain concessions that do not cohere well with the demands of applied linguistics. For instance, following long-standing practice in science, linguists have reduced the complexity with which they deal. One way they have done so is to segregate the systematic side of language from its unruly side. Saussure (1916 [1959]) distinguished *langue*, the shared social structure of language from *parole*, the actual use of language by people in their everyday lives, and declared the former to be the optimal focus of linguistic investigation. Chomsky (1965) later invoked a different dichotomy motivated by the same goal, i.e. to get at the systematic nature of language. Chomsky distinguished mental competence or the idealized native speaker's knowledge of his or her language from performance, the actual use of the language. Notice that for Chomsky, competence was an individual's knowledge, knowledge that arises from an innate language faculty, not the shared social structure of Saussure. The innate faculty was endowed with the principles of a universal grammar or UG, which was said to underlie all human languages. Chomsky rejected performance as the proper domain for linguistics because, as he noted, a speaker's performance was affected by dysfluencies and ungrammaticality stemming from the demands of online processing. Both Chomsky and Saussure (Weinrich, Labov, and Herzog 1968: 120–1) agree that the object of investigation should be homogeneous.

In addition to removing language from its context of use, linguists have been selective in the data that they choose to analyze and represent in other ways. Following from the interest in *langue*/competence, the data have been largely derived from linguists' intuitions about grammaticality, judgments about which made-up sentences are grammatical and which are not. In so doing, they segregated the morphosyntactic or grammatical subsystem from the phonological, the semantic, and the pragmatic subsystems of language. This was because Chomsky and his followers sought to construct the mental grammar of the individual in order to reveal the systematicity of language and to account for the fact that speakers can use their grammar to produce and comprehend novel utterances.

A third way that certain theoretical linguists have reduced the complexity with which they contend is by removing the dimension of time. By making synchronic language the object of investigation, the messiness that comes from variation-induced language change is lessened. 'Saussure made it quite clear that for his conception of a language as a "whole synchronic structure" to make sense at all, we must slough off all those domains, from phonetics to psychology that would make the subject unmanageable by received scientific standards, hence, the idealization away from *le langage* and indeed *le parole*, to *la langue*' (Toolan 2003: 125).

These three moves—decontextualizing, segregating, and atemporalizing—are all common enough in science, and some would say necessary, in order to cope with the complexity of what is being investigated and to fulfill the goal of accounting for the underlying system. Any representation of reality, scientific or otherwise, involves a simplification, just as we have done in examining language apart from its ecology. Yet the sum total of the three moves means that we are left with a compromised view of language with which to apply to our applied linguistics enterprise. In order to lend support to the major thesis of this book—that complexity theory offers a novel and more useful way of looking at applied linguistic concerns because there is no need to conceive of language in a decontextualized terminal state of frozen animation—we will first examine these three simplifying moves to see their effect.

Explaining the shape of language

Structural linguists enjoyed enormous success by restricting their domain of inquiry and showing that a particular linguistic subsystem had significant internal regularities. It is important to point out, though, that description and explanation are not the same. While a language may be described on its own terms, it does not follow that it can be explained without reference to factors outside of itself. Indeed, in an important way, the history of a language reflects the behavior of its speakers:

> The structure of language has emerged from the kind of messages speakers wish to convey and the kind of cognitive, perceptual, and articulatory mechanisms they have to convey them, either by biological evolution, or cultural evolution, or more likely by some combination of the two.
> (Nettle 1999: 13)

While it is admittedly difficult to correlate linguistic structure and lifestyle in the evolution of cultures, it is not inconceivable to imagine how different social forces might influence language. According to Bakhtin (1981), every use of language is marked by centrifugal (socially distinguishing, diversifying) and centripetal (societally unifying, standardizing) forces. While traditional disciplines such as linguistics emphasize the centripetal forces that centralize and unify a language, Bakhtin (1981: 293) emphasizes the centrifugal forces that decentralize and resist unity.

> For any individual consciousness living in it, language is not an abstract system of normative forms but rather a concrete heteroglot conception of the world. All words have the 'taste' of a profession, a genre, a tendency, a party, a particular work, a particular person, a generation, an age group, the day and hour. Each word tastes of the context and contexts in which it has lived in its socially charged life ...

Therefore, even if we accept Saussure's contention that the object of linguistics needs to be language studied 'in and for itself', it does not follow that the explanation should only be confined to the linguistic system (Nettle 1999: 14).[9] Explanations for the shape of language must have some social basis, for language is an abundantly rich resource for performing social action (Atkinson 2002). 'Human beings, in a socially differentiated world, necessarily pursue complex and conflicting interests. It is these human beings who determine how, and which, linguistic resources remain vital elements of social mediation' (Sealey and Carter 2004: 181). Locating language in the interstices between people, rather than only within individuals themselves, requires a different approach to thinking about and studying language from that of traditional linguistic approaches (Ahearn 2001).

A sociocognitive approach

As applied linguists, we are drawn to seeing the social side of language, in its full heterogeneity, for after all, applied linguists deal with issues of language use in the real world. Further, sociolinguists have convincingly demonstrated that humans live in linguistically heterogeneous environments and both learn and use their language under these conditions (for example, Weinreich, Labov, and Herzog 1968), resulting in socially differentiated language practices such as bilingualism, diglossia, and code-switching.[10] As Atkinson (2002: 537) writes 'Language and its interactions, from a sociocognitive perspective, would be seen in terms of "action" and "participation"—as providing an extremely powerful semiotic means of performing and participating in activity-in-the-world (Rogoff 1990, 1998; Lave and Wenger 1991)'.

This is not, however, to deny the importance of cognition. In a series of cross-linguistic studies, Slobin (1996) has convincingly demonstrated that the structure of a given language influences how speakers think and conceptualize. Language does not determine thought as in the Sapir-Whorf hypothesis, but our thoughts are influenced by the filtering effects of our language. In a collapsing of dichotomies, Slobin calls this 'thinking for speaking'. For example, Negueruela *et al.* (2004) show that 'even advanced language learners have problems appropriately indicating motion events when they have to cross typological boundaries between their target-languages and their native languages. English speakers learning Spanish, for instance, tend to express manner in Spanish as they do in English, which does not result in an error of form but which leads them to mark manner very differently from Spanish speakers.

Furthermore, the shape of language is surely affected by limitations of human cognitive processing. The fact that center embedding (such as when a relative clause modifies an object in the middle of a sentence) is less frequent than initial or final position embeddings, that suffixation of morphological affixes is much more common than prefixing and infixing (presumably due to the fact that lexical stems must be processed before the information derived from any affixes attached to them is usable) (Cutler, Hawkins, and Gilligan 1985), and that utterances begin with a theme, containing given information, which provides a point of departure for the message, all point to the cognitive impact on language. Then, too, assigning certain clausal constituents the status of old and new information, determining patterns, categorizing experience, prototyping, using conceptual schema, metaphors, and analogies, not to mention registering the language changes of which we have been speaking, could all be categorized as cognitive phenomena.

Indeed, we ourselves favor a sociocognitive approach, the lack of a hyphen signalling the fact that complexity theory encourages an integrative approach, rather than segregating the social from the cognitive (Larsen-Freeman 2002a, 2007b). Certainly there are some who choose to work either on the social side of language or on the cognitive side with little attention paid to the other. Although dealing with one apart from the other may allow for rigorous descriptions, it must be recognized that the description can only be partial. More problematic from a complexity theory point of view is that the dichotomizing leaves open the issue of how the two, cognitive and social, are connected—an issue of enormous importance when dealing with language development, language teaching, and language use. By looking at only one side or the other, a dualistic view of phenomena is promulgated and reinforced. Dualisms such as 'system and access' or 'knowledge and behavior' or 'competence and performance' or '*langue* and *parole*' or 'knowledge and control' or 'a property theory and a transition theory' or 'acquisition and use' are adopted. Such dualisms get in the way of seeing that members of each pair are two perspectives on the same underlying process. Language structure is shaped by the way that language is used, and its use in turn fuels further development. 'Structure-process', Bohm calls it (in Nichol 2003). As such, the dualistic thinking is unparsimonious and perhaps unnecessary. Clearly, then, speakers of a given language are constrained to some degree by the structures of their particular language, but just as clearly, languages change in a social context, sometimes much more rapidly than supposed, despite their self-reproducing natures. It is therefore helpful to look closely at the interconnections between the patterns in language and how language is used in order to gain a more thorough understanding of how people both reproduce and transform language, issues relevant to applied linguistics, particularly the three areas we have chosen to feature in this book.

Understanding the whole

The second assumption made by many linguists is that in order to account for the systematicity of language, they need to confine their investigation to only one autonomous subsystem of language at a time. Structural linguists, and transformational grammarians after them, conferred supremacy upon the formal system—keeping the semantic and pragmatic subsystems apart from grammar in an attempt to get at the essence of the latter. The division of language into autonomous subsystems is a problematic move, parallel to the one separating language from its context and structure from use, with no clear theoretical way to connect them. Such is the case with the distinction between the lexicon and grammar, a distinction that persists to this day as can be seen from O'Grady's summary of the position adopted currently by many linguists:

> There is a near-consensus within contemporary linguistics that language should be seen as a system of knowledge—a sort of 'mental grammar' consisting of a lexicon that provides information about the linguistically relevant properties of words and a computational system that is responsible for the formation and interpretation of sentences.
> (O'Grady 2003: 43)

As with the asocial view of language, this position has also been criticized by other linguists, some of whom have rejected the division between the lexicon and the computational system (for example, corpus linguistics, systemic-functional linguistics) and some of whom have rejected the exclusive focus on the formal system (for example, case grammar, cognitive linguists). In the early days of transformational grammar, generative semanticists sought (unsuccessfully, it turned out) to incorporate the semantic dimension into a generative model. In other traditions, such as case grammar, cognitive linguistics, and systemic-functional linguistics, meaning is of paramount importance, as it is also, or should be, with applied linguistics. Of course, this was recognized early on. Chomsky's lack of interest in language use data was rejected by many linguists, especially when conversation analysis (Sacks, Schegloff, and Jefferson 1974) and speech act theory (Searle 1969) were both revealing how language was as much restricted by social convention as it was by syntactic rules. Hymes (1972), too, made a bid to extend the boundaries of linguistic competence to communicative competence.[11] However, despite the broadening, there was still incommensurability between cognitive orientations and social orientations in Hymes' position, as was pointed out early on by Halliday (1978).

Treating the subsystems of language as autonomous runs contrary to an assumption we make from a complexity theory perspective, which is that it is impossible to understand the whole of a complex system by attempting to understand its parts independently. As we have seen in Chapter 2, the behavior of the whole of a complex system arises out of the interactions of the elements or agents that comprise it. When this notion is applied to language, it is clear that it will not work to treat the subsystems of language as autonomous, unravel the mysteries of each subsystem in turn, and then compile what we have learned about each in order to understand the whole of language. Because language is complex, what is evident at any one time is the interaction of multiple complex dynamic systems, working on multiple timescales and levels (Larsen-Freeman 1997; Lemke 2000b).

Of course, applied linguists should not only be naysayers. It is easy to be critical. We have to shoulder some responsibility and not merely adopt linguists' fixed and homogeneous theoretical units in the face of prevailing evidence that such a characterization of language is a normative fiction (Klein 1998). Still, though we may know better, we also often settle for methodological convenience, treating linguists' units as psychologically real. Tempting as it is, it is not helpful to analyze our data with ready-made categories. We will see how this is particularly misguided in the next chapter when we examine the language produced by learners.

Change throughout the system

Not only is the assumption of autonomy of the subsystems of language problematic, but so also is assumption of their immutability (although making such an assumption may be procedurally convenient, of course). Any dynamism that was present in early renditions of transformational-generative grammar was manifest in the application of transformations to derive surface structures from deep structures; however, this dynamism was operational in the model of grammar, not in the grammar itself. Moreover, the resultant surface structure was always judged for its well-formedness, i.e. how consistently it adhered to a finite set of grammatical/computational rules of a so-called 'end-state grammar'. What then about the dynamism present in a computational linguistic system itself? After all, the O'Grady quote (on p. 94) makes an implicit claim about dynamism by using process words such as 'formation' and 'interpretation'. Such an approach to sentence formation and interpretation conceives of a process that commences with an input to the system. The task for the system is to generate an appropriate output, and it does so via a sequence of internal operations culminating in the production of that output. However, a big difference is that a computational system of the input-output variety operates metaphorically as a serial-processing computer (see Chapter 1), one in which change is confined to just one variable, with most others remaining unchanged.

Conversely, processes in a dynamic system are distributed, with all aspects changing interdependently all the time, not just when some algorithm is applied. A dynamic system does not change as a result of some input mapping to some output at some later time, but rather in a dynamic system change is maintained throughout the system. One analogy to understanding patterned change this way is to think of eddies in a stream. A stream parts around a large rock in its bed. The eddies created are only visible in the flow of the water downstream from the rock. While they appear to be stable formations at one level, they are obviously constantly being formed with different molecules of water at another level. In other words, stable does not mean static. Language is forever being virtually updated, even though from all appearances, it remains the same language. As we have already seen with the beak of the finch, there is a perception of stasis, but it is really illusionary.

Interim summary

To sum up to this point, as we have already seen in the previous two chapters, complex systems are in a perpetual state of flux. They, or at least parts of them, settle from time to time into attractor states. When the system, or one part of it, changes from one relatively stable attractor state to another, a process we have called a phase transition, the point of transition/criticality can sometimes be marked with increased behavioral variability. As they pass through a phase transition, the systems are self-organizing, where the new organization that emerges may be novel, qualitatively different from earlier organizations.

The natural state of the linguistic system can be 'defined as a dynamic adaptedness to a specific context' (Tucker and Hirsch-Pasek 1993: 362). (Remember that the context is also changing.) Humans soft assemble or adapt their language resources to meet the present contingencies or specific goals, and to reflect who they are and how they wish to be seen by others. Adapting their resources sometimes means appropriating extant language-using patterns; at other times, it means innovating. As such, the resources are both variegated and variable.

As they adapt their language resources to new contexts, humans change language. Thus, the language system and its use are mutually constitutive. 'The act of playing the game has a way of changing the rules' is the way Gleick (1987) puts it when discussing naturally occurring complex systems. The rules referred to by Gleick are not linguistic rules; nevertheless, the analogy is useful for representing the self-evident fact that we change a language by using it. Of course, some aspects of language change faster than others. Then, too, much of language change is continuous, and so it escapes our conscious attention. That language use leads to language change is not revelatory; after all, how else could language change occur? However, by focusing on the 'in-between-ness', the nexus between use and change, rather than imposing artificial dichotomies borne out of methodological convenience (i.e.

distinguishing diachronic from synchronic or competence from performance), we come to understand that these are all manifestations of a common dynamic process operating in different time frames and at different levels.[12]

While such linguistic expressions as 'end-state grammar' may belong to an agenda where language description and representation are the goals, they are less germane to applied linguists, who are centrally concerned with issues of language use and development (White 2003). As such, applied linguistics would be well served with more dynamic models. This is because a static algorithm cannot account for the continual and never ending growth and complexification of language as it is used and as it develops (Larsen-Freeman 1997). Complexity theory offers us an approach to understanding systems in change. It affords us a way to preserve the notion of system without reification. By putting time and change back into our systems, we have new ways of understanding processes of using and learning language.

Continuing with a complexity-inspired view of language

Sensitive dependence on initial conditions

As we have seen already in this book, a complex adaptive system is sensitive to initial conditions and to subsequent changes of conditions, which means that a small difference at the beginning or along the way can lead to significantly different outcomes. Mohanan (1992: 636) recognizes this characteristic of language, referring to formal linguistic universals as 'fields of attraction', which 'allow for infinite variation in a finite grammar space'. It also allows universal principles to have gradient values in their language-particular manifestation in contrast to generative linguistics, which generally views parametric choices as discrete. Thus, for example, there is voicing assimilation in all languages. How the principle of voicing assimilation is realized, however, varies considerably from language to language. In English, for instance, the voiced consonant assimilates to the voiceless, (regressive in 'five' versus 'fifth', progressive in 'John'[z] here versus Jack'[s] here') whereas in Spanish and Russian, the first consonant assimilates to the second, regardless of which one is voiced (Mohanan 1992: 637). Certain core substantive universals, such as voicing assimilation, possibly define the initial conditions of the system and give shape to the attractor of human languages (Larsen-Freeman 1997). Although these universals of language are not identical to UG, Plaza Pust (2006), seeing a link between UG and dynamic systems theory, claims that it is the principles of UG that give human languages their stability.

This does not mean, however, that a language is forever restricted by its initial conditions. This is because what Steels (2005: 4) calls the 'communal meta-system' changes as well, which affects the global state of the language.

> For example, new word classes may appear (like articles which did not exist in Latin but then emerged in all derived Romance languages), or

grammatical systems may change, as happened in English, which shifted
from a case-marking system as in Latin to a word-order + preposition-
based system for the expression of event-argument structure. So here
again, we have to abandon the notion that there is a static meta-system in
favor of a complex, adaptive systems view.
(Steels 2005: 4)

Thus, while a system might show sensitivity to initial conditions, the conditions are reflexively updated. It should also be noted that, as with other
characteristics of complex adaptive systems, this same property of sensitive
dependence applies to different levels and timescales. For instance, the initial
conditions of an individual's language use can be a speaker's experience of a
particular language up to the present. Bakhtin's (1981) notion of dialogism
applies here. Bakhtin maintains that the words that we speak are 'half someone else's'. They do not become our own until we 'populate' the words 'with
our own intentions'.

The sensitive dependence on initial conditions could even be extended to
the utterance level.[13] For instance, if we begin our utterance with an article,
it is likely that a noun will follow soon after. The fact that each word in our
utterance places increasing constraints on that which follows makes 'garden
path' sentences so difficult to process. A 'garden path' sentence misleads
us; it leads us down the 'garden path' by encouraging us to make certain
inferences about what is to follow, only to find out that the inferences are not
borne out. An example is 'The old man the boat'. From the form itself, let
alone its meaning, we are led to expect a noun to follow the article 'the' and
the adjective 'old'. Thus, our initial reading of 'man' is as a noun. It is only
when we reach the noun phrase 'the boat' that we realize that we have been
led down the garden path. At that point, we have to go back and reanalyze
'the old' as a collective noun derived from an adjective, which serves as the
subject and 'man' as the verb. Thus, initial conditions can affect the life of the
language, the prior discourse of language use, and even the interpretation a
single utterance.

Emergence

One of the central puzzles in linguistics has been how complexity in a 'final
state' in child language acquisition can exceed the combination of the initial
state (allegedly a universal grammar) and the input. In the debate on this issue
(Piatelli-Palmerini 1980: 140), Fodor, adopting an innatist stance, claimed that
it was impossible—that complex structure must have been innately specified
if it could not have been inductively arrived at from the input. However, if
language is conceived of as a complex system, then it is entirely possible for
novel complexities to emerge.

The demonstration that structure can come into existence without either
a specific plan or an independent builder raises the possibility that many

structures in physical bodies as well as in cognition might occur without any externally imposed shaping forces. Perhaps cognitive structures, like embryological structures, the weather, and many other examples, simply *organize themselves* ...
(Port and van Gelder 1995: 27)

The self-organizing property, when applied to language, suggests that we should not view the emergence of complex rules as the unfolding of some prearranged plan (Tucker and Hirsch-Pasek 1993: 364) because all that is required to account for complexification is a sensitive dependence on initial conditions, an openness, and a context in which the system can adapt and change, and in turn transform. Any structure arises in a bottom-up fashion from frequently occurring patterns of language use rather than as a priori components of fixed, autonomous, closed, and synchronic systems. In this way complexity theory makes a case for the emergence of macroscopic order (indeed even that which has sufficiently stabilized to be labeled French or English) and complexity from microscopic behavior of language speakers (Port and van Gelder 1995: 29).

Competence and creativity

As insights from corpus linguistics show, the stabilities that speakers employ are diverse—words, phrases, idioms, metaphors, non-canonical collocations, grammar structures—a much more complex and diverse set of language-using patterns than the 'core grammar' of formal approaches. Thus, Tomasello (2003: 98–100) advises that 'the alternative is to look at linguistic competence, not in terms of the possession of a formal grammar of semantically empty rules, but rather in terms of the mastery of a structured inventory of meaningful linguistic constructions' that arise out of interaction.

How the inventory is structured at this point is a matter of speculation. What we do know is that humans are exquisite categorizers. It is likely that categories are created out of instances of pattern-using. Perhaps they are categorized based on the form-meaning-use features that they share with other constructions. Categories are graded (Rosch and Mervis 1975), with no single exemplar being identical to any other member of its group. Indeed, they are much more likely to be related through what Wittgenstein (1953/2001) calls 'family resemblances', 'a complicated network of similarities, overlapping and crisscrossing' (1953/2001: 66). Along these lines, Goldberg (2003) proposes a 'constructicon', which is an organized network of constructions whose elements are linked by inheritance hierarchies. This view allows for the existence of families of constructions (for example, Goldberg and Jackendoff 2004), in which similar, though different, constructions are at one and the same time linked to each other (in order to obtain the highest level of generalization) and separated (in order to grasp their more specific, or even idiosyncratic properties).

As the store of instances becomes large, instances appropriate to the
current task are more quickly and efficiently retrieved from memory, and
are therefore more easily and effectively applied to the task.
(Truscott 1998: 259–60)

Truscott notes that such an explanation is more in keeping with the attested
gradual incremental character of language learning than is a generative notion
of competence, involving resetting a UG parameter, which would register an
abrupt shift in a learner's grammar. Beyond this, it is difficult to say to what
extent abstraction occurs. Earlier, we talked about the abstract semantics of
the 'caused-motion' construction. Whether, in fact, language users abstract
the semantics as a conceptual schema or whether they simply analogize its
meaning to new verbs (a process we referred to earlier as inheritance) is
unclear. Certainly, we know from neural network modeling that it is possible
to elicit behavior that appears to be following rules, but has instead resulted
from induction of a pattern from many exemplars.

Indeed, we have known for some time that although speakers might possess
knowledge of linguistic rules and lexical items allowing them to produce an
infinite number of novel well formed utterances, in practice they do nothing of
the sort. Instead, they cobble together the constructions they have registered
earlier.[14] Essentially the same observation has been made many times since.
(See, among others, Bolinger 1976; Becker 1983; Pawley and Syder 1983;
Widdowson 1989; Willis 1990; Sinclair 1991; Nattinger and DeCarrico 1992;
Lewis 1993; Wray 2002.) The fluency and familiarity of native-like language
can be explained by the fact that it is generally not composed of wholly novel
combinations of words but rather of sequences that are 'sedimented' from
human speech interaction (Hopper 1998), though they are not static.

Words found together with a high frequency come to be processed as single
lexical units, what we have called language-using patterns. The following
patterns with 'what', for example, compiled by Bolinger (1976: 7), 'put the
hearer on notice as to what stance he is to adopt toward what he is about to
hear':

Know what?
Tell you what.
Tell you what you do.
Tell you what I am going to do.

For instance, the last one in this list says 'O.K. Let's make a fresh start. I'll
meet you more than halfway', etc. (Bolinger 1976: 7). This list could easily be
expanded. For instance, just the other day we heard an exasperated mother
say to a child: 'Now what?', a stance marker that signals to the child that the
mother is losing her patience.

It is clear that these language-using patterns, having emerged from interaction, are different from the way that we usually conceive of linguistic units
in competence or as the standard parts of speech, i.e. nouns, verbs, adjectives,

etc. However, just as we saw with the transitivity of verbs, we should observe that membership in standard linguistic categories has always been fuzzy as well. Hopper and Thompson (1984) note that a given word in a language is categorized as a noun or verb and inflected accordingly to the degree that a given instance of it approaches its prototypical function. This is not only true within a language, but across languages as well, so that in some languages what is an adjective in English might be manifest as a stative verb. Croft (2001) observes that although parts of speech such as noun and verb may be based in universal semantic-conceptual notions, for any given language, these categories can only be defined by the specific language constructions in which they occur. Indeed, Hopper and Thompson suggest that 'categoricality itself is another fundamental property of grammars which may be directly derived from discourse function' (1984: 703). Of course, not only categoricality, but also other properties of a pattern, such as its meaning, can be transformed through use. For instance, 'be going to' was earlier a marker of direction, and only later became the intentional future in English, thus another instance of grammaticalization (or grammaticization) (Bybee 2006), a process whereby the grammar of a language is affected by frequency of use. Other frequency effects can be illustrated with this pattern. Because of its frequency, 'be going to' has come to be processed as a single unit or chunk (N. Ellis 1996). This repackaging of its form results in its phonological reduction and fusion to 'gonna'. We know, of course, that agents reduce complexity by means of routinized behaviors (Holland 1995), which frees up attention to be directed elsewhere.

For after all, 'language is not a fixed code' (Harris 1996) that exists independently of its users, and that is ready-made for users before they start using it, but rather it is created, or at the very least assembled from conventional units, each time it is used. Often the creativity is produced by analogy. John Sinclair (personal communication 2006) offered the example of the analogic extension in the use of the verb 'manage'. In both American English (AE) and in British English (BE) one can 'manage an office' or 'manage one's affairs'. However in AE, unlike BE, one can 'manage' certain emotions, such as grief, which one cannot say in BE. In BE, one 'copes with grief', but one does not 'manage grief' — the two conveying somewhat different attitudes toward grief. Thus, comparatively speaking, the AE speakers have extended the scope of the verb 'manage' by analogy to deal with emotions.[15]

However, creativity extends beyond a single language. In fact, multilingual, multicultural contexts may favor creativity (Carter 2004). Carter points to Rampton's (1995) 'crossing' (a feature of cross-lingual transfers and creative mixing) adopted by urban adolescents in the South Midlands of Britain, which concerns the use of Creole by adolescents of Asian and Anglo descent, the use of Panjabi by Anglos and Afro-Caribbeans and the use of stylized Indian English by all three groups.

In Rampton's data, liminal exchanges take place in contexts which are socially fluid. They are fluid because normally ordered social life is loosened and normal social settings and interactions involving rules and purposes set by adults or by conventional social institutions do not apply. (Carter 2004: 171–2)

Where systems are stretched, where conventional rules are not upheld, where a point of criticality is reached, new forms emerge. At the 'edge of chaos' (Chapter 3 of this book; Lewin 1992; Waldrop 1992), systems are more flexible and responsive. New forms and patterns then become the resources of the community upon which members of the speech community can draw, exploit, and reshape to populate with their own intentions and the affordances of the new contexts.

Of course, there is also a great deal of non-creative, formulaic language use which provides stability and routinization to a communicative event. Formulaic language allows messages to be conveyed easily and straightforwardly, often when a transaction of information or phatic communion is the main purpose of the exchange, but at the same time formulaic language is also always available as a scaffold from which other language patterns can be built (Carter 2004: 133–4).

It is this sense that, as Bolinger has pointed out (1976), speaking is more similar to remembering procedures and things than it is to following rules. It is a question of possessing a repertoire of strategies for building discourses and reaching into memory in order to assemble them or to improvise. Notice that from a complex systems perspective, what is in memory are process representations, memories of acts of using language patterns. When we speak, we 'push old language into new' Becker (1983). Antilla (1972: 349) says it this way: 'Memory or brain storage is on a much more extravagant scale than we would like to think'.

Phylogenetic emergence

Emergence also occurs at other levels of scale and time—ontogenetic and phylogenetic. We will deal with ontological emergence in the next chapter, but let us briefly tackle the issue here of how language is emergent in the species. Before discussing the matter from a complexity theory perspective, let us understand the two fundamental positions on the issue. Chomsky has long maintained that humans possess an innate faculty of language in the narrow sense, a species-specific computational system. (See Hauser, Chomsky, and Fitch 2002, for an up-to-date discussion of this position.) Steels (1996) explains that the innate language faculty is seen as a kind of 'language organ' that 'came into existence due to a series of genetic mutations each giving an adaptive advantage or alternatively that there has been a single "catastrophic" mutation giving rise to syntax and thus full language …' (Steels 1996: 462).

As Pinker (1994: 18) clearly states: 'Language is not a cultural artifact ... . Instead, it is a distinct piece of the biological makeup of our brains'.

From an emergentist or complexity theory perspective, there is no need to posit an innate language faculty or a mental organ. Language can be seen to have emerged in humans in two senses of emergence: '(1) it could spontaneously form itself once the appropriate physiological, psychological and social conditions are satisfied and (2) it could autonomously become more complex, based on the same mechanisms that cause the growth of complexity' (Steels 1996: 462), such as self-organization.

Of course, it is difficult to adduce evidence to support one side or the other in the innatist/emergentist debate because no one really knows how language originated. However, there has recently been a great deal of interest in trying to understand its origin. One avenue of research is comparative—comparing animals and humans to see if there is anything biological that could explain the human capacity for language, which is allegedly different from animal communication. As it turns out, many of the biological differences between humans and animals, which might explain the language capacity difference, have been found to be true of both. For instance, it was once claimed that the descent of the larynx in humans enabled language. Now, however, it is known that larynxes descend in other species without spoken language such as red deer and chimpanzees (Nishimura, Mikami, Suzuki, and Matsuzawa 2003).

Another hypothesis advanced to explain the difference between human and animal communication is that humans possess a unique theory of mind, an awareness that others have private mental states which cannot be directly observed and the concomitant ability to 'read' and represent those. However, recent studies claim that certain animals have at least a rudimentary theory of mind, 'including a sense of self and the ability to represent the beliefs and desires of other group members' (Hauser *et al.* op. cit.: 1575), although this research has not always been corroborated in chimpanzees, for instance (Hauser *et al.* op. cit.: 1576). Still, recent research on the chimpanzee genome and findings from primatology suggest that there is a great deal of genetic overlap and behavior in common between chimpanzees and humans (de Waal 2005). In any case, Burling (2005) believes there to be no link between animal cries and human language, although there might be between gesture and human language (Arbib 2002).

Some scholars, more in line with an emergentist position on the issue, speculate that certain social or cognitive capacities were developed in tandem with that of language. For example, Logan (2000) argues that the origins of speech and the human mind emerged simultaneously at the bifurcation from percepts to concepts and in response to the chaos associated with the information overload that resulted from the increased complexity in hominoid life, due to the development of tool-making. Other emergentists imagine that certain social and cognitive capacities preceded the genesis of language and created the conditions for language to emerge. For instance, our social nature, our talent for imitation, our ability to segment audio stimuli, and our ability to establish joint attention on some common focus all develop during a child's first year of life, and may have been precursors to language in the species (Bates 1999). Then, too, 'our ability to create and manipulate symbols, letting one object, sound, or action stand for an object, event, or ideas that are not currently present or perceivable in the immediate environment' is clearly involved in the process by which language is acquired (Bates and Goodman 1999: 35) and may be a non-language ability that preceded the emergence of language. Thus, even though none of these basic cognitive and communicative abilities are specific to language, they permit the emergence of language. While they are not linguistic capacities, they may make language possible, just as a giraffe's neck allows it to occupy an environmental niche that no other ungulate can do (Bates and Goodman 1999).

Another approach to trying to explain the origin of language is to look at the history of language. This approach, complemented by the study of the genesis of pidgins and creoles (for example, Mufwene 2001; McWhorter 2001), to which Satterfield (2001) has contributed a complexity theory perspective, and recent studies of the rise of sign language in isolated communities (Senghas *et al.* 2004; Sandler *et al.* 2005) suggest that certain lexical items become grammaticized (Hopper and Traugott 1993) as function words and grammatical morphemes through usage, which can account for how syntax emerged from the use of lexical items throughout a long history of language development and change (Ke and Holland 2006). We saw this earlier in the example from Bybee (2006), in which the lexical verb of direction, 'go', eventually grammaticized as a marker of future intention, 'be going to'.

Turning the innate issue totally on its head, it may be the case, then, that more important than humans evolving for language is the fact that languages could have evolved to be learnable by humans. Seeing language as a complex adaptive system, Lee and Schumann put forth this argument:

> From our perspective, linguistic structure emerges as a complex, adaptive system from the verbal interaction of hominids attempting to communicate with each other. Individuals organize lexical items into structures, and if the structures are efficiently producible, comprehensible and learnable, then their use will spread throughout the community and become part of the 'grammar' of the language.
> (Lee and Schumann 2005: 2)

More recently (personal communication 2007) Schumann has pointed out that much of the complexity of syntax, such as 'gapping', which supposedly would require a sophisticated syntactic ability to handle, is actually true of the written language, but not that of the spoken language of conversation, which is much simpler and therefore more easily learnable. Thus,

> What the conversational interaction does is to insure that the forms that ultimately become part of the grammar are those that fit the cognitive and motor capacities of the brain (Kirby 1998). The vetting process inherent

in the interaction modifies the grammatical structures to fit the brain rather than requiring the brain to evolve a genetically based mechanism designed to specify the form of the language. The resulting language is a technology that is passed on to succeeding generations as a cultural artifact.
(ibid: 2)

Going a step further, Bates and Goodman (1999: 35) suggest that once some form of language finally appeared on the planet, it is quite likely that language itself began to apply adaptive pressure on the organization of the human brain. Perhaps, then, 'Languages have evolved with respect to human brains', (Deacon 1997: 110) and 'brains have been shaped to fit the demands of language as well' (ibid.: 327). Deacon adds 'the proper tool for analyzing language structure may not be to discover how best to model them as axiomatic rule systems but rather to study them the way we study organism structure: in evolutionary terms. ... [L]anguage structures may simply reflect the selection pressures that have shaped their reproduction' (Deacon 1997: 110–11; see also Christiansen 1994). Language and the capacity of humans for it have conceivably molded each other in a relationship of dialogic unity, yet another example of co-adaptation in complex dynamic systems.

Before concluding this chapter, there are several loose ends that we need to tie up, having to do with human agency, representation of language in the brain, and the fractal shape of language. We will briefly treat each of these in turn.

On humans and language use

With this talk of the beaks of finches and eddies in a stream and giraffe necks, it is reasonable to stop and ask if the language system somehow exists apart from human agents. Does it operate independently of humans, subject to natural laws such as any complex dynamic system—for example, the weather system—operating in nature? Our answer is an emphatic 'no'. Our concern is with how people use and learn language, and it is important not to leave the impression that languages exist apart from the humans who use them. Languages will only survive insofar as they have a role in furthering people's interests or obstructing those of others (Sealey and Carter 2004: 181). Without speakers, a language becomes endangered, as so many are today.

That does not mean, however, that we are always consciously aware of language as a tool with which to pursue our interests or that we deliberately impel language to change. One linguist (here conceiving of language in the abstract) has written, that language is 'one of the natural organisms of the world to be treated by the methods of natural science, one moreover that independently of its speakers' will or consciousness has its periods of growth, maturity and decline' (Schleicher 1863 in Robins 1967). While some might reject this claim as too animistic,[16] it is clear that languages as abstractions do exist before their current speakers were born and will remain after they die. Moreover, the changes that humans enact in their language-using patterns are not usually as deliberate as the coining of a new term.

In addition, humans register qualities and quantities about the language they participate in, the frequency of constructions (Larsen-Freeman 1976; N. Ellis 2002), for instance, and appear to be quite proficient at maintaining them. Elizabeth Bates writes:

> MacWhinney and I shared a belief that the competence-performance distinction within linguistics was deeply misleading. We sought instead to explain linguistic variability (both cross-linguistic and individual differences) by building statistical variation directly into the representations that subserve language use. In other words, we argued that linguistic knowledge was 'probabilistic all the way down' reflecting the statistics of language use (in the input) and language learning (through inductive learning).
> (Thelen and Bates 2003: 384)

As we will see in Chapter 6, repeated experiences of participating in talk lead speakers to have expectations about how talk will proceed. Indeed, lexical-functional grammarian Bresnan (2007) notes that speakers of a language have powerful predictive capabilities that enable them to anticipate the linguistic choices of others by instantaneously weighing multiple sources of information. 'These observations support an alternative view of linguistic competence as inherently variable and stochastic in nature rather than categorical and algebraic' (Bresnan 2007). Then, too, a basic assumption of Halliday's systemic-functional linguistics is that speakers have a sense of the frequency of particular choices in the language as a whole (Thompson and Hunston 2006). Halliday and James (1993), for example, claim that positive clauses outnumber negative ones in the ratio of 9:1 and that people are sensitive to this and to the frequency with which choices co-occur. Further, it is also maintained that when people produce or understand language, they are sensitive to whether choices and combinations of choices correspond to or depart from these norms. The probability that one term or another in a system will be instantiated within a text within a given register is always a matter of degree, of course, so there is always potential for change (Matthiessen 2006).

In short, whenever people seek or direct others to accomplish things, they must exploit what Halliday calls 'the meaning potential of language'. Whenever they do, they are engaging with the language resources available or accessible to them. Through this engagement, they experience these resources in enabling and constraining ways (Sealey and Carter 2004: 83). They may not be conscious of them, but the system can only operate through them.

Representation in the mind

Another of the issues that arises when entertaining a view of language as a complex system is what to do about the issue of representation of the system, i.e. as Gregg (2003: 96) says 'whether or not one must appeal to "representations" in one's explanation of language competence and acquisition; whether or not '... [e]xplaining language mastery and acquisition requires the postulation of contentful mental states and processes involving their manipulations' (Cowie 1999: 176)'. Gregg notes that behaviorists certainly rejected contentful mental states. Other modern theorists do, too, though for different reasons. For instance, Schumann *et al.* (2004) promote a neurobiology of language that connects anatomical and physiological mechanisms in the brain with behavior without the need to infer intervening cognitive explanations (that are not answerable to what is known about these mechanisms).

In contrast, other theorists are concerned with mental states and processes. They disagree as to their nature—for instance, as to whether they are properly conceived of as the manipulation of symbols by rules (Gregg 2003), whole phrases encoded in memory (Truscott 1998; N. Ellis 2003), or as patterns of activation across a pool of neuron-like processing units (Elman *et al.* 1996: 25)—but they agree that explaining linguistic capacities requires appealing to some sort of mental process. Of course, these three (rules, whole phrases, patterns of activation) reflect the diversity in the theorists' locus of explanation. From Marr's (1982) theory of vision, we know that the same object may be represented at different levels of detail. At one extreme, what is of interest can be treated in a very abstract way such as a generative rule; at another level, the focus of inquiry is treated with great detail, for example, specific exemplars stored in memory. At the lowest level of scales, it could be seen as patterns of connectivity in a neural network. What is important to remember is that all three are abstractions, necessitating some form of representation, which already filters out many of the details. A consequence of this is that we cannot simply talk about some language-using process having some property; rather, we must talk about whether, given a certain level of detail and a certain locus of explanation, it is seen to have this property.

In any case, symbolic accounts are the norm in our field, so it is difficult to know how to characterize an alternative. For example, should the current level of activation of distributed connection weights in subsymbolic connectionist systems be considered a mental state of some sort? We get help answering this question from Port and van Gelder:

> The crucial difference between the computational models and the dynamical models is that in the former, rules that govern how the system behaves are defined over the entities that have representational status, whereas ... dynamical systems can behave in a way that depends on knowledge without actually representing that knowledge by means of any particular aspect of the system.
> (Port and van Gelder 1995: 11–12)

The answer to our question, then, is 'yes'. Dynamic system theorists downplay the role of symbols and rules and have suggested that we think instead in terms of distributed dynamic processes that operate on non-representational internal states (Elman 2005: 112).[17] Spivey puts it this way:

> The reason I continue to use the term ['representation'] is largely to ease the intellectual transition from cognitive psychology's traditional information-processing framework to a dynamical-systems framework. I submit that the notion of trajectory through state space (a temporally drawn-out pattern of multiple 'representations' being simultaneously partially active) as a replacement for the traditional notion of a *static symbolic* representation.
>
> (Spivey 2007: 5)

While this may be difficult to understand, it might help to say that from our perspective, dynamic systems do not represent an independent world, they enact one (Varela, Thompson, and Rosch 1991: 139). This rhetorical move is accompanied by a different understanding of cognition. Cognition, from the newer perspective, is situated, is embodied action, and, importantly, is inextricably linked to histories, much like paths that are created by walking. 'Consequently, cognition is no longer seen as problem solving on the basis of representations; instead, cognition in its most encompassing sense consists in the enactment or bringing forth of a world by a viable history of structural coupling' (Varela, Thompson, and Rosch 1991: 205), 'structural coupling' being 'our history of recurrent interactions' (Maturana and Varela 1987: 138).

It is clear that the enactment of a world does not involve the mind alone. Clark (1997) finds that representation in the brain should not lead, as do more traditional computational models, to the separation of the brain from the body and from the environment in which it functions—including other people. Clark argues that cognitive activity should not be seen as autonomous and separate when it quite obviously is affected by a range of physical and contextual factors. We certainly share Clark's view in espousing the fully embodied mind.

Van Lier's 'ecological view', which, like ours, is a relational, not a material, view of language, is worth quoting in this regard:

> What does it mean to know a language, if not to possess a store of linguistic structures, rules, words, phrases, and so on? What are the linguistic contents of the mind? This is not an easy question to answer, either for the cognitivist or for the ecologist. I suppose that the ecologist will say that knowledge of language for a human is like knowledge of the jungle for an animal. The animal does not 'have' the jungle; it knows how to use the jungle and how to live in it. Perhaps we can say by analogy that we do not 'have' or 'possess' language, but that we learn to use it and to 'live in it'.
>
> (van Lier 2000: 253)

In this way, we can think of language as a process in which we participate, and that our minds/brains are shaped by language; they do not contain it. Of course to say that there is no need for representation in the form of rules in the mind does not mean that nothing endures. We have already entertained the idea that competence might be considered the memory of patterns of language using that change the likelihood of what people say at any point. What it does mean is that 'There is no principled distinction between representation on the one hand and processing or acquisition of information on the other, as the static and dynamic aspects of cognition are tackled jointly' (Hulstijn 2002: 4).

From a complexity theory perspective the crucial point not to be missed here is that linguistic knowledge is not *given* but adaptively *achieved* by the individual in the environment (Leather and van Dam 2003: 19). What this means is that meaning is not located in the brain, in the body, in the environment or in a particular linguistic form: it is a function of the global state of the system, and it emerges in the interaction (Varela, Thompson, and Rosch 1991: 149–50). To concretize this notion, let us say that we do not choose words that contain meanings and then place them on the table for our interlocutor to pick up, but rather we use words and phrases as 'prompts for meaning construction' (Evans and Green 2006: 214), selected and adapted in the dynamics of interaction. Thus, in the negotiation of meaning, which accompanies every dialogic interchange, new meanings are routinely created for old forms, both unintentionally and on purpose. We will revisit this theme in Chapter 6 when we apply a complexity theory perspective to discourse.

On power-laws and fractals

One of the gifts of a new theory is that it invites new questions. As we saw in the previous chapter, complexity theory makes use of spatial metaphors for heuristic purposes. In keeping with this heuristic, in this section, we entertain the question: what is the shape of a language trajectory in the landscape or state space of human language-using potential? Larsen-Freeman (1997) pointed to work on human language by Zipf (1935) to help us answer this question. Zipf showed that power-laws affect the frequency of use of words in any human language, as they do other natural phenomena, such as the magnitudes of earthquakes. A power-law signals a relationship, usually between two variables, which is scale-free. Zipf demonstrated that in texts of various lengths, there is an inverse relationship between the frequency of occurrence of a word and its frequency rank so that relatively few words occur often while others are comparatively rare. Power-laws are a signature of complex systems, and when their constants are iterated, they yield fractals, a geometric shape that is self-similar at different levels. Carlson and Doyle (2000) suggest that power-law distributions, as well as several other features of many complex systems (including language), may be the design or evolution of systems for optimal behavior due to their compressibility. Gilden (2007:

310) adds that 'Fractal organization endows a system with the flexibility to change and adapt to new circumstances'.

Notice that we are talking about language use as a fractal, not linguists' descriptions of language. For example, many linguists (such as tagmemicists and systemic functional linguists) make use of fractal systems of analysis, in which it is assumed that all levels of language, context, and culture can be described in ways that are theoretically consistent. Indeed, Thompson and Hunston point out that systemic-functional linguistics uses a common vocabulary of semiotic choice at all these levels and then underscores the interdependence among them (Thompson and Hunston 2006: 1). However, this fractal is metalinguistic—a description of language, not language itself.

For language use to qualify as a fractal, it must have properties that apply at all levels. In support of this, an especially interesting finding that Zipf (1935: 45) made, which reveals the fractal shape of language, is that

> ... when words of a vocabulary are ranked in the order of frequency, the average 'wave lengths' [the average number of words occurring between its average occurrences] (the reciprocals of the frequency) are approximately successive multiples of ten; that is, the wave length of the *nth* word is 10*n*. For example (on the basis of Eldridge's table of 43,939 English words)

> The first word has a 'wave length' of 10 (actually 10.2)
> The second word has a 'wave length' of 20 (actually 20.4)
> The third has a 'wave length' of 30 (actually 32.1).
> Etc.

Zipf (op. cit.: 46) adds

> One value of this method of plotting is that the average 'wave lengths' of the most frequent words remain approximately the same regardless of the extent of the samplings, provided of course that a sampling is taken of sufficient length and variety ... to be statistically significant. Thus the average interval between occurrences of the most frequent word will be approximately the same whether one counts 5,000 or 10,000, 100,000 or ten million words of connected English speech ...

Thus, clearly, as required by a fractal, there is a self-similar pattern at different levels. Interestingly, this same 'harmonic series' that Zipf found to be true of English, he also found in Latin and Chinese. This should not be surprising in that all information systems need to be fractal in shape in order to make them compressible and thus shareable (Winter 1994). Indeed, Ferrer i Cancho and Solé (2003) claim that Zipf's law is a fundamental principle common to all languages, accounting for the emergence of complex languages. They demonstrate that once a given threshold is reached, Zipf's law emerges spontaneously. In a later article, Ferrer i Cancho (2006) suggests that Zipf's law could be a manifestation of a complex system operating between order and disorder.

Zipf has also compared rank frequencies of words from a number of German texts from the ninth through the sixteenth century to English rank frequencies of words in texts from the ninth century to the twentieth. He found no fundamental statistical difference between them. It is worth quoting at some length what Zipf interprets from this finding:

> In short, although the original West Germanic had split apart long ago into the various dialects of England on the one hand and of Southern Germany on the other, and although with passing centuries these dialects changed phonetically, morphologically, semantically, and syntactically until they appeared as completely foreign tongues to one another, nevertheless in terms of dynamics as reflected in their respective rank-frequency distributions these languages remained fundamentally the same. Morever, if we step back further and include East Germanic as represented by Gothic, we find the same; and so too, as far as we know with the Greek.
>
> Thus we are finding for the acts of speech what physicists have long since found for the acts of inanimate nature: behind all the apparent diversity and complexity of the phenomena lies the sameness of fundamental dynamic principle.
> (Zipf 1949: 126)

Of course, words are only one type of language-using pattern, and as Zipf himself acknowledges, the pattern only emerges in a corpus of sufficient size and variety. Thus, questions about the extent to which there are fractals in language use remain.[18] Conceivably there are fractals in other language-using patterns, because every time a language user uses a pattern it affects the probability with which the pattern is used in the future. As Lemke (2000a) notes, certainly for biological systems, and probably for many others as well, the richness of their complexity derives in part from a strategy of organizing smaller units into larger ones, and these in turn into still larger ones, and so on. We will also see in the next chapter that this type of organization facilitates learning.

Conclusion

A complexity theory perspective views language using as a dynamic system that emerges and self-organizes from frequently occurring patterns of language use at different timescales from the milliseconds of neural connections to the millennia of evolution, and across a range of levels from the individual to interacting pairs to entire speech communities, rather than as a fixed, autonomous, closed, and atemporal system. Viewing language as a complex system makes us regard linguistic signs not as 'autonomous objects of any kind, either social or psychological', but as 'contextualized products of the integration of various activities by [particular] individuals in particular communicative situations' (Harris 1993: 311), what we have called their language resources. 'It logically follows that they are continually created to meet new needs and circumstances ...' (Toolan 2003: 125). Complexity theory encourages us to link real-time processing and all its variability to change over time. The value of this perspective is that language is no longer perceived as an idealized, objectified, atemporal, mechanistic 'thing' (Rutherford 1987). Many of the insights into language discussed in this chapter are not new—but complexity theory allows for a certain satisfying coherence among them. It also prompts additional questions (for example, 'How is language a fractal?'), and it allows one to develop or appropriate research tools (from other traditions), as we will see later in this book.

Perhaps no language is as unstable as an unfossilized language learner's interlanguage; however, a caveat we should make here is that while some of the characteristics we have been discussing in this chapter so far also apply to learner language, not all do, as there are clearly other factors at play in second language development, a point to which we return in the next chapter.

In this chapter, we have made the case for conceiving of language as a complex, adaptive, dynamic system. By so doing, we have been laying the foundation for claiming that the evolution of language, language change, language diversity, language development, language learning, and language use are emergent from the dynamic processes of change that operate in all languages at all times. In the remainder of this book, we will use this conception and this claim to inform areas of applied linguistics.

Notes

1   Any theory of language must be seen to be embedded in a theory of semiotics (van Lier 2004).
2   Which is similar to, though different from, Halliday's saying 'language is as it is because of what it has to do' (Halliday 1978: 19).
3   This is different from Labov's (1972) claim about upwards and downwards influences on language change. According to Labov, 'changes from below' are changes that are below conscious awareness, whereas 'changes from above' are changes to the language brought about consciously.
4   In fact, consciousness itself is an emergent property of distributed processes throughout the brain, not a property of the mind, or even a process in itself (Gazzaniga and Heatherton 2007).
5   At the neural level, this is stated as Hebb's law: 'When an axon of cell A is near enough to excite cell B and repeatedly or persistently takes part in firing it, some growth process or metabolic change takes place in one or both cells such that A's efficiency, as one of the cells firing B, is increased' (Hebb 1949).
6   Although Goldberg appears to change her position on this and says that frequently-occurring 'patterns must be stored as constructions even when they are fully compositional' (2006: 64).

7 This appears to be happening in modern-day American English in the pull between the present perfect and past tense for certain uses or in the tension in the use of negative prefixes such as 'dis-' and 'un-' before certain adjectives (for example, 'dissatisfied' and 'unsatisfied', 'disconnected' and 'unconnected').

8 Designed to teach French in institutes overseas, the Audio-Visual Method was informed by a modernized frequency count of French called *Le français fondamental*, which included a measure of how strongly people associated particular words with the situations in which they were likely to occur (Howatt with Widdowson 2004: 316–17).

9 It also does not follow that grammars that are descriptively adequate are psychologically real, an important point to which we return in the next chapter.

10 And even in the development of entirely new 'mixed' languages. Indeed, a new mixed language, Light Warlpiri, has emerged in a remote Warlpiri community in northern Australia. It is spoken by children and young adults in the multilingual community of Lajamanu and has developed within the last 30 years. Besides being a mixture of its source languages, it has developed an innovative auxiliary system, which draws on, but is not the same as, the systems in the source languages (O'Shannessey 2007).

11 Indeed, we should not fail to qualify our comments about linguists. Obviously, not all linguists see language in the same way. Certainly, language socialisation researchers (for example, Ochs, Schiefflin, Watson-Gegeo) and socioculturalists (for example, Vygotsky, Wertsch, Frawley, Lantolf, Appel, Pavlenko) as well as critical theorists (for example, Norton), and others regard language as a form of social action, a cultural resource, and a set of sociocultural practices.

If we add to this list of 'exceptions' those linguists who make meaning central to their understanding of language, and here we but mention examples of functional linguists (for example, Thomson, Chafe, Bybee, Hopper, Traugott), cognitive linguists and lexical semanticists (for example, Fillmore, Kay, Lakoff, Langacker, van Valin, Talmy, Givón, Fauconnier), systemic functional linguists (for example, Halliday, Hasan, Martin, Christie, Matthiessen) and functional grammarians, such as Dijk, we have identified linguists whose orientations and models are more socially oriented and semantically or cognitively based, linguists whose views are very helpful to applied linguists. However, it remains the case that language pedagogy and research, at least within North America, continue to rely on American structuralism and generative grammar for the most part.

12 See also Dickerson's (1976) case for the psycholinguistic unity of language learning and language change.

13 Trevor Warburton deserves the credit for pointing this out.

14   At least L1 speakers do; L2 speakers may translate or apply explicit grammatical rules that they have learned.

15   Although 'anger management' can be used in BE.

16   Humboldt also recognized that language must be viewed as 'energeia' and not as inert 'ergon', writing 'a language is to be identified with a living capability by which speakers produce and understand utterances, not with the observed products of the acts of speaking and writing'. (1949, cited in Robins 1967).

17   Although dynamic systems theorists' views on the need for mental representation have changed over the years (see Thelen and Bates 2003), and dynamic field theory (for example, Schutte, Spencer, and Schöner 2003) has allowed representational states to emerge from sensory-motor origins.

18   Another example of language as a fractal comes in the observation that variation within a single grammar bears a close resemblance to variation across grammars. For example, most recently, Bresnan, Deo, and Sharma (2007) have shown that individual patterns of variation in subject-verb agreement with affirmative and negative 'be' extracted from the Survey of English Dialects show striking structural resemblances to patterns of inter-dialectal, or categorical, variation.

5

Complex systems in first and second language development

In the previous chapter, we proposed that language be conceived of as a complex, adaptive, dynamic system, metonymically at least. It is the way it is because of the way it has been used, its emergent stabilities emerging out of interaction. We also suggested that these variegated stabilities or language-using patterns are enacted in specific contexts to deal with any contingencies and to take advantage of any affordances present in the context in the service of identity and meaning construction. Being enacted does not mean that the emergent stabilities are static wholes, of course. In fact, we referred to them as process representations—memories of the acts of using language, which are categorized through family resemblance and which are multiply linked in a dynamic network, to become our latent language resources for subsequent use. We call them 'latent' because they do not exist apart from the context in which they are used. Being our language resources also does not mean that they were memorized. How they become part of our language resources, then, is the focus of this chapter.

As a point of departure, we begin by sketching a nativist view of first language acquisition. Then, in order to understand what a complexity approach perspective offers, we outline what an emergentist/dynamic systems view of first language development looks like. Next, we repeat this sequence for second language acquisition (SLA), i.e. initially outlining a nativist view of SLA, and then offering a contrasting view of second language development, informed by complexity theory. Before concluding this chapter, we examine some data from a recent study to see how well our complexity theory-informed expectations are realized. Later, in Chapter 7, we will discuss the relevance of these observations for second language instruction.

Perhaps a brief explanation is in order before we embark on this ambitious agenda. In the preceding paragraph, we have deliberately differentiated the terms 'acquisition' and 'development'. While the former is commonly used in the research literature, from a complexity theory perspective, 'development' is preferred. One reason for this is that a complex systems view of language rejects a view of language as something that is taken in—a static commodity that one acquires and therefore possesses forever (Larsen-Freeman 2002a). Indeed, from a social perspective, one could equally well argue conversely: that language is never acquired; it is something in which one participates (Sfard 1998). However, the sociocognitive view that we have adopted does not accept the acquisition/participation dichotomy as an adequate description of reality. Instead, as with Atkinson *et al.* (2007), we seek to view mind, body, and world relationally and integratively—as constituting a single ecological circuit. As the anthropologist, Gregory Bateson (1972: 465) put it, 'the way to delineate the system is to draw the limiting line in such a way that you do not cut any of these pathways in ways which leave things inexplicable'.

As we saw in the previous chapter, when we drew a permeable line around language use, where to draw the line in a way that does not leave things inexplicable is a challenge for complexity theory, which adopts an integrative understanding. Nevertheless, as we shall see, at the very least, from a complexity theory perspective, we would not want to draw the line between a person and context because development is never a function of a person or context alone, but results as a function of their dynamic interaction (Thelen and Smith 1998: 575).

A second reason for preferring the term 'development' is that, as we have already emphasized in this book, language using is a dynamic system, continuously changing; therefore, its potential is always being developed—it is never fully realized. As we said in Chapter 3, the state space of a language-using system represents the landscape of possibilities of a system. Third, the use of the term 'development' is meant to recognize the fact that language learners have the capacity to create their own patterns with meanings and uses (morphogenesis) and to expand the meaning potential of a given language, not just to internalize a ready-made system. Finally, as we have seen already, a language is not a single homogeneous construct to be acquired; rather, a complex systems view that sees that the stabilities in the basin of attraction emerging from use foregrounds the centrality of variation among different speakers and their developing awareness of the choice they have in how they use patterns within a social context. Thus, as we saw in the previous chapter, language is an ever-developing resource, albeit one with some stability.

First language acquisition from a nativist perspective

Although there are several versions of nativist theories of first language acquisition, all of them hypothesize the existence of an innate component or universal grammar (UG), seen to be a genetic endowment of human beings. According to Chomsky (1986), it is the job of a linguist to explain 'I-language' or internal language that is in the mind, not 'E-language' or the external language utterances actually spoken in a speech community. In order to explain I-language, nativists posit a faculty of language, which must provide first, a structured inventory of possible lexical items (the core semantics of minimal meaning-bearing elements) and second, the principles that allow infinite combinations of symbols, hierarchically organized. The principles provide the means to construct from these lexical items the infinite variety of internal structures that enter into thought, interpretation, planning, and other human mental acts (Chomsky 2004).

Nativist accounts rest on the assumption that the capacity to learn language is a unique property of the human mind that is represented as a separate module in the brain, conceived of as an organ within the brain that performs specific kinds of computation (Chomsky 1971). Nativists believe that this modular architecture allows the shape and form of I-language to be largely independent of other aspects of cognitive processing or social functioning. They also believe that the fact that a UG is contained within the module accounts for the evolution within the human species and explains how native language acquisition can take place so expediently, given what they feel is a rather degenerative state of the input, filled with pauses and inchoate utterances and other dysfluencies, referred to collectively as the 'poverty-of-stimulus'. The impoverished input, combined with what is alleged to be an absence of negative evidence (i.e. evidence of what the system will not permit), leads nativists to argue 'that the complexity of core language cannot be learned inductively by general cognitive mechanisms and therefore learners must be hard-wired with principles that are specific to language' (Goldberg 2003: 119), although quite naturally, the search for what these principles are is an ongoing one, which has gone through several stages so far.

In an early stage of nativist accounts of first language acquisition, it was thought that the UG imposed narrow constraints on hypotheses that a child would entertain about the first language, such as conditions on wh-extraction from wh-phrases (relatives and interrogatives). Without such principled constraints, and given the absence of negative evidence, children would have no rational basis for rejecting different versions of rules that they hypothesize to exist based on the input they receive. In other words, it was assumed that there must be some narrowing of the hypothesis space for language acquisition to proceed inductively.

A later stage in the nativist account resulted from a fundamental shift in thinking (Chomsky 1981). Rather than children being seen to induce rules through a process of hypothesis formation and testing within the constraints of UG, Chomsky's 'principles-and-parameters' framework proposed a deductive solution to the same 'poverty-of-stimulus' problem, due especially to the problematic absence of disconfirming or negative evidence. This newer solution supposed that the UG already present in the child contained universal principles of grammar, which guide the child in the acquisition process. Once the process is triggered by linguistic input, children select among the parametric options made available to them by the UG principles. During parameter setting, children zero in on the exact shape of their native language by choosing the proper settings on a small set of binary oppositions. For example, a positive setting on the PRO-DROP parameter, which permits the subject in a sentence to be dropped if it is a pronoun, will select for languages like Italian or Chinese, whereas a negative setting will select for English. It is thought that acquisition of this I-language must take place within some critical period, just as birds must acquire their song before a certain age, for after this age, the hard-wired Language Acquisition Device is no longer operable.

For the time that nativism has held sway in recent history, it has been associated with generative linguistics. As such, it has been thought that the nature of I-language can best be revealed by studying formal structures independently of their semantic or pragmatic functions. Ever increasing layers of abstractness have characterized the formal representations, with minimalist claims by Chomsky (1995) most recently allowing only the principle of 'merge', an operation that takes n objects already constructed and constructs from them a new object. The merge principle is especially interesting because as Chomsky (2004) states, it is likely a more general cognitive principle, not at all limited to language.

First language acquisition from an emergentist, dynamic systems, and complexity theory perspective

The attempt to identify non-language-specific principles has moved nativism closer to an emergentist perspective on language and its acquisition. There does, though, appear to be an overlap in the way that both theories have come to characterize linguistic knowledge, with Chomsky referring to part of the language faculty as a structured inventory of lexical items; and emergentist Tomasello refers to language as a 'structured inventory of symbolic units' (Tomasello 2003: 105). However, significantly different is the fact that Tomasello's symbolic units are form–meaning composites since he rejects nativists' exclusive focus on grammatical form. Moreover, according to Tomasello (2003: 101), linguistic competence involves the mastery of routine formulas, fixed and semi-fixed expressions, idioms, and frozen collocations, all of which nativists see as peripheral, not core, to linguistic competence.[1]

Another fundamental distinction between the two positions is emergentists' insistence that there is no need to posit language-specific principles in a genetic endowment in order for language to have evolved or for successful first language acquisition to take place. They would say that general cognitive capacities will do nicely for both language phylogeny and ontogeny, capacities such as the ones that enable humans

- to establish joint attention
- to understand the communicative intentions of others
- to form categories
- to detect patterns, to imitate[2]
- to notice novelty (Tomasello 1999, 2003; Ke and Holland 2006), and

- to have the social drive to interact with conspecific caregivers, which may exist in other social animals, but be less powerful, or at least different, from that which drives humans (Lee and Schumann 2005).

Stepping back from language for a moment, consider MacWhinney's (2005) account of the well known discovery of Huygens in 1794 that two pendulums in clocks swinging in different arcs will eventually swing in synchrony, 'the one pendulum serving as the strong attractor that entrains the other pendulum to its periodicity' (2005: 192).

Relating this to language, MacWhinney notes that an infant begins to move its jaws rhythmically during a pre-babbling stage. During the babbling stage, the periodicity of this movement entrains a similar periodicity in the opening and closing of the glottis. As a result of this coupling, canonical babbling emerges (ibid.: 193). 'These epigenetic trajectories are the pathways of development trail-blazed for us by evolution, but recapitulated uniquely by every developing organism in interaction with its environment' (Lemke 2002: 70).

Emergentism thus calls for some genetic prerequisite to language onto-genesis, a big difference being, as we have just indicated, that the genetic contribution is not a matter of transmitting the principles of universal grammar through an organ in the brain; rather, it consists of more domain general capacities. While there are apparently substantive universals, which define the state space of all systems of language use (Mohanan 1992), when it comes to ontogeny, language-using patterns are seen to be learnable using domain-general capacities. To illustrate the domain-general capacity of pattern recognition, consider, for instance, Saffran, Aslin, and Newport's (1996) research that shows that neonates can detect patterned sequences of up to three syllables. Later, when presented with the same sequences, the infants recognize them, but they do not respond when the syllables are presented in a different order. It makes sense that for humans to detect patterns in language use, they would need to track frequencies and that frequency plays a role in developing patterns of language using that we wrote of in the previous chapter.[3]

Moreover, unlike nativists, emergentists are not convinced that the ambient use of language is all that impoverished. An emergentist account assumes that the positive evidence that children receive is sufficient for patterns to appear among a child's language resources initially on an item-by-item basis. Furthermore, 'young children's earliest linguistic productions revolve around concrete items and structures; there is virtually no evidence of abstract syntactic categories and schemas' (Tomasello 2000: 215). Later, upon increased exposure, children categorize the patterns and, perhaps, generalize from them. For example, when the language use of children who are acquiring English is examined, it is found that early on children's use of language is replete with frequently occurring 'light' verbs, such as 'go', 'do', 'make', 'give', and 'put'. The production of light verbs is not only true for children learning English, but has been found in children's speech in a variety of different languages—Finnish, French, Japanese, and Korean. Frequently-occurring forms are more accessible to children; they are also shorter than other forms, making them more manageable, a corollary to Zipf's law (frequency leads to shortening), which we introduced in Chapter 4.

Zipfian profiles

This would be as good a time as any to deliver on our promise to return to how a Zipfian type of organization in language may facilitate development. Recall that according to Zipf's law (1935), the more common words in a language account for geometrically more word tokens in a language than do the less common ones. Goldberg (2006) reports on research in which she and her colleagues analyzed a corpus of mothers' speech to their 28-month-old children. The analysis revealed that one verb, in particular, occurred with far greater frequency in a certain construction than any other verb. In the case of the intransitive motion construction (for example, 'We are going home'), it was the verb 'go'. For another construction, the caused-motion construction, the verb 'put' was far and away used more commonly than any other verb ('Let's put the toys away'), and for the ditransitive construction, which we discussed in the previous chapter, it was the verb 'give' ('I'll give you a cookie'). Research by Stefanowitsch and Gries (2003) concludes that the skewing of the data to this magnitude goes beyond what could be expected from these high frequency verbs. Goldberg suggests that the frequency-skewed data facilitates the learning of these constructions. The facilitation is due to the fact that not only do these particular verbs occur in a wide variety of contexts, but also that their semantics each convey 'a basic pattern of experience' (Goldberg 2006: 77) that is semantically prototypical for the constructions with which they are associated. Furthermore, the meanings of these verbs are associated with concrete actions, making their meaning clear to a child. In this way, children learn about the meaning of more complex constructions from their early encounters with these constructions in which relatively few frequently-occurring, semantically-concrete, short verbs are used.

   With the addition of supporting evidence from experiments, Goldberg (2006) concludes that Zipf's law applies within individual construction profiles to optimize the learning of the semantics of the construction due to the one very high frequency exemplar that is prototypical of the meaning of the construction.[4,5] In addition, the psychology of category learning suggests that acquisition is optimized by the introduction of an initial, low-variance sample centered upon prototypical exemplars (Elio and Anderson 1981, 1984). This low variance sample allows learners to get a 'fix' on what will account for most of the category members; then later, children can generalize the semantics of the construction through inheritance to include the full breadth of exemplars.

It turns out that the input need not be nearly as impoverished as is sometimes assumed; analogical processes can be seen to be viable once function/meaning as well as form is taken into account; there is good reason to think that children's early grammar is quite conservative, with generalizations emerging only slowly; and the ability to record transitional probabilities and statistical generalizations in the input has proven a powerful means by which to learn certain types of generalizations.
(Goldberg 2003: 222)

Probability and variation

Although much of the traditional linguistics literature describes languages as having deterministic rules, as we saw earlier, sociolinguists (for example, Labov 1972) and historical linguists (for example, Kroch 1989) describe rules as being variable or being used in a probabilistic fashion by individuals. Importantly, as Newport (1999: 168) notes, 'If these phenomena occur in natural languages, it must be the case that children are capable of acquiring such rules'. Probabilistic grammarians go a step further, claiming that variability and continuity enhance learning, making the learning task 'considerably more achievable' (Bod, Hay, and Jannedy 2003: 7). Thus, probabilistic linguists call into question the need for an innate language faculty in order to contend with the poverty-of-stimulus, showing that unlike categorical grammars, probabilistic grammars are learnable from positive evidence alone.

There has been a great deal of research of late on statistical language learning and infants. Earlier, we mentioned neonates' ability to learn sequences of three syllables. Infants can also capitalize on the statistical properties of language to detect the distribution of sounds in words, word boundaries, the order of word types in sentences, and even rudimentary syntax (summarized in Saffran 2003; see also Matthews *et al.* 2005). These findings have led Saffran and others to ask if it is possible that humans learn sequential structures better when they are organized into subunits such as phrases. They have determined that learners can indeed avail themselves of 'predictive dependencies', such as the fact that the presence of an article predicts a noun or a preposition predicts a noun phrase 'downstream'. In turn, these predictive dependencies—what in the previous chapter we called 'initial conditions'—can be used by learners to locate phrase boundaries. In a refrain that should be familiar to our readers by now, Saffran (2003: 110) suggests that those who hold a Chomskian perspective are correct in saying that the similarities across languages are not accidental; however, it is not true that the similarities are innate, 'Instead, human languages have been shaped by human learning mechanisms (along with constraints on human perception, processing, and speech production)'.

Further evidence for the fact that children can learn from variability in the language environment is the observation that children learn the phonemic contrasts of their native language even though they exhibit wide differences within and across speakers. Variability is not only important in the 'external' environment, however. Indeed, it is a basic tenet of dynamic systems theory that for change to occur, stable patterns must become unstable in the endogenous environment, or what we have called, the intrinsic dynamics, of the learner in order to allow the learner's system to self-organize in new ways. Thus, variability is not simply 'noise' in the external or internal environment, but instead may be crucial for language development and may in fact be the actual mechanism of change in development (Gershkoff-Stowe and Thelen 2004: 13).

Epigenetic landscapes

From a dynamic systems point of view, what is studied are not single variables, but rather changes in systems. What such an investigation focuses on are the intrinsic (for example, the infant's developing articulatory system) and extrinsic dynamics of the surrounding context at one timescale that can lead to a new development. We can expand on this point by looking at development from the perspective of Waddington's epigenetic landscape. (See Chapter 1.) Waddington meant for the surface of the landscape to reflect the changing probabilities arising from the dynamics underlying complex systems. Muchisky *et al.* (1996) have used Waddington's epigenetic landscape 'to conceptualize moment-to-moment language processing and language development as integrated phenomena' (Evans 2007: 137). Development is construed not as progression toward increasing stability, but as a series of *changes* of relative stability and instability. Figure 5.1 shows the evolving speech attractor landscape from Muchisky *et al.* (1996) as an infant moves from reflexive sounds to first words.

Each line of the attractor landscape is a *collective variable*,[6] a measure of the state of the developing system at that point in time. The depth of each valley on the line represents the stability at that point in time, and 'thus captures the probabilistic rather than rigidly fixed nature of behavioral and cognitive states' (Thelen and Smith 1998: 277). The shape of the lines depicts the dynamics of the moment determined both by the history of the child up to that point in developmental time and the particulars of the moment—i.e. motivational and attentional state of the child as well as the social and physical context (Thelen and Smith 1998: 276–7).

> The landscape represents one critical property of developing dynamical systems: the nesting of changes on multiple timescales. The contexts and conditions that determine the stability of the system at any point in time … constitute the initial conditions for the state of the system at the next instant of time … and so on. The system is thus reiterative; each state is dependent on the previous state.

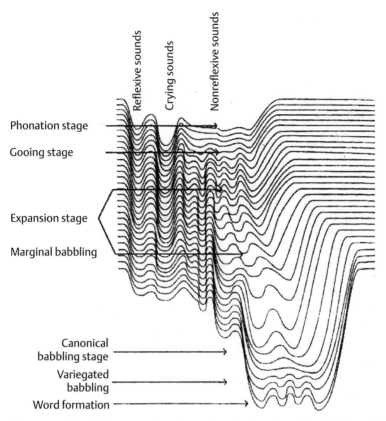

Figure 5.1 Evolving speech attractor landscape from Muchisky et al (1996).

Most important, this reiterative process occurs at all timescales. Thus, a landscape of evolving and dissolving stabilities just as easily depicts the dynamics of a real-time process, such as … producing a sentence … as it represents changes in those abilities over minutes, hours, days, weeks, months. In dynamic terms, the timescales may be fractal, or have a self-similarity at many levels of observation.
(Thelen and Smith 1998: 277)

Thus, the system changes from one moment to the next with the immediately preceding moment being the starting point for its next state. 'Although it is hard to conceive of a system that is not affected by its proceeding state, this iterative property is hardly ever taken seriously in … standard approaches to development' (van Geert 2003: 661). 'Each step in the process creates the conditions for the next step. In fact, there exists a kind of bidirectionality' between internal and external (van Geert 2003: 650).

Emergence of complexity

The bidirectionality allows for new patterns to emerge. As Tucker and Hirsch-Pasek put it

> [T]here is no attempt to appeal to the existence of information either in the environment or in the individual, as innate structure, to account for development. Structure or form (information) is *constructed* in development, and arises through the successive organizational adaptation of systems components to a specific context.
> (Tucker and Hirsch-Pasek 1993: 362)

In other words, what is striking from a complexity view is that the child produces language that is richer or more complex than the language addressed to the child (van Geert 2003: 659). This is a commonly observed property of all complex systems—systems in which the complexity emerges not only from the input to the system nor from an innate blueprint, but rather from the creation of order;[7] the development of a creole from a pidgin provides an example of this. Viewing language development as self-organization or structure formation in a dynamical system means that different learners may develop different language resources even when the ambient language is similar (Mohanan 1992). As Mohanan (1992: 653–4) puts it, 'Suppose we free ourselves from the idea that [first] language development is the deduction of the adult grammar from the input data, and think of it as the formation of patterns triggered by the data'.

While, frankly, we do not understand how exactly structure formation takes place (van Geert 2003: 658), it has been hypothesized that what motivates it is some discrepancy among the patterns that have been detected (Tucker and Hirsch-Pasek 1993). Two such discrepancies have been termed 'control parameters', i.e. parameters in a dynamic system that motivate a system-wide change. (See Chapter 3.) One such parameter is hypothesized to be the discrepancy that children note between patterns that they encounter and ones that they produce. For example, the fact that the subjects of most English sentences are agents establishes itself as a pattern in the child's language. Later, it may be noted by the child that subjects are not always agents. Such observations will eventually force the child to abandon strict reliance on semantic categories in favor of syntactic ones (Tucker and Hirsch-Pasek 1993). A second hypothesized control parameter is a discrepancy between what the child wants to say and what she or he is able to say (Bloom 1991). 'Note, however, that these discrepant moments, as control parameters, are instigators of change only. The reorganizations themselves and the forms that emerge are not determined by these cues, merely enabled by them' (Tucker and Hirsch-Pasek 1993: 378).

Inventories and networks

Our complex systems view aligns well with emergentists such as Elman *et al.* (1996), Bates (Bates and Goodman 1999), MacWhinney (1999), Goldberg (2003), and Tomasello (2003) in seeing the process of first language development as resting on general cognitive principles (not specific to language) as being sensitive to frequency and in this way probabilistic and inductive, and for giving due accord to meaning (Ellis and Larsen-Freeman 2006). However, we are not especially drawn to conceiving of language resources as a 'structured inventory of symbolic units', although we do agree that each language-using pattern participates in multiple relations with many others, and in this sense is structured (Langacker 1987: 57). In fact, it is within the multiple relations that a niche for a pattern is created in the ecology of a language (Taylor 2004). For this reason, we prefer Goldberg's (2003) network metaphor or 'constructicon'.

However, from our perspective, in addition to the fact that we prefer the term 'patterns of language-using' over 'constructions' (see the previous chapter), there are two things that are missing from Goldberg's network metaphor. The first is that 'In learning a language, one does not learn features of stratal subsystems in isolation from one another; rather, one learns them as clusters of features that work together' (Matthiessen 2006). Thus, other strands of the network must relate constructions by contingency, i.e. there must be a way to connect constructions with others with which they co-occur in language use. Secondly, we believe any network metaphor should reflect the social environment as well. Humans do more than simply record their past experiences in frequency tables (Elman 2003). As we saw in Chapter 4, it must be recognized that if we follow Bakhtin in conceiving of language 'as a dynamic force that derives from generalized collective dialogues …' then 'one must recognize how expressions are situated in, and carry the force of this form of dialogue', not only through one's own activity and context creation, but also through the interconnection of these with others.

We also depart from Goldberg, in at least one other respect. Goldberg (1999) explicitly distances herself from Hopper's emergent grammar. She does not believe that grammar is constantly emerging during ongoing discourse as Hopper does, and as we do. Instead, she believes that grammar emerges primarily during initial acquisition. Once it is acquired, it is assumed to be highly conventional and stable. As we have indicated thus far in this book, we believe that language-using patterns change at some level and at some timescale with every instance of use. For this reason, one can never say that a system is fully acquired. While it is convenient to use a simplifying container metaphor and conceive of the language system contained somehow as a static entity in someone's head, we think that this metaphor is not an apt way to think of a person's language resources. Of course, there may be patterns of neural connections in the brain and, based on our past experience with someone, we come to expect them to use their resources in a certain way;

however, we can never be certain that they will do so on any given occasion. As such, one's language resources only reflect latent potential; it is not until they are realized in language use that we know about a person's language resources, and then, of course, we only know about them with regards to that particular instance of use. We will have more to say about the notion of language resources as latent potential in the next chapter.

Co-adaptation

We would also want to remind our readers that for us, a central concern is language in use, language within socially and culturally meaningful activity, such as referred to in the previous chapter as Wittgenstein's language games. Through a skilful use of situated language, one makes choices that construct one's stance towards real or potential interlocutors. Through language use, one constructs one's identity, on an ongoing basis. Through language use, one reveals one's beliefs and values—developing skilful language use in these areas and others is part of language development.[8]

For this reason, as we have written, the social dimension of language is indispensable. It is not merely a source of 'input' to the system, though Tomasello (2003: 90) points out that social contexts (and their inherent routines, artifacts, and grammatical constructions) do 'serve to constrain the interpretative possibilities' available to the child. Another significant contribution of the social context, from a complex systems perspective, is the possibility it affords for co-adaptation between an infant and an 'other', early on its caregiver. As a child and its caregiver interact, the language resources of each are dynamically altered, as each adapts to the other. Dynamic systems theorists refer to this as the 'coupling' of one complex system to another. This is not about the acquisition of rules, nor is it about conformity to uniformity (Larsen-Freeman 2003). It is also not about the acquisition of a priori concepts, which cannot be known separately from our perception of their emergence in the ongoing flow of experience (Kramsch 2002). Rather, it is about alignment (Kramsch 2002; Atkinson *et al.* 2007), or the term we prefer, co-adaptation. In infancy, the child does not respond verbally; nevertheless, the caregiver interprets the child's non-verbal behavior as a response and continues the 'conversation'. This co-adaptation is an iterative process, with each adjusting to the other over and over again.

Gleitman, Newport, and Gleitman's (1984) early work showed how the quality of child-directed speech changes as the child grows, coming to approximate more closely adult-directed speech—importantly, though, never becoming isomorphic with it. Here is evidence that caregiver speech and the child's developing patterns of language use are mutually-constitutive, with each changing to accommodate the other through co-adaptation. This characterization of environmental language is different from static depictions that tend to regard the environment as a triggering mechanism, fostering the maturation of innate structure. It also differs from theories that regard the input as primary and which suggest that the communicative context and highly structured input propel the system forward (Tucker and Hirsch-Pasek 1993).

To illustrate this point, let us cite some recent research by Dale and Spivey (2006) using three English corpora from the CHILDES database. The researchers showed how the child and his or her caregiver produce sequences of words or syntactic phrases, during a conversation, that match those being heard ('syntactic coordination'). Especially interesting from our perspective is that the researchers found a Zipf-like distribution in the patterns that were shared with each child and caregiver pair. In other words, there are highly frequent sequences of word classes guiding the recurrent patterns in conversation. The other important finding is that advanced children are often leaders, whereas children earlier in development might be guided by caregivers. Therefore, who initiates the behavior that is adapted to is not a one-way street—the child is actively involved in shaping the context, particularly when the child reaches a higher level of grammatical development.[9]

Dale and Spivey discuss other coordinative patterns in human communicative behavior. Indeed, coordination or synchronization applies to many phenomena in the natural world as well. Kelso (1999: 111), for example, writes of the synchronous flashing of fireflies that occurs among certain species in Malaysia and Thailand, which anyone fortunate to witness will not soon forget:

> These insects have the ability to synchronize their flashing with either an outside signal or with other fireflies of the same species. A propensity for rhythmic communication is evidently shared by humans and fireflies. Of course, on a cellular level, such behavior is not only ubiquitous but important, as in the case of pacemaker cells that coordinate their electrical activity to maintain the heartbeat.

Systems as diverse as pendulum clocks, singing crickets, fireflies, cardiac pacemaker cells, firing neurons, and applauding audiences exhibit a tendency to operate in synchrony. These phenomena are universal and can be understood within a common framework based on modern non-linear dynamics (Pikovsky, Rosenblum, Kurths 2001).

Co-adaptation applies to a longer timescale as well, that of a lifetime. 'The life cycle of an organism is developmentally constructed, not programmed or preformed. It comes into being through interactions between the organism and its surroundings as well as interactions within the organism' (Oyama, Griffiths, and Gray 2001: 4):

> Taking a systems perspective on developmental processes means, among other things, attending to the ways in which the developing organism functions as a resource for its own further development. The organism helps determine which other resources will contribute to that development, as well as the impact they will have. The roles played by the

vast and heterogeneous assembly of interactants that contribute to a life-course are system-dependent and change over time.
(Oyama, Griffiths, and Gray 2001: 5)

On yet a longer timescale, co-adaptation can be seen as co-evolution. There is a

softness (permeability) of the boundary between inside and outside [that] is a universal characteristic of living systems ... organisms do not find already existent ecological niches to which they adapt, but are in constant process of defining and remaking their environments. Thus organism and environment are both causes and effects in a co-evolutionary process.
(Lewontin 2000: 125–6)

Bifurcations

Applying this systems perspective to the language-learning situation, we see that many resources are needed to support the development of language use in a child. The process requires time, a working memory, attention, effort, a language usage to be developed, support from a more competent other, etc. These are all constrained to some extent. For instance, the participants' working memories are limited compared with the complexity of the language that is produced in the adult–infant dynamics. Resource limitation is an important factor in explaining the dynamics of the process, and when resources change, so do the attractors or trajectories of dynamic systems. An increase in working memory due to neurological maturation of the child, for instance, may result in the system's fluctuating between two mutually exclusive states in phase space, a bimodal distribution. Bimodality can signal that there is about to be a transition in the system. At this point, a phase transition or what dynamic systems theorists call a 'bifurcation' (see Chapter 3) may take place. 'Bifurcations occur whenever the system can be in two qualitatively different states or stages at the same time. They are characteristic of qualitative change in development' (van Geert 2003: 658). When resources change, a discontinuous switch, what we have called a phase transition, from one to the other possible state may take place. As Elman *et al.* (1996: 218) explain

The relevance of bifurcations for our purposes should be obvious. Children often go through distinct stages in development, exhibiting qualitatively different behavior in each stage. It is tempting to assume that these stages reflect equally dramatic changes and reorganization within the child. Bifurcations illustrate that this need not be the case; the same physical system may act in different ways over time merely as a result of small changes in a single parameter—in this case, the young child's working memory.

U-shaped learning curves

This observation is reflected in the familiar U-shaped learning curve commonly observed in development. A well-documented example of this occurs with the learning of the past tense in English. Children initially produce correct irregular past tense verb forms ('slept') in English. Later, they commit overgeneralization errors, applying the '–ed' to irregular verbs (*'sleeped'). However, as they experience more verb forms, they appear to discover the regular pattern and the irregular 'exceptions' and thus their performance improves on both. Such a discovery has been interpreted as the children having induced the 'rule' of past tense formation. This has led to the proposal that the representation of language entails the existence of two separate mechanisms—rule learning for regular verbs and rote learning for irregulars (Pinker and Prince 1994).

By contrast in dynamic systems, 'qualitative distinctions between regular and irregular patterns of behavior can *emerge* through the operation of a *single* mechanism' (Elman *et al.* 1996: 131). The U-shape results from a dynamic competition between regular and irregular verbs. Initially, learners fail to mark past tense morphologically (i.e. they fail to use the verb + '–ed' construction) due to the frequency of irregular verbs in the language addressed to them. Later, the irregulars disappear in their production, as the type frequency of regular verbs overwhelms the token frequencies of the irregular forms, displaying the characteristic dip in the U-shaped learning curves and the analogical overgeneralization of '–ed' to irregular verbs. In other words, the U-shaped dip in the learning curve occurs around the point in development in which there is a change in the proportional strength of regular '–ed' compared to other mappings. As the number of verbs in the competition pool expands across the course of learning, there is a shift in the relative type frequency of regular and token frequencies of irregular forms, a quality which is registered in the virtual updating of language resources, and the irregular forms reappear (Ellis and Larsen-Freeman 2006).

Vocabulary bursts

A dynamic systems view offers new, simpler explanations for other developmental phenomena as well. For instance, a common phenomenon in child language development is the so-called 'vocabulary burst', a period of great vocabulary expansion on the part of the language-learning child when the child is usually between 14 and 24 months of age. The initial acceleration occurs around the 50-word level, after which words are added to the child's repertoire at a very rapid pace. Similar bursts have been reported for grammatical development between the ages of 20 and 36 months of age. A number of explanations have been proposed to account for the vocabulary burst. They include 'insight' theories (i.e. the child suddenly realizes that things have names), theories based on shifts of knowledge, categorization, and phonological abilities (Elman *et al.* 1996: 182). However, as van Geert

(1991) has argued, there is no need to posit such causes to explain this kind of growth. The real impetus for the acceleration that we commonly observe between 50–100 words may be the fact that any increase is proportional to the child's total vocabulary size—the more words you know, the easier it is to learn others. Other factors may play a role, but they are not essential to account for non-linear change in a dynamic system. The point is the behavior of the system can appear to be different at different points in time, even though the same mechanisms are always operating. Their relative impact, however, depends on the state of the system resulting from its interactions with the environment and its internal dynamics. This mutuality is often responsible for much of the non-linearity that is so characteristic of developing systems in general (van Geert 2003: 658).

Connected growers

Of course, the vocabulary expansion cannot continue to follow this growth function indefinitely. For if it did, the child would have a vocabulary size of two billion words by the time she or he enters kindergarten! Since this clearly is not the case, the burst must come to an end at some point. Dromi (1987) has proposed that this damping occurs because the child has switched her or his attention from vocabulary to grammar. In support of this proposal, it has been found that similar bursts occur for aspects of grammatical development between 20–36 months of age. Thus, the deceleration of vocabulary growth is offset by the rapid increase in grammatical development, an example of how dynamic systems are interconnected (Robinson and Mervis 1998).

This notion of 'connected growers' also explains the link between the development of language and other capacities, such as sensori-motor skills:

> Studies of language development and breakdown suggest that sensori-motor and language processes develop with similar trajectories (i.e. the ability to manipulate an object in a certain way emerges at the same time in development as does production of a certain language structure); conversely, lesions causing language deficits often cause problems with other sensori-motor skills (i.e. patients with aphasia are very likely to have problems producing gestures or interacting with objects …).
> (Dick *et al.* 2005: 238)

In addition, progress in object categorization changes rapidly at the same time as children's object name vocabularies also expand rapidly (Smith 2003), suggesting possible links between these two processes. It is clear, then, that the ability to produce and comprehend language

> is based upon an interwoven constellation of skills that emerges from everyday human behavior: social, physical, and linguistic interactions with the environment (exogenous) combined with the consequent

interactions among neural systems (endogenous).
(Dick *et al.* 2005: 238)

Knowledge is a process

Time and time again when researchers conduct experiments, they find that children's abilities differ from one experiment to another, depending on who the experimenter is, where it is being conducted, the precision and type of instructions, the task variation, the child's motivation and attention, etc. People often show dissociations in their behavior, seeming to know things when they are tested in one way, while seeming unaware of the same information when they are tested in another way (Munakata and McClelland 2003). Observations concerning the fluidity of children's abilities have led researchers to posit a distinction such as the one that certain linguists make between performance and competence. They theorize that competence, or what a child *really* knows, can only be seen by stripping away performance and contextual variables. However, from a dynamic systems account, the competence-performance distinction is both unnecessary and insufficient.

> Because behavior is always assembled *in time*, there is no logical way of deconstructing what is the 'essential', timeless and permanent core, and what is only performance and of the moment. Because mental activity has developed in time from the fundamentals in perception and action, and because mental activity is always tied in real time to an internal and external context, there is no logical way to draw a line between these continuous processes. The essence of knowledge is not different from the memory, attention, strategies, and motivation that constitute the knowing.
> (Thelen and Smith 1998: 594)

We conclude this section by underscoring the point once again that, from a complexity theory perspective, it is a mistake to assume that the result of the language acquisition process is an autonomous static competence or a fixed inventory of symbolic knowledge. As van Geert explains:

> Knowledge [in a child] say, for example, of the object concept is not some internal symbolic structure that causally guides actions. Knowledge is a process. It is the result of the dynamic process of interaction between a specific context and a specific body (a body with a specific past and history). The process unfolds by the continuous transaction between the context and body, and both body and context change during that interaction and by so doing provide new conditions in the process.
> (van Geert 2003: 661)

While retrieving an object is a physical action, it seems to us the lesson also applies to language. If we are left with only constructing a mental grammar or lexicon, we still need to explain its activation. If instead, we see knowledge as a process of language using, we will have streamlined the process and remained truer to a language-using sense of language. As Toolan (2003: 125) asserts disapprovingly, it is not the case that the child is learning the adult language system for 'there is no fixed system anymore than a child's or adult's diet is fixed or a system'. The idea of language as a fixed system, with stable or largely stable mapping of forms onto meanings, was most powerfully articulated by Saussure in his *Cours de Linguistique Générale*, and it has predominated in western academic linguistics ever since.

Second language acquisition from a nativist perspective

It is time now to turn our attention to second language acquisition. It will not surprise readers that a complexity theory perspective leads us to expect second language acquisition (SLA) to be different from first, given that the language-using system has already entered into a basin of attraction in state space. It is also the case that second language acquirers are a diverse group, which makes generalizing about the SLA process a potentially flawed proposition. Indeed, because learners and learning are experientially interconnected, there will be considerable variation from one learner to another and from one learning situation to another. We will return to this point later in this chapter. On the other hand, if linguistic systems are dynamic systems, there should be some qualities about the learning process that transcend all learners. Before considering these, we start off with a reprise on the theme of nativism, with which we began this chapter.

Long (2007) identifies three different views of nativism prevalent in SLA: special, hybrid, and general nativism. Many researchers who hold a special nativist view of first language acquisition continue to posit an influence of an innate UG on the second language acquisition process. One subset of these has assumed that second language acquirers are able to access a genetically transmitted UG even in adulthood. As we saw earlier, one prominent rendering of the UG is that it is hypothesized to include general abstract syntactic principles and the parameters along which languages vary. Another subset of these researchers believes that UG principles and parameters are still accessible to second language acquirers, but mediated through the first language, i.e. second or additional language learners begin with the parameter settings already established in first language acquisition.

A second group of nativists, hybrid nativists, believes that there is a 'fundamental difference' (Bley-Vroman 1990) between first and second language acquisition such that while UG may have operated for the former, it no longer does so for the latter. A third group consists of what Long (2007) calls general nativists. This group holds that SLA proceeds without UG or any such language-specific innate knowledge and abilities, and is instead accomplished through use of general cognitive mechanisms (for example, O'Grady 2003).

Second language development from a complexity theory perspective

Sensitive dependence on initial conditions

We have already laid claim several times in this book to being general nativists. We think that humans' genetic inheritance consists of general cognitive mechanisms and social drives that interact with the environment to organize the development of complex behavior.[10] Certainly, holding a complex systems perspective makes us accept the sensitivity to initial conditions of complex dynamic systems. This same acceptance makes it plausible that just as visual deprivation in early years profoundly alters lifelong abilities in animals and in humans (Mayberry and Lock 2003: 382) so also can 'a lack of language experience in early life seriously compromise development of the ability to learn any language throughout life. These findings mean that timely first-language acquisition is necessary, but not sufficient, for the successful outcome of second language learning'.

As we do, Mayberry and Lock (2003: 382) suggest that '... the development of language capacity may be an epigenetic process whereby environmental experience during early life drives and organizes the growth of this complex behavioral and neurocortical system'. Mayberry and Lock's position is consistent with a complex systems position that previous experience shapes the present in significant ways. Such shaping in SLA has traditionally been referred to as transfer, whereby learners' initial experience in using their first language leads to a neural attunement to the first language, which affects their second language learning experience (Ellis and Larsen-Freeman 2006). Of course, the effects of this experience can occur in third and subsequent language acquisition as well, making the mix of these dynamic systems all the more complex.

There are many factors responsible for the visible effects of the experience with the first language: the typological proximity of the languages, the learners' perception of the proximity, the competition in frequencies among lexical items from the languages, the amounts of exposure to the languages, the learners' proficiency, the learners' orientation and goals, the cognitive and social demands of a given task, etc. There are not only many factors, each on its own contributing a part, but also the factors interact, sometimes overriding each other, sometimes converging as powerful multiple effects (Andersen 1983a; Selinker and Lakshmanan 1992). And, as Ellis and Larsen-Freeman (2006: 560) note, they do so always as a function of time (MacWhinney 1999), time on all scales: in thousands of years—the recency of the diachronic divergence of the first language from the second or additional languages in the evolution of these languages; in years—the age of the learners and their length of exposure to the language; in milliseconds—the particular point in language processing in dynamical patterns of interactive-activation, both excitatory and inhibitory (McClelland and Elman 1986; Green 1998; Dijkstra 2005). As we have seen before with complex systems, change takes place on all timescales and on all levels of a system.

Multilingualism

Before leaving the topic of multiple language-using systems interconnecting, we should acknowledge that the assumption of monolinguals speaking the same language acquiring an equally homogeneous target-language is another one of those convenient reductionisms, often adopted by researchers. As we know, though, with increasing globalization, initial language development and certainly subsequent language development is increasingly taking place in environments where multilingualism or plurilingualism is the norm.

From a complex systems perspective, language use in the multilingual situation, which has been common in the past and likely will become almost universal in the future, is not a matter of translation between totally discrete and distinct language systems. For example, Meara's (2006) bilingual lexicon modeling, which allows for some interaction of two lexicons (at even a low level of 'entanglement'), shows how general properties of lexical networks can emerge such that even relatively small amounts of input in one language can effectively suppress the other language without building in some special 'language switch'. MacWhinney (2005: 195) makes the point that 'multilingual processes can be viewed as emerging from within-language resonance … When we code-switch from English to Spanish, the initial moments of speaking Spanish are still under the influence of resonance operating in English (Grosjean and Miller 1994)', or overlapping state spaces.

Whether or not there are separate but interacting language-using systems in bilinguals or whether the two systems are integrated into one is still a matter of contention; nevertheless, the point is that from a complex systems perspective the two systems are coupled, with the use of one affecting the use of the other. It is therefore a misconception to see a bilingual speaker as two monolinguals joined together, a point made clear in Herdina and Jessner's (2002) dynamic model of multilingualism, which operates within a similar theoretical frame to ours.

The second language development process

Not only does complexity theory regard systems as interconnected, but also as dynamic, often unstable, 'far from equilibrium' as the Nobel-prize-winning chemist Prigogine has put it. In contrast, much SLA research has proceeded as if a static and complete set of grammar rules were available and that its acquisition was the goal of language acquisition. Such projections as the learner's acquisition of verb tenses, and so on, continue as if the learner were filling out details of an already existing paradigm. But this is not likely to be the case from the learners' perspective. From a complexity theory point of view, not only do we get a more variegated portrayal of language-using patterns, we also get a different, more emic, or learner-centered, account of their development. Learning is not the taking in of linguistic forms by learners, but the constant adaptation of their linguistic resources in the service of meaning-making in response to the affordances that emerge in the communicative situation, which is, in turn, affected by learners' adaptability.

There is no consistent level at which patterns are fixed—their boundaries may or may not coincide with the constituent boundaries of linguists' grammatical descriptions, which is why we have adopted the general and flexible term 'language-using patterns'. Still, the question arises as to their psychological status, i.e. are they psychologically real for language learners? Gries and Wulff (2005) have conducted research that suggests that they are. Despite having more restricted exposure to the second language than do native language acquirers, second language learners are still able to arrive at generalizations that can be explained by patterns. 'In addition, in spite of various differences between first and second/foreign language learning, the probabilistic nature of the results and their similarity to that obtained for native speakers provide strong additional support of exemplar-based theories of second/foreign language acquisition in which frequency of exposure to, and use of, constructions play a vital role ...' (2005: 196).

Indeed, as we have already seen in the work of Goldberg and her colleagues, the distribution of verb frequencies within constructions facilitates the acquisition of the semantics of constructions. Slobin (1997) also notes that high frequency correlates with shorter forms (Zipf 1935), leading highly frequent forms to be easier to learn and to use. Thus, the scale-free distributions that Zipf found not only resulted in the emergence of complex language phylogentically, but may also optimize the learning of language ontogenetically, and perhaps it is the case, as we see now in the work of Gries and Wulff in second language acquisition as well. In other words, the natural structure of language is precisely the structure that would enable humans to learn.

A study of second language development

So far this book has been text heavy. It would be useful at this point to examine some second language data in light of the position just taken. The following data were collected as one part of a study conducted by Larsen-Freeman (2006b).[11] The table below shows the written linguistic production of participant 'U', a 37-year-old female engineer from the People's Republic of China, living in the US and studying English. U was asked to write a story for her ESL teacher. She wrote the story four times over a six-month period, with an interval of approximately six weeks between each. Three days after writing each story (i.e. the same story each time), U was asked to tell the story orally. Both renditions were untimed. Furthermore, U received no feedback on her performance. Her oral performance was recorded and transcribed, but the data being reported on here will largely be drawn from the written narratives.

The narratives were analyzed into 'idea units', mostly full clauses, 'a message segment consisting of a topic and comment that is separated from contiguous units syntactically or intonationally' (Ellis and Barkhuizen 2005: 154). Arraying the corresponding idea units side by side for each telling of the story reveals how the narrative is constructed each time and how it differs over time. (See Table 5.1 below, where the spelling and punctuation of the original is preserved.) Of course, there is no way to distinguish the effect of telling the story previously from actual language development (although from a complex systems perspective, perhaps it does not matter), but by having U tell the same story, at least the variation due to task differences was minimized, though not eliminated, of course, because this is not to say that U saw the task the same way each time, her mutable motivation and engagement with the task being part of the changing context. U brings with her her own unique history and will move on from these storytelling experiences in some way changed by her participation.

	June	August	October	November
			An Old Friend	An old friend
1	Two years ago, I lived in Detroit.	Two years ago, I lived at Detroit.	I lived in Detroit two years ago.	When I came to the U.S.A three years ago, I lived at Detroit.
2				There were a lot of Chinese studied or worked at metro Detroit.
3				We used to celebrate holidays with some friends; namely, we always had parties in holiday season.
4	Someday, my friends invited me to go to a celebration for Chinese Holiday.	One day I went to a party for celebrating Chinese holiday.	One day, one friend invited me to a party to celebrate a Chinese holiday.	Two years ago, one of my friends invited me to a party to celebrated Chinese New Year.

5	There were about 200 persons in that celebration.	There were about 200 persons at the party.	There were about two hundred persons in the party.	There were about two hundred persons at the party.
6	Of course, we had a Chinese dinner together.	Of course, we had some Chinese dishes.	Like every party, we got a lot of delicious Chinese food.	Like every times, we had a lot of Chinese food.
7	When I was picking up my dishes I saw a lady past by me.	When I was picking up my plate, I saw a lady	When I was taking my food, a lady past by me,	When I was picking up my food, a lady past by me,
8	I felt I met her before,	and felt I knew her,	and I had a feeling that I knew her,	and I had a strong felling I knew her,
9	but I couldn't figure out.	but I couldn't remember who she was	but her name just was on my tongue I could say it.	I could not mention who she was.

Table 5.1 The first nine idea units in U's written story

Many observations can be made about these 7–9 idea units. Certainly, it is easy to detect the influence of first language use, in the alternation over time between 'in' and 'at' in the first and fifth idea units, Chinese not distinguishing these meanings with different prepositions. Then, too, the pattern beginning with 'there' in the second idea unit is commonly found in Chinese-English interlanguage,[12] reflecting the topic-comment word order of Chinese (Schachter and Rutherford 1979). Clearly U's English speech is affected by the initial conditions of Chinese, and her attention is, not surprisingly, in tune with it in some regards.

We can also discern some stable second language-using patterns. In idea unit 1, although its position and number changes, it is the case that the construction '# + years + ago' endures. The same holds for 'about two hundred persons', a pattern embedded in the 'there were' pattern in idea unit 5. Some language-using patterns are more variable. For example, in idea unit 4, the phrase commenting on an event is reported as 'a celebration', 'for celebrating', 'to celebrate', 'to celebrated', the last one perhaps being primed by the 'invited' preceding it. In other instances, we see a partial iteration, with some differences. In idea unit 7, for example, each utterance begins with 'When I was', but each initial clause has a different predicate, i.e. 'picking up my dishes', 'picking up my plate', 'taking my food', 'picking up my food'. Of course, there are also different degrees of variability. Look at the pattern in idea unit 8, 'I had a feeling that …' in October, which was only slightly modified in November, 'strong' being added in the slot before 'feeling', spelled 'felling'.

While a complex systems view would encourage us to confine our comments to the changes that take place in a learner's enactment of language-using patterns, as we have just done, it is traditional in interlanguage studies to talk about progress from a target-language perspective. There are, after all, two additional idea units in the November telling of the story, perhaps as a result of attentional resources having been freed up so that more elaboration was possible. Of course, the task was untimed, so time constraints were not necessarily an encumbrance on performance. However, it is known that with iteration, speakers start to consolidate constructions into larger units, just as chess masters are able to develop schemata about the attack or defense configurations of chess pieces, which increases their fluency and frees up their attentional resources to go elsewhere.

Another move in the direction of target-language performance can be found in the move from the incorrect 'someday', used in June in idea unit 4 to the correct 'one day' in August and October, to its replacement in November with the more precise 'two years ago'. Again, from a target-language perspective, one can also find examples of regression. For instance, in idea unit 9, U's 'I just couldn't remember who she was' in August was more target like, and perhaps more closely matched what she intended to say, than what she did say in November, i.e. 'I could not mention who she was'. However, progression and regression are problematic concepts from a complex systems perspective. It is well known that at any given time, speakers have language resources that are heterochronous, practices and patterns considered typical of many earlier and later stages co-exist and interact and are differentially produced in different contexts (e.g., Lemke 2000b). This is true of interlanguage as well, as evidenced, for example, in learners' 'scouting' and 'trailing' behaviors (Huebner 1985). Language development is not only uneven but also proceeds at multiple rates simultaneously. In addition, a more superficial target-oriented analysis of interlanguage forms might obscure the significant target like and non-target like changes that are taking place in semantic and pragmatic mappings. One instance of this in U's data is in idea unit 6, where the semantics of 'of course' is maintained, but reformulated as a prepositional phrase in October ('Like every party ...') and November ('Like every times ...'); also, U's attempt to use an adverbial logical connector in idea Unit 3 in November ('namely') is semantically acceptable but fails on pragmatic grounds from the perspective of target-language use.

The shift from 'of course' to a prepositional phrase beginning with 'like' is interesting in another regard. From a complex systems perspective, one needs to look 'down' a story, not only across time from one telling to another. One wants to look to see to what extent patterns are clustering. What motivated the shift is impossible to say from these data alone; however, the consequence of this shift is that U can adopt a more consistent theme-rheme discourse organization 'down' her story. This can be seen, for example, in her October story, where the shift allows for the repetition of thematic 'party' (see idea units 5 and 6) as does the thematization of 'food', in the next two idea units (idea units 7 and 8). In addition, from a complex systems perspective, one would also want to investigate what motivates the telling of the story in this way. While the social influence is perhaps more evident in dialogic activity—see the next chapter for its influence in oral discourse—there are a few things that can be seen even from the limited data here. One obvious difference is U's use of a title in the October and November writing of her story. This written convention helps the reader (the teacher) of the story to understand what she is about to read. It is also perhaps noteworthy that U tells the story in November in such a way that the reader understands that she has come to Detroit from another country (idea unit 1), something the teacher, of course, knows, but something that was unreported in earlier written versions of the story, though it was mentioned in the oral ones—see data below. U also lets the reader know that she is Chinese when she uses 'we' in idea unit 3; again, the teacher knows this, of course, but it is possible for other readers not to know this from the way she has told her story in June, August, and October.

Much more could be said about change, stability, and variability in this limited set of data. For example, we have not even commented on U's use of verb tenses or English determiners, both of which were highlighted in the instruction that U was receiving. It is also unlikely the case that U's entire performance could be explained solely as simple associative learning processes applied again and again. Although they likely play an important role in implicit learning (N. Ellis 1998), since U is a second language learner in an instructional context, doubtless there are other mechanisms at play. It is not improbable that U has memorized certain fixed units. For example, although not in these data, a few idea units later in the story in November, U uses the idiom 'from the bottom of my heart', acceptable in both Chinese and English. Then, too, as an older second language learner, U may very well have availed herself of grammatical rules she had learned. For instance, her use of 'used to' in idea unit 3 in November follows directly from her receiving instruction on using 'used to' for past habits. It is unclear whether U meant to imply that she no longer celebrates Chinese holidays with friends, as 'used to' does, but this is doubtful. It is more likely the case that she has not quite mastered the semantics of this phrasal modal.

It is also possible that U translated directly from Chinese into English. Such is likely the case when she said in idea unit 7 in October that she 'was taking her food', where an English speaker would have used 'getting'. The Chinese verb *na*2 (2 = use of the second tone) is used in this context, and it is usually translated in English as 'take' because the Chinese 'get' verb, *de*2 *dao*04, means 'obtain' and would not be used in the context of getting food. Also, as mentioned above, a few idea units later in her story told in November, U writes 'Some things from the bottom of my heart came out', a direct translation from Chinese, which would not be acceptable in English, but which does include the correct English pattern 'from the bottom of my heart'. One final example of the complexity that we will cite here is in idea unit 9 in the story told in October. U writes '... her name was just on my tongue'. This expression is neither Chinese (translated into English as 'her name was just beside my mouth'), nor is it English ('her name was just on the tip of my tongue'), but perhaps some amalgamation of the two or a partial rendition of the English pattern.

This amalgamation reminds us to make the point that formulaic language (Wray 2002) that arises through self-organizing processes in first language use can also do so within the second language. These processes over time produce emergent stabilities that we notice as expressions with some degree of fixedness in learners' language resources. Since complex systems of different sorts obey the same principles, similar self-organizing processes in second language learning-and-using can also be expected to produce stabilized, formulaic second language. An example of a second language formula is the use of the question tag 'isn't it?' for all numbers and persons. The initial and ongoing conditions are different in the case of the first and second language use. When second language learners use formulaic language, they may use a narrower system in a restricted range of contexts and have their first language as an additional element in the system. Thus, while formulaic second language may look the same as that found in first-language data, it may be quite different in form or in the amount of variation around the stability.

In any event, what should be evident from this brief sample and analysis is that as a complexity perspective would lead us to expect, U uses heterogeneous language patterns, leaving us to conclude that what is psycholinguistically real for learners does not align well with standard units in linguistic theories. What we also see is the waxing and waning of language patterns. Language learning is not a linear, additive process, but an iterative one (de Bot, Lowie, and Verspoor 2007), the iteration no doubt exaggerated in these data given the repeated task. We need to take into account the 'messy little details' (de Bot, Lowie, and Verspoor 2007: 19). It is by looking at these that we see that behavior is variable and context dependent (van Dijk 2003). Further, 'It is very well possible that if we look close enough that the general developmental stages individuals go through are much less similar than we have assumed so far' (de Bot, Lowie, and Verspoor 2007: 19) and may, instead of being governed by rules, be 'pastiches of various kinds of item-based constructions' (Tomasello 2000: 76). As we saw in Chapter 3, the degree of variability around an attractor becomes an important measure of system stability. It becomes data, rather than noise around an ideal performance.

Whether or not the messy little details in U's language-using patterns, the continuities and discontinuities, are indicative of lasting development is, of course, unclear. The differences might be due to a range of factors other than learning, for example, the fading of memory of the previous story or its transformation, as each time we retrieve and restore a memory, it can be subtly altered. Then, too, the particular contextual enactment of those resources varies from one time to another. Perhaps, upon reflection, U has changed her interpretation or opinion about the event. What we *can* say from the complex systems view we are proposing in this book is that U's language resources are self-organizing as the system moves through another region of its state space. This allows us to avoid a deficit view of language proficiency or the comparative fallacy (Bley-Vroman 1983). We do not have to infer that learners have or have not reset a particular parameter. We do not have to speculate on whether improved performance has resulted from U's gaining better access to a steady-state competence. We do not have to set arbitrary thresholds for determining when something is acquired. We do not have to talk about language as something to be taken in by saying that she has 'gotten the past tense'. Rather, we see language learning as continuous and never ending. One can investigate, indeed researchers and teachers need to investigate, a learner's language-using patterns at a particular point in time, just as we have done with U. Such investigations will inform pedagogical decisions (as we will see in Chapter 7) or researchers' inferences, but we do not have to treat a linguistic form as a commodity to be possessed once and for all. The important question remains, of course, as to whether improvement on this storytelling task will allow U to enact her language resources more effectively in future language-use situations (Larsen-Freeman 2002a), but we believe that this can and needs to be established without language being commodified.

U's data illustrate the variegated forms, the variety of influences, and the non-linear development of second language learners. The data collected for this study do not allow us to address the question of whether improvement on this task has led to U's being able to enact her resources on a longer timescale, nor do they permit observations about more socially-situated second language development, in which one might look at turn-taking, for instance. Further, this study cannot speak to the issue of alignment in second language acquisition, one that is no doubt important (Atkinson *et al.* 2007). Admittedly, also, the analysis of U's data is primarily focused on linguistic features. Further, the data do not permit us to zoom in on the local level of change in the moment, where one can see the real motors of development underway. As such, it is difficult for us to make full use of the tools from a complexity perspective, identifying the collective variable, for instance. However, being able to make full use of what a complexity theory offers is the goal for our next studies in which denser and more varied corpora will be gathered.

Although, as we have just seen, progress in SLA has traditionally been viewed as the degree to which a language learner's interlanguage conforms to the target-language, it should be acknowledged from a complex systems view that there will never be complete convergence between the two systems. For one thing, there may be little reason for a learner to attempt to emulate native-speaker norms (Cook 2002; Seidlhofer 2004), and for another, there is no fixed, homogeneous target end state to language evolution or development (Larsen-Freeman 2005). There is no 'final state' for processes that are always still ongoing in language learning and development (Lemke 2002: 84). That does not mean, of course, that patterns cannot become entrenched (MacWhinney 2006), whereby with repeated use, they become more fixed. This is particularly true, when the second language develops at first as parasitic or dependent on the first. In Chapter 3, we talked about this as the system sometimes occupying deep valleys in the state space of complex systems.

None the less, if the system of language use remains open, it continues to evolve. Thus, from a complex systems perspective, what invites explanation is fossilization, not change. While we would not wish to argue that there are no maturational constraints on SLA, the finiteness implied in the term 'fossilization' forces us into the comparative fallacy and a static view of finite linguistic competence, rather than looking for alternative explanations for the observed behavior. Because there may be a great deal of flux in the system, this does not mean that there is no stability. For after all, language is at least partially conventionalized and must have some rigidity in order to assure efficiency of processing (Givón 1999), not to mention its learning. To quote psychologist Esther Thelen at some length, in a dynamical systems approach to development, it can be seen that

> Some of the resulting self-organized patterns of action and thought are very stable because of the intrinsically preferred states of the system and the particular situation at hand. Such patterns of thought and action may be thought of as strong attractors in the behavior space…performance is consistent and not easily perturbed … . Other patterns are unstable, they are easily perturbed by small changes in the conditions, and performance with the same subject is highly variable and not dependable … .
> Development, then, can be envisioned as a changing landscape of preferred, but not obligatory, behavioral states with varying degrees of stability and instability, rather than as a prescribed series of structurally invariant stages leading to progressive improvement.
> (Thelen 1995: 77)

This view perhaps provides a new way of thinking about fossilized forms, then, as stable, but not static, patterns. Clearly, the neural commitment of the first language, and the ensuing entrenchment, may lead to a deep valley or well. However, any fossilized form should be seen against a backdrop of the boundlessness of potentiality (Birdsong 2005; Larsen-Freeman 2005) that is the hallmark of an open, dynamic system, one in which learners actively transform their linguistic world, not just conform to it (Donato 2000).

Also, while we have seen there are no discrete stages in which learners' performance is invariant, there are periods where certain forms are dominant, periods that have been referred to as stages in the acquisition of certain grammatical structures. Then, too, the existence of well attested sequences of development in SLA must be explained. One hypothesis is that the building blocks need to be in place in sufficient critical mass to move the system to a period where a different form dominates (Marchman and Bates 1994). Mellow (2006) shows how the initial use of complex syntactic structure is facilitated by the prior acquisition of the components of the construction. From these constructions, gradually learners develop linguistic abilities that can be described as grammaticized, generalized linguistic constructs (cf. Goldberg's account of the role of light verbs). Also, connectionist modeling by Elman (1993) reveals that neural networks function optimally when the input is limited to take into account the status of the system. However, rather than being a disagreeable limitation, Elman states that 'developmental restrictions on resources constitute a necessary prerequisite for mastering certain complex domains'. This, of course, is a central assumption of Pienemann's (1998) processibility theory—the emergence of new forms in a learner's second language and the degree to which such forms are variable are determined by the processing skills available to the learner at each stage.

The dominance of certain patterns may arise through a gradual building up process or through a period of fluctuation among competing patterns, followed by a phase shift in the system when a certain critical threshold is crossed, and some wider reorganization is triggered (McLaughlin 1990). The sudden discontinuity of the phase shift illustrates the non-linearity of complex systems, arising from the interaction of variables, whose modulating, mediating, attenuating, and amplifying effects on each other in positive feedback relationships (Ellis and Larsen-Freeman 2006), causes a phase transition to be reached, which results in a change of state. The change of state is difficult to predict because, as Ellis and Larsen-Freeman put it the

> effect of variables waxes and wanes ... goals and subgoals are set and met, strong motives once satisfied fade into history ... . The correlation between 'cause' and 'effect' might be negligible at one point in time, or in one particular context, but substantial at others. All individuals, all phenotypes, all genotypes react differently to different environmental conditions, making simple generalizations impossible. There is not one environment; individual agents select their own environments; the world inhabited by living organisms is constantly being changed and reconstructed by the activities of all those organisms (Lewontin 2000). (Ellis and Larsen-Freeman 2006: 563)

In this way, every organism is changing and determining what is important in its world-creating and remaking the world in which it lives (Lewontin 2006).

Quantitative analysis of data from second language development study

At this point, it would be helpful to return to some SLA data to illustrate this point. There were four other women in the study in which U participated. Four measures were calculated for all five participants' written stories: fluency (average number of words per t-unit, a t-unit being a minimal terminal unit or independent clause with whatever dependent clauses, phrases, and words are attached to or embedded within it), grammatical complexity (average number of clauses per t-unit), accuracy (the proportion of error-free t-units to t-units), and vocabulary complexity (a sophisticated type-token ratio—word types per square root of two times the words—that takes the length of the sample into account to avoid the problem that regular type-token ratios are affected by length (Ellis and Barkhuizen 2005). These indices have been determined to be best measures of second language development in writing. (See, for example, Larsen-Freeman and Strom 1977; Wolfe-Quintero, Inagaki, and Kim 1998.)

Group averages on the four measures, shown in Figure 5.2, indicate that learners are making improvements in each. Over the six-month period of this study, participants are writing more fluently and accurately, and their writing has become more complex in grammar and in vocabulary.

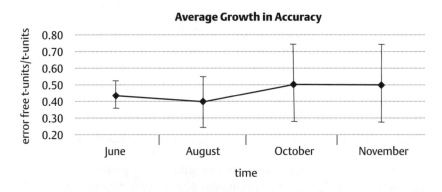

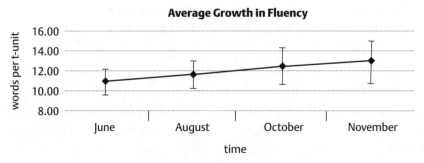

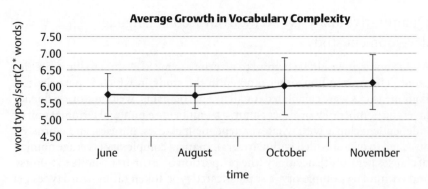

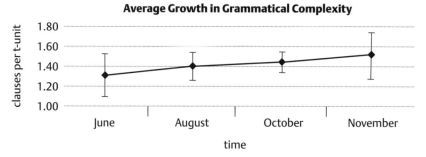

Figure 5.2 Group averages (± 1 SD) over time on 4 indices using written data

Of course, it is well known that group averages can conceal a great deal of variability, which can be seen by the standard deviations mapped onto Figure 5.2. Averaging group data has its limitations. Group data may often describe a process, or a functional relation, that has no validity for any individual (Sidman 1960). Thus, if we were to disaggregate the data, we would see a rather different picture.

Interindividual variability is clearly reflected in the different trajectories in Figure 5.3. Whereas group averages can be represented by a more or less smoothly ascending curve, some individual performances regress and progress, and others remain somewhat unchanged over time.

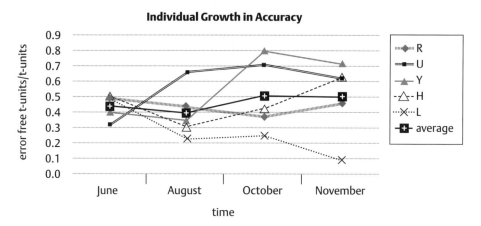

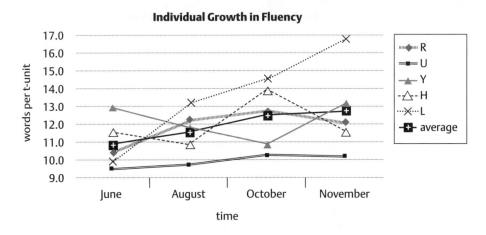

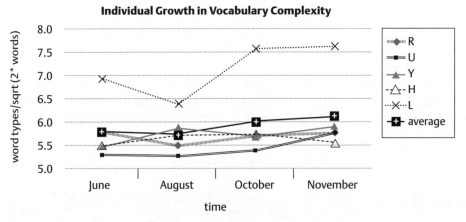

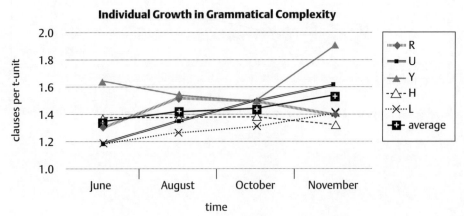

Figure 5.3 Interindividual variation over time and the average for 5 participants on 4 indices using written data

As with the search for SLA indices of development (for example, Larsen-Freeman 1978), those generalizations that exist at the group level often fail at the individual level. These graphs show that the assumption of progressive conformity to target-language norms does not pertain. In its place, we see that different participants are following different routes to SLA. Even in first language acquisition, of course, this is the case.

> Although [developmental milestones] may characterize the timing and sequence of events *on the average* ('the modal child'; Fenson *et al.* 1994: 1), the reality is that there is massive variation in both *when and how* children move through these important language milestones ...'
> (Marchman and Thal 2005:145)

Marchman and Thal (2005: 150) go on to explain that

> slight differences in the relative rate, strength, or timing (chronotopic constraints) of the component achievements can result in relatively significant differences between individuals in behavioral outcomes ... . Instead, from an emergentist view, children differ in language learning skill not because of domain-specific knowledge that they either have or don't have, but because of variations in how and when the pieces of the process were *put together* during learning.

Such variation is only magnified in SLA, of course, where there is an influential first language, not to mention a cognitive and experiential maturity and different orientations on the part of learners that affect the process. Thus, although it could be said that the learners were exposed to similar instructional procedures during the course of this study, they actually exhibit diverging patterns of development, due perhaps to the way that individuals have chosen to allocate their limited resources.

Of course, variation is a familiar theme to anyone doing SLA research. As a result, some SLA researchers have been inspired by variationist linguistics as conceptualized by Labov (1972) and Bailey (1973). (See Chapter 4.) For instance, Preston (1996) reminds us that early Labovian quantitative variation analysis in SLA was first done by Lonna Dickerson (1974). Wayne Dickerson (1976) followed, drawing a parallel between stages in interlanguage development and linguistic change and noting that the use of the variable rule was appropriate to such study. Stauble and Larsen-Freeman (1978) wrote variable rules for second language learners of Spanish learning English, and Tarone (1982) made use of Labov's stylistic continuum in her continuous competence model. Schumann (1978) and Andersen (1983b) applied ideas on variation in the processes of pidginization and creolization to second language acquisition, and there have been others, too numerous to mention here.

Bailey's (1973) wave model has also been applied to SLA. Its earliest application was that in Gatbonton's (1978) gradual diffusion model, which offered a dynamic view of second language phonological learning as a particular form of diffusion throughout a learner's speech. Recently, Trofimovich, Gatbonton, and Segalowitz (2007) found support for the 1978 model and pointed to cross-language similiarity between the first and the second language and lexical frequency in the second language as factors accounting for the gradual diffusion. From a complexity theory perspective, the finding of two interacting factors makes a great deal of sense. Importantly, though, only 40 per cent of those researched in the 2007 study were found to match the predicted pattern. By adjusting the factors so that they were more comparable to Gatbonton's original study, the researchers raised the percentage to 60 per cent. Thus, clearly there is a pattern there, and it is not our intention to be critical of this valuable work.

We must point out, though, that from a complexity theory perspective, no matter which variationist approach is applied, we would want to know how variation works at the level of the individual as well—why individuals conform and why they do not—to expected patterns (de Bot, Lowie, and Verspoor 2007). As de Bot, Lowie, and Verspoor say, 'a system will never be fixed and it is not the possible causes but the degree of variability in itself (which may be systematic, free and unsystematic) that is taken as providing insight in the developmental process' (2007: 53). Looking at variation not so much to discover its systematicity, but to discover what variation can tell us about the second language development is critical from a dynamic systems perspective. (See, for example, R. Ellis 1985.) This is because one of the tenets of a complex systems approach is that it is when the process is relatively unstable or teetering on the brink of chaos that the organism is free to explore new behaviors in response to task demands. Indeed, it is the flexibility to discover new solutions that is the source of novel patterns (Thelen 1995). From a complexity theory perspective we also do not expect that we will ever exhaustively account for the number of factors at play in SLA.[13] Indeed, Tromfimovich, Gatbonton, and Segalowitz noted that additional factors, besides phonetic contrasts and their frequency in the second language, may play a role.

Of course, because language is complex, progress cannot be totally accounted for by any one factor or by performance in any one subsystem. As we said in Chapter 2, the complexity in the language-using system arises from components and subsystems being interdependent and interacting with each other in a variety of different ways. What is evident at any one time is 'the interaction of multiple complex dynamic systems, working on multiple timescales and levels' (Larsen-Freeman 1997; Lemke 2000a; Cameron and Deignan 2006). Furthermore, there are also many dimensions to language proficiency—accuracy, fluency, and complexity being three that are theorized to have independent status in performance in that learners can have different linguistic goals at different times when performing in a second language (Skehan 1998; Robinson 2001). Not to be overlooked, though, are abilities with regards to discourse practices, genre structuring, and conversation structure.

Dimensions of language proficiency, language socialization/discourse practices, and even individual patterns of language use interact in ways that are supportive, competitive, and conditional (van Geert and Steenbeek 2005). They are supportive in that development in one of these subsystems, dimensions, practices, or patterns might depend upon the development in another. We saw this earlier in this chapter with regard to first language acquisition, for example, in the relationship between lexical spurts and grammatical development. Seeing the two subsystems as 'connected growers' (Robinson and Mervis 1998) demonstrates the importance of understanding not only static relations between variables, but also relations that change throughout the course of development. However, while mutual, the relationship is not necessarily symmetrical, in that after a while, the development in one subsystem may have a competitive relationship with development in another. The competition is due to the inherent limited resources that humans can and will invest in learning a new skill or solving a task (Robinson and Mervis 1998), such as humans' limited working memories, attention, and time-on-task (MacWhinney 1999; van Geert 2003). This can result in, for example, at one point in time, higher performance on one dimension of proficiency—say accuracy—which can seemingly detract from performance in others—say fluency and complexity. We will see how this plays out shortly.

Patterns in variation

Earlier we mentioned the fluctuation in U's use of 'in' and 'at'. Table 5.2 displays the first idea unit from her written narratives, once again, and Table 5.3 shows the same for her oral narratives.

June	August	October	November
1 Two years ago, I lived **in** Detroit.	Two years ago, I lived **at** Detroit.	I lived **in** Detroit two years ago.	When I came to the U.S.A three years ago, I lived **at** Detroit.

Table 5.2 Participant U: written story data at four times (first idea unit)

June	August	October	November
1 Two years ago, I lived **at** Detroit...	When I came to United States three years ago I lived **in** Detroit.	Three years ago I came to the United State and I lived **in** Detroit .	When I came to the United States I lived **at** Detroit.

Table 5.3 Participant U: oral story data at four times (first idea unit)

It is clear from these idea units that 'in' and 'at' are in competition in U's language resources, and no growth seems to be taking place. At least for U, there appears to be a bimodal attractor (Bassano and van Geert, unpublished manuscript) operating, with 'in' dominating at one time, giving way to a dominant 'at' another time. Indeed, Fischer and Bidell (1998: 514) point out that 'Just as individuals are beginning to develop a new type of skill, they shift between two different representations or two different strategies, each of which is only partly adequate to the task ...'.

However, when we take the level of magnification one level lower, we see that the system is not as free as it might seem. What might at first be called free variation, with *in* and *at* competing for 'air time', lessens when we examine the instances of 'in' and 'at' one by one. There still is some variation that is not easily explicable; for instance, in June, U uses 'in Detroit' in writing, but 'at Detroit' in speaking three days later. From a target-centric perspective, she also incorrectly puts *in* in the phrase 'in that celebration' in June—see idea unit 5 in Table 5.1. However, in this same month, U uses 'in' correctly when it is in a fixed phrase. She says 'keep in touch' at one point in the oral telling of her story (data not displayed here). Also, when she uses 'at' correctly in June, she does so where there could be no other logically semantic alternative, i.e. she says 'sit down at a table' and 'stared at me'; 'in' simply would not work semantically in these contexts. Here again, though, these two might also have been learned as a form-based pattern (i.e. the co-occurrence of verb + preposition) instead of through any sort semantic generalization. What this approach does show is that U knows some individual items that might allow her to build toward a more target like system. They may begin as holophrases, for example, 'keep in touch', and later become the basis for semantic generalization. It also shows what insights can be obtained by careful analysis at different levels of magnification, including the observation that even when things appear to be in a bimodal attractor at one level, there may be other sorts of dynamics within the system taking place at another level, even at the neurobiological level. As we said in Chapter 2, dynamic systems change all the time, sometimes continuously, sometimes discretely. Even systems in equilibrium are continually adapting to contextual changes and may change internally as a result of co-adaptation with the environment. We might not see a tree growing if we watch it, even for a long time, yet we know, in fact, that at a level that escapes our perception, there is a great deal of growth taking place.

In any event, it is easy to see other differences among the different versions of the story. What one would like to know as an applied linguist is if any of this variation is indicative of the instability that precedes a phase shift in the system. It is here where a pedagogical intervention might be optimal. This may be especially true when the variation that is taking place within a short period of time (i.e. within the three days between the writing and telling of the story) mirrors that over the six months of this study. For instance, the alternation in use of the prepositions 'in' and 'at' by U suggests that she might benefit from focused instruction on the difference between using the two prepositions in locative phrases. Such a pattern invites a microgenetic experiment (Vygotsky

1962), 'where the researcher deliberately facilitates (or even retards) the discovery of ... new ways' of behaving 'through coaching, training, practice, or scaffolding support' (Thelen and Corbetta 2002: 6) to see what effect it has on the system. Promoting U's 'noticing' (Schmidt 1990) might allow her to build novel representations from language-using patterns.[14]

Of course, this attractor state, even one exhibiting bimodality, may be relatively stable. When the second learner is made aware of the error, the learner may be able to correct it at the time, but then the learner may well fall back to the error state. Van Geert (2007: 47) notes

> An attractor state can be reached from many different starting points. The typical error of the L2-speaker may also result from different acquisition trajectories in different speakers. Finally, an attractor state may change if the system is dramatically altered or enriched or if a significant perturbation is applied. Thus, a typical error may disappear if the speaker receives extensive training or moves to a different linguistic environment in which the exposure to the L2 by L1-speakers is considerably greater.

Of course, had a successful pedagogic intervention taken place with U, there is no guarantee that it would necessarily work with the other learners. Depending on when it occurs and with whom, a similar intervention can lead to highly diverging patterns of development (de Bot, Lowie, and Verspoor 2005). Teachers know this, and researchers also know this from the many classroom-based SLA studies, such as those using focus-on-form interventions. In any case, the alternation between 'in' and 'at' illustrates the 'effect of competition between sometimes deeply entrenched rivals' (Sharwood Smith and Truscott 2005: 237), such as that which obtains where the native language does not make the distinction at all, and we know to expect 'extended periods where alternative forms exist side by side' (Sharwood Smith and Truscott 2005: 237).

Learner factors

Variation also results from learner factors—age, age of arrival, length of residency, goals, motivation, perception of the social status of one's interlocutor—all these and many others influence learner production, contributing to its variability.

Even among these factors of course, we must deal with complexity and dynamism. Take, for example, motivation to learn another language, which has always been thought to play a formative role in SLA. Today, it is commonly acknowledged that the simple integrative versus instrumental distinction introduced in the pioneering work of Gardner and Lambert (1972) is too simple for the multifaceted nature of motivation (Larsen-Freeman 2001). Dörnyei (1998), for example, has argued that we need to take into account social group factors in determining the motivation of second language learners, not to mention personal factors such as the need for achievement and self-confidence, and situational factors such as the interest and relevance of course-specific materials in instruction. Even such factors as students' perceptions of their teacher's communicative style were found to have a bearing on students' intrinsic motivation (Noels, Clément, and Pelletier 1999). Then, there is the matter of the dynamism of these factors. 'During the lengthy process of mastering certain subject matters, motivation does not remain constant, but is associated with a dynamically changing and evolving mental process ... [there is] motivational flux rather than stability within the individual' (Dörnyei and Skehan 2005: 8).

From a complex systems perspective, flux is an integral part of any system. It is not as though there was some norm from which individuals deviate. Variability stems from the ongoing self-organization of systems of activity. As Fischer and Bidell (1998: 483) observe

> A person carrying out activities does not possess one fixed level of organization. The types and complexities of organizations found in dynamic skills are always changing because (a) people constantly vary their activity systems as they adjust to varying conditions and coparticipants, and (b) people are commonly in the process of reorganizing their skills to deal with new situations, people, and problems. For instance, a tennis player will play at top level one day— after a good night's rest, on an asphalt court against a well-known opponent. The same player will play at a much lower level the next day, with a bad night's sleep, on a clay court, against a new adversary. This reduction in the player's skill is a real change in the organization of an activity. It is not an illusory departure from some 'more real' underlying stage or competence. There is a change in the actual relationships among the participating systems of perception, motor anticipation, motor execution, memory ... and so on. These relations constitute the true dynamic structure of the skill. The level of organization of tennis skills varies because coordination among the systems is different on two different days. It is not necessary to posit any additional layers of abstract competence or stage structure to explain this variation. It is accounted for by the dynamic properties of real activity systems.

In Chapter 1, we questioned whether it was indeed even possible to separate the learner from learning. Perhaps this quote from Fischer and Bidell makes clear why this question is pertinent. It should also be clear by now why we favor a 'person-in-context relational view' (Ushioda 2007) when studying learner factors. Such a view of motivation, for example, would mean

> a focus on real persons, rather than on learners as theoretical abstractions; a focus on the agency of the individual person as a thinking, feeling human being, with an identity, a personality, a unique history and background, a person with goals, motives and intentions; a focus on the interaction between this self-reflective agent, and the fluid and complex

system of social relations, activities, experiences and multiple micro- and macro-contexts in which the person is embedded, moves, and is inherently part of. My argument is that we need to take a relational (rather than linear) view of these multiple contextual elements, and see motivation as an organic process that emerges through the complex system of interrelations.
(Ushioda 2007)

Such an approach, we believe, would be something that Kramsch (2006) would favor as well. In her book on multilingual subjects, Kramsch discusses how SLA research has given relatively little attention to individuals as opposed to the process of language learning, and when it has attended to learners, it has often separated their minds, bodies, and social behaviors as separate domains of inquiry.

Individual attractors

Traditionally, intra-individual variability was seen as a form of measurement error. However, from a complex dynamic systems approach, intra-individual variability is an important source of information about the underlying developmental process (van Geert and Steenbeek, in press; Bassano and van Geert, unpublished manuscript). For instance, in examining the data from the study of the learners of English, it is possible to discern distinctive orientations and paths that learners exhibit over time. That is, although there is variability from one time to the next, it is also possible to identify attractors or preferred paths within individual performances. This can best be seen by mapping the performance of the five participants on two of the indices, which were scaled to allow comparability. When grammatical complexity is plotted against vocabulary complexity (Figure 5.4), for example, it is clear that subject L has focused on vocabulary complexity (whether consciously or not) while all the others were doing the same with grammatical complexity, although meeting with varying degrees of success. Plotting fluency against grammatical complexity (Figure 5.5) shows that L improved in fluency, subject U made more gains in grammatical complexity, and the others fell somewhere between.

Thus, L, a 27-year-old with a masters degree in biology earned in the PRC, has improved in what might be called an expressive dimension (fluency and vocabulary complexity), whereas subject U, a 37-year old engineer, appears to have developed in grammatical complexity, while her level of expressiveness—fluency and vocabulary complexity—have remained rather unchanged. Quantitative analyses reveal that while overall the group is making progress, at least if progress is defined as becoming more fluent, accurate, and complex from a target-language perspective, each member of the group is following a somewhat different path.

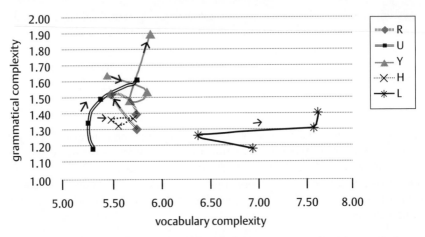

Figure 5.4 Change of grammatical complexity compared with vocabulary complexity for 5 participants using written data

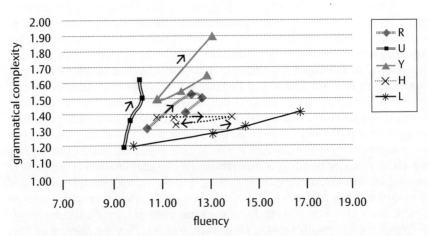

Figure 5.5 Change of fluency compared with grammatical complexity for 5 participants using written data

By producing network models based on corpus data, Ke and Yao (forthcoming) were able to corroborate this finding for first language. Using the Manchester corpus from the CHILDES database, they modeled language development over time, exploring its growth and connectivity in a network. Among other things, they found that children cannot be simply classified as early or late talkers by one or two measures. They may develop faster in one dimension, but slower in another dimension. They conclude by observing that children follow different paths in multidimensional space.

Individual developmental paths, then, each with all its variation, may be quite different one from one another, even though in a 'grand sweep' view, these developmental paths appear quite similar (de Bot, Lowie, and Verspoor

2007). One consequence of this is that generalizations about learning can be deceptive and are not likely to hold for all learners (Larsen-Freeman 1985).

Situational differences

This would be a good time to deliver on our promise to return to the question of how different SLA is for different learners due to situational differences. Leather and van Dam (2003) outline four different types of learning situations (first language acquisition, early SLA, instructed SLA, and SLA by adult migrants) and say unequivocally that the course of language acquisition cannot be separated from the specific circumstances of acquisition. 'There is *always* a context of acquisition that must be taken into account, and it is always complex, dynamic and in principle emergent' (2003: 19). While it is possible, of course, to separate context and person for the purpose of analysis, such separation requires the untenable assumption that the two are independent (van Geert and Steenbeck 2005).

Certainly a fundamental difference when it comes to second languages is the contrast between instructed and uninstructed development (overlooking for the moment the great variety of conditions and experience that exist within each of these types). Although there is SLA research that shows evidence of developmental processes applying both within and outside the classroom (for example, Felix 1981), it is also the case that interactional demands differ in different social contexts. Different types of interaction can affect not just the rate, but also qualities of second language development (for example, Pica 1983) and even different routes. For instance, data in Tarone and Liu's (1995) study contradict those found by other researchers in that the participant in their study produced English questions that were out of the natural developmental order. They suggest that this is because of the different interactional contexts in which the participant engaged, which included a number of question types from later stages of development. Thus, the participant's language developed differentially in different interactional contexts, as he entered into different role relationships and responded to different demands from his interlocutors. Tarone and Liu's 'claim implies that external social demands can be so strong that they can cause an alternation in internal psychologically motivated sequences of acquisition—even so-called universal sequences of acquisition' (Tarone and Liu 1995: 122).

A complex systems approach then, in common with ecological approaches (Leather and van Dam 2003: 13), 'takes a view of the individual's cognitive processes as inextricably interwoven with their experiences in the physical and social world. The *context* of language activity is socially constructed and often dynamically negotiated on a moment by moment basis'. In contrast to this embedded view of development, SLA researchers have adopted a compartmentalized research agenda, with some researchers concentrating on understanding learning and others attempting to account for learners' differential success[15] despite the fact that early on Selinker warned that 'A theory of second language learning that does not provide a central place for individual differences among learners cannot be considered acceptable' (Selinker 1972: 213, fn. 8). However, it may no longer be sufficient to talk about individual differences in SLA as a backdrop to a universal learner and learning situation (Kramsch 2002). Difference and variation need to move to the center of language acquisition research.

Other theories

Complexity theory is not the only approach to treat language use in a more dynamic fashion. There are other approaches that support a new metaphor as well. For instance, as we claimed in Chapter 1, Smith and Samuelson (2003) find a complementarity between connectionism and dynamic systems theory. One problem with connectionist modeling, however, is that many connectionist models lack the persistence of memory to learn sequentially; therefore, they cannot be used to investigate how a previously learned language may influence the learning of one encountered later (Nelson 2007). Biologically-inspired, adaptive resonance models (Grossberg 1976), on the other hand, overcome this disadvantage (Loritz 1999; Nelson 2007). Because such models can embody a learning history, they can be employed to better understand how first language conditioning of learned attention may affect later learning of a second language.

The most relevant example of a model of language development, which was 'paleo-connectionist', but which 'has now merged into the river of connectionism' (Thelen and Bates 2003), is the competition model (Bates and MacWhinney 1989). Core competition model beliefs about language and its development, which echo several of the themes in this book, are that language is function-, rather than rule-driven, that language is learned from input in a statistical or probabilistic way, and that language learning is non-linear, whereby gradual changes can lead to emergent properties (Thelen and Bates 2003: 385).

In this chapter, we have also discussed UG. While a language-specific innate mental organ is not consistent with seeing language as a complex adaptive system, our perspective does accommodate innate cognitive capacities and social proclivities. Even long-term generative grammarians, such as Culicover and Jackendoff (2005), now include among a child's full internal resources for language acquisition a 'broad UG' (p. 12), which includes various social skills and the capacity for imitation, leaving a 'narrow UG' for language-specific resources, which guide, but do not determine the course of language acquisition. The principles of UG in their account serve as 'attractors' for the process of generalization. Interestingly, contrary to traditional generative accounts, but much more in line with the case being made in Chapters 4 and 5 of this book, Culicover and Jackendoff's 'simpler syntax' assumes that a child is able to extract statistical regularities from the language environment and that generative grammar's traditional distinction between lexicon and grammar is mistaken. It may be the case that a new consensus in linguistics is coming about in which the distinction of convenience between competence and performance is giving way to 'a theory of competence ... embedded in a theory of performance—including a theory of the neural realization of linguistic memory and processing' (Culicover and Jackendoff 2005: 10).

Besides UG-inspired research, an influential theory in SLA is interactionism (Long 1996; Gass 1997; Gass and Mackey 2006). We believe that the interactionist position, in seeing the importance of interaction as a source of energy for the developing system, fits with a complex systems perspective. However, while an interactionist approach maintains that learners use interaction to get comprehensible input from which they can learn, a complex systems view is that any interaction is a mutual one with the language resources of both participants being changed in the encounter. Moreover, the social context of language use is not just a site in which acquisition takes place; it has a formative influence on language development (Firth and Wagner 1997). With a complexity theory perspective, we claim that language use, language development, language learning, and language change are all situated, co-adapting dynamic processes occurring on different timescales and at different levels (Larsen-Freeman 2003), which is different from what we take the interactionist perspective to be, in that interactionists feel it is important to distinguish acquisition from use (Long 1997; Gass 1998).

Another difference may be that complexity theorists emphasize the simultaneous changes that are taking place throughout the total system, although how to actualize this in practice, is admittedly an issue. Interactionists, on the other hand, tend to be more focused on linguistic units that shift from one form to another as a learner's interlanguage increasingly conforms to the target language. Importantly, in complexity theory, the endpoint is less of interest (because, it is claimed, it does not exist) than how behavior unfolds in real time. A complexity theory perspective views learners' development not as an act of conformity to some common endpoint, but rather as a process of dynamic adaptedness to a specific context, in which the context itself is transformed, and which is accomplished by volitional agents, who may choose other than to conform to the norms of a particular speech community in any case.

Another approach, receiving much attention these days, is a Vygotskyan perspective on SLA. (See, for example, Lantolf and Thorne 2006.) Complexity theory and sociocultural perspectives align well in certain respects. Both embrace Hopper's views on emergent grammar (Lantolf 2006a: 717). Both try to unify the social and the cognitive, although they do so in different ways, and neither is exclusively a theory of SLA (Lantolf 2006a). Whereas for sociocultural theory, internal mental activity has its origins in external activity[16], a dynamic systems perspective holds that development entails the ongoing interaction between internal cognitive ecosystems and external social ecosystems (de Bot, Lowie, and Verspoor 2007), where development is always being co-constructed between humans and their environment

(Larsen-Freeman 2007a). Further, unlike what we understand to transpire in the ZPD of sociocultural theory, in which a learner is enabled by a partner to perform a task beyond his or her current level of competence,[17] complexity theory sees alignment as mutual, a process we have called 'co-adaptation', where both the learner's and the partner's language resources are transformed through their participation, though not necessarily in a way that is beneficial for learning. (See Chapter 7.)

Also, although both reject the notion that development is a cumulative process, conceiving of it, instead, as a synthesis of heterochronic processes, complexity puts great stock in self-organization not only at multiple time-scales, but also at multiple levels from the neural to the greater speech community. The contribution of the brain to human thought in sociocultural theory up to the present has not received much attention (Lantolf 2006a: 726), understandably, given what little was known about the functioning of the brain during Vygotsky's tragically short life; but for complexity theorists, the brain is very much a part of the dynamic system, which itself keeps changing.

Conclusion

Clearly, there remains a great deal to work out with regards to a complexity view of development. We acknowledge imprecision in some places and gaps in others. None the less, we think that complexity theory presents a new and interesting enough way of looking to motivate us to do the hard work that comes next. In this chapter we have entertained a view of language development within a complexity approach. From this point of view what is studied are not single variables, but rather changes in systems. 'Emergence of language abilities and real-time language processing are the same phenomenon differing only in the timescales at which they are observed' (Evans 2007: 131). Embodied learners soft assemble their language resources interacting with a changing environment. As they do so, their language resources change. Learning is not the taking in of linguistic forms by learners, but the constant adaptation and enactment of language-using patterns in the service of meaning-making in response to the affordances that emerge in a dynamic communicative situation. Thus, this view assumes that language development is not about learning and manipulating abstract symbols, but is enacted in real-life experiences, such as when two or more interlocutors co-adapt during an interaction. During co-adaptation, the language resources of both are transformed. A developing system functions as a resource for its own further development, which calls into question, at least, whether it is possible to separate the learner from learning.

The difference among learners is not 'noise', but rather a natural part of dynamically emergent behavior assembled by the individuals with different orientations, grounded in social relationships with other people, and in keeping with historical contingency. From a complex systems perspective, flux is an integral part of any system. It is not as though there was some norm from which individuals deviate. Variability stems from the ongoing self-organization of systems of activity. To honor this, we need to look at the 'messy little details' that make up the 'here and now' of real time. We need to take into account learners' histories, orientations and intentions, thoughts and feelings. We need to consider the tasks that learners perform and to consider each performance anew—stable and predictable in part, but at the same time, variable, flexible, and dynamically adapted to fit the changing situation. Learners actively transform their linguistic world; they do not just conform to it. This view of development might be better served by conceiving of it as a web rather than a developmental ladder (Fischer and Bidell 1998; Fischer, Yan, and Stewart 2003).

> The metaphor of a web is useful for dynamic models because it supports thinking about active skill construction in a variety of contexts as well as types of variability. Unlike the steps in a ladder, the strands in a web are not fixed in a determined order but are the *joint product* of the web builder's constructive activity and the supportive context in which it is built (like branches, leaves, or the corners of a wall, for a spider web). (Fischer and Bidell 1998: 473)

Such an image depicts development as a complex process of dynamic construction within multiple ranges in multiple directions, a point we will expand upon in Chapter 7. Before doing so, in the next chapter we carefully examine language in use.

Notes

1 There are different types of emergentism. While we find O'Grady's (2005) syntactic carpentry account intriguing, we do not feel that a computational account is necessary or desirable to account for the emergence of order.
2 Consider, for example, 'mirror neurons' in the brain, which fire not only when an individual is performing some imitation of another's actions, but also when the individual observes someone else performing the same action.
3 Tomasello (2003) notes that this ability to detect abstract patterns in auditory and visual input is not unique to humans. Other primates such as tamarin monkeys also have this skill. Therefore, pattern finding is a cognitive capacity that has a deep evolutionary history and certainly cannot be seen as a specific adaptation for language.
4 Ellis, N., F. Ferreira, Jr., and J.-Y. Ke, in an unpublished paper 'Form, function and frequency: Zipfian family construction profiles in SLA', have tested this for naturalistic second language learners of English in the ESF corpus (Perdue 1993) and confirm these profiles.
5 Ninio (2006) also shows that children recreate the power-law distribution of the mothers' network for the same construction, concluding that syntax grows in a fractal manner.

6 It is called a collective variable because it is macroscopic, rather than microscopic. It allows the system to be described with fewer variables than the number needed to describe the behavior of the original components, which in a complex system are abundant and at different levels of scale, for example, molecules, cells, individuals, communities, species, etc. (Thelen and Smith 1998: 587). See also Chapter 3.

7 Mohanan (1992), for example, invokes Menn's (1973) crystal formation metaphor for phonology.

8 And, of course, you cannot make such meaning only with the formal linguistic system; other semiotic means are always functionally coupled with language use in real activity (Lemke 2002).

9 Co-adaptation can be a process internal to an individual as well, such as that which takes place when there is a continuing adjustment between the language being used and the idea being talked about (Slobin 1996).

10 Although, of course, the genetic inheritance is at one and the same time the result of evolution and a source for further evolution.

11 Some of the analysis and discussion in what follows have been drawn from Larsen-Freeman (2006b). Larsen-Freeman was assisted in data collection by Agnieska Kowaluk and in the preparation of the figures by JinYun Ke.

12 We are using 'interlanguage' not in Selinker's original sense of the grammatical part of learner language (Selinker 1972), but rather more loosely to cover all that has been learned of the second language. We are also not assuming that there is an interlanguage continuum spanning the distance from the first to the second language.

13 For learner factors alone, Schumann (1976) mentions 4+; by 1989, Spolsky lists 72.

14 Caleb Gattegno, the originator of the Silent Way, made this point years earlier when he discussed the essentialness of awareness.

15 With regard to this last point, we note that from the genesis of the field of second language acquisition, the study of SLA was to 1. account for the acquisition process, and 2. account for the differential success of learners (Hatch 1974). These two foci have been widely interpreted by the research community as constituting two separate research agendas.

16 There is some controversy as to whether Vygotsky's thinking was dialogic or dialectic (Wegirif, forthcoming). If it is the latter, then this is an important difference between complexity theory and sociocultural theory because complexity theory assumes no ultimate grand synthesis between the internal and the external, but rather that there exists an ongoing dynamic interaction between them.

17 Although neo-Vygotskyans, such as Donato (1994), point to the long-term development that results from collective scaffolding among peers. See also Swain and Lapkin (1998) and Watanabe and Swain (2007) for how peer interaction during 'language-related episodes' encourages development.

6

Complex systems in discourse

This chapter adopts a complex systems perspective on discourse. It suggests the various different complex systems at work in discourse and how they interrelate. Discourse events familiar to applied linguists, as sites for research or in their own lives, are seen as complex dynamic systems in action, with people as agents in social systems, using other complex systems—of language and other semiotic means—in interaction with each other.

In Chapter 4, we considered language as emergent patterns stabilized from use. Here we focus on the processes that give rise to that emergence in a complex dynamic system in which several individuals interact over time in language-using processes. We start from conversation as joint action (Clark 1996), although seeing this action as utterances in speech communication (Bakhtin 1986), human action in the microgenetic moment mediated through language (Wertsch 1998), or talk-in-interaction (Schegloff 1987), rather than through a transmission or code model of language, as Clark from his psycholinguistic viewpoint seems to do (Edwards 1997).

This starting point has already proved fruitful for dynamic views of discourse in the work of Scandinavian scholars, particularly the edited collection entitled *The Dynamics of Dialogue* (Markova and Foppa 1990) and the more recent theoretical framework for a dialogic view of language (Linell 1998). This work builds on that of Russian scholars writing in the earlier part of the twentieth century, including Voloshinov, Vygotsky, and Bakhtin, who stressed the importance of the dialogic aspect of discourse, i.e. that language use is hardly ever a totally individual affair. Bakhtin's dialogism also influenced Kristeva (1986) in developing her theory of intertextuality—how texts and words influence each other in the processes of use: 'any text is constructed as a mosaic of quotations; any text is the absorption and transformation of another' (ibid.: 37). For a dynamic view of language in use in pragmatics, see, for example, Verschueren (1999).

This chapter aims to bring these and other work together in a complexity perspective, and pushes further to show how this perspective not only combines earlier work but also offers ways to think about people using language in interaction as nested within multiple systems. A description of discourse is developed as multiply interconnected language-using activity. For talk, this means that any moment of speech action is connected across multiple timescales and levels of human and social organization through nested and interacting complex systems. Connection across timescales implies that the historical and the neurological, and all timescales in between, are connected into the moment of activity. Connection across levels of human and social organization implies that individual action is connected into all groups that influence the individual, from the partners engaged in the talk, to the global speech community and all sociocultural groups in between.

A pair or group of people engaged in speech communication or talk-in-interaction are seen as a coupled system, with the individuals as component subsystems. Moving inside the coupled system of talk-in-interaction, the talk of each individual is seen as a complex dynamic system that emerges from the interaction of subsystems of body, brain, and mind with language resources contributing as one of many complex systems that interact in the brain/mind system during talk-in-interaction (Thompson and Varela 2001; Gibbs 2006; Spivey 2007). The individual is not seen as a bounded entity but connected out into the environment. The environment or context of discourse is, in line with complex systems theory as set out in Chapters 2 and 3, inseparably part of the complex dynamics, with systems reacting to changes through soft assembly and co-adaptation.

What is discourse?

From a complexity perspective, discourse is complex dynamic language-using activity. The mapping of complex systems as set out for complexity thought modeling in Table 3.1 allows us to explore this idea more precisely. In order to begin to answer the first questions about the nature of complex discourse systems, we begin with current thinking about 'discourse'. The introduction to a recent major handbook on discourse analysis (Schiffrin *et al.* 2001: 1) groups the many definitions of discourse into 'three main categories: (1) anything beyond the sentence, (2) language use, and (3) a broader range of social practice that includes non-linguistic and nonspecific instances of language'.

These categories are problematic in various ways from a complexity perspective,[1] which emphasizes the interconnectedness of individual language use with the products of language use as texts and with social language use. A concern with language use needs to reflect on how social practices affect individual language production, and a concern with broader social practices needs to understand the contribution of instances of language use to those evolving practices. The first sense of the term 'discourse', that focuses on units larger than the sentence, betrays a written language bias, evidenced in much of linguistics (Linell 1988). The concern here would seem to be with longer stretches of writing or talk (for the time being passing over the written language bias), and how sentences or equivalent units of talk combine together. This sense is problematic for a complexity perspective in that such 'discourse' appears to be static, about products of language use, rather than dynamic. A complex systems perspective might see a product of language in use—text or a completed conversation, for example—as an emergent attractor in the trajectory of a dynamic system (as described in Chapter 3), but in order to understand emergent attractors we need to understand the dynamic 'discourse system' that produces them. Sense (1) then becomes an epiphenomenon of the discourse activity of the system. For example, when we consider two people engaged in talk, their 'conversation' emerges from the dynamics of how they talk to each other, while what they say reflects and constructs who they are as social beings.

Senses (2) and (3) are inseparable in a complexity perspective where they would be seen as referring to discourse activity in a complex dynamic adaptive system at different, but interacting, levels of human and social organization and timescales. The second sense of 'discourse' requires that product and processes of language using are considered together—the production, interpretation and the text by individuals (Fairclough 1989). The third sense, what Gee calls 'Discourse with a big D' (Gee 1999: 38) includes ideological assumptions alongside conventionalized social practices and uses of language.

The three senses of discourse can thus be brought together by seeing discourse as action in complex dynamic systems nested around the microgenetic moment of language-using. Discourse is no longer to be treated as an afterthought, an ugly duckling sub-area, that does not really fit the theoretical mold of other levels, which are described as autonomous simple linear systems, or in which discourse has been forced to fit by being squeezed into hierarchical rank and scale models. The pragmatics of language use does not have to be the 'wastepaper basket' category of linguistics (Yule 1996) but instead is intimately involved with the study of the local social practices and patterns of discourse systems (van Lier 2004).

The work of this chapter is to develop this idea of discourse as a complex dynamic adaptive system, and to explain various discourse phenomena through processes such as self-organization, emergence, co-adaptation, and reciprocal causation. We address the questions posed at the start of this section by focusing on face-to-face conversation as the primary site of discourse action and thus as the focal level and scale of discourse as complex system. Conversation is examined in detail in terms of coupled dynamic systems, and then we move to other levels and timescales of discourse, and to other types of language use. We map findings from discourse and conversation analysis on to a complexity perspective, to suggest what a discourse system landscape might look like and which discourse features act as attractors in the landscape of talk. We see how local routines, established to reduce the complexity of systems, connect upwards into social conventions of discourse through emergent patterns of use, and through reciprocal causation, how social discourse conventions act downwards to constrain what happens in the moment of language use. We apply ideas of patterns of stability and variability, central to working with complex systems, to findings from discourse analysis. Towards the end of the chapter, we briefly address the use of simulation modeling for the study of discourse.

We move now to look in more detail at one particular system that can be considered focal among the multiple systems of discourse: face-to-face conversation.

Face-to-face conversation

It has been suggested that face-to-face conversation should be taken as the primary type of language use from which all others spring (Clark 1996; Schegloff 2001; van Lier 1988, 1996, 2004). Clark argues that conversation is 'the basic setting for language use' and should be taken as primary, as the starting point from which to build descriptions of other types of language use. Other types of language use, he contends, require specialized skills and some process of learning:

> … face-to-face conversation … is universal, requires no special training, and is essential in acquiring one's first language. Other settings lack the immediacy, medium or control of face-to-face conversation, so they require special techniques or practices.
> (Clark 1996: 11)

For Schegloff as well, 'talk in interaction' is foundational to social life and action, and to language learning. His programmatic statement of this status prefigures much of the content of this chapter:

> Conversational interaction may then be thought of as a form of social organization through which the work of the constitutive institutions of societies gets done—institutions such as the economy, the polity, the family, socialisation, etc. It is, so to speak, sociological bedrock.
> (Schegloff 2001: 230)

He continues by describing conversation as 'the basic and primordial environment for the development, the use, and the learning of natural language—both ontogenetically and phylogenetically' (ibid.: 230).

In developing a complex systems view of discourse, we work from Clark's premise that face-to-face conversation must be characterized first and that characterization used to build descriptions of other discourse settings. Other discourse settings beyond conversation that will be of interest to readers of this book include literacy events that involve writing and reading, and learning settings such as the language classroom. Later in this chapter and the next we move to these other discourse settings, extrapolating the complexity approach to discourse from the 'basic setting' of people engaged in conversation. First, though, we start here with an extract of face-to-face conversation and use it to draw out an overview of the various discourse systems that are interacting across other levels and timescales.

Extract 6.1 shows two people, who are meeting for the second time, talking about the impact of their first meeting, referred to as 'it' in line 54. This stretch of talk comes from early in the conversation as the two speakers settle into talking together and work their way into what becomes an extended topic. The setting of the talk is post-conflict reconciliation in Ireland, and the speakers are Patrick Magee (PM) and Jo Berry (JB). Patrick Magee had been responsible for the death of Jo Berry's father twenty years earlier, when, as a member of the Irish Republican Army (IRA), he had planted a bomb targeted at members of the ruling British Conservative party. (See Cameron 2007.)

Extract 6.1[2]

```
51 PM   like .. having to handle that.
52      .. you know,
53      and er,
54      ... (1.0) or the .. enormity of it.
55 JB   [hmh]
56 PM   .. [perhaps],
57      you know,
58      .. the- there's nothing prepares you for it.
59 JB   .. [no].
60 PM   .. [of course] that's er --
61 JB   ... (1.0) no.
62      well I felt [..] com- completely the same.
63 PM   [hmh]
64 JB   ... (1.0) and that --
65      .. in the last two weeks I have walked down the street,
66      and I have just been struck,
67      ... (1.0) by what's happened.
68 PM   .. hmh
69 JB   and I just looked at people,
70      and,
71      .. and just thought,
72      ... (1.0) I haven't --
73      ... (1.0) it's like --
74      .. I can't ...(1.0) integrate,
75      what what happened between us.
76 PM   [hmh]
77 JB   .. and just [normal] life [[going]] on around me.
78 PM   [[hmh]]
79 JB   .. you know,
80      I just --
81      it's just been too different.
```

In this extract, which lasted about 30 seconds, the two speakers collaborate in 'joint action' (Clark 1996) that produces talk around the topic of the impact of their first meeting. On the timescale of turns of talk, here around 6 seconds, we can see the mental planning and skills involved in joint conversational action as speakers anticipate when the other will end a turn and prepare to speak, sometimes producing overlaps as in 55/56 and 59/60. The mechanics of turn-taking contributes to speakers' collaboration on ideational and affective dimensions, as they co-construct (Jacoby and Ochs 1995) a perspective on the topic of their first meeting. The co-construction process is made explicit in line 62 where JB aligns herself with PM: 'I felt completely the same'. Through their language choices, the speakers agree that the impact of their first meeting was significant: PM talks of 'the enormity' of the fact of the meeting (line 54) and adds a further extreme case formulation in line 58: 'nothing prepares you for it'. After her explicit agreement, JB then elaborates in some detail on her reaction to the meeting, using a strong metaphorical verb phrase 'just been struck' (line 66) and an extended, emphasizing contrast between everyday actions such as walking down the street and the extraordinary nature of the event of meeting (from line 69 to the end). During this elaboration, around line 77, PM interjects two supportive minimal responses, represented as 'hmh', which acknowledge JB's expression of the affective impact of the meeting. JB does the same while PM is speaking in lines 55 and 59.

The interaction of the two people involves them in coordinating their contributions, interpreting the other person's contribution, and responding to it in the moment. The way in which they engage in the conversation enterprise is 'dialogic' (Bakhtin 1981; Linell 1998) in its interconnectedness. It is more than two individuals doing their own thing while adjusting timing, as happens in an action like synchronized swimming; all aspects of using language, whether in interpretation or in responding, involves some construction of the other person in one's mind in order to speak in a way that caters specifically for him/her:

> The speaker breaks through the alien horizon of the listener, constructs his (*sic*) utterance on alien territory, against his, the listener's, apperceptive background.
> (Bakhtin 1981: 282)

In a later section, this dialogism is described in complex systems terminology as the 'coupling' of individual systems into a single system that is the process or activity of the conversation.

The nesting of levels and timescales of discourse

Their first meeting, talked about in Extract 6.1, had a huge impact on the two speakers. Jo Berry had wanted the meeting to take place for many years because of her wish to understand the motivation that had led to the bombing, but she had had to wait until Patrick Magee was released from prison and had negotiated the terms of meeting. Patrick Magee had a different initial motive in agreeing to meet—he wanted to explain the political reasons that had led the IRA to embrace violence. The two individuals came to their first meeting and first conversation with these differing motivations. As the talk progressed, they came to allow the legitimacy of each other's motivation, resulting in a combined joint motivation. This 30 second extract of talk thus has a powerful history, both in the long term over the twenty years since the bombing, in the medium term over the three months since the first meeting, and in the short term over the minute from the start of the talk. The extract also has a future, partly available to the researcher through the rest of the transcription.

The interconnectedness of the lives of Jo Berry and Patrick Magee is rather more dramatic than that between most partners in everyday conversations, but serves well to exemplify the idea that each speaker is part of the context or environment in which the other operates. The outline of their situation in the previous paragraph equates to the 'initial conditions' or intrinsic dynamics of the system(s) at the start of the conversation from which Extract 6.1 was taken. Figure 6.1 tries to capture in a diagram the multiple systems at various timescales and levels that are active and that contribute to the minutes of talk in Extract 6.1. These 'interacting systems … mesh in the current moment' of the face-to-face conversation (MacWhinney 2005: 191).

The moment of conversation appears in Figure 6.1 as the central process, portrayed as a sequence of 'slides' between the two black arrows. The diagram uses the visual convention of a series of slides to represent a discourse event, although the event itself is of course continuous.[3] The active language (and related) systems of each individual that come together in the coupled system of talk are represented as shaded dots within the discourse environment. The moment of talk (one slide) forms part of the conversation, i.e. it is a small distance on the trajectory over the conversation landscape. Extract 6.1 is transcribed into 'intonation units' (du Bois *et al.* 1993; Chafe 1994), each lasting around two seconds. Once completed, the conversation becomes one discourse event in a continuous series of connected discourse events, shown as a series of cylinders in the bottom left of Figure 6.1. In our example, the conversation is one of a series of meetings and conversations between the two speakers, sometimes private, sometimes in public with an audience or an interviewer. Extract 6.1 comes from the second meeting, which took place in the year 2000, and the two have since continued to meet and talk in a range of contexts. Each conversation or meeting contributes to a longer, bigger 'conversation', the complex dynamics system of their ongoing inter-action. Each person engaged in the face-to-face conversation can be seen as a complex system of interacting subsystems of continuous ideational, emotional, and physical activity, from the cellular and neural levels upwards to the physical being encountered in the conversation. This individual comes to the conversation from, and with, his or her ontogenetic history (shown as

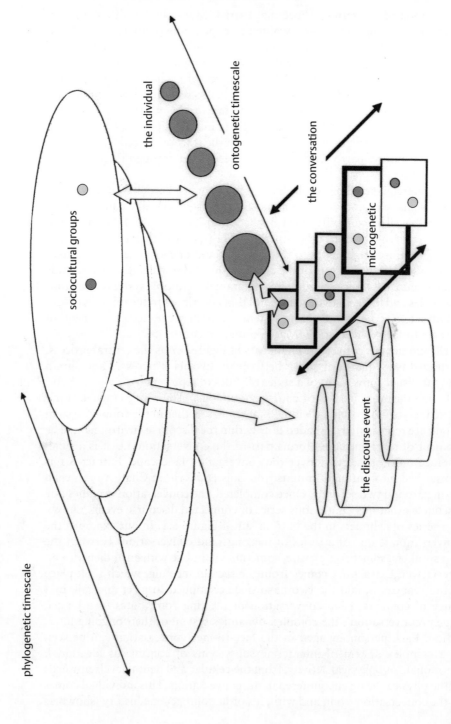

Figure 6.1 Interacting timescales and levels of human and social organization in the dynamics of discourse

receding circles in the top right of the diagram), and will move on from the conversation, changed in some way by participating in it.

The timescales relevant to face-to-face conversation between two people are:

- the mental processing timescale of milliseconds
- the microgenetic timescale of online talk
- the discourse event timescale: the 'whole' conversation, on the scale of hours
- the series of connected discourse events, on the scale of weeks, months, and years
- the ontogenetic scale of an individual's life, and
- the phylogenetic timescale.

At each of these timescales, we can see different levels of social systems at work, where by 'level' we refer to the size of the group that the individual is participating in. The individual can participate in the dyad, and in sociocultural groups and institutions of various types and sizes all the way up to the society and speech community.

The various systems at play in discourse are more usefully seen as 'nested' systems (Bronfenbrenner 1989) in which influence can pass in many directions, than as hierarchically-arranged, with only 'downwards' influence from higher systems to lower ones.

The soft assembly of dynamic systems in the microgenetic moment of talk

At the microgenetic timescale of conversation, speakers soft assemble their contribution, through the adaptation of these subsystems in the moment and 'on the fly' (Thelen and Smith 1994). Soft assembly, it will be recalled from earlier chapters, describes an adaptive action in which all aspects of context can influence what happens at all levels of activity. In Chapter 3 we used two examples of soft assembly: that of a horse and rider continuously adapting their motion in response to factors such as the condition of the ground, the physical health and energy levels of person and animal, and the weather; and that of an infant soft assembling reaching and grasping movements in response to the position and shape of the toy he or she wants to get hold of. Interconnected subsystems change as a whole when the person (or horse) adapts in response to whatever obstacles or challenges are thrown up by the task in hand. What we see and hear happening in the conversation are the observable traces of interior physical, emotional, and cognitive activity continually adapting to the discourse environment, which includes the topic, oneself, and 'the other'. For example, the movement of tongue, mouth, and jaw in a person's speech production system 'can compensate adaptively for disturbances or perturbations encountered by one part of the system by spontaneously readjusting the activity of other parts of the system' (Saltzman 1995: 157). At a cognitive level, there is two-way feedback and adaptation between the grammar of the language being used and the idea being talked about (Slobin 1996; Chapter 4 of this book), and between the ideational/ conceptual or pragmatic and lexical choices. One person's understanding of the other person's contributions to the talk is a continuous and adaptive process that makes use of all available information of all types, linguistic and non-linguistic (Spivey 2007).

The microgenetic soft assembly of talk in Extract 6.1 shows itself in the transcript as 'non-fluency' features, which suggest something of a struggle: several pauses of around one second in length, which is quite long for face-to-face conversation, together with several instances of false starts, notably around lines 72–74, where a speaker seems to begin an utterance but then abandons it and starts another version. At other points in the conversation, talk flows much more easily, so we might infer that something is causing a challenge here, perhaps getting started into the topic or recalling a memory with strong emotional content.

At the beginning of the chapter, we referred to the interconnectedness of discourse activity: across levels of social organization, across timescales, and out into the physical environment as embodiment blurs the boundary of the individual person. The embodied nature of discourse is seen in the, often subconscious, adjustments of speakers' physical posture and position in response to other people; if one person in a group places his or her hands behind his or her head, the likelihood is that other members of the group will follow this action. This kinaesthetic mirroring illustrates how physical systems are active in conversation as well as systems of language. Work on gesture in talk (for example, McNeill 1992; Cienki 1998) and on ellipsis and deixis (for example, Koike 2006) reveals the interdependence of these systems with language systems. Research into how gesture co-occurs with language shows that the two systems work together:

> the gesture and its synchronised co-expressive speech express the same underlying idea but do not necessarily express identical aspects of it. By looking at the speech *and* the gesture, jointly, we are able to infer characteristics of this underlying idea unit that may not be obvious from the speech alone.
> (McNeill 1992: 143)

Koike's analyses of videotaped tripartite conversations of Japanese speakers show how each individual uses his/her body and language together (Koike 2006). If we looked solely at language in the conversation of a group, we would identify multiple instances of ellipsis, so-called 'missing' elements of language, such as the grammatical subject of an utterance. However, such missing elements are often provided by gesture or gaze, so that the speaker's contribution to the conversation is realized through the coordinated use of these various subsystems. Seen as the outcome of multiple, interacting systems, conversation has less missing or omitted than a language-oriented approach might suggest; in fact, speakers who are dynamically co-adapting can be expected to include sufficient cues to understanding, distributed through the multiple systems that comprise conversational contributions.

Each person is also a social being, shown in Figure 6.1 by the arrows connecting the individual level to the sociocultural group level. An individual comes to a conversation as a member of various sociocultural groups (collectives and aggregates), and having played a range of roles within groups: families, school classes, political groups, peer and friendship groups, speech communities, etc. A person's history of interactions in these various groups builds up collections of experiences through other conversations and through other events that contribute to the language, cognitive and affective resources available to be drawn on in future talk. As a participant in the conversation in Extract 6.1, Jo Berry brings her experiences as a daughter, sister, and mother; as a parent counselor and educator; as a peace activist and so on. Patrick Magee brings his experience as family member; as former member of the IRA; as ex-prisoner, and so on. These histories and experiences influence talk in the moment; for example, Jo Berry's counseling experience leads her to react in certain ways to things said by Patrick Magee and to make particular use of reformulations, in which she plays back to him words, phrases, or ideas that he has spoken earlier, often as a way to go back to a topic. Patrick Magee uses some phrases that reflect current or earlier social identities: he speaks of 'the struggle' to mean the political conflict between Irish Republicans and the British government and army, and 'the movement' to mean the Irish Republican Army (Cameron 2007).

Each of the collectives or groups that people belong to can be seen as complex systems (Sealey and Carter 2004), in which individuals or smaller groups function as agents, and from which emerge 'discourses' of various types (Gee 1999), and which have trajectories or histories as groups. The cessation of political violence by the IRA is being followed by expansion of their discourses to include the discourse of involvement in mainstream political processes. Jo Berry and Patrick Magee have, as what we might call an ensemble, become part of a loosely connected group of 'people engaged in post-conflict reconciliation'; a recent program for television brought together people affected by the conflict in Northern Ireland with Archbishop Tutu who led the South African Truth and Reconciliation Commission, connecting the two very different geographical and socio-political contexts. A complex dynamic systems perspective on the language of social groups will be used later in this chapter to explain the emergence of group ways of talking.

When we return to the talk of Extract 6.1, having looked at the multiple complex dynamic systems involved in face-to-face conversation, we see that the transcription, and the recording from which it was made, are 'traces' (Byrne 2002: 36) of the soft assembly of these systems in successive moments of talk. As language users, we are those systems, responding to other people at all the different scales of time and levels of size, through processes that include feedback, co-adaptation, self-organization, and reciprocal causation and that operate mostly below the level of conscious awareness. As researchers, we collect traces of this system activity in order to try to reconstruct the dynamic processes of discourse. When we reach into the complex system of face-to-face conversation, to analyze a part of it or as teachers to work with some aspect of it, we are reaching into a churning, changing mass of interconnected systems, rather as a surgeon reaches into the complexity of the human body in order to carry out an operation on some organ within it. Although we may pull out and deal with parts of the complex whole separately, we have to remember that the parts are not independent of each other or of the larger whole. If we consider a part in isolation from its role in the whole, we will not be able to understand it fully. Conversely, understanding the interconnections among parts and whole may yield new ways of understanding how people use language in discourse.

A complex systems perspective reminds us that, instead of focusing on what, linguistically, may be 'missing' in conversation, we should look for how dynamically co-adapting speakers provide sufficient cues to understanding, distributed through the multiple systems that comprise conversational contributions. A fuller trace of conversational system activity would include information from various subsystems, levels and timescales. For example, from the individual as system, information on movements and gesture, gaze, facial expression, voice patterns, and even, as in lie detectors, temperature and sweating; from the social group level, information on group membership and affiliation; from ontogenetic history, information on influences over childhood, and so on. Of course, such increased information has a cost in terms of research time and expertise needed to interpret it, which in turn impacts on the amount of data that can be processed. An informed choice will need to be made about what, of all that is involved, should be selected as data. And having made such choices, the researcher needs to remember that the data that are collected and analyzed are a partial trace of the activity of multiple interacting systems.

The next section develops in more detail a complexity perspective on interaction of individuals at the microgenetic scale of talk.

Face-to-face conversation as a coupled system

The previous section took an extract of conversation and showed how a complexity perspective might describe the discourse system as resulting from the interaction of the systems of the two individuals, each of which can be seen as comprised of various physical and mental subsystems, and in turn as part of larger systems. We noted that the basic setting of language use, conversation, is dialogic—the individuals do not function independently in their talk together, since each affects the other continuously as the talk proceeds. Speakers influence each other on various dimensions, including the physical, emotional, and conceptual or ideational, when they formulate talk contributions with the other person 'in mind', designing utterances that, for example, will not offend, that will explain adequately and appropriately, or that will be effective in achieving goals. (See also Grice's maxims (Grice 1975) and relevance theory (Sperber and Wilson 1986).) There is subconscious influence across speakers when they adapt their accent or loudness, or when they adjust gaze or position in response to the other. As people listen to each other in talk, they may make non-verbal responses to what they hear, through supportive back-channel responses or through facial expression. In this way, each contribution to talk and each act of interpretation is dialogic and 'interindividual', partly designed for the other and a property of the talk rather than just of the individual (Morson and Emerson 1990: 129).

The complexity version of this dialogism is that the two speakers in face-to-face conversation form a 'coupled system', a term we first introduced in Chapter 3. To explore the nature of coupled dynamic systems, we start from a concrete example. In Chapter 5, we used the example of two pendulum clocks, that begin by swinging in different arcs and come eventually to swing in synchrony. The explanation for this is that each pendulum causes vibrations to pass through the wall to the other, perturbing each other's rhythms until they gradually reach 'a co-operative state of entrainment' (Saltzman 1995: 154; van Gelder and Port 1995). In this example, the dynamics that led to the co-adaptation of the clocks into a coordinated rhythm were purely mechanical, and thus predictable in ways that people are not. Studies of human sensori-motor coupled systems, in the domains of speech production (Saltzman 1995), of finger movement (Kelso *et al.* 1981), and knee-joint movement (Schmidt *et al.* 1990), show how coupled human systems shift from one preferred or 'natural' pattern of activity to another preferred pattern. With these human systems, the adjustment is controlled, not by mechanical vibrations as with the clocks, but by perceptual information, which may be either visual, as when one person synchronizes movement by watching another, or spatial, as when one person synchronizes movements of different parts of the body. For researchers of physical adaptive systems, the use of perceptual information to control adaptation and self-organization of the coupled dynamic systems links bodily coordination inseparably to cognition through an intention to coordinate actions. The motivation to coordinate leads to visual or spatial information feeding back into the physical action and prompting adaptation.

> The result is a coupled, abstract, modal dynamical system that seamlessly spans actor and environment. It is tempting to speculate that this perspective applies quite generally across the spectrum of biological behaviors.
> (Saltzman 1995: 168)

As applied linguists, it is tempting for us to push the speculation slightly further still and suggest that language-using systems work in similar ways—that conversation is helpfully seen as a coupled dynamic system, with each speaker being part of the 'environment' of the other. The intention to participate in conversation creates a flow of context-specific information, non-linguistic and linguistic, that influences the use of language by participants, such as adhering to the Gricean maxim to 'be relevant'.

An intriguing further connection between gesture and language use is suggested by Arbib (2002). Brain researchers have found links between movement and mirror neurons found in Broca's area, a critical language center in the left hemisphere of the human brain. This has led to speculation that the mirror neuron system is the biological foundation on which human language is constructed, which in the course of evolution went from gesture to gesture + speech to speech accompanied by gesture.

Language use as a property of the discourse not of the individuals

An important implication about discourse follows from seeing speakers within a conversation not as autonomous systems but as part of a larger coupled system. The language that is used can be seen as a property of the coupled system of the conversation.

> ... properties of the coupled system cannot in general be attributed to either subsystem individually, an agent's behaviour properly resides only in the dynamics of the coupled system ... and not simply in the dynamics of [either subsystem] alone.
> (Beer 1995: 132)

So, if the language use must be seen as a property of the coupled system and not as a property of either of the individual speakers, who 'possesses' the language? Beer's answer is intriguing:

> ... we must learn to think of an agent as necessarily containing only a latent potential to engage in appropriate patterns of interaction. It is only when coupled with a suitable environment [or other system] that this potential is actually expressed through the agent's behaviour in that environment.'
> (ibid.: 132)

Translating the last part of the quote back into the domain of discourse: as we saw in the previous chapter, a person has 'a latent potential' to use language. It is only in a suitable discourse environment that this potential is actually realized through the talk in that environment. This latent potential to engage in discourse includes[4] what we have so far in this book called a person's 'language resources'. These resources are virtual and do not exist

separately of their manifestation in use. All we have is language-using behavior in particular contexts or discourse environments. Each occasion of
language-using behavior is dependent on the specific discourse environment,
and conversely each discourse event is unique.

The microgenetic trajectory of a discourse system

We remain with face-to-face conversation as the primary setting for discourse
to explore conversational activity and patterns in terms of the trajectory
of a complex dynamic system. If it is possible and useful to see face-to-face
conversation as a complex dynamic and adaptive system, then we should be
able to understand how talk works in terms of dynamics. An initial sketch of
face-to-face conversation as the trajectory of a discourse system, continuously
changing and adapting, will be developed in this section, drawing on empirical
studies of talk and showing how details can fit into a complexity approach.

Visualization of a complex discourse system invokes the image of a
multidimensional landscape with hills and valleys, over which the system
roams, creating a trajectory (as in Figures 3.1, 3.5, 3.6). The landscape
represents the probabilities of various modes or phases of discourse behavior,
and the trajectory is carved out as a particular conversation moves from one
mode to another. The trajectory is a trace of the conversation, showing the
choices made and directions taken. It represents the immediate history of the
talk, and is another way of visualizing the series of 'slides' that make up the
discourse event in Figure 6.1.

The dimensions of the conversation landscape will be multiple, and include
the linguistic, ideational, affective, and physical. The system's 'modes of behavior' operate simultaneously on these dimensions, and are described in
terms of these dimensions as parameters. The intrinsic dynamics or initial
conditions of the discourse system dictate the particular state space landscape
for a particular conversation. Different conversations take place on different
landscapes. For example, the second conversation between Jo Berry and Pat
Magee had a landscape of possibilities that was partly a result of their first
conversation. The size and shape of hills and valleys represent the probability
that a system will enter a particular mode and, having once entered it, the
probability that it will remain there. The valleys are attractors in the system,
preferred modes of conversational behavior that the system tends to return to.
A valley with steep sides indicates a stable mode of conversational behavior
that will be difficult to move out of; for example, talk between disaffected
couples or warring neighbors may quickly move into argument no matter
where it begins. A hill indicates an unstable mode of conversational behavior
that will require effort to maintain for any length of time; it might be expected
that highly original and creative poetic talk might occupy this kind of region in
a state space of face-to-face conversation since it would require considerable
effort. A system can move along calmly, avoiding deep valleys and steep hills,

but may suddenly move into one of the attractors in a more dramatic phase shift. Conversations that 'run out of steam', as when exchanging pleasantries with strangers, can be seen as moving into a fixed point attractor, i.e. they stop. A change of topic may move the conversation into a different region of state space; if the topic is difficult to talk about, for example, involving face-threatening acts such as asking and responding to requests to borrow money, the attractors in that region will feature diffident and hesitant patterns of talk. The system is changed by its move into the attractor—new patterns emerge. Around the edge of some attractor basins are areas of state space that display self-organized criticality (Chapter 3) and that would represent highly variable modes of conversational behavior—what we have referred to as Kauffman's 'edge of chaos' (1995). Here, the system is highly unpredictable as it adapts rapidly, or self-organizes, in response to a changing landscape.

The idea of 'critical' points in discourse was discussed by Candlin (1987). Cameron and Stelma (2004) found that clustering of multiple metaphors indicated critical points in the reconciliation conversations. For example, at one point Patrick Magee began to appropriate the metaphor of 'healing' to refer to his accepting of responsibility; the 'healing' metaphor had until then been the 'discourse property' of Jo Berry, used to refer to her recovery from grief at her father's death. The act of metaphor appropriation potentially pushed the relationship between the speakers out of equilibrium, and Patrick Magee seemed at some level to be aware of this possibility. The critical moment was resolved by Jo Berry acknowledging his right to make use of 'her' metaphor in an episode that showed a significant degree of metaphor clustering; the trajectory of talk moved away from the edge of the attractor that might have represented an abrupt end to the conversation. In a finding suggestive of fractal shapes, the statistical analysis of metaphor clustering showed this occurring at two scales: around 5 intonation units and across longer episodes of around 25 intonation units (Cameron and Stelma 2004).

Talk is influenced 'downwards' by sociocultural and historical factors that operate over longer timescales than the conversation, and we may image this influence as a slow changing of the landscape itself. The hills and valleys can themselves change shape, or new ones emerge, as social and cultural influences of various kinds influence the types of choices available to participants in conversation. The evolution of the landscape occurs at a slower timescale than the conversation, although dramatic changes may sometimes occur. For example, system-level grammatical changes, as we saw with the adoption of the 'do' verb for questions (Chapter 4) take place over centuries, whereas technological developments such as the spread of social networking websites may lead to more rapid changes, altering the state space landscape of conversation over a period of weeks or months—still much more slowly than the microgenetic timescale of actual conversations.

In the next sections, we keep this phase space landscape in mind, as we fit some of what is known about face-to-face conversation into this topological representation of complex discourse systems.

Local routines in the coupled system of talk: adjacency pairs and sequences

The most detailed descriptions of the local workings of the complex dynamic system of face-to-face conversation, in terms of language choices, come from conversation analysis. Through meticulous study of detailed transcriptions of talk, conversation analysis has revealed patterns of behavior of the conversation as a system, co-constructed by speakers in coupled systems. The 'adjacency pair' is perhaps the simplest example of a discourse system construct. An adjacency pair consists of two turns of talk in which the second turn is the response to the first, be this an informational question and its answer, an invitation and its acceptance or decline, or a compliment and response. The adjacency pair is a unit of the talk; each speaker contributes to it, but the meaning and function of what is said comes from its role in the adjacency pair. So, for example, 'I don't know where I'm staying next week' could, as an isolated sentence, be used for many different purposes in conversation, but as part of an adjacency pair, it will be understood in specific and different ways if it is heard as a response to an information-seeking question: 'Where are you staying next week?' or as a response to an invitation: 'Would you like to meet up on Thursday?', when it sounds more like a refusal or at least a non-acceptance.

Other conversation analysis constructs that describe attractor basins in the trajectory of talk include sequences and pre-sequences. In a pre-announcement sequence, for example, speakers work out between them whether what one of them has to say will be news to the other or not. The speaker with 'news to tell' may begin with a pre-announcement like 'Guess what?', to which the response may be either an invitation to proceed with telling, for example, 'What?', or a blocking response that inhibits further telling, for example, 'I heard' (Schegloff 2001). The talk then moves into either a news telling sequence, or, if this has been blocked, begins a new sequence on some other topic. The trajectory of a face-to-face conversation will feature many such routinized sequences and pre-sequences, particularly at its start and at its close. Sequences that are routinized in conversation will be gentle attractors that the talk system moves into and out of as the conversation proceeds. Local routines help reduce the complexity of the system by narrowing down choices for participants. A familiar opening to a pre-sequence enables speakers to recognize from past experience what type of talk they can expect to hear next. Processing capacity is freed up as expectations facilitate interpretation and production. Routinized behaviors emerge in the trajectory of interaction as a way of reducing complexity and at all levels, including phonological adaptations, such as contractions, and lexical phrases that become routinized and formulaic, such as we saw with 'gonna', and discourse level routines, such as parent and child bedtime stories (Bruner 1983).

Limit cycle attractors: extended and interactional talk

In this section, we push the analogy between conversation and a coupled dynamic system to suggest that face-to-face conversation has preferred 'modal patterns' that act in a similar way to limit cycle attractors in a complex system. We first explain the idea of limit cycle attractors in another type of human coupled system, and then connect the idea to work in discourse analysis on modes of talk in conversation.

Coupled systems of gesture and movement, such as finger movements or moving a leg and an arm together, have two preferred states or modes of behavior, which are their 'limit cycles' (Kelso *et al.* 1981; Thelen and Smith 1994; Saltzman 1995). The system prefers to move in one of these two patterns, and, when perturbed out of one pattern, will shift into the other. In Kelso's study of finger movement (Kelso 1995; described in Cameron 2003a), participants were asked to move just their index fingers in a rhythmical movement, from vertical, through ninety degrees to horizontal, and back to vertical, rather like the movement of windscreen wipers on a car. Two starting points were given: the fingers of both hands at the same angle (in-phase) and the fingers at ninety degrees to each other (anti-phase). Once people started moving their fingers, they were asked to increase the speed of movement; the frequency of oscillation was the control parameter of the coupled system. If people started in anti-phase, they could keep moving with the ninety degrees between the fingers, but if they gradually speeded up the movement, there would come a point where the relative movement of the two fingers would suddenly shift into phased oscillation. If they started in-phase, this position could be maintained as speed increased. The moving fingers as a coupled system has two limit cycle attractors or stable patterns: either in-phase with each other or in anti-phase, maintaining the ninety degree angle between them. At low frequencies, both patterns are (relatively) stable attractors; at higher frequencies, the system has only one stable attractor, the in-phase movement. When perturbed away from the anti-phase mode, the coupled system moves into the more strongly preferred in-phase pattern, presumably as a result of constraints of cognitive attention and perceptual input.

The reader will recall that systems can be described by collective variables that bring together several parameters of the system into a single value. The finger oscillation phase difference works as the collective variable to describe the moving finger system. When the fingers are moving in-phase, the difference is zero; when they are in anti-phase the difference is ninety degrees. In analogy with the finger moving study, Cameron (2003a: 48) suggests that a 'collective variable' for dialogue might be 'alterity', a construct of otherness or difference between self and other (Wertsch 1998; Bakhtin 1981, 1986).[5] Alterity will have multiple dimensions, which might include, for example, ideational or conceptual alterity (difference in understanding of a concept), attitudinal or affective alterity (difference in feelings about what is being said).

Patterns of discourse and language use are larger and more complicated than the sensori-motor systems described above, but we may usefully understand conversation as oscillating between preferred modes of discourse behavior that act as attractors in the discourse system. Conversation trajectories do not arbitrarily move across the state space landscape, but are drawn to particular areas of the state space by these limit cycle attractors. Candidates for such attractors would seem to be the two types of talk labeled 'extended' and 'interactional' talk. In the interactional modal pattern, conversation proceeds as a series of short exchanges where each person attends to and understands the other. This type of talk can be seen at the beginning of Extract 6.1, from 51–63, and would also be characteristic of the informal chat that might take place when people come together for a meeting but before the formal business begins or when people talk with strangers at a bus stop. The extended modal pattern of talk would be typified by longer anecdotes or narratives told by one person, as happens from line 64 in Extract 6.1. Chafe (1994) suggests that the two patterns of talk differ not just linguistically but also cognitively, in connecting to two types of consciousness, one around what is immediate and present and one concerned with what is remembered or imagined that manifests itself in talk in the form of narratives with pre-sequences and evaluations. Snow (1996) found important differences between the two modes in first language development. By the age of two years, young children's different family experiences with discourse correlated with differential development of interactional versus extended talk. Children in families where people engaged in extended talk, for example, telling stories about their day around the dinner table, showed more development in their own extended talk patterns. As in Figure 6.1, an individual's discourse experiences on the ontogenetic timescale impact on language resources available for use in discourse at any particular moment.

Attractors in the discourse space landscape: the IRF pattern

Conversation analysis, by offering careful description of the micro-level of face-to-face talk as a single coupled system, is compatible with the complex dynamics systems approach to discourse being developed here and provides an important starting point for assembling a complexity toolkit for discourse. However, the kinds of joint action, adjacency pairs and various types of sequences, described by conversational analysts, do not just happen 'out of the blue', but take the form they do partly because people come to talk with expectations derived from previous experiences as members of sociocultural groups. These sociocultural forces have pre-shaped the landscape on which conversation takes place, and so work 'downwards' on to the microgenetic timescale. As an illustration of this idea of the shaping of the discourse landscape, consider another pattern of talk that has proved to be a robust finding of discourse analysis in classrooms, the 'IRF' pattern (Sinclair and

Coulthard 1975; Mehan 1979). This pattern of talk has three parts to it: Teacher Initiation, Student Response, Teacher Feedback (sometimes called Evaluation and hence IRE). In Extract 6.2, we see an instance of the IRF pattern from an episode of teacher-fronted classroom talk with 10-year-old students:

Extract 6.2
1 T   (1.0) but do you know what happens to butter?
2   (.) it does
3   (.) there are two things it does
4   (.) which are like volcanic rocks when they're being
      <XXX>
5 S   it bubbles
6 T   it bubbles
7   (.) well done
8   (.) yes
(Cameron 2003a: 103)

The Initiation in line 1 by the teacher takes the form of a question and acts as a request for information. The response does not come immediately and the teacher adds some clues to help students answer in lines 2–4. The student Response in line 5 is received with positive Feedback in lines 6 and 7: a repetition of the response and an explicit evaluation: 'well done'.

The IRF pattern has been found in many empirical studies of classroom talk in the USA and the UK; it seems to operate as an attractor basin in the state space landscapes of the discourse being studied. It is found in its 'basic', or stabilized, form of question–answer–evaluation, but also with many small variations, such as the inclusion of clues to the answer in Extract 6.2 or extended versions in which the teacher seeks further information after the Feedback step. Sinclair and Coulthard (1975) tried to fit such discourse patterns into a rank and scale hierarchy that, as part of a formal linguistic system, would extend across from phonology through grammar up to discourse. This structural approach to discourse, which does not allow for non-linearity, dynamics, openness and connection to context, could not explain adequately why such patterns emerge (Adger 2001). A full explanation needs, we suggest, to include the context, in which a teacher is talking with a class of 30 or more students at the same time and must control the social interaction through the use of language, keeping attention focused and not diverted, while at the same time providing a learning experience in which students encounter new ideas or consolidate concepts and understandings. These social, cultural, pedagogic forces contribute to the shape of the state space landscape on which the talk takes place. The trajectory of the classroom talk system on the discourse landscape is pulled into the IRF attractor basin from various regions of the state space—see Figure 3.6. The attractor has emerged in answer to multiple needs. The larger sociocultural level exerts influence in the form of accepted ideas that learning is enhanced by active participation and that contributing to classroom talk promotes such active participation and is thus to be positively valued. At the same time, the teacher has to control the class, involving students in classroom talk in order to motivate them, but holding responsibility for the ideational content of the talk, for the talk not becoming too noisy, and for staying on topic. Adapting to these various forces produces talk with fairly short turns, and the IRF pattern, as a particularly 'fit' (in evolutionary terms) response to the situation. In the IRF pattern, the Initiation step focuses the attention of students on a specific learning point; the student Response allows one person to voice what others may be thinking; the Response then receives a Feedback or an Evaluation by the teacher to help avoid students learning something inappropriate. Classroom lessons often include episodes of teacher-led talk at certain key points, for example when recalling previous work on a topic or when bringing a lesson to a close. These episodes will feature multiple instances of the IRF pattern; the trajectory of the classroom discourse system returns again and again to the IRF attractor.

The potential for disruption created by placing 30 or so students with a single teacher, particularly in social contexts that value freedom of thought and some indulgence of youth, means that the landscape of classroom discourse looks very different from the system landscape of two co-operating adults in conversation. There will be many more hills—unstable and dispreferred modes of talk—and fewer but probably deeper valleys—attractors that represent reliably successful ways of talking and may be passed on explicitly through teacher training. The IRF pattern is an attractor that shows variability around a very stable pattern, as it is adapted in response to particular classroom contingencies. The discourse system will tend to return to the IRF attractor because it is a pattern that works; it is a preferred behavior of the system. There are other patterns of behavior in classroom discourse (for example, Mercer 2004), but the IRF is one of the strongest in that it has been found in many locations, at different ages and levels of education, at different points in lessons (van Lier 1996).

In a state space landscape, the relative depth of valleys reflects the strength and stability of the attractor, how easily the system is perturbed from its behavior in the attractor. To see perturbation around an IRF pattern, Extract 6.3 shows the teacher–student talk immediately prior to Extract 6.2, with the last line of Extract 6.3 being the first line of that extract:

Extract 6.3
1 T do you know what happens?
2   (.) I did it at the weekend (.) so I know what happens
3 S is molten lava like wax?
4 T yes
5   (1.0) it can be a bit like wax
6   (1.0) but do you know what happens to butter?
(Cameron 2003a: 103)

Extract 6.3 superficially resembles an IRF pattern, starting with a question as Initiation in the first line, a student Response in line 3 in the form of a question, and teacher Feedback in lines 4 and 5. However, the content of the student's talk does not respond to the teacher's initiating question but to an earlier section of talk in which lava was compared to runny butter and to sticky treacle. The student here offers a further comparison, with molten wax. The teacher accepts the student question, with some hesitation, and a rather unenthusiastic evaluation, and then returns to her initiating question, repeating and extending the lexicogrammatical form of line 1 in line 6. The student turn pushed the discourse system away from the intended IRF sequence but only briefly. The system stabilizes and returns to the attractor when the teacher re-asks the question and the IRF pattern proceeds as in Extract 6.2. The IRF attractor is a relatively deep well in the discourse system landscape, with perturbations not easily pushing the system into other paths.[6]

In Extract 6.3, the teacher's repeating of the Initiation step is likely to lead students to understand that the first Response was not appropriate in some regard. Using human abilities to detect patterns and to extract probabilistic information about frequency of occurrence, people come to have expectations about how talk will proceed from their repeated experiences of participating in discourse. As a result, an initiating question may be interpreted as the first move in an IRF pattern, with expectations thereby activated as to appropriate responses. Experience of patterns of talk also assists participants in recognizing and dealing with deviations from those patterns, such as occurred with the student initiation in line 3 of Extract 6.3.

Emergent attractors in a discourse system: conceptual pacts

In cognitive psychology and psycholinguistics, laboratory experiments are used to study language use under controlled conditions. By definition, such studies are not centrally concerned with broader social practice involving language which was the third meaning of 'discourse' discussed at the beginning of the chapter. Neither do most such studies concern themselves much with the first sense of discourse, extended talk beyond the sentence. Furthermore, accounts of language processing developed in these fields have until recently relied largely on findings about language used non-dialogically (Pickering and Garrod 2004).

In an exception to this trend, studies carried out by Clark and various colleagues have explored how speakers collaborate in the joint action of talk on controlled tasks. One aspect of this is how speakers converge on a way of talking-and-thinking about objects they are jointly concerned with. Brennan and Clark (1996) had people in pairs describe sets of pictures of common objects to each other under varying task conditions involving choosing and matching pictures. The experiments thus created a laboratory version of dialogic discourse over a timescale, albeit rather short. They were interested to find out how the objects were referred to and how reference changed over time. They found that people established 'conceptual pacts', by which they mean 'a temporary agreement about how they ... are to conceptualize that object' (1996: 1491).

Conceptual pacts are evidenced by the use of lexical items for example, 'a shoe' might be referred to as 'a pennyloafer', 'a casual shoe' or 'our old shoe' (ibid.: 1491). Speakers come to agree on a conceptualization through a process in which one person proposes a term and the other person then either agrees to it or an alternative is requested or suggested. Looking at this through a complex dynamics perspective we can see that what is being talked about is variability between people in how they understand and refer, and reducing that variability to a stabilized agreed form-meaning-use composite. The coupled system self-organizes to an agreed conceptualization, and lexical reference, for the object being talked about.

Conceptual pacts, as described by Brennan and Clark, fit our category of emergent phenomena in face-to-face conversation. They are a property of the coupled discourse system in several ways: they are jointly agreed by speakers and addressees; they are accessible to both partners in talk; they are established through adaptive interaction with a specific partner. They emerge as attractors in the discourse system through self-organizing processes in which references are modified over repeated trials, becoming shorter and more efficient. They are stable as attractors but the system shows variability around the stability, as when earlier labels are suddenly returned to under changed task conditions.

For Brennan and Clark, conceptual pacts account for the phenomenon of lexical entrainment, the process by which people come to use the same terms in talk. They make the important point that use of lexical items in coordinated conversation is not just about reference and getting the other speaker to attend to the right object. They also want the other person to think about the object in the 'right' way for what is happening in the conversation at the time, so that was is said about the object will be understood. However, in naming these attractors 'conceptual pacts', they seem to go too far in the opposite direction and lose the interconnectedness of language use and thought, especially since lexical evidence is used to establish the existence of conceptual pacts. Pacts may be better considered as both lexical and conceptual—in Cameron's terms, pacts of thinking-and-talking (Cameron 2003a).

Shared metaphors as attractors in discourse systems

A specific type of lexical/conceptual pact, making use of figurative language, has been observed in studies of face-to-face conversation in classrooms and other contexts (Cameron 2003a; Cameron 2007; Cameron and Deignan 2006). Metaphors are particularly suited to acting as lexical/conceptual pacts because they bring together information from two different domains into a compact, memorable, and vivid phrase (Ortony 1975). The interaction of the conceptual domains serves to 'hide and highlight' (Lakoff and Johnson 1980);

a particular conceptualization of an idea is isolated as certain properties are foregrounded while others are backgrounded. At the same time, the conceptualization can be rich, often carrying affective information as well as ideational. While all kinds of language stabilize into patterns through use, metaphorical language patterns appear to be more stabilized in their lexicogrammatical form than non-metaphorical language (Deignan 2005).

Cameron's study of talk between a teacher and her class of 9–11-year-old students (2003a) captured the emergence of a shared metaphor in the dynamics of the classroom discourse system. The teacher initiated the process when she gave feedback to a student (A) on her drawing of trees which were sketched in an overly simple way as circles on top of vertical lines. The feedback consisted of a comparison with 'a lollipop':

Extract 6.4a
T (to student A) go back to your memory
                  of the tree that you're trying to draw
                  because that's tended to
                  to look like a lollipop
                  hasn't it
(Cameron 2003a: 117)

A couple of seconds later in a further utterance, the teacher repeats and re-formulates, reducing the form from a comparison to a metaphorical phrase:

Extract 6.4b
T   when I was a very young teacher
                  and I kept on saying to a little girl
                  will you please stop doing lollipop trees
(ibid.)

The phrase is now a compact form that captures the conceptualization of simply drawn trees, together with the affective force of a (gently) negative evaluation and the idea that there are better ways to draw trees. The use of 'lollipop' carries with it, not just the shape that could have been improved, but a 'stylistic aura' (Bakhtin 1981) of something playful and childish, which may serve to foreground the inappropriacy of such drawings in an academic setting.

Up to this point in the talk, only the teacher had used the phrase in talking with student A. Shortly afterwards, the teacher moved to look at a picture being drawn by another student (B) and was about to give student B some feedback when the microphone recorded a third student (C), who had been a peripheral participant in the first 'lollipop trees' exchange and was some distance from student B, making use of the phrase under her breath and to herself:

Extract 6.4c

T (to student B)	it's lovely that one
	don't spoil it
	the only thing that I'm going to criticize is
STUDENT C	<u>lollipop trees</u>

(ibid.)

The use of the phrase by student C suggests that 'lollipop trees' had stabilized, albeit only briefly, in the classroom discourse system as a lexical/conceptual pact. This may have been only a temporary stabilization and the data do not provide evidence of how widely it spread across the students, but it serves to show the self-organizing processes of discourse at the local level, 'constrained by the grammatical affordances of the language and driven by the contingencies of the pedagogic interaction' (Cameron and Deignan 2006: 677).

Cameron and Deignan (2006) introduce the label 'metaphoreme' for phrases like 'lollipop trees' that emerge in the local dynamics of talk, and argue that the same processes of self-organization in talk give rise to metaphoremes on the larger phylogenetic scale—we return to this idea later in the chapter.

Discourse as complex system: interim summary

The account developed so far in this chapter has taken face-to-face conversation as the primary type of discourse. We have shown how people talking together, in face-to-face conversation and in other types of talk, can be seen as a coupled system with a trajectory across a landscape. Attractors in the landscape include conventionalized patterns of talk that shape the landscape and emergent features such as local routines, conceptual pacts, and shared metaphors. The dynamic system of talk is driven by multiple factors, which may include attempted alignment with the other person (Pickering and Garrod 2004), a search for coherence (Meadows 1993), a desire for emotional equilibrium (Damasio 2003), the reduction of alterity (Cameron 2003a), and a range of discourse purposes such as persuasion or informing.

Any instance of discourse activity is connected to systems at a range of timescales and levels that impact on the moment of talk. Before moving to suggest how different timescales and levels interact, we next extrapolate to discourse systems other than face-to-face conversation, in particular to written text.

The dynamics of written discourse

So far in this chapter, we have focused on face-to-face conversation as the basic setting for language use, with some diversions into other types of talk. In this section, we move to written discourse and ask how that might be seen from a complex systems perspective. As before, this requires us to identify complex systems and subsystems around written text, the agents and relations in these systems and the interactions among them that produce trajectories and patterns of variability and stability. The traditional division of discourse into written versus spoken is overly-simplistic. Discourse is increasingly multi-modal, with people using a mix of gestures, spoken language, images and written text in order to 'say what they mean' (Kress *et al.* 2001). Electronic communication in particular affords multiple modality, and the interaction of human and machine systems. What is said here about written discourse can be extended to multi-modal discourse.

The notion of 'literacy event' (Barton and Hamilton 2005) fits well into a complexity perspective since it incorporates the social and the cognitive by focusing on the uses of texts. In a literacy event, people produce or use texts as part of some human discourse activity. In other words, a literacy event is the unfolding of a social, coupled discourse system in which a text or texts serve as elements. The shape of the state space landscape is influenced by phylogenetic processes in which certain patterns of written discourse emerge as stabilized attractors.

Learning to read and learning to write are phase shift type events on the ontogenetic timescale of an individual's discourse development. While not considered further here, we note that processes of literacy development (themselves complex and dynamic) contribute to the intrinsic dynamics or initial conditions for any specific literacy event.

When we move from spoken to written discourse, we move from something instant and intangible to something delayed and concrete. A written text is not in itself dynamic—it is fixed and unchanging. However, a text can be part of multiple dynamic systems, through its composition and through its reading and use. In this section, we describe some of the complex dynamic systems around written discourse. In the next section, we move up the scale to discuss the written language system and its evolution.

Reading a text as a dynamic process

The act of reading can be seen very differently in different situations, influenced by cultural values and contextual expectations. Reading may be silent or voiced aloud. Finding personal meanings in texts may be privileged or may be discouraged. Religious texts held as sacred repositories of ideas may not be open to varied interpretations or to translation. Different interpretations of a poem can be arrived at with each reading. Reading in school classrooms often requires reading out loud through turning written symbols into spoken words, and a child may read successfully out loud without understanding all of what is spoken.

In a meaning-centered view of reading, the goal of reading is for the reader to reach an understanding of the text. Looking at this from a complexity perspective, the process of reading of a written text can be seen as a complex dynamic system moving across a state space landscape that consists of all possible interpretations of the stretch of text being processed. Understanding the whole text is also seen as a complex dynamic system that produces the multidimensional state space landscape on which the reading process moves. The experience of reading the text changes the landscape as the reading process co-adapts with current understandings of the whole text. Meaning is constructed from the text at different levels using the reader's previous experiences of literacy, of texts, and of the world; the reader searches for a coherent meaning for the whole as the parts are processed. Attractors in the landscape represent stable interpretations and each will have a degree of variability. Some attractors may be quite weak, with large amounts of variability where parts of the text are open to multiple interpretations.

Composing a written text from a complex systems perspective

The project of producing a written text is a dynamic process involving multiple interacting complex systems. In producing the text, the writer draws on his or her resources, in the particular discourse environment, 'to bring thought into existence on a concrete plane' (McNeill 1992: 18). The dynamic processes of composition are like the trajectory of a complex system, in which the 'final' text emerges as a fixed point attractor. This compositional system contains multiple interacting subsystems. Composing in the moment arises through the meshing together of systems and subsystems working at various levels and timescales. Imagine the process of writing a newspaper article or book. Interacting dynamic systems and subsystems would include the individual people involved as writers, readers, publishers, etc; their language and other resources; the publishing system. Each system or subsystem may have human agents, material elements such as computers, paper, pens, and intra-individual elements such as written language resources and skills. Within each system, agents and elements are connected through multiple relations: writer and publisher are connected through publishing contracts; the writer's language resources are connected to physical elements through such relations as computer skills or repetitive strain injury. The state space landscape of the compositional system is influenced by history and convention in the form of previously emerged routines and patterns, both ontogenetic and phylogenetic.

As the text is composed, it moves through different versions, changing and adapting in the process of composition. This dynamic operates not just at the whole text level but with variability at all levels, selecting the best word, trying out several ways of writing the same idea, adapting syntactic formulations of clauses and sentences, moving around paragraph content and sections. Eventually the text stabilizes into a form that stops changing, and that we can see as a fixed point attractor in the compositional trajectory. Various pressures ensure that most texts are finalized, even though potentially endless further variation will have been possible.

Writing a text connects with the basic discourse mode of face-to-face conversation—for example, in listening to how an idea sounds when written down and in composing a text with specific readers in mind—but it is very different from it, in many ways more complicated and demanding. To construct written text, people need to know about the written language and how it can be deployed. Writers engage in 'asynchronous joint action' (Clark 1996: 90) when they compose a text for readers displaced in space and time, requiring an act of dialogic imagination to construct readers' reactions as part of the composing process.

The emergence of discourse phenomena

Previous sections of this chapter have suggested how we might understand discourse as a complex dynamic system. We adopted face-to-face conversation as the basis for other types of language use and discourse, and as the starting point for developing a complex dynamic systems view, and then extended it to the use of written texts. We saw that the probability landscape over which conversation moves is influenced by multiple linguistic and non-linguistic (social, cognitive, affective, etc.) factors, and that conversation between people can be seen as a coupled system that adapts and organizes locally.

Taking a complexity perspective motivates us to look for changing patterns of stability and variability in the systems under scrutiny. We have already met several emergent discourse phenomena arising from face-to-face talk, including patterns of classroom talk that stabilize in particular classrooms and across classrooms, and lexical-conceptual pacts and metaphors that stabilize over the timescale of a discourse event. In this section, we discuss further discourse phenomena that emerge upwards from discourse in the moment to the sociocultural level and phylogenetic timescale.

Although we are moving our attention to more macro levels and timescales, to periods of time longer than that of face-to-face talk and to larger social groups, the complex systems perspective leads us to expect that the mechanisms that accounted for discourse phenomena at micro scales and levels will explain discourse phenomena at these more macro scales and levels. We look for self-organization of dynamic systems into stabilized patterns, accompanied by degrees of variability, which function as attractors in system trajectories, and thus act downwards in reciprocal causality from macro-level to constrain language use at lower levels (Barr 2004). It has sometimes been proposed that an explanation for social conventions requires conventionalized, common knowledge which members of social groups have as mental representations (Lewis 1969; Clark 1996). Recent evidence that speakers in conversation behave egocentrically rather than from such assumed common knowledge has led to a search for alternative, complexity-based, theory for the emergence of shared patterns:

common knowledge is not necessary for the emergence of symbolic
conventions, ... instead ... semantic representations are coordinated
through use; that is, as a by-product of individual attempts at
coordination among speakers and listeners which are distributed over
time and across the language community.
(Barr 2004: 939)

This is a very similar position to that of Hopper, whose emergent grammar we
have referred to several times already in this book. Barr employs multi-agent
simulation modeling to show how convergence can emerge as a possible by-
product of local interactions. Rather than needing common knowledge as
global representation, language-using agents have language resources that
are updated on the basis of individual successes or failures to communicate
over multiple instances of interaction. Just as flocking patterns emerge from
local actions of individual birds, so repeated local adaptations in response to
a conversation partner works upwards in the modeled system to 'maintain
cohesion in semantic space for the language community' (Barr 2004: 942).
The emergent coordinated patterns also work downwards to construct and
constrain the system in action at local level, through reciprocal causality, 'the
active power that wholes exert on parts' (Juarrero 1999: 26).
   We now explore some examples of such emergent discourse patterns and
the local rules that give rise to them.

Speech genres

Genres are abstract, socially recognised ways of using language.
(Hyland 2002: 16)

The idea of genre has been particularly productive and influential within the
teaching of writing but applies across all modes of language use. Historically,
the notion of 'speech genres' can be traced back to the work of the Russian
scholars, Medvedev and Bakhtin, who were themselves reacting to the closed,
rather mechanical idea of genre as structure in formalist literary theory
(Morson and Emerson 1990). They wanted the idea of genre to capture both
the tendency of language use to 'crystalize' into patterns and the potentiality
or openness of language that allows it to continue changing. A genre is more
than a 'template' for how to use language, but 'a specific way of visualizing
a given part of reality' (Morson and Emerson 1990: 275). A genre organizes
how we conceptualize and understand the world, and 'speech genres' are
stabilized ways of expressing the world (Bakhtin 1981, 1986; Swales 1990).
   Speech genres can be seen as attractors in the discourse systems we have
elaborated in this chapter, that involve language, the social and interpersonal,
the affective, the attitudinal, and the cognitive. Through use and adaptation
in multiple micro-level interactions over time, certain ways of understanding
and talking about the world emerge as relatively stable patterns or genres.

The relative stability of genres reflects their 'fuzzy' nature in practice (Swales 1990). The following quote illustrates how Bakhtin's ideas resonate with complexity theory; he is concerned with connecting the detailed richness of ordinary language use with higher level generic patterns, and his (metaphorical) conception of discourse is essentially dynamic (Morson and Emerson 1990; Cameron 2003a):

> Genres are the residue of past behavior, an accretion that shapes, guides, and constrains future behavior. ... Their form is not mere form, but is really 'stereotyped, congealed, old (familiar) content ... [that] serves as a necessary bridge to new, still unknown content' because it is 'a familiar and generally understood congealed old world view' (Bakhtin 1986: 159–72).
> (Morson and Emerson 1990: 290–1)

When we make use of genres in speaking or writing, we use the stabilized patterns but exploit the variability around them to create what is uniquely needed for that particular literacy or discourse event.

Genres are observable through stabilized ways of using language but, in Bakhtin's version, are more than that. They work socially and cognitively as frameworks for discourse; we speak through genres and with genres. They are learned by infants with the learning of first language(s) and need to be learned as part of learning a second language: 'Each genre implies a set of values, a way of thinking about kinds of experiences, and an intuition about the appropriateness of applying the genres in any given context' (ibid.: 291–2).

The term 'genre' is sometimes restricted to describe types of written text, an impoverished use of the construct in comparison to the Bakhtinian version. Speech genres incorporate conventions of language use but are much more than that. Conventional styles and registers of written text, such as 'the small or classified ad' or 'the academic essay', are emergent stabilities in the trajectory of social group written discourse. Genres are themselves dynamic and continue changing through use. Their stability is combined with variability, and it is this variability that provides the potential for growth and change. Bakhtin attributed wisdom and memory to genres, a personification that emphasizes how social history may be recorded or embedded in the changes that genres go through. Complexity theory suggests that we look at what happens when a stable genre is perturbed, whether it returns to stability or whether it moves away from its attractor to some new stability. We should pay attention to changes in genres, to how new energy or change from outside affects the stability. For example, economic and social changes have interacted with the genre around the 'CV'—the curriculum vitae document that job seekers compile and send to possible employers. What used to be a rather formal list of qualifications and experiences often begins now with an eye-catching personal statement that aims to sell the applicant rather than merely to describe: 'I'm a self-starter, looking for a position that will utilize my excellent communication skills ...'.

Periods of rapid change in genres, either in individual use or in social history, suggest potentially important areas for investigation and research. Genres that are changing and adapting fast and frequently may indicate that the discourse system is 'at the edge of chaos', about to move into a new attractor or to dissolve and reform in some other shape altogether. Such may be the case, for instance, with the genre of the text message, which is only a few years old. The limitations of early generation mobile phones led to text messages with reduced and abbreviated form, such as 'C U 2morro'. Technology now allows speedy, accurate texting through predictive spelling programs, so one receives fewer abbreviated texts. The genre is developing in another direction that lies somewhere between email and texts through the sending of messages on social network websites and through instant messaging. Where the affordances of technology will take the genre next is unpredictable—it may undergo a phase shift to some new form, or stabilize.

The richness of the concept of genre explains how it can be disputed when applied to literary study or to language learning and teaching. Different groups of scholars attend to particular aspects of genre—some to the communicative purposes, others to typical forms and structures of texts or speech events (Hyland 2002). Any simplification of the notion of genre loses something of its complexity. The particular simplification which focuses on the stabilities of a genre in order to describe a typical speech or textual pattern may be helpful to learners, but backgrounds the variability or potential of the genre, which is the source of creativity, individuality and growth in use. Complexity theory reminds us that understanding variability is crucial to understanding dynamics, and that understanding genres must include understanding their flexibility as well as their stability. It may be that corpus linguistic techniques can be used to uncover something of the range and flexibility of language use in a genre, but corpora can only evidence what has already been done in discourse, not its potential.

Once again we face the issue of predictability in complex systems. We can predict that genres will evolve and change, with new stabilities emerging out of earlier ones. We cannot predict what these will look like, only that they will happen. We can, however, establish patterns of change through examining the trajectories of genres over time, looking for regularities.

Conventionalized metaphor

Earlier in this chapter, we saw how metaphorical phrases can emerge from the local dynamics of talk as stabilized forms that are re-used with shared meanings, and we suggested that the same complex systems processes could be used to explain metaphor on the broader, social scale. Metaphors emerge as attractors in discourse through situated language use, stabilized in particular forms that capture particular ideational content along with particular sociocultural, pragmatic, and affective qualities (Cameron and Deignan 2006). For example, the metaphorical proverb: 'a stitch in time saves nine', is often abbreviated to 'a stitch in time' and typically used to comment on how some potentially difficult situation was avoided by timely action. Its form (and its possible variation) has stabilized, but, behind the form, we also find a stabilized idea, attitude, values, and manner of use.

In addition to the very fixed forms of proverbs, we find 'metaphoreme' attractors in discourse that have more complicated stabilities with variability. In a study that combined corpus analysis of stabilized forms with detailed discourse analysis of variability in particular instances of use, Cameron and Deignan (2006) showed how the following conceptual, linguistic and affective regularities have stabilized around the metaphoreme <(not) walk away from>:[7]

- it is used hypothetically to talk about an action that could have been taken but usually was not: 'I was prepared to walk away from the struggle'
- the things that might have been 'walked away from' are difficult, traumatic and/or burdensome, or tempting: 'struggle', 'a rocky marriage', 'an offer'
- 'not walking away' is the more difficult option
- the verb is usually not inflected, either because it is in the infinitive form or because a modal, such as 'can't', is used
- strong adverbs, such as 'simply' or 'never', are often used in close proximity, adding to the sense of burden or difficulty.

The various lexicogrammatical regularities operate with differing degrees of probability; some occur almost always, others are used frequently but not always. In other words, the relative stability operates with degrees of variability that can be exploited by speakers in actual situations of use. The precise details of stability and variation found in any particular metaphoreme are unpredictable. What is predictable is that language use leads to emergent stabilities of this type that exploit the full potential of language in discourse.

Other emergent discourse phenomena

At the start of this chapter, a complexity view of 'discourse' was set out, and we have exemplified how social discourse practices can be seen as in a relationship of reciprocal causation with local situated discourse, whereby local rules give rise to emergent stable patterns of activity at higher levels of the system, with continuing change made possible through the variability associated with the stabilities. We have discussed the examples of metaphors and genres, and how these can be seen as arising from face-to-face talk and other micro-level language use. Many other discourse phenomena may also be candidates to be seen as emergent attractors in discourse systems:

- shared jokes (and ways of making jokes) that are in the moment, micro-level instances of shared amusement and then pass around a speech community
- discourse markers of various sorts that come to be idiosyncratic or more generally accepted ways of marking talk and text: for example, 'absolutely'

appears to have entered some people's speech as an alternative to 'yes' to mark agreement

- referencing conventions for groups of people: for example, our experience in writing together suggests that the use of third person plural pronominal forms to refer to individual people without marking for gender, as in 'each person should give their picture to their partner' is currently more established in British English than in American English where the singular is still preferred: 'each person should give his or her picture to his or her partner' or avoided altogether as in 'you should give your partner your picture ...'
- the development of discourse patterns in subcommunities and institutions, such as prisons, schools, specialist hobby or skill groups, for example, talk around music or particular sports.

Modeling the complexity of discourse

The descriptive application of a complexity perspective to discourse undertaken in this chapter is just a starting point. Describing discourse in terms of complex dynamic systems is the first step, involving identification of possible systems and their dynamics, the agents/elements in the systems and the various types of relations among them. From this, it becomes possible to check that patterns of change in the real-world system also map on to the types of change found in complex dynamic systems. These steps establish a working metaphor that connects the real-world system to a complex dynamic system. Social systems like this are not likely to be quantitatively modeled (Chapter 2)—there are too many variables and too much that cannot be captured. They may be amenable to qualitative modeling (see Chapter 8), with multi-agent simulations for example, and the modeling process will take the metaphor further, perhaps developing theory in the model building process and perhaps enabling modelers to try out different scenarios of change in the system.

We would argue that there are benefits to seeing discourse through a complexity perspective even if the metaphorizing process does not proceed to actual modeling, since it offers a framework and metaphor for understanding how language users interact locally to produce discourse outcomes. The complexity perspective enables another way of understanding language use and discourse within social institutions, another way of understanding the connections between local action and global structure, and another way of understanding possibilities for influencing change in the system. A complex systems approach to discourse requires us to connect empirical findings and theories across cognitive psychology, sociolinguistics, conversation analysis, and pragmatics.

Discourse systems are more accessible to applied linguists than ever before, with increasingly effective methods for recording, storing, and handling large amounts of language use data, through data digitalization and methodologies such as those developed by scholars working in corpus linguistics. The history of linguistics is not unaffected by the technology of the time, and it would seem that technology is now offering us the possibility of understanding discourse in all its senses: in use, beyond the clause, and across social groups.

Analysis or investigation of discourse from a complex systems perspective does not require us to throw away other approaches and their techniques. Indeed, multiple types of analysis are needed to work with information from systems at different scales, and new ways of blending methods (see Chapter 8) are needed to explore simultaneous activity on several scales. For example, several projects are underway to find ways to describe gesture in relation to speech (for example, Carter, Knight, and Adolphs 2006; www.togog.org), and we have seen in this chapter how corpus linguistic methods can be combined with close analysis of episodes of talk to track connections between individual use of language and conventions at the social group level.

Notes

1 Not just from a complexity perspective of course. Adherents of particular schools of discourse analysis would find objections to each of these senses.

2 The project, 'Using visual display to investigate the dynamics of metaphor in conciliation talk', was supported by the UK's Arts and Humanities Research Board under its Innovation Award scheme. We acknowledge that support, and also thank the participants in the talk for giving permission to use the data.

Symbols used in transcripts:

The ends of intonation units are marked with the following symbols:

, = continuing intonation contour
. = final intonation contour
-- = a truncated (incomplete) intonation unit
[ ] indicates an overlap
.. indicates a short pause
... indicates a longer pause with time in seconds in brackets, for example, (2.0)

3 Picturing a continuously dynamic conversation as successive, discrete slides, as per the graphic convention, is somewhat inappropriate. However, there seems no obvious alternative given the limitations of a two-dimensional diagram on a page—readers are encouraged to make the diagram continuously dynamic in their minds as they view it.

4 We also need a larger construct of 'discourse resources' which captures the potential to engage in discourse.

5 Alterity contrasts with 'intersubjectivity' in describing what lies between people engaged in social interaction. Intersubjectivity refers to a shared focus of attention and perspective (Rommetveit 1979; Rogoff 1990;

Smolka *et al.* 1995; Wertsch 1998). Pure or complete intersubjectivity is problematic; it must be a fiction since we each see the world through our own experiences, but a search for intersubjectivity can be taken as motivating much face-to-face conversation (Rommetveit 1979). The idea here is that alterity is not a fiction but is always present as the perceived disparity between self and other that is to be resolved (Cameron 2003a).

6 Work in interactional sociolinguistics has shown how speakers use various cues and signals in talk to infer what the other person intends and to plan and produce their own turns (for example, Goffman 1974, 1981; Gumperz 1982). Gumperz describes the discourse system not as a landscape as a complexity perspective suggests, but rather by using an alternative metaphor of ecology: 'Speaking ties into a communicative ecology that significantly affects the course of an interaction' (Gumperz 2001: 221).

7 Metaphoremes are placed inside triangular brackets; the brackets around *not* are to suggest it is preferred but not essential.

7

Complex systems and the language classroom

Introduction

This chapter takes complexity theory into the language classroom, applying the perspectives on language, discourse, and language development that we have so far developed. By 'the language classroom' we mean situations of second (including foreign) language learning, either instructed learning with direct teaching of the second language or situations where students may not be taught the second language directly but are expected to learn it through participation in curriculum subject classes. This latter would include CLIL (content and language integrated learning) or content-based learning situations where the second language is learned through content instruction, and 'mainstreaming' situations where students from minority ethnic communities are taught in the majority language.

Taking a complexity theory perspective on the language classrooms places the focus on action: communicative and speech action, teaching action, language-using, thinking, task action, physical action.

Is there a complexity method?

A complexity approach does not automatically translate into a complexity method for teaching language. (At least we do not have one.) The reason for its absence is not because we do not believe in the value of methods; on the contrary, we think that methods, post-method macro-strategies, and approaches are excellent heuristic devices. When methods are seen as sets of coherent principles that link to practice, they help act as a foil whereby teachers can clarify their own principles and beliefs, they challenge teachers to think in new ways, and they provide associated techniques with which teachers can experiment to come to new understandings (Larsen-Freeman 2000b).

One reason that we do not think a complexity method is likely is because we think limiting the teacher or learners to certain techniques or activities is antithetical to complexity theory. Because of the complexity of language and learners, a resourceful teacher will need to call upon a wide range of activities and techniques that support learning. However, we are not simply saying that a complexity-compatible approach to language teaching is eclectic and that anything goes. A complexity approach is not relativistic (Cilliers 1998). Almost anything goes in the abstract, but any particular moment in a lesson can be rich with learning potential and some directions to take may be better than others if a more efficacious way of learning a language, which still honors the quality of life in a classroom (Allwright 2003), is the aim.

Another reason for not advancing a particular method here is because we think that such an effort would be futile. As with language, methods are dynamically adaptable in use. This has always been the case, of course. Anyone who has visited classes (even a few) in which teachers profess to be practicing communicative language teaching will attest to the fact that what is taking place in such classrooms is very different, one from another. Thus, any methodologist should anticipate, indeed encourage, adaptation. Perhaps the worth of a method should, in part, be a measure of this—how easily adaptable it is.

A complexity approach to language classroom action

Complexity theory offers interesting and potentially important ways of thinking about classroom action and the role of the teacher. We suggest the following four components as a useful starting point for building a complexity approach to language teaching and learning:

1 It's all connected

A complexity perspective on the language classroom highlights connections across levels of human and social organization, from individual minds up to the socio-political context of language learning, and across timescales, from the minute by minute of classroom activity to teaching and learning lifetimes. Any action in language teaching and learning is tied into this web of connections to multiple systems which can influence and constrain it; understanding classroom action requires those connections to be uncovered. In particular, learning involves the connected brain-body-world of continuity psychology (Gibbs 2006; Spivey 2007) and ecological approaches (van Lier 2000; Kramsch 2002; Clarke 2007).

2 Language is dynamic (even when it's frozen)

We have said in other words in this book that language as a separate entity is a normative fiction (Klein 1998); it only exists in the fluxes of language use in a given speech community. For the language classroom this implies that what has previously been taken as the goal of learning, the 'target language', ceases to exist in any simple form and we are faced with several problems to solve: do we remove language dynamics to produce a static or frozen version of a language for learning and/or do we try to teach the dynamic system of the living language (see Larsen-Freeman's 2003 concept of 'grammaring')? Whose language (living or frozen) becomes the goal of language learning?

The statement however insists that 'language is dynamic'. What we mean by this is that, even if a frozen or stabilized version of the language is used in a syllabus, grammar book, and test, as soon as the language is 'released' into the classroom or into the minds of learners it becomes dynamic.

Inside the language classroom, the dynamics of language-using by teachers and students lead to the emergence of individual learners' growing language resources and of classroom dialects, and, beyond the classroom, to the emergence of lingua franca varieties (Jenkins 2000; Seidlhofer 2001, 2004).

3 Co-adaptation is a key dynamic

Co-adaptation appears to be a particularly relevant type of change in the dynamic systems of the language classroom. As we saw in Chapter 3, co-adaptation is change in connected systems, where change in one system produces change in the other. In Chapter 6, we saw how people engaged in speech action co-adapt. Language classrooms are full of people co-adapting—teacher with students, students with each other, teacher or students with learning contexts. Stabilized patterns of action, including language action, emerge from co-adaptation on various timescales.

Like other kinds of change in complex systems, co-adaptation is inevitable but not necessarily for the benefit of learning; all sorts of forces may push a system to stability. Understanding how and why co-adaptation happens will shed light on patterns of classroom action and help work out how intervention might be successful. Our debate about human agency comes full circle here—because co-adaptation is neutral or undirected, i.e. it can be for good or for bad, there is no escaping the need for agents in the system to take ethical responsibility for its dynamics. It is also improtant to point out that the goal of language teaching is not to bring about conformity to uniformity (Larsen-Freeman 2003) by assuming that what we are trying to do is to transpose what is in the teacher's head to the students' heads.

4 Teaching is managing the dynamics of learning

The first three points suggest that teaching can be seen in a complexity approach as managing the dynamics of learning, exploiting the complex adaptive nature of action and language use while also ensuring that co-adaptation works for the benefit of learning. Attending to variability around stabilized patterns can suggest how patterns of classroom action might be changed to increase the benefit to language learning, by finding ways to perturb systems out of attractors and into new trajectories.

As we will see later in this chapter, even when teachers appear to be in control of interaction, they are subject to the dynamics of the complex system of the classroom. Teachers do not control their students' learning. Teaching does not cause learning; learners make their own paths (Larsen-

Freeman 2000b, 2006). This does not mean that teaching does not influence learning, far from it; teaching and teacher–learner interaction construct and constrain the learning affordances of the classroom. What a teacher can do is manage and serve her or his students' learning in a way that is consonant with their learning processes. Thus, any approach we might advocate would not be curriculum-centered nor learner-centered, but it would be learning-centered—where the learning guides the teaching and not vice versa.

Due to the non-linearity of a complex dynamic system as it moves through state space, small perturbations (teacher interventions) can make a big difference. Of course, it also can happen the other way around. Teachers and students may work very hard on some aspect of language using, with little apparent success. One day, though, the point of criticality may be reached and the system self-organizes in a new way. Learning is not cumulative in any simple way and a great deal of synchronic variability is to be expected.

The four components of a complexity approach are taken forwards through the rest of the chapter, illustrated and developed through examples and elaboration.

Chapter outline

The next section presents an overview of complex systems in and around language classroom action, carrying out the first step of complex system thought modeling set out in Table 3.1. Other steps in the process are illustrated in three examples of action in language learning situations taken from our experience and re-interpreted through a complexity approach. We aim to demonstrate the particular kind of understanding produced by recasting these situations in a complexity framework and how these understandings can lead through intervention to improved learning opportunities. The four aspects of the complexity approach delineated at the start of the chapter are used to guide and structure these interpretations and discussions.

Before concluding, we make some brief points about the language that is being learned, language assessment, and modeling classroom systems.

Connected complex systems and the language classroom

Let's take an imaginary, at this point rather unspecified, language classroom and identify possible complex systems that radiate inwards and outwards from classroom action. Suppose we drop in on the class—learners and their teacher—in an institution such as a secondary school one Tuesday afternoon in February. If we look through the door of the classroom, we can see the learners sitting and listening to their teacher. As we watch, some hands go up, some learners speak, the teacher speaks. The teacher talks some more, learners move around and sit in groups, open their books and start talking to each other about a text and picture in the books. The complex systems in this scenario are everywhere and at every scale. They are connected, dynamic, and co-adaptive. All are bound by the same general principles and can be described with the same set of tools that should, by now, have become familiar: agents and elements; relations among elements; trajectories; self-organization; emergence; stability and variability; attractor states.

- The language class or lesson event that takes place that Tuesday afternoon can be seen as the trajectory of a sociocognitive complex system. The elements and agents of the system include the learners, the teacher, the books, the language items being used, the physical environment. Whole class talk and group talk are just two modes of interaction from the many types of relations between the learners as agents that occur during the class. In that interaction, learners and teacher soft assemble their language resources for the action at hand. The lesson as a whole is the completed trajectory of the class as complex system over a state space landscape. The lesson event connects to previous events and to events yet to happen (van Lier 1988, 1996, 2000; Charles 2003; Mercer 2004; Seedhouse 2004; Chapter 6 of this book).
- Teachers frequently talk about a group of students as a single entity, reflecting our experience that placing individuals together in a group and treating them as an ensemble leads to group patterns of behavior that may be quite different from the styles and norms of the individuals who make up the group. We also know from experience that a class can behave quite differently for one teacher than for another. One teacher may be respected for her serious attitude to learning and receive quiet, disciplined responses in lessons; another may be more extrovert and active in style, producing enthusiastic and lively responses from the class. Each style may be more or less successful, the point being that connections between teacher and class give rise to distinctive, emergent patterns of behavior in the coupled system.
- When four or five learners come together as a group to carry out a task, the group acts as a coupled system with its own dynamics emerging from the adaptation of individual systems (Foster and Skehan 1999; Bygate, Skehan, and Swain 2001; Edwards and Willis 2005). Collective variables will describe the action of the group, while the task requirements act as a control parameter that can shift the nature of that action.
- If we go to a lower level or scale from the lesson, the action of each person in the class can be seen as the trajectory of a complex system over a state space. Each engagement in action provides language exemplars and language use that may stabilize attractors in the state space as learning emerges across timescales from use (Cameron 2003a; N. Ellis 2005; Atkinson *et al.* 2007; Chapter 5 of this book). Complexity thinking can be extended to constructs usually seen as individual factors but in need of connecting to other timescales and levels of human organization, such as personality, motivation (Dörnyei 2003; Lamb 2004; Ushioda 2007), style of learning

or teaching, ability, intelligence, background, etc. Each of these might be understood as arising from self-organizing systems and as dynamic.

- On a yet lower scale, going inside the individual, the body consists of multiple subsystems. The brain is one of these complex systems, coupled to other physical systems and self-organizing through neural activity to contribute to the 'shape' of the living, functioning human being (Gibbs 2006; Spivey 2007).

- If we move outwards or upwards from the lesson to larger systems, we can think of the individual, group, and class as nested in the school as a complex system, with elements that include, as well as the obvious people and buildings, the parents, laws and guidelines, finances, and so on (Bronfenbrenner 1989; Lemke 2000b).

- The national curriculum for foreign languages (where one exists), one of the elements in the 'lesson system', might itself be seen as a complex system, and as an emergent outcome of a curriculum-producing system (Mitchell 2000; Littlewood 2007). In a complexity theory approach, an analytic syllabus such as a process syllabus, where emphasis is placed upon helping students to develop their capacity for communication, rather than accumulating items (Breen and Candlin 1980; Long and Crookes 1993) would be preferred. The teacher's role as a manager of learning is to nudge the students' developing system into a trajectory through state space that is consonant with the students' goals and the goals of instruction. This is not a one-time proposition, of course, but happens moment by moment. It is also not as if the teacher is getting all the students to move in the same direction at the same time. Recall the metaphor of the web with which we concluded Chapter 5. Unlike the steps in a ladder, the strands in a web are not fixed in a determined order but are the joint product of the web builder's constructive activity and the supportive context in which it is built. This suggests that any syllabus is unique, emerging from interactions and teachers' and learners' decisions. A standard synthetic syllabus could be used as a checklist rather than as a prescribed sequence (Larsen-Freeman 2003).

- We can go further out still to the socio-political context in which the education system is situated, nationally and globally. On this scale, we might, for example, examine international English language teaching as a complex dynamic system, or examine the impact of international migration on national provision of ESOL teaching (Brumfit 2001; Pennycook 2003; Baynham 2005; Holliday 2005; Cooke 2006). Language classrooms often find themselves affected by storms that blow down from higher, socio-political, levels. These are aspects of what Bakhtin called the 'centripetal forces' on language that counterbalance its centrifugal tendencies to flux and change (Bakhtin 1986: 668). They often have other types of goals than educational: for example, building (or dismantling) social cohesion across a multilingual or multi-dialectal nation.

- The foreign language that is being taught can be conceived of as a complex system, as can the first language(s) that the learners and teachers use. A recent debate reaching down into the classroom concerns the use of English by non-native speakers and the construct of English as a lingua franca (ELF) that emerges from adaptation in such use (Jenkins 2000; Seidlhofer 2001, 2004). Since language-using patterns emerge from the speech community, the concept of an idealized native speaker speaking a homogeneous language, at least when it comes to a lingua franca like English, can no longer fully define language or what needs to be learned.[1] Any decision concerning these matters must be a local one, negotiated as appropriate in the context where the instruction takes place.

In applying the complexity lens to an aspect of classroom action, we will need to select, out of all that is connected and interacting, particular systems to focus on. Other aspects or systems become the dynamic environment in which these focal systems operate, but are still connected to and able to influence them. The 'initial conditions' of the focal systems, i.e. the state of a system when it commences the activity we are interested in, are very important to understand, since these conditions form the system's initial landscape and influence its trajectory as it changes over time.

Co-adaptation in language classroom interaction

The soft assembly of resources in language classroom action is the source of second language development. As we saw above, the microgenetic moment of action is nested in multiple sociocognitive systems. As these systems change over time, agents and elements will adapt and self-organize, sometimes resulting in the emergence of phenomena across levels of human organization and timescales. A message of this section is that these dynamics are *always* at work (or at play) in language classrooms. Complexity theory can help us notice and more fully understand the processes of adaptation and emergence that construct and constrain language classroom action.

Students need opportunities to work with the language-using patterns of the designated speech community because using and learning them are congruent processes. Students in a classroom are immersed in an environment full of potential meanings. These meanings become available gradually as the students act and interact within the environment (van Lier 2000). They do so by constantly adapting their language resources in the service of meaning-making by attending to the affordances in the context—perhaps to the content in content-based/CLIL-based instruction, or to the tasks in task-based instruction, or to the themes in theme-based instruction. These are customary types of instruction nowadays, and, as always, we would still want for them to be meaningful and engaging. However, what might be special from a complexity theory perspective is how students experience these approaches. An affordance is neither a property of a specific context nor of the learner—it is a relationship between the two. Thus, the teacher would be a facilitator of a given activity, but it is the students who would directly engage with the second language as a dynamic system, shaping their second language resources through working with them, soft assembling in response to what they perceive the affordances to be for different tasks and purposes. Each experience of soft assembly leaves a trace and changes the latent potential of the learners' language resources. Complexity theory applied to the language classroom, along with sociocultural theory (Lantolf 2006b) and conversation analytic perspectives (Firth and Wagner 1997; Seedhouse 2004) thus argues that how the language is used in classrooms affects how language resources develop.

This section highlights, too, the inevitability and disinterestedness of self-organization and emergence. Complexity theory does not suggest that using language automatically leads, through self-organization of the learner's system of language resources, to the emergence of effortless accuracy in the second language. Self-organization happens; it does not happen necessarily for the best. It happens because the agents and elements are connected together and into their environment, because they are how they are, and because they continually adapt. Sometimes it is easier to understand self-organization and co-adaptation when they can be seen to be not entirely beneficial for language learning but to have other outcomes such as the establishment of classroom dialects (Harley and Swain 1984). We use examples here to illustrate firstly how co-adaptation can operate and what results from it. While we also discuss how these situations might be managed to prompt different dynamics in the systems, the main aim in this section is to raise awareness of the inevitability of the dynamic processes themselves.

Co-adapted talk in a language classroom

The example we use here for illustration draws on observation and recorded data from a foreign language lesson in a small class of 11-year-old students in a village school in northern Norway (adapted from Cameron 2001: 42–51). In the lesson, the teacher wanted students to talk in English about polar animals, using content and language that they had encountered through previous work with textbook reading passages and exercises. To prompt talk, the teacher asked the learners, one after another, to select a particular animal and then talk about it to the rest of the class. The adaptation of tasks in the classroom was noticed long ago; Breen (1987) distinguished tasks as plans from tasks as actually carried out, while Coughlan and Duff (1994) noted that task activity is different each time it is repeated, and also that interaction on a task is co-constructed by participants, here the teacher and individual learner.

The system and its dynamics

The complex system that we are focusing on here is action on a task[2] and so has the components: teacher, class, task. Relations among these components produce the emergent 'talk-on-task' that serves as a learning opportunity or affordance for that individual. The trace of the talk, in the form of recording and transcription, represents the trajectory of the system over its state space landscape, i.e. all possible outcomes of the task in that classroom. Each interactional episode with an individual learner shows the teacher's talk co-adapting to the learner's talk through interaction on the task. The data show how the system starts from the expectation of extended talk but quickly adapts and a not particularly helpful, but rather stable, attractor of limited questions and answers emerges. An exception to this pattern allows us to speculate as to what may be driving the system and how it could be adjusted.

The lesson began by the teacher setting out an oral task in two steps, shown in the first extract. First, he asks the class to 'think of any animals you know' (lines 6–8), and asks two learners to write an animal name on the board:

Extract 7.1[3]
```
 1  T  (4.0) there were some
        (1.0) polar
        (3.0) some some animals
        there mentioned
 5      (2.0) er
        (2.0) could you please
        (2.0) think of
        (3.0) any animals (.) you know
        (2.0) um
10      (3.0) A
        and then B
        could you please
        (2.0) go to the blackboard
        and write (.) down
15      (2.0) the name of an animal you know
```

In the second step, which starts at line 10, the teacher goes on to ask two boys, here called A and B, to each write the name of an animal on the board. A writes 'foks', which is corrected to 'fox', and B writes 'reindeer', assisted by the teacher. At this point in the unfolding of the teacher's task plan, the learners do not know what will follow this second step. This is soon revealed when the teacher asks the boy A, who is standing with B near the board at the front of the class:

```
16  T  while you are on the blackboard
        could you please tell us a little about (.) arctic fox
        what kind of animal is it?
```

Here then is the oral task as initially set out by the teacher: the learner is to speak about the (polar) animal he has chosen to write on the board. This initial plan is adapted as learner A tries to respond. While the teacher's request might seem intended to produce an extended description, A's difficulties in talking about the arctic fox lead to the teacher adapting the nature of the task. We see the start of this adaptation in the second extract which begins with a very open question. The learner's limited response to this question prompts the teacher to offer interactive assistance by reducing the scope of the question in line 7 to 'describe it' with further assistance in the structuring of the description through the closed questions in lines 8 and 9, 'is it big? is it small?':

Extract 7.2

```
 1 T  what kind of animal is it?
   A  it's (.) fox
   T  it's a fox?
      yes it is (laughs)
 5    um
      (3.0) could you tell us
      describe it?
      is it big?
      is it small?
10    (1.0) how does it (.) look like?
   A  little
      and white
      er
      (5.0)
15 T  is it a big or a small (.) animal?
   A  little one
      (1.0)
   T  a small one
      yes
20    rather small
      compared with
      (1.0) for instance
      polar bears
      yes
```

A's response to the question comes in lines 11–13 in the form of two adjectives 'little and white', followed by a long pause. This response acts as feedback to the teacher who reacts (line 15) by asking another closed question, this time about size rather than appearance and including a choice of 'big' or 'small'. The learner could choose between the alternatives provided by the teacher. In fact, he produces a different lexical item in response: 'little one' (line 16) which is then recast in a short response-feedback sequence to 'a small one' (line 18). A reformulation follows (lines 20–24) in which the teacher expands the idea of 'small' to a comparison with 'polar bears'. After another pause, the teacher asks two further questions (at line 25 and lines 31–34) to extract parts of a description from the learner:

25 T have you seen an arctic fox?
  A no
    er
    on TV yes
  T not (.) the real one?
30   no
    (2.0) do we have
    the arctic (.) foxes
    in (.) Norway?
  A I don't think so
35 T no I don't think so too
    I think
    you have to go to
    further
    further north to get them
40   (2.0) yes thank you

The interaction between the teacher and learner A concludes with a comment by the teacher on where arctic foxes live (lines 36–40).

The task landscape was changed with the use of language in the interaction. What began as an invitation from teacher to learner to produce an extended description changed into a jointly constructed description in which the teacher helped the learner by asking increasingly closed questions and offering his own comments. In observing a series of such interactions between the teacher and other students, Cameron found that, with one exception, what started as an open invitation each time became a sequence of questions from the teacher with short answers from the student, sometimes added to by further comments from the teacher, in a similar pattern to that seen in the above extracts.

Applying complex systems thinking to the unfolding lesson, we can see the teacher–learner interaction as co-adaptive, with each response constructing a feedback loop between participants. The 'talk-on-task', or interaction, is a trajectory over the state space landscape of the subsystem {teacher + learner + task}, and the landscape is evolving as the interaction proceeds and adapts. The move from an open description task to a series of questions and answers can be seen as a move to a stable attractor in state space landscape of talk-on-task, since most of the interactions between teacher and individual student ended up in this way. This mode of interaction may be preferred because it avoids uncomfortable silences, because it makes it possible for the learner to say something, because the teacher feels he is suitably supportive, and/or for other reasons we cannot know.

Possible collective variable to describe the system

To describe the system in action, moving from the unstable interactional mode to the more stable, limited question and answer mode, we need to find a suitable collective variable for the system, i.e. one that brings together teacher and learner talk-on-task into one measure. A collective variable that describes a system's trajectory must be observable from the data and may need to be quantifiable depending on the methodology being employed (Thelen and Smith 1994: 251). A candidate for a collective variable for this interactional system is derived by comparing the actual language used by the learner and with the expected language as set up by the teacher's utterances.

The idea of a collective variable that derives from a difference between variables in the individual systems is inspired by Kelso's work on finger movements. (For more on this, see Kelso 1995; Cameron 2003a: Chapter 2; Chapter 6 of this book.) The candidate collective variable to describe the interaction and its shifts in the Norwegian classroom task is, in analogy with Kelso's phase differential, labeled 'interaction differential' and reflects the differences in lexico-grammatical and cognitive content of expected and actual utterances. Most of the teacher's utterances are elicitations and these can be graded in terms of the demands they make on the learner expected to answer them (Cameron 2001): more open questions (for example, 'tell us about a fox') make more demands, both lexicogrammatically and cognitively, than more closed questions (for example, 'is it big or small?'). The elicitations used by the teacher are rated in terms of the demands they make, from 1 for a confirmation request to 8 for an open elicitation. As we saw in the extracts, very open elicitations may actually be responded to by silence or short answers. Learner utterances, mostly responses to teacher elicitations, can be rated in terms of their lexicogrammatical and cognitive content, with credit given for clause-length rather than phrase or single word replies and for use of content-related lexical items new to the interaction. The 'interaction differential' collective variable then takes values that reflect the difference between what the teacher's elicitations appear to expect and the learner's actual response.

The elicitation-response pairs in the interaction between teacher and learner A could be calculated as follows:

(1) T could you please tell us a little about (.) arctic fox
   no response from A
   Elicitation: open request for information (rated 8)
   Response: silence (rated 0)
   Interaction differential: 8

(2) T what kind of animal is it?
   A it's (.) fox
   Elicitation: more specific description request (rated 7)
   Response: clausal, minimal information content (rated 3)
   Interaction differential: 4

(3) T is it big?
   is it small?
   no response from A

Elicitation: choice of answer given in question (rated 3)
Response: silence (rated 0)
Interaction differential: 3

(4) T (1.0) how does it (.) look like?
    A little
       and white
    Elicitation: question about specific aspect (rated 6)
    Response: word length, two new (to event) lexical items (rated 4)
    Interaction differential: 2

(5) T is it a big or a small (.) animal?
    A little one
    Elicitation: choice of answer given in question (rated 3)
    Response: phrase length (rated 2)
    Interaction differential: 1

(6) T have you seen an arctic fox?
    A no
       er
       on TV yes
    Elicitation: yes/no question (rated 2)
    Response: single word + phrase (rated 2)
    Interaction differential: 0

(7) T do we have
       the arctic (.) foxes
       in (.) Norway?
    A I don't think so
    Elicitation: yes/no question (rated 2)
    Response: formulaic clause (rated 2)
    Interaction differential: 0

(8) The interaction then concludes with further information from the
    teacher:
    T I think you have to go to further north to get them
    Rated using the same criteria as learner responses, the interaction
    differential of this would be graded 6 (two clauses + two non-finite verbs
    + two new lexical items 'further' and 'north').

The trajectory of teacher and learner as complex system

Figure 7.1 shows the successive values of the interaction differential and
represents the overall trajectory of the interaction.

    As the lesson proceeded, interaction between teacher and successive students
about their choice of arctic animal followed much the same pattern of starting
with a wide differential and quickly narrowing down to a stable attractor
of a sequence of teacher elicitations followed by limited learner responses,

with concluding information from the teacher. This concluding information increased in complexity and length. Successive episodes produced similar trajectories to Figure 7.1.

The final student to speak in the lesson (learner D) interacted quite differently with the teacher, by taking control of the task from the start and talking about his pet budgerigar (which is a tropical bird and not a polar animal). This learner adapts the task. He talked much more and used more complex language,

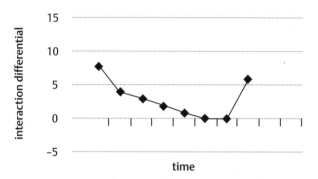

Figure 7.1 Trajectory of teacher interaction with learner A on the task, described in terms of the interaction differential

and the teacher responded with fewer elicitations and more responses in his own talk. (For details, see Cameron 2001.) The interaction differential again usefully describes the talk as a collective variable (Figure 7.2). The spike in the middle of the interaction is the teacher telling a short anecdote, and at the end him adding some information. The negative values represent places where learner D offers information in language that is lexicogrammatically more advanced.

The interaction differential takes on a wider range of values in this interaction, and does not follow the pattern of a large differential that is rapidly closed down. There would seem to be two contributing factors to the different trajectory of this learner's talk: his proficiency level in English was higher, and he was thus able to participate in the task as planned without it needing to be adapted into a simpler mode; and he had a great deal of knowledge of the topic he was talking about, which he had managed to select through subversion or manipulation of the planned topic.

If we zoom out to a larger level of social organization and timescale, we can put together the successive trajectories to get the trajectory of the larger system of teacher and class interaction on the task. In this larger system, the pattern of tightly-structured, relatively closed teacher elicitation followed by limited learner response appears to be a stable attractor to which the interaction adapts. The interaction with learner D is an unstable attractor, a hill in the landscape that the system moves to only briefly.

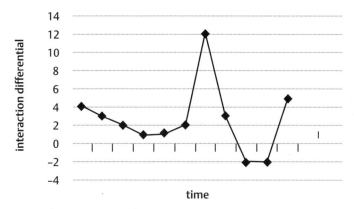

Figure 7.2 Trajectory of teacher interaction with learner D on the task, described in terms of the interaction differential

Managing the dynamics of learning

There are many pedagogic reflections that could be made about the choice of task and language—see Cameron 2001. We restrict ourselves here to those that relate to a complexity interpretation of the lesson.

Having developed a (very rough) 'complexity thought model' of the system, we can now proceed to use it to consider other possible ways to run the task. We explore how the system parameters might be adjusted and what might happen as a result of the adjustments. For example, we might hypothesize that content knowledge is a control parameter in this system; knowing more about the animals might push the interaction into more useful modes, as it did for learner D. The reference to 'knowledge' and not 'language' here is deliberate—successful learner D did not know all the English words and phrases that he wanted to talk about the budgie but, knowing what he wanted to say, he was able to say something close enough, stretching his language resources in the process. This challenge reveals his latent potential (see Chapter 6) in English through participation in the interaction, while the talk of the other learners did not seem to offer the same opportunity to stretch their resources and show the full extent of their latent potential.[4] Obviously, the learners need a certain amount of language around the topic, but it may be that what they have is sufficient if it can be brought into use. This hypothesis could be tested in the classroom by spending time on the topic of the animals, i.e. increasing the control parameter, and then trying the task again. If content knowledge does work (for these learners) as a control parameter, increased knowledge will cause the system to avoid the less helpful attractor of limited questions and answers and move to other areas of the state space where the learners' latent potential is more fully revealed.

In designing task-based, content-based, or theme-based activities (for example, Beckett and Miller 2006), teachers as managers of learning would want to think about how to adjust the control parameter of discrepancy. The gap between how students want to use their language resources and what the context warrants can provide the impetus for students' finding, creating, and learning new patterns of language using. In order to create the discrepancy, the activities would always have to challenge learners to exploit the meaning potential of their developing systems in new ways. Two examples of how to do so would be to reduce the planning time given students before they engage in a task again (Foster and Skehan 1999) or to increase the information density of a given task (Larsen-Freeman 2003).

In re-running the task, the teacher might also choose to manage the co-adaptation of language proactively to adjust the collective variable of the interaction differential in a contingent manner (van Lier 1996). Instead of closing down the talk by asking very restricted questions, the teacher could adapt to the student by gradually opening up questions. Successful talk about the animal topic would look more like Figure 7.2 than 7.1, with the interaction differential taking values of between plus and minus 3 or 4, i.e. the teacher asking questions of a type and content that stretch the learners without incapacitating them and reducing them to silence.

Studies have shown the value of having students do a task more than once or tell or listen to a story more than once, particularly where, as here, the task or story is too complicated for simple repetition. Arevart and Nation (1991) conducted a study where students were asked to deliver a four-minute talk on a familiar topic to a partner. They then changed partners and delivered the same talk to a different partner, but with a three-minute time limit. Finally, they changed partners again and delivered the same talk in two minutes to their new partner. Delivering the same talk under increasingly severe time constraints was effective not only in enhancing fluency but also, somewhat unexpectedly, in improving accuracy. The result is that a structure is built up, a structure of language-using patterns at different levels of scale. Note that when we say the 'same talk' it is never really 'the same', nor is it the case that the talk is repeated. It is helpful to distinguish between repetition and recursion in this regard (Larsen-Freeman 2007d). Repetition is designed to improve set performance. Its frame is closed. Recursion is a transformative process. Its frame is open. (Doll (1993). See also Ochs and Capps 2001, 'living narratives', narratives that are shaped and reshaped in the course of the telling.)

By viewing tasks as dynamic systems, we move away from a static view of task as frame (Bygate 1999) to one of task as an evolving, open dynamic structure offering various affordances to learners. Task-based learning argues that classroom tasks provide frameworks for individual language-using activity, and that this will facilitate language learning through use (for example, Edwards and Willis 2005). Looking at the use of language tasks through the lens of complex systems allows a dynamic view in which the idea of task as frame is converted to the idea that the task sets the initial state space landscape of the complex system of task action. The initial landscape across which the system will move as work on task proceeds is shaped by the task as planned by the teacher and by the language resources that each student brings to the task. Hills in the landscape may be challenges that the task presents to language use: for learner A, the task landscape has very steep hills in the form of open questions. The landscape's valleys are attractor states that represent preferred modes of behavior on the task. However, attractors are not necessarily useful, as we saw above, or as in the use by students of their first language to complete a task noted by several researchers as a tendency (for example, Littlewood 2007). A fixed point attractor somewhere on the landscape represents the end of the task where, all goals achieved, language use terminates.

As the learners work on the task, using language to do so, the system moves across the task-based landscape. In the static view of task as frame, unfolding task action would be the trajectory across a stationary landscape. Such a representation is only adequate for very rigid tasks, such as coloring in a picture through dictation or reciting a poem learned by heart. The kind of evolving landscape that we have seen before for coupled, co-adaptive systems better represents language tasks that are designed to engage and involve learners by giving them some degree of choice. In these tasks, the group talk changes the task as they begin to do it, and the task is constructed through the doing of it. For example, a pair of learners engaged in a 'spot the difference' task may adapt to each other and to the pictures they are using, and evolve efficient ways of establishing differences (Pinter 2007).

Co-adaptation in content-based classroom interaction

The second set of illustrative examples draws on experience in a UK secondary school, in an area of low socio-economic status where nearly all the students came from settled minority ethnic communities and used English as an additional language with Gujerati as the major home language (documented in Cameron *et al.* 1996; Cameron 1997). Students did not receive formal language instruction in English, since official policy is that English language skills would develop through participation in classroom activities and main-stream curriculum subject lessons. However, national and local limits on education spending at that time had led to many mainstream subject teachers working, not just without language support teachers or aids, but largely with-out training in how to support additional language development through curriculum subject classes.

A group of researchers including the second author of this book was invited to act as consultants to work with mainstream teachers on improving their support for English language development through the curriculum. At the start of the project, we gathered information about the initial conditions by asking teachers for their perceptions of issues and problems, and by classroom observations and recordings of lessons. (There was also some consultation with students.) The striking contrast between what was said and what was observed prompted a complex dynamics perspective on the classroom issues. In brief, mainstream teachers reported problems with students, while observations revealed that these problems were not located just with the students, but seemed to emerge from the self-organizing dynamics of teacher-led classroom activity embedded in the particular socio-political contexts of school, community, and urban area.

Minimal responses as attractor in classroom interaction

Teachers reported that classroom discussions were unsatisfactory because students only gave short answers to their questions or did not answer at all. When we transcribed classroom discourse, many responses to teachers' questions were indeed 'minimal'—single word answers or silence. However, when we analyzed the discourse, possible reasons for this phenomenon became apparent. Questioning sessions were teacher-led and, while the teachers may have prepared them, for students, these sessions were completely spontaneous: they had no prior knowledge of the questions that might be asked, nor were they given planning time to answer them. Teachers' questions tended to be open or difficult: for example, when reviewing a previous topic, one teacher asked the class: 'What is a food chain?' A student faced with this question, without time to prepare an answer, could not be expected to do much more than produce single word, minimal responses, such as 'fox', 'chicken'. These answers showed that students did recall the concept of a food chain, but they did not satisfy the teacher's expectations of an appropriate answer. The teacher's response to short answers was either to give the answer herself, or to ask one of the brighter students to give an answer. These actions may have served to further discourage students from struggling to construct an answer, since experience showed them that, if they did not answer, they would soon get to hear a good answer from someone else.

Seen from a complex systems perspective, the 'minimal response scenario' that had emerged as a school-wide phenomenon was self-organizing out of the classroom dynamics. We saw in Chapter 6 that the Initiation–Response–Feedback (IRF) pattern, has been found in a wide range of classrooms. In this school a particular type of IRF pattern had become an attractor state, not just for specific episodes of interaction, but in classrooms across the school (and more widely, given how often teachers in similar schools greet the description with recognition). It seemed to have emerged from the co-adaptation of the coupled subsystems of students and teacher. The second language learners adapted to teachers' difficult questions by saying something, possibly relevant to the question but not elaborated; the teachers adapted to receiving short responses by giving the answer herself or selecting one of the most able students to provide the answer. Co-adaptation occurred over several timescales. On the timescale of the questioning session within a lesson, a teacher, faced with minimal responses from students, tended to select a student who could give a fuller answer or to provide the answers themselves through elaboration of the single word answers, thus satisfying the learning goals of the questioning, for example, recall or revision of content. Over timescales of weeks and months, students became accustomed to this mode of operating and became less and less motivated to try to find an answer to a teacher's question, having adapted their behavior to wait for a 'star' student or the teacher to answer the question. As teachers realized, the emergent and self-organized minimal response scenario was not beneficial for language or for cognitive development.

Framing the problem in terms of co-adaptation offers a different view and a way forward. While teachers spoke of students as the locus of the problem: 'they only give short answers', the problem was observed to concern both teachers and students in their adaptation to each other. The agents in the system most able to instigate a different trajectory were the teachers, and it was via the teachers that intervention in the whole system was planned and instigated. In the next subsection, we illustrate one aspect of intervention. We then move to the level of the school to see the connections between classroom action and larger issues.

Intervention in the dynamics of interaction: wait time

Intervention in the minimal responses scenario described above involved perturbing the system out of its stabilized attractor state through changes in teacher action. In a multi-strategy approach, teachers' awareness was raised of the demands that their questions made on students, of the types of questions they used, and of alternatives; teachers tried to make their expectations about responses explicit to students, explaining that they wanted students to try to answer questions even if they were not sure their answers were correct; students were given more time to construct their answers; students were encouraged to discuss answers in pairs before offering an answer in the public forum of the class discussion. The changes in behavior required did not come easily; teachers had to consciously adjust what they did until it became familiar.

One of the strategies tried was to take 'wait time' as a possible control parameter of the system and see if increasing it would change the nature of the interaction. Wait time is the length of time that the teacher waits after asking a question and before giving up and providing a clue, providing the answer herself or asking another student. It has long been known that increasing wait time is useful (for example, Fanselow 1977; Rowe 1986). For learners, wait time can be thinking time; it gives time to find an answer to the question and to formulate it in the required language. The more complicated the question, the longer wait time learners need. When a teacher worked at lengthening the time waited after asking a question, we observed improvement in the quality of student answers, contributing to improvement in the overall quality of the classroom talk. Her change to the control parameter had shifted the classroom interaction system out of the minimal response attractor and into a different trajectory. At a human level, though, because the teacher's mode of interaction was strongly entrenched, she did not find it easy to change. She was very conscious of the physical effort involved in waiting and how strange it felt at first.

Co-adaptation at school level: expectations and motivation

Patterns of behavior at the classroom level interact with patterns of behavior at the institutional and, beyond that to the socio-political level and historical timescale.

The school-based project described above was initiated to address problems of low achievement. As well as the minimal response scenario, teachers described other problems relating to student participation, such as students not bothering to do homework, or coming to lessons without the right equipment. Once again, observation showed that these were not solely student issues but whole system issues, resulting from co-adaptation over time among the coupled subsystems around the school. Exploring the issue of homework showed that, indeed, many students did not complete homework set by teachers, but it also showed that some teachers had come to assume that homework would not be completed and so started lessons by giving answers to homework rather than collecting it to mark. As a student in such classes, there had come to be little point in doing homework, since any work that mattered would be repeated in class. The teachers' action, which had resulted from some students not completing homework, may have led to even fewer students being motivated to do the work, which would in turn reinforce teachers' views that going over work in class was necessary. The outcome of this vicious circle of co-adaptation was misconstrued as a lack of commitment by students when it also involved low expectations of students on the part of some teachers.

Similarly, teachers complained that students came to class without the proper equipment such as pencils and rulers. Teachers adapted to this situation by providing equipment in class; and students had in turn adapted to this provision of equipment by paying even less attention to what they should bring. Again a downward spiral through co-adaptation produced a negative situation that was construed as a problem of the students rather than of the larger system.

Connected to these co-adaptations on a longer timescale and a broader social level were the low expectations of the ethnic minority students expressed by some teachers; they were not expected to achieve particularly well in class or in public examinations. The culture of low expectations may have affected (as well as being affected by) how the teachers taught, including the questions they asked, the amount and type of homework they set, the provision of equipment, and many other less observable decisions. It is also likely to have affected students' expectations and identities, contributing to their desire to comply, or not, with teachers' requests. Teacher expectations are likely to be connected into larger systems too, bearing on the history of minority ethnic communities in the area, attitudes, and politics.

Effective intervention to shift the system out of the attractor state of low expectations was again driven by the socially more powerful group in the school, i.e. the teachers, particularly the deputy head teacher who adopted various interventions such as working to involve reluctant teachers, re-arranging the schedule so that teachers could participate in seminars, involving parents, etc. Intervention is not likely to be needed just on one occasion since the attractor state is likely to draw the system back to a mode of low expectations. Instead, expectations have to be consciously and continuously raised in order to shift the trajectory of the coupled system away from its tendency towards low achievement.

The dynamics of emergent language-using patterns

The final example of complexity thinking applied to language classroom phenomena turns our attention to language patterns. The type of adaptation considered here involves learners' language resources for the communicative situation they find themselves in. The arguments of Chapters 4, 5, and 6 are applied to discuss how these adaptations in the moment produce emergent language-using patterns in the resources of individuals and groups.

The language patterns discussed here were found in the course of research projects carried out in the UK into the writing of students using English as an additional language[5] at ages 10 and 16 years (Cameron 2003c; Cameron and Besser 2004). Samples of writing were collected from 'advanced bilingual' students, i.e. who (a) used English as an additional language, and (b) had been in the UK for at least five years. Comparisons were made with samples from students who used English as a first language, and between writing by higher achieving and lower achieving students using English as an additional language.[6] Major first languages were Punjabi, Urdu, Bengali, and Gujerati. The writing samples were subjected to detailed analysis of features including (a) as whole text—use of genre, cohesion, paragraphing; and (b) text-internally—use of clause grammar, lexis, spelling, punctuation. Qualitative and, where appropriate, statistical analyses of the results were carried out on the differences between groups.

The emergent language patterns

One of the most robust findings was significant differences between writing in English as an additional language and writing in English as first language in the number of errors[7] made in the specific area of formulaic sequences and collocational conventions, often in the use of prepositions. Separate measures of errors in use of prepositions and delexicalized[8] verbs, such as 'do', 'make', 'put', 'give', etc., also showed significant differences across language backgrounds. In the study of writing by 16-year-olds, significant differences were also found in accurate use of inflections on nouns and verbs, and in use of determiners such as 'a' and 'the'.

Below are examples of forms marked as errors; in complexity terms these are variations around the stabilized forms of British Standard English (BSE). Alternatives that would have been appropriate to the discourse context appear in brackets:

> *pouring with tears down their faces (with tears pouring down)
> *brown chocolate eyes (chocolate brown)
> *he was driving his mum crazy for it (over)
> *I went flying on the floor (on to)
> *his best of all friend (best friend of all)
> *they waited for a lot of time (for a long time)
> *a bundle of people (a crowd/? bunch of people)
> (Cameron and Besser 2004: 73–5)

Some of the examples have a different word order from the standard forms, while others use different prepositions from the standard first language patterns of these particular expressions and their intended meanings. In the third example, two formulae 'driving someone crazy' and 'crazy for x' seem to be blended together; in the context of the story, it is not 'his mum' who is 'crazy for' anything, but her son's longing for a game ('it') that is driving her crazy. The last two examples collocate lexical items that are not usually used together; in contrast, the first four examples would be lexicogrammatically and pragmatically appropriate in different discourse contexts, for example:

> pouring with *rain*
> brown chocolate *tastes better than white chocolate*
> he was crazy for *her*
> *lying* on the floor

Errors in the use of delexicalized verbs included the use of an inappropriate but similarly frequent verb and the use of a delexicalized verb where a more highly lexicalized verb was needed, for example:

> *it will do a really good help to us   (be)
> *schools don't give enough interest   (show)
> *It would be a great idea if you all make some kind of meeting (had/held)

The language patterns found to be different across the English as an additional language and first language groups are patterns of variation from standard written British English in (i) word order and/or elements of semi-fixed collocations, and (ii) the use of prepositions and determiners (labeled with the more pedagogically-friendly term 'small words' by Cameron 2003c).

These findings are somewhat counter-intuitive. After all, the writers are largely from the second or third generation of immigrants who moved to England from the Indian sub-continent, rather than newly arrived. Most had been in an English-using school environment since preschool, an average of 7 years and 2 months in the UK education system for the 10-year-olds, and 10 years and 4 months for the 16-year-olds. They had passed through the period of 5–7 years that research into bilingual language development in North America suggests is needed for language skills to reach parity with first language peers (Collier 1987).[9] And yet the patterns of use found in the writing data differ from the standard forms that these learners might be expected to have encountered many times.

A complexity interpretation of the findings

A complexity theory interpretation starts from the premise that the learners' multiple experiences with these words and phrases in meaningful communicative situations have led to the patterns that appeared in the writing data. To explain or understand the nature of the patterns, we need to investigate the nature of the experiences that produced them.

The complex systems of relevance here are those of children from minority ethnic communities using and learning their second or additional language in mainstream school contexts in England. Their language-using patterns result from the dynamic and adaptive process of soft assembly of language resources 'in the service of meaning-making in response to the affordances that emerge in the communicative situation' (Chapter 5: p. 135). For these learners, the communicative situation has been the curriculum subject classroom (or in lower grades, the primary school classroom) as in the school described in the previous illustration; specialized language support is provided for those new to English but is not widely available past the beginning stages.

Meaning-making occurs during participation in classes. Over time, the continual adaptation of language resources through soft assembly in the microgenetic moment of participation leads to phase shifts that stabilize particular patterns of the second language; this study revealed those patterns that are most different from those of first language users. A simple version of frequency effects (N. Ellis 2002) is clearly not sufficient to explain these patterns, in a variation of Zipf's law, more errors are occurring with the use of words that are more frequently encountered and in multiple linguistic contexts. It may be that the use of these words in semi-fixed formulaic sequences (Wray 2002) accounts both for frequency and for the variant patterns. Word order and collocations found in formulaic sequences that have sedimented out of language use over long timescales and large levels of social organization (as in Chapter 4) often seem quite random: the words do not follow the more regular patterns of use that they have in 'open choice' language (Sinclair 1991), and so need to be learned as specific exemplars. If frequently used words are also frequently encountered in semi-fixed formulaic sequences, it may be more difficult for learners both to generalize accurately (Ellis 2005) and to learn the multiplicity of specific, semi-fixed uses. Put another way, the affordances for learning these aspects of language are many, but they are so varied that generalization is difficult, and the lexicogrammar is so specific that generalizing would not be enough any way.

The dynamics of the language-using situation also contribute to explaining the language patterns found in writing by students using English as an additional language. Firstly, in the content lessons where the students develop their English, teachers of history or science, for example, are concerned with emphasizing content vocabulary, often using lists of 'key words' to support teaching on a particular topic. Students see these key words highlighted in isolation, rather than with their common collocates. Secondly, and particularly for younger students, much input is oral, meaning that endings and 'small words' like determiners and prepositions are unstressed and may disappear in the flow of speech (Cameron and Besser 2004). What makes L1 learning easy makes L2 hard as Ellis and Larsen-Freeman (2006) put it. Students may not notice small words and endings in teacher talk, and conversely, teachers may not notice whether they are used in student talk. Since subject content is the main concern in the language-using situations, student answers to teacher questions may be accepted on the basis of their conceptual content rather than lexicogrammatical accuracy.

The very low salience of these language features in school communication means that it is unlikely that they will be noticed or attended to, and explicit learning is unlikely to happen (Schmidt 1990; N. Ellis 2005). Combine this with the difficulties of implicit learning of many different and specific semi-fixed collocations and we have a possible interpretation for the findings of the writing project. This explanation does not just consider individual language processing but connects this with the dynamics of the language learning situation and the nature of teacher-led activity to account for patterns of language that develop and emerge over time.

Complexity theory applied to the language classroom, along with sociocultural theory (Lantolf 2007) and conversation analytic perspectives (Firth and Wagner 1997; Seedhouse 2004), argues that how the language is used in classrooms affects, through self-organization and emergence, how language resources develop. This study reminds us that the specific details of language-using matter. Learners' attention to language adapts in response to classroom demands.

As we have said before, every use of language changes language. As we saw in Chapter 5, development occurs through repeated activity in slightly different situations. In the classroom, this translates as 'every use of language changes the language of learners; over time, successive uses of language lead to the emergence of language-using patterns across groups and in the language resources of individuals. Students learning English through participation in subject classes have different language-using experiences from students learning English as a foreign language, and will develop different language-using patterns. Of course, there will be overlap: for example, determiners and endings seem to cause problems in many contexts. But this does not mean that the specificities of learning and using contexts are irrelevant and need not be taken account of, just that the specificities are sufficiently similar for these aspects of English to produce similar outcomes.

Atkinson *et al.* (2007) suggest that a mechanism they call 'alignment' is necessary for second language learning. Alignment is defined as:

> ... the complex process through which human beings effect coordinated interaction, both with other human beings and ... environments, situations, tools, and affordances.
> (Atkinson *et al.* 2007: 169)

However, when we see how emergent language patterns are tightly connected to the specifics of their use, it is clear that alignment is not a straightforward process in which learners match their language to that of their interlocutors. Alignment may be necessary but it is far from sufficient. We have thus preferred to use the notion of co-adaptation, inevitable but neutral, and able to capture situations where adaptations are less than beneficial for learning as well as those where learning can be observed.

Managing the dynamics of emergent patterns

The literature contains a range of possible ways of addressing the emergence of problematic features of language, from teachers giving corrective feedback and recasts (for example, Lyster and Ranta 1997) through directing learners' attention to features of language through form-focused tasks (for example, Swain and Lapkin 1998) to accepting these as dialectal variations and thus not necessarily in need of attention (for example, Jenkins 2000; Seidlhofer 2004).

A complexity approach, that traces emergent features back to the dynamics that gave rise to them, can contribute to selecting or adapting from this range of possible activities by focusing on the dynamics in the microgenetic moment of use and seeking to manage those dynamics to produce the desired outcome. This might mean, for example, presenting key words for science or history topics in their most useful collocations rather than in isolation, or focusing on topic-related semi-fixed formulaic sequences in group writing activities to direct attention to precise forms. Activities that encourage precision at the moment of use include shadowing and dictogloss. In shadowing (e.g., Schmidt 1990), the students repeat as closely as possible after the teacher exactly what the teacher says and does. Such practice has been shown to be effective for learning the suprasegmental patterns of language using and the accompanying gestures. Dictogloss (e.g., Kowal and Swain 1994) has students work in pairs to reconstruct in writing a text read aloud by the teacher. It was shown to prompt students to focus on and talk about form.

Language is dynamic (even when it's frozen)

In the additional language situations described above, learners encounter language as a dynamic system, and this produces particular kinds of developmental patterns and co-adaptations. In situations of instructed language learning, the language that is the goal of learning is rendered less dynamic:

> ... the rules of language use, and much of the language system, are inherently fluid and negotiable, but the teaching of languages has to act as if they are stable and unnegotiable in order to offer a supportive base for learners.
> (Brumfit 2001: xi)

It seems inevitable that, as Brumfit says, the complexity of the dynamic system that is a living language will need to be reduced in some ways for the purposes of learning and teaching. Moving targets are notoriously difficult to hit, so learners need to be presented with something less fearsome, often a static model of the foreign language, frozen or crystallized in time and reduced in complexity. The static, reduced model is presented to learners in textbooks, grammars, dictionaries, recordings, curriculum goals, and other sources. Even though what is offered to students may appear static, complexity and dynamism re-appear as soon as the language is re-animated through its use in classroom action.

In addition, however, we have to consider whether there are ways for learners to experience language dynamics, or at least to be aware of change and variation in the living language, so that at some stage of proficiency learners can deal with a more dynamic model. Learning is not the taking in of linguistic forms, but the continuing dynamic adaptation to the context, which is also changing. In order to be able to use language patterns beyond a given occasion and thereby overcome 'the inert knowledge problem' (Larsen-Freeman 2003), students need experience in adapting to multiple and varying contexts. Working with a variety of partner configurations in the class is one way to make this happen. Another way is to plan a mix of activities in-class, project work outside of class, and computer-mediated communication, where learners can send and receive messages in real time.

Writing of 'the grammar of choice', Larsen-Freeman (2002b) discussed the way that many factors come into play when deciding which language-using patterns to use. Students need to become aware of the choices they have and of change and variation in the dynamics of language use—in a way commensurate with their ability to understand. Larsen-Freeman (2003) advises teaching 'reasons, not just rules'. Reasons help students see why speakers made choices to use the patterns that they did. One way to do so is to have the teacher and other students use a 'think aloud' technique, freezing the action momentarily and explaining the choices that exist in the moment of language use and what consequences might follow if one were to exercise one option or another. Another is to raise students' consciousness by having them understand grammar as a process of decision-making, not only by its products (Rutherford 1987), a process that is part of what Larsen-Freeman (2003) has called 'grammaring'.

Language assessment

Assessment, especially formative assessment, and feedback are important practices in a complexity approach to language learning. Students have to be helped to go beyond what they can already do, and to go beyond, they will benefit from receiving feedback from others. In fact, it is this feedback from teachers, students, and others with whom they interact, which keeps their developing language-using patterns intelligible, just as the greater speech community keeps its users' idiolects from moving to completely different regions of state space. While the process of morphogenesis (the development of new forms) may be aided by interaction and negotiation of meaning with peers, to prevent the creation of an unhelpful classroom dialect, there should also be opportunity for interaction with, and feedback from, more proficient language users.

Formal language assessment, as an educational function and as a commercial enterprise, has huge effects on language teaching, and vice versa, that could be analyzed as co-adaptation in complex dynamic systems. Several examples of this co-adaptation were discussed in Chapter 3, including the phenomenon of 'washback', when teachers 'teach to the test'.

Finding out about the language resources of each student

Seen from a complexity perspective, second language testers try to find out about the second language resources that are unique to each student. Each student brings his or her unique intrinsic dynamics to the testing situation, and the test is the trajectory of the system of student and test over the landscape that is all possible responses to the test. These language resources, however, are only latent potential until realized in the particular discourse environment of the test.

From this perspective, it is important to begin by recognizing the limitations of tests.

> (No) test or task that lasts but a few minutes or an hour gauges what we can do with language across the full range of human timescales. Nor can any test or task separate language skills from the social skills and cultural knowledge needed for every task.
> (Lemke 2002: 84)

Nevertheless, testers and teachers want to understand the dynamics of what students know and what they do not know. Discrete point tests, which usually rely on dichotomous scoring, treat learning as an all or none affair. Recently, it has been proposed that scoring items polytomously, so that learners receive partial credit for what they do know, would yield information about learners who have an intermediary knowledge of what is being tested, rather than their being treated as if they have no knowledge at all (Purpura 2006). This is a very promising prospect from a complexity point of view for one would expect progressive attainment not either/or acquisition, since from this perspective, there is no static independent and measurable 'thing' to measure, test, evaluate, or codify.

The social dimension of language testing

Most language tests have ignored the social use dimension of language and have followed traditional psychometric methods in measuring isolated pieces of grammar and vocabulary knowledge; however, measuring test takers' ability to use language in social contexts is seen to be increasingly important (McNamara and Roever 2006). Importantly, this awareness goes beyond extending the construct being measured. A social view of performance is incompatible with the traditional view of performance as a simple projection or display of individual competence. Increasingly, therefore, language testers are questioning whether it is possible to isolate the contributions of test takers from those of the test takers' interlocutors, say in oral proficiency interviews. The interconnectedness of interviewer and interviewee, and the resulting co-adaptation is, from a complexity perspective, inescapable. Further, the particular discourse environment of the test, which includes the tester as interlocutor, is part of what determines, out of all the possibilities in the latent potential of the individual's language resources, what is actually used. This places a huge responsibility on test and tester not to prevent the testee from showing what he or she is capable of.

Along somewhat similar lines, Lantolf and Poehner (2004) call for 'dynamic assessment', arguing against the assumption that the best sort of assessment is that of independent problem solving. Since higher order thinking and language use emerges from our interactions with others, it makes sense to test the examinee before and after an intervention, designed to teach the student how to perform better on the test. The student's final score represents the difference between pre-test (before learning) and post-test (after learning) scores, a way of measuring the student's latent potential. This is a promising new development in language assessment because, from a complexity perspective

> ... the whole point of gauging language development is to act with respect to the future: to recommend what to do next, to set a course of learning for a longer future period, to develop expectations of what learners can do with the language in various possible futures.
> (Lemke 2002: 85)

Modeling the language classroom

Language classroom systems will challenge modelers, both in finding valid ways to reduce the complexity to fit into possible models and in accounting for the human aspect of the systems. Agent-based simulation models appear to offer most promise (for example, Barr 2004; Ke and Holland 2006). Even if a productive computer simulation does not materialize, the process of constructing a model can be very fruitful because it pushes the modelers to make decisions about the nature of the systems, about their interconnections and about which explanatory theories are appropriate to describe them.

What we have called 'complexity thought modeling' and have exemplified in our interpretations of language classroom systems (and outlined in Table 3.1) can lead to understandings of behavior patterns in terms of the systems that produce them. The process may also help generate hypotheses to be investigated through classroom research—see Chapter 8. Teachers or trainers may find complex systems helpful in making sense of what they experience in language classrooms, in order to think about intervention in classroom systems, perturbing them away from unhelpful patterns or attractors and back on the move towards language learning.

Conclusion

As we have said before in this book in concluding sections, much remains to be done. Well, that is the nature of the enterprise we have undertaken in developing a complexity theory approach to applied linguistics. As with the other areas that we have written about, we are only at the opening stages of the adventure. We have suggested four components of a complexity approach that we think are particularly salient when applying complexity theory to the language classroom, and have identified a fifth *en route* about the influence on language development of the local and specific detail of how language is used and experienced:

- it's all connected
- language is dynamic (even when it is frozen)
- co-adaptation is a key dynamic in classroom systems
- teaching is managing the dynamics of learning
- the specifics of language use and experience matter.

These have guided the presentation of examples from language and content classrooms that have been described and interpreted from the complexity perspective throughout the chapter.

We have seen how microgenetic action in language classrooms connects into multiple nested systems that range from the neurological to the socio-politics of migration and testing. The dynamics of these systems show features common to complex systems including trajectories into stabilized attractors of behavior. Some of the examples highlighted how the attractors may or may not be beneficial for learning, emphasizing the vital role of the teacher in managing the dynamics.

The idea that difference may be used in finding collective variables and control parameters of complex systems was further developed in this chapter. Difference may be significant because it prompts change. In the language development systems of Chapter 5, difference appeared as 'discrepancy', and in the talk systems of Chapter 6 as 'alterity'. Here 'interaction differential' was used as a collective variable in teacher–student talk-on-task.

We also took up the idea that language resources of individuals exist only as latent potential to engage in appropriate patterns of interaction until realized in specific discourse environments, which first appeared in Chapter 6. The challenge is for interaction, tasks and tests to be designed, planned, and managed so as to push and stretch an individual's language resources to the edge of their current potential.

The specifics of language-using action reverberate through all the connected systems in and around the language classroom, as emergent stabilized patterns reflect the conditions in which they developed: not only does language learning emerge with language-using, but what is learned depends on the conditions and nature of use. To suggest a particular ethical implication of this specificity, we return to the writings of Bakhtin (1993). For Bakhtin, ethics does not operate at a global level of the system but in the specificity of local action (Morson and Emerson 1990). Local specificity requires an ethical responsibility that is active in response to every contingency and decision:

> if ethics is real, and is located fundamentally in particular situations, then real work is *always* required. That work of judging necessarily involves a risk, a special attention to the particulars of the situation and a special involvement with unique other people at a given moment of their lives. It is precisely in such a nexus that morality, like love, lives.
> (Morson and Emerson 1990: 26)

This feels to be a satisfactory response to the issue of human agency raised in earlier chapters. Complexity theory, in connecting local and the global, keeps active what is specific about individuals and their actions. Since each action or decision has the power to affect all that it is connected to, our ethics must apply at that local level. Ethical responsibility is thereby placed on agents and actors in complex systems, as we hold that we all are, and is to be applied to all actions and decisions, in the language classroom as elsewhere.

Notes

1 Prodomou (2007) warns of the dangers of arguing from a reductive simplification—there is no reason to assume a homogeneous variety that is a lingua franca across all non-native speakers. A complexity view of ELF raise interesting questions in this regard: if, as is sometimes suggested, the patterns that emerge under certain conditions (i.e. ELF) are adopted

as content for teaching, what will result? Dynamism will continue, with no guarantee that ELF patterns would be used or learned as such; they will continue to evolve into some other set of patterns as yet unknowable. Conversely, if what is labeled ELF is indeed a set of stable and emergent patterns then they should continue to emerge if standard English continues to be taught.

2 We admit to using the term 'task' rather loosely here. It seems more appropriate than 'activity' which does not have the same sense of clear, planned goals for communication on a topic relevant to the students' physical environment.

3 In these transcriptions, pauses shorter than a second are marked as (.); longer pauses are given to the approximate length in seconds as (2.0) etc. The names of students are replaced by A, B, etc.

4 The idea of a task that stretches language resources and reveals a learner's latent potential in the second language overlaps with the Vygotskyan notion of the zone of proximal development.

5 In the UK context, 'additional language' is the form used to refer to a language other then the first.

6 The projects were aimed at investigating possible linguistically-related underachievement by these students who had been in the school system for a relatively long time.

7 The term 'error' is used to refer to forms that do not match standard written British English. The status of 'errors' within a dynamic view of language is discussed later in the section.

8 The most frequent verbs in English are 'delexicalized' (Sinclair 1991) in that they have multiple uses that constrain their meanings; also known as 'light' verbs. (See Chapter 5.)

9 The idea that the goal of learning English as an additional language is parity with native speakers is, of course, questionable, from a complexity perspective on second language development (Chapter 5) and from other perspectives (for example, Rampton 1995; Seidlhofer 2004).

8

Researching complex systems in applied linguistics[1]

In this book, we have used the term 'complex systems' to refer to systems that have different types of agents and elements which interact in different ways over time. Such systems are dynamic, open, non-linear, and adaptive. They change over time, sometimes steadily, while at other times, they change suddenly and dramatically. Through the sudden change, or phase transition, the system self-organizes, generating new, emergent, modes of behavior. As we have seen, complexity theory has been used to study naturally occurring systems, such as the weather and the rise and fall of animal populations, and it has also been more recently applied to human behavior in, for example, the disciplines of economics and epidemiology. (See Table 2.1.) While, in many ways, predator-prey interactions influencing animal populations and the spread of disease are different, they have in common dynamic properties of systems.

Understanding change in language use, language development, and language learning is central to applied linguistics, too. As we have seen throughout this book, many of the phenomena of interest to applied linguists can be seen as complex systems. For example, if we see the speech community as a complex system, then it will also have within it sociocultural groups that themselves function as complex systems; individuals within these subgroups can be seen as complex systems, as can their individual brain systems. There are complex systems 'all the way down' from the social to the neurological levels. Languages, as socio-politico-cultural constructs that are named as entities, for example, 'Spanish' or 'Arabic', can be seen as complex adaptive systems. Because applied linguists deal with complex, adaptive, dynamic systems, we believe complexity theory offers a helpful way of thinking about applied linguistic matters.

Once one decides to research a complex system, a 'complexity toolkit' (Wilson 2000) offers various concepts and empirical methods that can be used to examine the dynamics of the focal systems. Guidelines include:

- When focusing on a particular aspect of a complex system, other aspects or systems are taken as the environment in which the focal aspect or system changes. This lets the background continue to be dynamic while we focus on foreground activity.
- The 'initial conditions' of the system are very important, i.e. how the system is set up when it commences the activity we are interested in, since these conditions form the system's landscape and influence the trajectory of the system as it changes.
- Connections and relations underpin change and dynamics in the system, both among the system's components and outwards into other systems. They need to be understood in order to understand why the system behaves as it does and how further change might be instigated.
- It is important to look for
  o co-adaptation between linked systems
  o emerging patterns of stability, and variability around stability, as the various language classroom subsystems evolve and self-organize
  o points of change or transition when a system shifts from one behavior to another.
- In understanding a complex dynamic system, all possible influences on any behavior of a system need to be considered, not just the most obvious.

Turner comments on chaos/complexity theory:

> What the new science has done, in effect, is to place within our grasp a set of very powerful intellectual tools—concepts to think with. We can use them well or badly, but they are free of many of the limitations of our traditional armory. With them we can dissolve old procrustean oppositions—ordered and random, for instance—and in the process reinstate useful old ideas such as freedom. New concepts, such as emergence, become thinkable, and new methods, such as non-linear computer modelling, suggest themselves as legitimate modes of study.
> (Turner 1997: xii)

In this chapter, we first examine how these powerful concepts necessitate changes from traditional approaches to research. Then, we offer some general methodological principles for investigating issues in applied linguistics. Before concluding this chapter and this book, we make some suggestions for how to take extant methods and apply the new principles to them so that they are suitable for a new ontology. Core to all these is the dynamic nature of complex systems—change becomes the heart of what is investigated.

Changes from traditional research

Nature of explanation and prediction

A first major area of difference between a complex systems and a traditional approach to research involves how we understand and attempt to explain the phenomena that are observed—the nature of explanations and the level of explanations. In complexity theory, theory and laws work at an abstract and general level. Because many complex systems are interconnected and coordinated, it is not always possible to explain behavior, and changes in behavior, by detailing their separate components and roles in a reductive or what Clark calls 'a componential' explanation (Clark 1997: 104). To return to the analogy that we first introduced in Chapter 3, when a sand pile avalanches, we can never know which particular grain of sand will produce the avalanche that collapses the pile. What we know is that if sand keeps being added to the pile, eventually a large avalanche will occur. We also know about avalanche patterns. Because we know these things, we can articulate an explanation at a higher level, i.e. our explanation of sand pile avalanches is expressed in terms of the structure and stability of the sand pile, rather than about the behavior of individual grains of sand.

Such a perspective is antithetical to the common reductionist approach in science, which relies on a central principle that one can best understand an object of inquiry by taking it apart and examining its pieces. From a complexity theory perspective, knowing about the parts individually is insufficient because complexity theorists are interested in understanding how the interaction of the parts gives rise to new patterns of behavior. In addition, reductionist explanations can never be exhaustive or complete because the behavior of every part of the system cannot be fully known. Moreover, even if it were possible to know about the behavior of the individual parts and their interaction, the individual parts do not make a consistent contribution to interactions over time. They also do not make a proportionate contribution, contrary to what one might expect. This last point, to which we have referred several times in this book, is known as 'the butterfly effect', the notion that even a small action, such as a butterfly's flapping its wings in one part of the world, can have a large influence on meteorological conditions somewhere else. Turner (1997) states that a fundamental assumption underlying prediction is that the chain of causes is recoverable. In the case of complex systems, this cannot be assumed. The 'unknowableness' in complex systems, together with their non-linearity, which leads to discontinuity and self-organizing change, make them unpredictable in the conventional sense of predictability.

Systems and behavior can, of course, be described retrospectively, once change has happened, and doing so is the central work of a complexity approach, which we illustrated with language development data in Chapter 5, language use data in Chapter 6, and classroom data in Chapter 7.[2] What we can observe is what has already changed—the trajectory of the system. This is a 'trace' of the real system, from which we try to reconstruct the elements, interactions and change processes of the system (Byrne 2002). Such a process is retrodiction (or retrocasting), rather than prediction (or forecasting), explaining the next state by the preceding one.

In conventional reductionist science, explanation produces prediction in the form of testable hypotheses. In complex systems approaches, once a system has changed or evolved, the process can be described and then explained through an appeal to such notions as self-organization, but new predictions are not necessarily a consequence. Of course, we may have expectations of how a process will unfold, or even of its outcomes, based on prior experience, but we cannot tell exactly what will happen (Stewart 1989). Essentially, adopting a complex systems perspective brings about a separation of explanation and prediction.

Of course, because the future is unknowable, it does not follow that there is no continuity from the past. 'Some continuities will be sufficiently robust that contingencies will not deflect them ...' (Gaddis 2002: 56). For example, gravity will continue to operate to keep us on the ground. However, when it comes to actions that people take, when consciousness itself is at issue, forecasting is a highly risky business.

Causality

Closely related is the matter of causality. In the traditional approach to research, a key type of scientific explanation is that 'Cause X produces outcome Y'. The researcher searches for a critical 'element whose removal from a causal chain would alter the outcome' (Gaddis 2002: 54) and that can thus be said to be the cause of the outcome. To suggest that an event may have had many antecedents or causes is not considered doing good research. Gaddis quotes a recent guide to social science research to illustrate how this traditional view of causality translates into methodology:

> A successful project is one that explains a lot with a little. At best, the goal is to use a single, explanatory variable to explain numerous observations on dependent variables.
>
> Reductionism implies, therefore, that there are indeed independent variables, and that we can know what they are.
> (Gaddis 2002: 55)

Viewing the research foci of applied linguistics as complex systems would encourage us, at least, to question this approach to causality.[3] The unknow-ableness and interconnectedness of systems makes it much more difficult, if not impossible, to isolate independent variables that act in causal ways.

Since agents and elements in complex systems are interconnected, it is highly unlikely that a single cause will give rise to a complex event. The grain of sand may trigger an avalanche, but it does not on its own cause it. Rather, there are likely multiple and interconnected causes underlying any shift or outcome.

> We may rank their relative significance, but we'd think it irresponsible to seek to isolate—or 'tease out'—single causes for complex events.
> (Gaddis 2002: 65)

In fact, some would go even farther. Byrne (2002) argues that social scientists' adoption of 'variable centered analysis', in which some variables are held to work as causative or determining forces, is ill-advised. He urges: 'death to the variable', and then continues:

> ... let us understand clearly, once and for all, that variables don't exist. They are not real. What exists are complex systems, which systems are nested, intersecting, which involve both the social and the natural, and which are subject to modification on the basis of human action, both individual and social.
> (Byrne 2002: 31)

While dealing a death blow to variables might be more extreme than some applied linguistics researchers would like, there is no doubt that complex systems types of explanation, which do not allow prediction in the traditional sense, differ from what we are used to. The construct of a collective variable, however, can be helpful. Collective variables are 'actions and responses that index the cooperativity of a multidimensional system' (Thelen and Smith 1994: 99). They describe dynamic patterns, of varying and changing stabilities. The mutual phasing of gaze direction during social interactions is one example. Instead of investigating single variables, we study changes in systems that include self-organization and emergence. Emergent properties or phenomena occur when change on one level or timescale of a system leads to a new mode on another level or timescale. For example, when a new lexical item is first used by individuals and then, through iteration and adaptation, it later becomes established in the language—as with 'emotional baggage', a metaphorical phrase referring to long-term issues that are still active in a person's mind. This phrase has emerged fairly recently in English, influenced by social changes and language uses (Cameron and Deignan 2006). This particular phrase cannot have been predicted to arise, using the usual definition of prediction; nevertheless, the genealogy of such phrases can be studied and their origin sometimes explained in retrospect. We can offer reasons that a particular phenomenon has risen, but not necessarily causes that predict it.

One type of causality that is operable in complexity theory we have labeled 'co-adaptation'. Co-adaptation describes a kind of mutual causality, in which change in one system leads to change in another system connected to it, and this mutual influencing continues over time. For example, a native speaker may adjust pronunciation, speed, and lexicogrammar when speaking with a non-native speaker, and the non-native speaker may adjust in response as the language she or he is hearing becomes easier to process. As we saw in Chapter 5, co-adaptation between an infant and an 'other' (who would in the early stages be its caregiver) occurs routinely in first language development. As a child and its caregiver interact, the language resources of each are dynamically altered, as each adapts to the other. Then, too, we saw in Chapter 7 that in classrooms, teachers and students continually co-adapt—to establish routines or in the explanations of new constructions or the initiation of an activity. From co-adaptation of the teacher and student complex systems, emerges the joint behavior of the system that we might call 'the lesson'. Similarly, moving down one level, within the student as an individual, co-adaptation of multiple subsystems leads to the emergence of a language skill such as reading.

Van Geert and Steenbeek (in press) describe a particular type of co-adaptation when they appeal to the notion of 'superposition', in which a phenomenon is characterized by two (apparently) incompatible properties at the same time. Their example is the construct of intelligence, which is, they argue, 'at the same time (almost) completely determined by the environment and (almost) completely determined by genes' (ibid.: 5). This apparent paradox is resolved once it is seen that 'genes and environment are locked in a complex chain of steps over time and that they cannot be conceived of as variables that make mutually independent contributions to development' (ibid.: 5).

Van Geert and Steenbeek also adopt the idea of mutual or reciprocal relationships in modeling first language development. Development is seen as

> a web of interacting components that entertain supportive, competitive and conditional relationships. The relationships are reciprocal but not necessarily symmetrical. For instance, it is likely that an earlier linguistic strategy bears a supportive relationship to a later, more complex linguistic strategy. The latter, however, may have a competitive relationship with its predecessor … . By modelling such webs of reciprocal action, it is possible to understand the emergence of stages, temporary regressions, inverse U-shaped growth and so forth.
> (ibid.: 9)

Foreground and background

We have made the point several times in this book that claims for the whole system cannot be made by examining one part of it because its subsystems or components are interconnected. It does not follow, however, that every subsystem or component part will have an equal impact on another. Thus, saying that subsystems are interconnected should not lead to a paralyzing holism in which nothing gets done because one cannot figure out how to take in the whole from one vantage point. The Gaia hypothesis (see Chapter 2) would have us believe everything in the universe is interconnected. If we accept this in principle, it does not mean that we cannot investigate the structure of a conversation between two interlocutors without consulting a star chart or what is happening with the stock market that day. As was said in the first bulleted point above, one can—indeed, one needs to—foreground a focal point, while allowing the background to continue on its dynamic trajectory. However, there are three caveats to choosing a focus. First, as we have just said, claims about the whole system cannot be made from examining a subsystem. Second, we need always to be open to looking for explanations from outside the focus, such as we did in Chapter 4 in trying to understand why language has evolved in the way it has. After all, it is possible that if the interlocutors are heavily invested in the stock market, and the stock market is behaving chaotically that day, and the interlocutors are aware of it, that such behavior might influence the conversation, even if the topic of the stock market is never broached. We cannot know this a priori, of course, but as we have said, we need to remain open to seeking explanations for observations from outside of the focal subsystem. Third, what is determined to be focal needs to be thoughtfully considered and justified.

In Chapter 5 we noted that where one draws the line around a focal area is crucial. It is important to determine the ecological circuit in which one is interested. We have already stated that for us we would not wish to draw the line between an embodied mind and context because as we have said, we do not believe that one can understand one without the other. As in biology:

> we cannot escape from the dialectical relation between parts and wholes. Before we can recognize meaningful parts we must define the functional whole of which they are the constituents. We will then recognize quite different ways of breaking up the organism depending on what we are trying to explain. The hand is the appropriate unit for investigation if we are concerned with the physical act of holding, but the hand and eye together are an irreducible unit for understanding how we come to seize the object that is held.
> (Lewontin 1998: 81–2)

Generalizability

Because where we draw the line is so critical, it may be helpful to think of causation as contingent, rather than categorical (Gaddis 2002). Any causal statement must have a number of qualifications. In other words, as we saw in Chapter 7, we should think in terms of 'particular generalizations', not universal ones. We might acknowledge tendencies or patterns, but resist claiming applicability for our applied linguistics findings beyond specific times and places. The teacher's reply to a question about whether a particular teaching technique is effective, i.e. 'It all depends ...' is particularly apt in illustrating this point. For the success of a given technique does depend: it depends on the characteristics and goals of the particular individuals who comprise the class; it depends on the school and community in which the class is situated; it depends on the day of the week that the technique is used, even on the time of the day, etc. If one thinks in terms of reality as a web, then everything is connected in some way to everything else (Gaddis 2002: 64).

> The social sciences have too often dealt with this problem by denying its existence. They've operated from the conviction that consciousness and the behaviour that results from it are subject, at least in general terms, to the workings of rules—if not laws—whose existence we can detect and

whose effects we can describe. Once we've done this, or so many social
scientists over many years have assumed, we'll then be able to accomplish
in the realm of human affairs at least some of the tasks of explanation and
forecasting that the natural sciences routinely perform.
(Gaddis 2002: 56)

The hope of doing so, though, rests on spurious assumptions concerning
human behavior: that it is always rational, that decisions are always based
on accurate information, that human behavior is immune to cultural and
individual differences, and that it does not change. None of these is true.
Instead, Byrne takes 'a localist' perspective, which recognizes that:

> knowledge is inherently contextual and that a crucial component of the
> specification of any item or system of things and relations known is the
> delimitation of the spatial and temporal boundaries within which that
> knowledge might hold.
> (Byrne 2002: 163)

Sealey and Carter contrast Byrne's localism with claims made in second
language acquisition.

> The characteristics of motivation have been discussed as a 'learner trait'
> or with reference to 'situated language identity theory' …; researchers
> debate how accurately different sub-components of motivation have been
> identified, how to distinguish between goals, motives, and orientations,
> and so on.
>   [For instance, researchers from one study] conclude that 'orientations
> explained 41 per cent of the variance in motivation'… The study has
> many of the characteristics of the traditional approach to SLA research,
> including the identification of variables, the quantification of their relative
> weightings, and a quest for some generalisable findings about the nature
> of motivation in SLA.
> (Sealey and Carter 2004: 195)

However, Ellis and Larsen-Freeman (2006) have pointed out that it is rarely
the case that researchers get correlations that exceed 0.40, which explain
just 16 per cent of the variance, in any case. This is because there is no single
cause that explains a particular phenomenon. Each variable is but a small
part of a complex picture of many interacting sources. Multivariate analyses
can raise the percentage of variance that is accounted for, of course, but even
so, a great deal is left unexplained. This is not to say that the findings in
one context in one study cannot be relevant to another, but saying they are
relevant is not claiming some cause will produce the same effect. Rather, it is
saying that what generalizes from one context to another is the need to look at
dynamic interactions and the possibility of connected emergent outcomes. In
other words, what generalizes are the mechanisms and dynamics of complex
systems.

Replicability

One of the ways that scientists establish the validity of their claims is through replicability. If they or another team of researchers repeat an experiment and obtain the same results, the original results are deemed valid. By now it should be clear that the position of complexity theorists, especially those preoccupied with the study of human behavior, is that there can be no absolute replicability—the initial conditions are always different. Of course, there are sciences that rely on virtual rather than actual replicability as a means of verification. For instance, hypotheses like Darwinian natural selection emphasize relationships among many variables, some of them continuous, others contingent. Both regularity (genetic inheritance) and randomness (mutations) co-exist in such hypotheses. While natural selection does not yield predictions that can be tested and results that can be replicated, such hypotheses do explain, and generate consensus (also controversy, mostly from non-scientists) as to their validity. Perhaps these hypotheses that explain and generate consensus are what we should be seeking as complexity theorists. Thus, validity does not come about through obtaining replicable results, but rather, taking a cue from qualitative researchers, from the trustworthiness of our accounts, their adequacy in including data on all relevant systems, subsystems, agents, elements and in describing the relations among them and that the explanations used to account for them (in words or in mathematical functions) are compatible with a complexity approach. (For more on validity of mathematical modeling, see below.)

In short, in the classical scientific paradigm, theories are developed in order to describe, explain, and predict the real world. Hypotheses are tested empirically, and studies are replicated in order to prove or disprove theories. But in a complex world, much of this changes: we abandon the goal of predictability; the nature of explanation changes; cause and effect work differently; reductionism no longer operates effectively to explain the emergent and self-organizing systems. Instead of static laws and rules that social scientists and applied linguists have, following the natural sciences, traditionally sought to uncover, we are faced with tendencies, patterns, and contingencies. Instead of single causal variables, we have interconnecting and self-organizing systems that co-adapt and that may display sudden discontinuities and the emergence of new modes and behaviors. A good application of complexity theory describes the system, its constituents, their contingencies, and also their interactions. Teasing out the (local) relationships and explaining their dynamics are key tasks of the researcher working from a complex systems perspective.

Data and evidence

A complexity view of language and language development has implications for research methodology beyond the nature of explanations, predictions, causality, generalizability, and replicability. Adopting a complexity perspective shifts our view of what is seen to be in need of empirical investigation, in particular the role of stability and variability, the context and the environment, and timescales and levels. It changes what we notice in the behavior of systems: flux and variability signal possible processes of self-organization and emergence; sudden phase shifts signal important changes and can direct attention to the conditions that lead up to them.

Stability and variability

Even when a complex system is in a stable mode or attractor, it is still continually changing as a result of change in its constituent elements or agents and change in how they interact, and in response to change in other systems to which it is connected. A complex system will show degrees of variability around stabilities, and the interplay of stability and variability offers potentially useful information about change in the system. From this perspective, variability in data is not noise to be discarded when averaging across events or individuals, or the result of measurement error (van Geert and van Dijk 2002), but is part of the behavior of the system, to be expected around stabilities, and particularly at times of transition from one phase or mode of behavior to another. Changes in variability can be indicators of development. If we smooth away variability, by averaging for example, we lose the very information that may shed light on emergence (Larsen-Freeman 2006b). If, instead, we pay attention to the nature of changes in stability and variability, we may find new ways of understanding language learning or development processes. For example, Fischer and Bidell question the static notion of stage structure in relation to cognitive development. They call for research that investigates the wide-ranging variability within and across individuals. And they ask, 'Why have there been so few efforts to account for systematic variability in developmental patterns?' (Fischer and Bidell 1998: 470). We might ask the same question about the systematic variability of language development as some second language acquisition researchers are already doing. (See Chapter 5.)

Variability and its relations with stability in a complexity approach can be measured in two ways. First, the degree of variability around the mean serves as 'an index of the strength of the behavioral attractor' (Thelen and Smith 1994: 86–7). If variability increases, with concurrent loss of stability, the system may be about to enter a transition to a new mode. A second measure uses the outcome of perturbing, or pushing, the system away from its stable behavior. The more stable the system is, the more likely it is to return to its customary attractor following the perturbation. A less stable system is more likely to shift into a different behavior. Around times of transition, the system will be more easily perturbed when pushed out of its path (ibid.). Lack of stability in knowledge or performance may suggest something interesting happening in the developing language use system. Investigation of variability occurs in dynamic modeling (see below) and can indicate potentially fruitful points in longitudinal data for in-depth investigation.

The changed nature of context

From a complexity perspective, context includes the physical, social, cognitive, and cultural, and is not separable from the system. Context cannot, for example, be seen as a frame surrounding the system that is needed to interpret its behavior (Goffman 1974). The connection between system and context is shown by making contextual factors parameters or dimensions of the system. Complex systems are often sensitive to changes in context and adapt dynamically to them in a process of 'soft assembly'. For example, as we have suggested, the children observed learning to reach and grasp by Thelen (Thelen and Smith 1994) adapted their movement dynamically to the local conditions of each task, such as the slope of the surface or the distance at which an object was placed. Furthermore, these local adaptations to contextual conditions are the foundation for emergent change, i.e. development, on a longer timescale. From repeated adaptive experiences in the 'here-and-now' of context, attractors emerge in the system that represent a more 'global order', i.e. at a higher level of motor, cognitive, or social organization or longer timescale.

In our applied linguistics context, any use of language can be seen as the soft assembly of language resources in response to some language-using activity. Use of language need not be verbal production but would include any activity, inside or outside the classroom, that involves mental activity around language: understanding, speaking, recall of language, practicing, and so on. Language learning or development emerges over time with these adaptive experiences of language use.

The context of a language learning or language-using activity includes: the intrinsic dynamics of the learner, i.e. what individuals bring to the activity, for example, their cognitive context, (for example, working memory); the cultural context (for example, what roles teacher and students play in this culture); the social context, including relationships with other learners and the teacher; the physical environment; the pedagogical context, i.e. the task or materials, the socio-political environment, among others. Many of these 'contextual conditions' will also be complex, dynamic, adaptive systems. The students in action will soft assemble their language and other resources in response to these contextual conditions, and the teacher and other students (to the extent that they can) will adapt in response to the students' actions. We thus cannot separate the learner or the learning from context in order to measure or explain it. Rather we must collect data about and describe all the continually changing system(s) involved. 'While it is unrealistic to aim to record all of these non-linguistic variables all of the time, it is possible to keep constantly alert to the significant changes that they both signal and codetermine in the discourse situation' (Leather and van Dam 2003: 19). In holding learner and context as inseparable, a complex systems perspective makes a similar argument to sociocultural (for example, Lantolf 2006b) and ecological approaches (for example, van Lier 2004), but perhaps emphasizes a different facet, seeing learner and a complex context as interacting, co-adaptive dynamic systems.

The complexity perspective also puts a slightly different slant on the claim that learning, as change, is at once individual and social. On the one hand, each individual is unique because he or she has developed his or her physical, affective, and cognitive self from a different starting point and through differing experience and history. Each individual thus acts as a unique learning context, bringing a different set of systems to a learning event, responding differently to it and therefore learning differently as a result of participating in it. In averaging across individuals, we lose detailed information about how those systems change in response to changes in context. At the same time, when an individual participates in a group, the group as a system both affects and is affected by the individual. So to understand language learning processes, we need to collect data about individuals (as well as about groups), and about individuals as members of groups as well as working alone. When researching groups, we need to see them as interconnecting systems of individuals. As van Geert and Steenbeek say:

> Although it is statistically possible to separate context- and person-aspects, such separation requires the assumption of independence of persons and contexts. This assumption is untenable under a dynamic interpretation of performance. On a short timescale, context affordances and person abilities result from the real-time interaction between the two and are, therefore, inherently dependent on one another. On a longer timescale, persons tend to actively select and manipulate the contexts in which they function, whereas contexts on their turn help shape the person's characteristics and abilities.
> (van Geert and Steenbeek in press: 12)

Nested levels and timescales

One other special consideration must be made with regard to the study of language and its development from a complex systems perspective, and that is the matter of nested levels and timescales. Human and social organization can be seen in terms of systems operating at various levels of granularity, from macro-level to micro-level; for example, from ecosystem to subatomic particles. The various systems operate at different levels but are interconnected or 'nested' one within another (Bronfenbrenner 1989). When attempting to explain the behavior of the system, each of these levels may contribute. In this example, cited in Sealey and Carter (2004), the spread of tuberculosis is explained through invoking four nested, interacting levels:

In accounting for who gets TB and in what contexts, Byrne argues, we must first acknowledge a biological aetiology (people must be exposed to the bacillus) and a genetic component (some people will have a natural resistance to the bacillus). However, whether particular individuals contract the disease or not will be socially contingent, since it will depend on the interaction between these features and other levels of the social world. Byrne identifies four such levels—the individual, the household, the community and the nation-state—existing in a nested hierarchy.
(Sealey and Carter 2004: 198)

As well as nested levels, the complex systems researched by applied linguists operate on a range of timescales, from the milliseconds of neural processing through the minutes of a classroom activity to change on an evolutionary timescale. For a particular study, certain levels and scales will be focal, but be affected by what happens on other levels and scales. Then, too, it must be borne in mind that

... certain events widely separated in linear time may be more relevant to meaningful behaviour now than other events which are closer in linear time.
(Lemke 2002: 80)

Since activity on one level and scale influences what happens at other levels and scales, with phenomena sometimes emerging at a particular level or scale as a result of activity at a lower level or earlier period, it is important when we are conducting research within a complex systems approach that we seek to find relationships within and across different levels and timescales. When we are able to do so, the results will be all the more powerful.

To summarize thus far, in complexity theory we search for ways to access the relational nature of phenomena, which is not the same as the pursuit of an exhaustive taxonomy of factors that might account for behavior of any given phenomenon. Further, we attempt to distinguish between contingent and necessary outcomes. Thus, the nature of explanation changes, cause and effect no longer operate in the usual way, and reductionism does not produce satisfying explanations that are respectful of the interconnectedness of the many nested levels and timescales that exist.

Methodological principles for researching language and language development

From this complex systems perspective, certain methodological principles follow:

1 Be ecologically valid, including context as part of the system(s) under investigation.

2 Honor the complexity by avoiding reductionism. Avoid premature idealization by including any conceivable factors that might influence a system. Always be open to considering others.

3 Think in terms of dynamic processes and changing relationships among variables. Consider self-organization, feedback, and emergence as central.

4 Take a complexity view of reciprocal relationships, rather than invoking simple, proximate cause-effect links.

5 Overcome dualistic thinking for example, acquisition versus use or performance versus competence. Think in terms of co-adaptation, soft assembly, etc.

6 Rethink units of analysis, identifying 'collective variables' or those that characterize the interaction among multiple elements in a system, or among multiple systems, over time.

7 Avoid conflating levels and timescales, yet seek linkages across levels and timescales. Include thinking heterochronically.

8 Consider variability as central. Investigate both stability and variability to understand the developing system.

Modified research methodologies

We now move to consider practical implications for the empirical investigation of language development, such as measuring the effectiveness of pedagogic interventions or tracking stabilities and variation in learner language. When enacted, some of the methodological principles above will no doubt lead to innovations of which we are currently unaware. Some methods, however, are already in existence with designs that make them useful for investigating complex systems. Others will need some modification.

Ethnography

In many ways, qualitative research methods, such as ethnography, would appear to serve the understanding of language as a complex dynamic system well, in that they 'attempt to honor the profound wholeness and situatedness of social scenes and individuals-in-the-world' (Atkinson 2002: 539), by studying real people in their human contexts and interactions, rather than aggregating and averaging across individuals as happens in experimental and quantitative studies. Atkinson cites as examples of applicable ethnographic methods the work of Davis and Lazaraton (1995), Holliday (1996), and Ramanathan and Atkinson (1999).

Agar goes further, arguing that ethnography is itself a complex adaptive system, that evolves and adapts as the researcher uses it:

> (it) will lead you to ways of learning and documenting that you had no idea existed when you first started the study. You will learn how to ask the right question of the right people in the right way using knowledge you

didn't know existed. You will see that certain kinds of data belong together in ways that you would never have imagined until you'd worked on the study for a while ... methods 'evolve' as local information about how to do a study accumulates. Ethnography does this. Traditional research prohibits it.
(Agar 2004: 19)

Importantly, ethnographers seek emergent patterns in what they study. Agar suggests that ethnography is a fractal-generating process. What ethnographers are looking for are processes that apply iteratively and recursively at different levels to create patterns, variations which emerge from adaptation to contingencies and environment.

One possible modification of ethnographic method, from a complexity theory perspective, however, is the assumption that applied effectively ethnography can produce objectivity. From our perspective, no matter how a researcher tries, total objectivity—a view of matters apart from who he or she is—can never be achieved. A complex system is dependent on its initial conditions, and this includes the researcher. Accounts of the 'same' phenomenon will differ when produced by different ethnographers (Agar 2004). This is not a problem, just a fact.

Formative experiments

Conventional experiments are problematic from a complexity theory perspective because of their ecological invalidity. Further, they can only, at best, lead to claims about proximate, linear causes, while not allowing for multiple or reciprocally interacting factors, which change over time. While we would not wish to discount experimental claims, we do need to problematize them in light of the fact that any cause and effect link that is 'found' might actually occlude fundamental non-linearity (Larsen-Freeman 1997).

Who can say, for example, on the basis of a pre-test/post-test design that a particular experimental treatment works or does not work? If the results are non-significant, the effects of the treatment may not yet be manifest; if the results are significant, they may have followed from an experience prior to the pre-test. A further limitation of conventional experiments occurs when researchers attempt to control context and situation, rather than investigating adaptation to the unique particularities of context:

They try to ensure that an intervention is implemented uniformly despite different circumstances; and they focus on post intervention outcomes instead of what happens while the intervention is implemented.
(Reinking and Watkins 2000: 384)

Qualitative and ethnographic studies, which carefully document instructional practices, are the means traditionally looked to for offsetting these limitations. However, Reinking and Watkins claim that these studies sometimes fail to tease out factors that affect success or failure in educational interventions, and to then explore how interventions might be adapted in response to those factors in order to be more effectively implemented.

A different type of experiment, called a 'formative experiment' (Jacob 1992 in Reinking and Watkins 2000), focuses on the dynamics of implementation, using the ideas of soft assembly and co-adaptation, and might thus be capable of overcoming these limitations. Using Newman's words, they define it as follows:

> In a formative experiment, the researcher sets a pedagogical goal and finds out what it takes in terms of materials, organization, or changes in the intervention in order to reach the goal.
> (Newman 1990, in Reinking and Watkins 2000: 388)

This (neo-)Vygotskian idea appears to be compatible with a complex systems perspective. Formative experiments attempt to investigate the potential of a system rather than its state; it accepts that change in one system can produce change in other connected systems, attempts to describe the interconnected web of factors influencing change, and investigates processes of co-adaptation in response to changed pedagogic goals.

Design experiments and action research

Another research method that has some characteristics compatible with a complexity approach is what has been called design-based research or a design experiment. Barab (2006) explains that in learning environments, it is difficult to test the causal impact of particular variables with experimental designs. Design-based research 'deals with complexity by iteratively changing the learning environment over time—collecting evidence of the effect of these variations and feeding it recursively into future design' (Barab 2006: 155).

Lobato (2003) discusses how design experiments differ from traditional experiments in that the focus of investigation is shifted from the products or outcomes of learning to learning processes. Teachers are encouraged to respond flexibly to what is taking place in the classroom, as they might ordinarily do, not to follow some experimental treatment protocol. In this way, a design experiment shifts 'from a reductionist cognitive view of learning to one that is also social in nature' (Lobato 2003: 19) and one that seeks to retrodict, rather than predict (Larsen-Freeman 2007c).

Better known, perhaps, is action research. Although often motivated for socio-political reasons (Kemmis 2001), action research is also concerned with possibility rather than prediction, and with the study of systems. Researchers, who may be practitioners rather than outside experimenters, deliberately introduce 'noise' into the system to see what transpires. They choose a problem in their teaching to study and apply the Lewinian cycle of diagnosing/action planning/action taking/evaluating/specifying learning (Baskerville and Wood-

Harper 1996). Action research takes place in the system environment and investigation of the system's response to a perturbation contributes to a deeper understanding of the system dynamics.

Longitudinal, case-study, time-series approaches

Another research methodology that might be useful, when modified for complex system purposes, is a longitudinal, case-study, time-series approach, which enables connections to be made across levels and timescales. In contrast, interlanguage studies often tend to be cross-sectional, denying us a portrait of individual growth and variability.

It is not sufficient to simply lengthen the amount of time that behavior is sampled. There is a need to identify appropriate timescales on which data are collected—does the change show itself over a period of days, or months, or does it take a lifetime (Ortega and Iberri-Shea 2005)? There is also a need to select appropriate sampling intervals, which will depend on the rate of change. Willett (1994) suggests that a researcher

> must assemble an observed growth record for each person in the dataset. If the attribute of interest is changing steadily and smoothly over a long period of time, perhaps three or four widely spaced measurements on each person will be sufficient to capture the shape and direction of the change. But, if the trajectory of individual change is more complex, then many more closely spaced measurements may be required.
> (Willett 1994: 674)

In addition, to be true to a complex systems approach, any longitudinal study must be set up to capture variability at various levels and timescales, from the general shape of the development process over a long period of time to the short-term variability that takes place between data-collection intervals, to the within-session variability that inevitably arises. Van Geert and van Dijk argue that a study should attend to all timescales since variability may be different on each scale: for example, '... a developmental variable may be slowly oscillating while gradually growing, while another variable may increase discontinuously with sharp day-to-day fluctuations' (2002: 346).

Capturing variability is made easier by the powerful computational tools now available. Van Geert and van Dijk (2002) show how we can use computerized databases, graphing, and statistics to track complex patterns of variation in second language learners over time. Cameron and Stelma (2004) show how cumulative frequency graphs and other types of visual data displays can assist analysis of the dynamics of discourse. Techniques, statistical and otherwise, used in analysis need to be suitable for genuinely longitudinal data rather than cross-sectional comparisons. We need to adopt and develop more appropriate ways of analysis to allow for the non-linearity of the process, such as multivariate time-series modeling, growth curve analysis or latent factor modeling (Nick Ellis, personal communication).

Methods of analysis of variability in dynamics systems, compiled by van Geert and van Dijk (2002), include: 'moving min-max' graphs, which, by plotting moving minima, maxima, and averages, show the data using the bandwidth of observed scores; graphs of score ranges show the change in the range width which might reflect various kinds of developmental phenomena; and standard deviations and coefficients of variation.

We would need to employ these and other innovative ways to deal with variability because as Sealy and Carter say:

> ... case-driven' does not equate with 'idiosyncratic', and 'complexity' does not equate with 'randomness'. We would expect studies of many different kinds to illustrate similar kinds of relations between contexts, mechanisms, and outcomes.
> (Sealey and Carter 2004: 210)

Microdevelopment

One approach to the study of change in behavior over a relative short time-scale is microdevelopment. It has become increasingly clear that in order to study 'motors of change' (Thelen and Corbetta 2002: 59) what are needed are not only longitudinal corpora, but also dense corpora that involve highly intensive sampling over short periods of time. Thelen and Corbetta suggest that the data which such an approach yield will not only allow us to fix the 'when' of developmental milestones, but, importantly, the 'how' of development by making development more transparent.

Thelen and Corbetta (2002) observe that in traditional research, change is often inferred from an endpoint measurement. Conversely, an assumption of researchers using a microdevelopment approach is that there are moments in the evolution of behavior where we can directly observe change happening. Furthermore, since change works at multiple timescales, these small-scale changes can illuminate change at a longer timescale. Also a problem with traditional approaches is that children (or adults) can use multiple routes to the same outcome; however, the routes may be equally, or more interesting than the endpoint, per se. Microdevelopment allows us to capture important developmental differences among learners, both children and adults.

Finally, a microdevelopmental approach assumes that the system—at least at times—is open to influences from the environment such that we can manipulate certain variables and see effects. For this reason, often micro-development is accompanied by microgenesis experiments, where the researcher deliberately facilitates (or even retards) the discovery of new ways within one or several experimental sessions through coaching, training, practice, or scaffolding support.

Computer modeling

Computer simulations or models offer an important approach to researching complex dynamic systems. Although still in its infancy, modeling in applied linguistics shows great promise. This approach builds a computer model of the real-world complex system under investigation and takes it through multiple iterations, replicating change over time. The model is designed and adjusted so that the outcomes over time reflect what is known of the real-world system. Further iterations or changes in parameters then allow the researcher to explore how the model system responds to changes in conditions. In a further step, the processes of development seen in the model are examined and may be hypothesized as representing change in the actual system.

Turner (1997: xxv–xxvi) contrasts the modeling process with conventional approaches to research. He points out that we have had models before:

> But such models have until now been fixed and inflexible, and based as they are on a linear conception of cause and consequence, they are confirmed or deconfirmed in an all-or-nothing way … .
>
> But now we have the technology—the computer, capable of endless, fast, accurate iterations of operations involving many mutually dependent elements—but also some of the theoretical machinery of fractal math and chaos science that are needed to transform modeling from a necessary nuisance into a fully fledged part of science.

The beauty of computer models is that instead of

> creating a hypothesis, testing it on the experimental and observational facts until a counterexample shows its flaws, and then trying another, we can create an accurate facsimile of reality by successive tweakings of the variables and the connections among them, run the model in a computer as long as we like, check that its behavior continues to resemble that of the reality, and then read off what those parameters are. This procedure reverses the top-down theory-to-phenomena approach of classical science, and thus can provide an admirable complement to it.
> (Turner 1997: xxv–xxvi)

The activity of building a model is an important part of the research process, since it requires explicit statements of theory and the most accurate empirical knowledge about the real systems and processes being modeled. As a result, the model is only as good as the assumptions built into it. Inevitably, the model differs from the actual system, being idealized or simplified in some respects, approximated in others. This raises new issues for applied linguistics around the validity and robustness of computer models of language development.

The two main types of models currently in use are neural network (or connectionist) models and agent-based models. Neural network models can replicate the learning of an individual brain and the emergence (or learning) of categories through self-organization. From very simple rules and initial conditions, the models can produce outcomes that closely resemble human learning and development in areas including vocabulary learning (Meara 2004, 2006), morphological learning (Rumelhart and McClelland 1986), and the emergence of syntax from lexical learning (Elman 1995). A major limitation of neural network models is their representation of the individual learner as isolated and as only cognitive, rather than as also an affective and social being. They also work with discrete change, whereas mental processes are continuous (Spivey 2007).

Computer platforms, such as SWARM, enable researchers to construct detailed, robust agent-based models, involving a population of embodied computer agents who engage in scripted interactions situated in a specific open-ended environment, and thus simulate the global consequences of local interactions. These agent-based models have helped to advance our understanding of the evolution of language in social groups (Ke and Holland 2006), of the development of creoles (Satterfield 2001), self-organizing vocabularies (Steels 1996), and the acquisition of language from complex, situated input (Marocco, Cangelosi, and Nolfi 2003).

The validity of a simulation model is checked by comparing the outcomes produced by the model with the outcomes of the real-world human system. If the model reflects the real-world behavior, it is said to be 'valid'. Gilbert and Troitzsch (2005) set out some of the issues around model validity. These include: the uncertainty introduced by the stochastic nature of processes in both real-world and model systems; the 'path-dependence' of simulations, i.e. the sensitivity of a model to its initial conditions; the possibility that the simplification involved in model construction leads to its being incomplete in some important way; and the possibility that the real-world data used to build the model were themselves incorrect or based on incorrect assumptions. This last may be particularly important for our field, since empirical data about language learning that we may need to build into the model may have been collected and analyzed under theoretical assumptions that differ greatly from those of the complex systems perspective.

Choices are made at each step in the building of a simulation model, from choosing and describing the real-world system to be modeled, through programming the rules for interaction among the agents in the model, to adjusting the parameters of the model and interpreting outcomes. Each choice can affect the model's validity and needs to be scrutinized and justified. Theoretical assumptions built into the model should be clearly stated in published papers so that readers can evaluate this aspect of validity.

The further step, of inferring back from the model to the real world about the processes of development, raises issues beyond what we might call 'outcome validity', as described above. Similar outcomes may be produced by computer models and human systems through very different processes. For example, neural network models have an internal structure very different from a human learning system, and similarity of outcomes would not justify claiming similarity of internal processes. 'Process validity' in simulation modeling is a more difficult construct than outcome validity. Inspecting the processes of simulation models may lead to areas worth investigating back in the real-world system, but claims of similarity should be treated with caution. How we label and talk about processes and parts of simulation models also needs to be done with care to avoid unwarranted or premature theoretical inferences: for example, van Geert's (forthcoming) choice of the term 'generators' to describe processes established through model building prompts resonances with a specific theory of language development that might lead researchers' thinking in particular directions, whereas a more neutral term might be less constraining.

As will have been apparent from the discussion above of validity, both simulation and neural network modeling are essentially metaphorical ways of understanding complex systems involving partial mappings between domains; to be valid, the outcomes of the model and the system being modeled must map on to each other although the internal processes may not. The technical detail of computer models and the high level of skills needed to develop them do not exempt them from the risks inherent in any metaphorical construction set out in Chapter 1 and revisited below.

Simulation modeling of complex dynamic systems is clearly going to be very important for applied linguistics. Validity issues need careful attention and, because the methodology and technology are still unfamiliar and difficult for many researchers, the onus of validation will inevitably fall on the modelers themselves. Then, too, language classroom systems will challenge modelers, both in finding valid ways to reduce their complexity to mathematical descriptions and in accounting for the human aspect of the systems. Even if a computer simulation does not materialize, the process of constructing a model can be very fruitful because it pushes the modeler to make decisions about the nature of the systems and connections involved and about which explanatory theories to use to describe them.

Brain imaging

Technological advances in brain imaging, including improvements in the temporal and spatial resolution of electro-encephalographic (EEG) and functional Magnetic Resonance Images (fMRI) are allowing detailed descriptions of the dynamics of brain activity, promoting a shift of emphasis from knowledge as static representation stored in particular locations to knowledge as processing involving the dynamic mutual influence of inter-related types of information as they activate and inhibit each other over time (Nick Ellis, personal communication). Brain imaging may contribute a useful tool to researching microdevelopment, although currently it is an expensive resource, often difficult for researchers to access.

Combining methodologies

Combinations or blends of methodologies (Mason 2002) would seem to be particularly appropriate to the study of complex systems, allowing different levels and timescales to be investigated. We outline three possibilities.

Discourse analysis and corpus linguistics

Large corpora of language use give us access to stabilized patterns and variability around them. While acknowledging that a corpus is a static collection of attested language and cannot show the dynamics of language as it unfolds in use nor its future potential (Larsen-Freeman 2006a), a corpus can serve to some extent as representative of the language resources of members of the speech community where it was collected. We can then combine corpus linguistics with close analysis of actual discourse, to trace the genesis and dynamics of language patterns, such as the conventionalization and signaling of metaphors (Cameron and Deignan 2003, 2006).

Second language acquisition and corpus linguistics

The field of SLA needs to make more use of computer-searchable longitudinal corpora for addressing theoretical issues. Rutherford and Thomas (2001) and Myles (2005) advocate the use of CHILDES tools for second language acquisition (SLA) research. Mellow (2006) illustrates the impact of large new computerized corpora such as CHILDES and TalkBank (MacWhinney, Bird, Cieri, and Martell 2004) on theories of second language learning. A corpus of adult ESL learners in a classroom setting is also a powerful aid in helping us to better understand adult language learning (Reder, Harris, and Setzler 2003).

Second language acquisition and conversation analysis

Conversation analysis (CA) attends to the dynamics of talk on the micro-level timescale of seconds and minutes. In a special issue of *The Modern Language Journal* (Markee and Kasper 2004), it was argued that joining a conversation analysis perspective on interaction with a long-term view of language development holds great promise (Larsen-Freeman 2004; Hall 2004). CA offers a rich description of 'the most basic site of organized activity where learning can take place' (Mondada and Pekarek Doehler 2004: 502). If these analyses were to be done with a sufficient density and rigor so that retrospective microdevelopmental analyses could be conducted, it would offer another means of connecting synchronic dynamism to its over-time counterpart.

*

Clearly, each of the approaches just discussed has its advantages and its drawbacks. Conversation analysis offers an in-depth view of conversational interaction, but it ignores any insights that a conscious introspection would permit. Corpus linguistics offers rich usage data, but the data are attested; they do not demonstrate the potential of the system. Others of these, such as brain imaging and neural network modeling, illustrate or simulate the dynamic patterns of brain activity, but do so by isolating the learner's brain from society and its normal ecology of function. Agent-based computer models might be more encompassing in this regard, in allowing for a social interactive dimension, but they, too, involve ecologically reduced ways of representing reality.

We began this chapter by proposing that the methods of inquiry of the natural and social sciences need to be modified by applied linguists whose theoretical commitment is to understanding complex, dynamic systems. We have pointed out that different assumptions, for example, about causality, underlie traditional research methods used in both the natural and the social sciences and those that are more suitable from a complex systems perspective.

What we can aspire to at this point in time is to entertain the principles we have enumerated earlier in this chapter while blending and adapting methods, a trend that is increasingly adopted across the social sciences. It should not be surprising that researchers are entertaining the possibility of using multiple blended methods. It is, after all, a pragmatic solution to the demands of a theoretical perspective that seeks to understand the dynamics of change in complex systems.

Conclusion

In this chapter, we have compared the assumptions underpinning a complexity approach to research with that of more conventional approaches. We have also considered research methods that appear to be more consistent with complex systems, although we recognize that we ourselves have only just begun to make use of these methods in addressing our own areas of research. In the future, we expect to see more computer modeling undertaken in applied linguistics and the development of newer, hybrid, or blended methods that do justice to the complex dynamic systems that we aim to elucidate.

As we conclude this chapter, and therefore this book, we take a moment to step back and to summarize our position. We have called here for complexity theory to be taken seriously for the useful theoretical and practical insights it affords applied linguists. We feel that seeing the evolution of language, its development, its learning, and its use as complex, adaptive, dynamic, non-linear processes rings truer to us than the theories in which we were trained or in what our professional experience has been since. We think that we are not alone in this regard.

We set out below some of the areas of applied linguistics that, prompted by a complexity perspective, we see in need of change, and then summarize the changes in understanding and approach that we hope complexity theory can bring to these areas.

What no longer seems appropriate

In common with many applied linguists, we have been dissatisfied with the decontextualizing, segregating, and atemporalizing, not only of language, as we have claimed in Chapter 4, but more generally, in the limiting assumptions in applied linguistics. From where we sit now, we object to the sanitizing of data, the removal of variability or the dismissal of that part of it that cannot be explained by correlation coefficients and ANOVAS. We do not find compelling evidence for an innate language-specific mental organ, although we do acknowledge that the state space of human language using may be circumscribed. We do not believe that language can be understood apart from the way it is used by its users and learners. Generalizations about language use across groups are not valid as descriptions of how individuals use language. Learners and their learning cannot be studied independently. We also do not accept that instruction can be treated as one more factor to be explained in language development. Neither do we respond well to the assumption that there is a unidirectional causality whereby language learners are 'done unto' rather than having autonomy and following their own paths in realizing their own goals. Additionally, we question the assumption of native speaker norms and target-centric views of learning, no matter whose norms are being followed. We know that teaching does not cause learning, although this does not in any sense mean that teachers can abrogate their responsibility for managing their students' learning in a way consonant with the negotiated and mutable goals of instruction. Furthermore, we do not think that the language that emerges—especially first and second language learners' language—can be successfully accounted for by using linguists' taxonomies. We find it unhelpful to construe the learning process as exclusively cognitive and disembodied, or for that matter, exclusively social. We do not think we can draw a line between individual and context and sweep variation into the category of individual differences. Learning must take place in a social context, and yet at the same time what gets learned must be usable beyond a single context. We have suggested that experience with the process of co-adaptation between learner and context is what makes it so. Finally, we no longer believe that simple causality underlies the problem areas we are concerned with or that research can be conducted in which one variable is singled out to be manipulated while all else is held constant—and that even if this could be done, that the results would in any way be useful.

What complexity theory offers

In a complexity approach, whose conceptual tools broadly includes dynamic systems theory, an ecological understanding of phenomena, a learning-from-use theory, and a sociocognitive perspective, we have found concepts that are much more resonant with the way that we view matters of concern to applied linguists.

Recognizing that language-using is not a fixed normative system, we do not choose to characterize language use as if someone takes in and then possesses language, but rather that someone can use language, or to be more specific, realizes their language-using potential in particular discourse environments. There is no fixed homogeneous state in the use of these language-using patterns (When someone develops physical fitness, we do not ask them where their fitness lies. We see it in the way that they are changed and in what they can do.) We have presented the case that language-using patterns emerge from the soft assembly of language resources in particular instances. These local actions of its users and the resources that emerge then entrain the subsequent pattern-making in a process of reciprocal causality, producing order at more global levels. They also shape the attractor or modes of behavior that the system prefers. We recognize that a dynamic system can continue to maintain its order, indeed give rise to new order, through self-organization, if it is open to energy from outside itself. The trajectory of a complex dynamic system, though, is characterized by non-linearity due to the interactions of its agents and elements and the fact that they change, as does their relationship within the complex system. It is the variability of the system that shows that it has the potential for further change and development. Complex systems also construct the contexts of which they are a part.[4] The system and its environment co-evolve over time through co-adaptation in time.

Complexity: metaphor or more?

In Chapter 1, we asserted the power and necessity of metaphor to shift thinking and build theory, and suggested that the complexity metaphor offers a replacement for the computational or information processing metaphor that has underpinned work in the field over last decades. We elaborated some of the risks associated with the use (or over-use) of metaphor and would like to review here how we have dealt with those risks and where we think the metaphorical future lies.

Chapters 2 and 3 explained ideas and technical terms from complex systems theory in order that they can be used with understanding and confidence by readers wanting to use complexity theory in their thinking and practice. Developing these explanations has not always been straightforward; apart from the technical difficulty of some of the ideas, complexity theory's contributing fields of physics and biology themselves employ 'quite different metaphors to describe the dynamics of change' (Goodwin 1994: 156) and these have had to be combined or adjusted.

Throughout the book we have tried to use complexity terms carefully to avoid conflating everyday and technical senses, for example, in the use of 'chaos'. There is an interesting reason why this is sometimes difficult and that lies in the aesthetics of the complexity metaphor. For example, the idea that 'a system roams across its landscape of possibility' is aesthetically very engaging. The poetic language and image tempts one to respond poetically, but we have not thought this book the place to do so. Perhaps elsewhere and some other day, the poetics of complexity will be given freer rein.

We have acknowledged the fact that, since a metaphor both hides and highlights its target domain, a single metaphorical concept will never be sufficient to serve alone as theory-constituting. Hence our welcome for an ecological metaphor applied to language use in context and for a particular type of connectionist metaphor applied to brain processes. The work of selecting and adapting further metaphors to fit applied linguistic needs is part of the future agenda of a complexity approach.

To become more than metaphor, complexity theory needs to convince applied linguists of its relevance and potential for the field. Clearly we ourselves are already convinced; for us, complexity theory has brought together many of our understandings, has addressed many of our concerns, and has stimulated new thinking. We see the application of complexity as going far beyond just adding to our vocabulary; it offers a revolutionary way of thinking and provides unique conceptual tools. In Chapter 1, we suggested that future development of a complexity approach, in which metaphor becomes theory, will require field-specific classifications, terminology, and explanatory theory. For example, the construct of 'interaction differential', used as a collective variable to describe teacher–student talk in Chapter 7, adapts a metaphorical analogy with a system from the field of motor movement, and grounds it in applied linguistic field-specific data. Further work will determine whether the idea of interaction differential is useable and useful in complexity approaches to data analysis.

The possible steps in what we have called 'complexity thought modeling' set out in Table 3.1 include the metaphorical or analogical mappings from the complexity source domain that are available for application in our field. It is hoped that this book will enable the use of 'complexity thought modeling' of applied linguistics research questions, i.e. thought experiments that make use of complex systems tools and ideas. Such thought modeling will involve the identification of systems, their components and connections, the visualization of change over time as the systems evolve and adapt, and will offer hypotheses to make sense of outcomes and behavior patterns in terms of emergent stabilities and phase shifts.

Complexity theory for applied linguistics is itself a complex dynamic system, and in its non-linear trajectory of development will continue to select, adapt, and stabilize concepts and terminology.

Closing words

Some of the complexity ideas now seem less radical than when we first began our exploration of chaos/complexity theory a decade or so ago. In fact, saying that language is a complex, adaptive, dynamic system might almost seem self-evident, as is saying that learning is a sociocognitive process in which the learner and the context interact. However, these ideas have not been axiomatic in certain influential theories in linguistics and applied linguistics, so it seems worthwhile considering them as a new way of thinking here.

Furthermore, to say language is a dynamic system or learning is a socio-cognitive process does not tell the whole story for applied linguistics; to serve applied linguistic work across the range of real-world situations in which we explore language use (Brumfit 1995: 27), we need to build a broader complexity theory framework that includes dynamics systems theory. This is what we have tried to do with different kinds of data in Chapters 4–7, indicating possibilities while acknowledging that these preliminary efforts are bound to be incomplete and inadequate. The complexity way of viewing our work is new to us, too, and the full implications of it remain to be discovered. As we said at the beginning, our purpose in writing the book at this point in time is not to have the last word but to open the conversation.

Notes

1 Portions of this chapter are to appear in a special issue of *The Modern Language Journal*.
2 Familiar tools were used in doing so. We suggest later that new blends of old tools will complement new tools in implementing a complexity approach.
3 Gaddis is an historian, not an applied linguist, but he is insightful about the nature of research in a way that we think is helpful to applied linguists. We thank Gad Lim for bringing Gaddis' book to our attention.
4 Lewontin gives a fascinating example of how humans literally construct their physical environment. When schlieren lenses (which can detect differences in the optical density of air) are used to photograph the human body, a layer of higher density air surrounding the body can be seen. The air moves slowly upward and off the top of the head. It is warm and moist and is created by the body's metabolic heat and water.

> The consequence is that the individual is not living in the atmosphere as we normally think of it, but in a self-produced atmosphere that insulates it from the outer air. The existence of this layer explains the wind-chill factor, which is a consequence of the insulating layer being stripped away by the wind, leaving the body exposed to the actual surrounding temperature. In normal circumstances it is the warm, moist, self produced shell that constitutes the immediate space within which the organism is operating, a space that is carried around with the individual just as a snail carries around its shell.
> (Lewontin 1998: 54)

Bibliography

Adger, C. 2001. 'Discourse in educational settings' in D. Schiffrin, D. Tannen, and H. Hamilton (eds.). *The Handbook of Discourse Analysis*. Oxford: Blackwell.

Agar, M. 2004. 'We have met the other and we're all nonlinear: Ethnography as a nonlinear dynamic system'. *Complexity* 10/2: 16–24.

Ahearn, L. 2001. 'Language and agency'. *Annual Review of Anthropology* 30: 109–37.

Allwright, D. 2003. 'Exploratory practice: Rethinking practitioner research in language teaching'. *Language Teaching Research* 7: 113–41.

Andersen, R. 1983a. 'Transfer to somewhere' in S. Gass and L. Selinker (eds.). *Language Transfer in Language Learning*. Rowley, MA: Newbury House.

Andersen, R. (ed.). 1983b. *Pidginization and Creolization as Language Acquisition*. Rowley, MA: Newbury House.

Antilla, R. 1972. *An Introduction to Historical and Comparative Linguistics*. New York: Macmillan.

Arbib, M. 2002. 'The mirror system, imitation and the evolution of language' in C. Nehaniv and K. Dautenhahn (eds.). *Imitation in Animals and Artifacts*. Cambridge, MA: The MIT Press.

Arevart, S. and P. Nation. 1991. 'Fluency improvement in a second language'. *RELC Journal* 22/1: 84–94.

Atkinson, D. 2002. 'Toward a sociocognitive approach to second language acquisition'. *The Modern Language Journal* 86/4: 525–45.

Atkinson, D., E. Churchill, T. Nishino, and H. Okada. 2007. 'Alignment and interaction in a sociocognitive approach to second language acquisition'. *The Modern Language Journal* 91/2: 169–88.

Baake, K. 2003. *Metaphor and Knowledge*. Albany, NY: State University of New York.

Bailey, C. J. 1973. *Variation and Linguistic Theory*. Washington, DC: Center for Applied Linguistics.

Bak, P. 1997. *How Nature Works: The Science of Self-organized Criticality*. New York: Oxford University Press.

Bakhtin, M. 1981. *The Dialogic Imagination: Four Essays*. Austin, TX: University of Texas Press.

Bakhtin, M. 1986. *Speech Genres and Other Late Essays*. Austin, TX: University of Texas Press.

Bakhtin, M. 1993. *Toward a Philosophy of the Act* (V. Liapunov, Trans.). Austin, TX: University of Texas Press.

Barab, S. 2006. 'Design-based research: A methodological toolkit for the learning scientist' in R. Sawyer (ed.). *The Cambridge Handbook of the Learning Sciences*. Cambridge: Cambridge University Press.

Barlow, M. and S. Kemmer (eds.). 2000. *Usage Based Models of Language*. Stanford, CA: CSLI Publications.

Barr, D. 2004. 'Establishing conventional communication systems: Is common knowledge necessary?' *Cognitive Science* 28: 937–62.

Barton, D. and M. Hamilton. 2005. 'Literacy, reification and the dynamics of social interaction' in D. Barton and K. Tusting (eds.). *Beyond Communities of Practice: Language, Power and Social Context*. Cambridge: Cambridge University Press.

Baskerville, R. and T. Wood-Harper. 1996. 'A critical perspective on action research as a method for information systems research'. *Journal of Information Technology* 11: 235–46.

Bassano, D. and P. van Geert. 'Modeling continuity and discontinuity in utterance length: A quantitative approach to changes, transitions, and intra-individual variability in early grammatical development'. Unpublished manuscript.

Bates, E. 1999. 'Plasticity, localization and language development' in S. Broman and J. Fletcher (eds.). *The Changing Nervous System: Neurobehavioral Consequences of Early Brain Disorders*. New York: Oxford University Press.

Bates, E. and J. Goodman. 1999. 'On the emergence of grammar from lexicon' in B. MacWhinney (ed.). *The Emergence of Language*. Mahwah, NJ: Lawrence Erlbaum Associates.

Bates, E. and B. MacWhinney. 1989. 'Functionalism and the competition model' in B. MacWhinney and E. Bates (eds.). *The Cross-Linguistic Study of Sentence Processing*. Cambridge: Cambridge University Press.

Bateson, G. 1972. *Steps to an Ecology of Mind*. New York: Ballantine.

Bateson, G. 1991. *Sacred Unity*. New York: Harper Collins.

Battram, A. 1998. *Navigating Complexity*. London: The Industrial Society.

Baynham, M. 2005. 'Contingency and agency in adult TESOL classes for asylum seekers'. *TESOL Quarterly* 39/4: 777–80.

Becker, A. L. 1983. 'Toward a post-structuralist view of language learning: A short essay'. *Language Learning* 33/5: 217–20.

Beckett, G. and P. Miller (eds.). 2006. *Project-based Learning in Foreign Language Education: Past, Present, and Future*. Greenwich, CT: Information Age Publishing.

Beer, R. 1995. 'Computational and dynamical languages for autonomous agents' in R. Port and T. van Gelder (eds.). *Mind as Motion: Explorations in the Dynamics of Cognition*. Cambridge, MA: The MIT Press.

Bernstein, R. 1983. *Beyond Objectivism and Relativism: Science, Hermeneutics, and Praxis*. Philadelphia, PA: University of Pennsylvania Press.

Birdsong, D. 2005. 'Why not fossilization' in Z-H. Han and T. Odlin (eds.). *Studies in Fossilization in Second Language Acquisition*. Clevedon: Multilingual Matters.

Black, M. 1979. 'More about metaphor' in A. Ortony (ed.). *Metaphor and Thought*. New York: Cambridge University Press.

Bley-Vroman, R. 1983. 'The comparative fallacy in interlanguage studies: The case of systematicity'. *Language Learning* 33/1: 1–17.

Bley-Vroman, R. 1990. 'What is the logical problem of foreign language learning?' in S. Gass and J. Schachter (eds.). *Linguistic Perspectives on Second Language Acquisition*. Cambridge: Cambridge University Press.

Bloom, L. 1991. 'Meaning and expression'. Plenary address, Jean Piaget Society, Philadelphia, May.

Bod, R., J. Hay, and S. Jannedy (eds.). 2003. *Probabilistic Linguistics*. Cambridge, MA: The MIT Press.

Bolinger, D. 1976. 'Meaning and memory'. *Forum Linguisticum* 1/1: 1–14.

Bourdieu, P. 1989. 'Social space and symbolic power'. *Sociological Theory* 7/1: 14–25.

Boyd, R. 1993. 'Metaphor and theory change: What is "metaphor" a metaphor for?' in A. Ortony (ed.). *Metaphor and Thought*. New York: Cambridge University Press.

Breen, M. 1987. 'Contemporary paradigms in syllabus design: (Parts 1 and 2)'. *Language Teaching* 20/2: 91–2 and 20/3: 157–74.

Breen, M. and C. Candlin. 1980. 'The essentials of a communicative curriculum in language teaching'. *Applied Linguistics* 1/2: 89–112.

Brennan, S. and H. Clark. 1996. 'Conceptual pacts and lexical choices in conversation'. *Journal of Experimental Psychology: Learning, Memory, and Cognition* 22: 1482–93.

Bresnan, J. 2007. 'Rethinking linguistic competence'. Course description for the Linguistic Society of America's 2007 Summer Linguistic Institute.

Bresnan, J., A. Deo, and D. Sharma. 2007. 'Typology in variation: A probabilistic approach to *be* and *n't* in the survey of English dialects'. *English Language and Linguistics* 11/2: 301–46.

Brinton, L. and E. Traugott. 2005. *Lexicalization and Language Change*. Cambridge: Cambridge University Press.

Bronfenbrenner, U. 1989. 'Ecological systems theory'. *Annals of Child Development* 6: 187–251.

Brügge, P. 1993. 'Mythos aus dem Computer'. *Der Spiegel* 39: 156–64.

Brumfit, C. 1995. 'Teacher professionalism and research' in G. Cook and B. Seidlhofer (eds.). *Principle and Practice in Applied Linguistics*. Oxford: Oxford University Press.

Brumfit, C. 2001. *Individual Freedom in Language Teaching*. Oxford: Oxford University Press.

Bruner, J. 1983. *Child's Talk: Learning to Use Language*. Oxford: Oxford University Press.

Burling, R. 2005. *The Talking Ape: How Language Evolved*. Oxford: Oxford University Press.

Bybee, J. 2006. 'From usage to grammar: The mind's response to repetition'. *Language* 82/4: 711–33.

Bygate, M. 1999. 'Task as context for the framing, reframing and unframing of language'. *System* 27/1: 33–48.

Bygate, M., P. Skehan, and M. Swain. 2001. *Researching Pedagogic Tasks: Second Language Learning, Teaching and Testing*. London: Pearson.

Byrne, D. 2002. *Interpreting Quantitative Data*. London: Sage.

Cameron, L. 1997. 'Critical examination of classroom practice to foster teacher growth and increase student learning'. *TESOL Journal* 7/1: 25–30.

Cameron, L. 1999. 'Operationalising metaphor for applied linguistic research' in L. Cameron and G. Low (eds.). *Researching and Applying Metaphor*. Cambridge: Cambridge University Press.

Cameron, L. 2001. *Teaching Languages to Young Learners*. Cambridge: Cambridge University Press.

Cameron, L. 2003a. 'Challenges for ELT from the expansion in teaching children'. *ELT Journal* 57/2: 105–12.

Cameron, L. 2003b. *Metaphor in Educational Discourse*. London: Continuum.

Cameron, L. 2003c. *Advanced Bilingual Learners' Writing Project*. London: OFSTED.

Cameron, L. 2007. 'Patterns of metaphor use in reconciliation talk'. *Discourse and Society* 18/2: 197–222.

Cameron, L. and S. Besser. 2004. *Writing in English as an Additional Language at Key Stage 2*. No. 586. London: Dept for Education and Skills.

Cameron, L. and A. Deignan. 2003. 'Using large and small corpora to investigate tuning devices around metaphor in spoken discourse'. *Metaphor and Symbol* 18/3: 149–60.

Cameron, L. and A. Deignan. 2006. 'The emergence of metaphor in discourse'. *Applied Linguistics* 27/4: 671–90.

Cameron, L., J. Moon, and M. Bygate. 1996. 'Language development in the mainstream: How do teachers and pupils use language?' *Language and Education* 10/4: 221–36.

Cameron, L. and J. Stelma. 2004. 'Metaphor clusters in discourse'. *Journal of Applied Linguistics* 1/1: 7–36.

Candlin, C. 1987. 'What happens when applied linguistics goes critical?' in M. A. K. Halliday, J. Gibbons, and H. Nicholas (eds.). *Learning, Keeping and Using Language: Selected Papers from the 8th World Congress of Applied Linguistics*. Amsterdam: John Benjamins.

Candlin, C. 2002. 'Commentary' in C. Kramsch (ed.). *Language Acquisition and Language Socialization*. London: Continuum.

Carlson, J. M. and J. Doyle. 2000. 'Highly optimized tolerance: Robustness and design in complex systems'. *Phys.Rev.Lett.* 84: 2529-2552.

Carter, R. 2004. *Language and Creativity*. London and New York: Routledge.

Carter, R., D. Knight, and S. Adolphs. 2006. 'Head-talk: Towards a Multi-Modal Corpus'. Paper delivered at the Joint Annual Meeting of the British Association for Applied Linguistics and the Irish Association for Applied Linguistics conference, University College, Cork, Ireland, September.

Casti, J. 1994. *Complexification*. London: Abacus.

Chafe, W. 1994. *Discourse, Consciousness and Time*. Chicago, IL: University of Chicago Press.

Chambers, J. K. and P. Trudgill. 1980. *Dialectology*. Cambridge: Cambridge University Press.

Charles, E. 2003. 'Can we use a complex systems framework to model community-based learning?' *ACM SIGGROUP Bulletin* 24: 33–8.

Chomsky, N. 1965. *Aspects of a Theory of Syntax*. Cambridge, MA: The MIT Press.

Chomsky, N. 1966. 'Linguistic theory'. *Reports on the Working Committees, Northeast Conference on the Teaching of Foreign Languages*. New York: MLA Materials Center.

Chomsky, N. 1971. *Problems of Knowledge and Freedom: The Russell Lectures*. New York: Vintage Books.

Chomsky, N. 1981. *Lectures on Government and Binding*. Dordrecht: Foris.

Chomsky, N. 1986. *Knowledge of Language*. New York: Praeger.

Chomsky, N. 1995. *The Minimalist Program*. Cambridge, MA: The MIT Press.

Chomsky, N. 2004. 'Three factors in language design'. Unpublished manuscript.

Christiansen, M. 1994. 'Infinite Languages, Finite Minds: Connectionism, Learning and Linguistic Structure'. Unpublished Ph.D. thesis. University of Edinburgh.

Cienki, A. 1998. 'Metaphoric gestures and some of their relations to verbal metaphoric expressions' in J-P. Koenig (ed.). *Discourse and Cognition: Bridging the Gap*. Stanford, CA: CSLI Publications.

Cilliers, P. 1998. *Complexity and Postmodernism*. London: Routledge.

Clark, A. 1997. *Being There*. Cambridge, MA: The MIT Press.

Clark, H. 1996. *Using Language*. New York: Cambridge University Press.

Clarke, M. 2007. *Common Ground, Contested Territory*. Ann Arbor, MI: University of Michigan Press.

Cohen, J. and I. Stewart. 1994. *The Collapse of Chaos*. London: Viking.

Collier, V. 1987. 'Age and rate of acquisition of second language for academic purposes'. *TESOL Quarterly* 21/4: 617–41.

Cook, G. 2000. *Language Play, Language Learning*. Oxford: Oxford University Press.

Cook, V. 2002. *Portraits of the L2 User*. Clevedon: Multilingual Matters.

Cooke, M. 2006. 'Where talk is work: The social contexts of adult ESOL classrooms'. *Linguistics and Education* 17/1: 56–73.

Cooper, D. 1999. *Linguistic Attractors: The Cognitive Dynamics of Language Acquisition and Change*. Amsterdam/Philadelphia: John Benjamins.

Coughlan, P. and P. Duff. 1994. 'Same task, different activities: Analysis of a SLA task from an Activity Theory perspective' in J. Lantolf and G. Appel (eds.). *Vygotskyan Approaches to Second Language Learning Research*. Norwood, NJ: Ablex Publishing Company.

Cowie, F. 1999. *What's Within? Nativism Reconsidered*. Oxford: Oxford University Press.

Croft, W. 2001. *Radical Construction Grammar: Syntactic Theory in Typological Perspective*. Oxford: Oxford University Press.

Croft, W. and A. Cruse. 2004. *Cognitive Linguistics*. Cambridge: Cambridge University Press.

Culicover, P. and R. Jackendoff. 2005. *Simpler Syntax*. Oxford: Oxford University Press.

Cutler, A., J. Hawkins, and G. Gilligan. 1985. 'The suffixing preference: A processing explanation'. *Linguistics* 23: 723–58.

Dale, R. and M. Spivey. 2006. 'Unraveling the dyad: Using recurrence analysis to explore patterns of syntactic coordination between children and caregivers in conversation'. *Language Learning* 56/3: 391–430.

Damasio, A. 2003. *Looking for Spinoza: Joy, Sorrow and the Feeling Brain*. New York: Harcourt.

Davis, K. and Lazaraton, A. (eds.). 1995. 'Qualitative research in ESOL'. *TESOL Quarterly* 29/3.

de Bot, K., W. Lowie, and M. Verspoor. 2005. *Second Language Acquisition: An Advanced Resource Book*. London: Routledge.

de Bot, K., W. Lowie, and M. Verspoor. 2007. 'A dynamic systems theory approach to second language acquisition'. *Bilingualism: Language and Cognition* 10/1: 7–21 and 51–5.

de Waal, F. B. M. 2005. 'A century of getting to know the chimpanzee'. *Nature* 437/7055: 56–9.

Deacon, T. 1997. *The Symbolic Species*. New York: W. Norton and Co.

Deignan, A. 2005. *Metaphor and Corpus Linguistics*. Amsterdam: John Benjamins.

Dick, F., N. Dronkers, L. Pizzamiglio, A. Saygin, S. Small, and S. Wilson. 2005. 'Language and the brain' in M. Tomasello and D. Slobin (eds.). *Beyond Nature-Nurture: Essays in Honor of Elizabeth Bates*. Mahwah, NJ: Lawrence Erlbaum Associates.

Dickerson, L. 1974. 'Internal and external patterning of phonological variability in the speech of Japanese learners of English'. Unpublished Ph.D. thesis. University of Illinois.

Dickerson, W. 1976. 'The psycholinguistic unity of language learning and language change'. *Language Learning* 26/2: 215–31.

Dijkstra, A. 2005. 'Bilingual visual word recognition and lexical access' in F. Kroll and A. De Groot (eds.). *Handbook of Bilingualism: Psycholinguistic Approaches*. Oxford: Oxford University Press.

Doll, W. 1993. *A Post-modern Perspective on Curriculum*. New York: Teachers College.

Donato, R. 2000. 'Sociocultural contributions to understanding the foreign and second language classrooms' in J. Lantolf (ed.). *Sociocultural Theory and Second Language Learning*. Oxford: Oxford University Press.

Donato, R. 2004. 'Collective scaffolding in second language learning' in J. Lantolf and G. Appel (eds.). *Vygotskyan Approaches to Second Language Learning Research*. Norwood, NJ: Ablex Publishing Company.

Dörnyei, Z. 1998. 'Motivation in second and foreign language learning'. *Language Teaching* 31: 117–35.

Dörnyei, Z. 2003. 'New themes and approaches in second language motivation research'. *Annual Review of Applied Linguistics* 21: 43–59.

Dörnyei, Z. and P. Skehan. 2005. 'Individual differences in second language learning' in C. Doughty and M. Long (eds.). *Handbook of Second Language Acquisition*. Malden, MA: Blackwell.

Dromi, E. 1987. *Early Lexical Development*. Cambridge: Cambridge University Press.

Du Bois, J., S. Schuetze-Coburn, S. Cumming, and D. Paolino. 1993. 'Outline of discourse transcription' in J. Edwards and M. Lampert (eds.). *Talking Data: Transcription and Coding in Discourse Research*. Hillsdale, NJ: Lawrence Erlbaum Associates.

Duranti, A. and C. Goodwin. 1992. *Rethinking Context*. Cambridge: Cambridge University Press.

Edwards, C. and J. Willis (eds.). 2005. *Teachers Exploring Tasks in English Language Teaching*. London: Palgrave Macmillan.

Edwards, D. 1997. *Discourse and Cognition*. London: Sage.

Elio, R. and J. R. Anderson. 1981. 'The effects of category generalizations and instance similarity on schema abstraction'. *Journal of Experimental Psychology: Human Learning and Memory* 7/6: 397–417.

Elio, R. and J. R. Anderson. 1984. 'The effects of information order and learning mode on schema abstraction'. *Memory and Cognition* 12: 20–30.

Ellis, N. 1996. 'Sequencing in SLA: Phonological memory, chunking, and points of order'. *Studies in Second Language Acquisition* 18/1: 91–126.

Ellis, N. 1998. 'Emergentism, connectionism and language learning'. *Language Learning* 48/4: 631–64.

Ellis, N. 2002. 'Frequency effects in language processing: A review with implications for theories of implicit and explicit language acquisition'. *Studies in Second Language Acquisition* 24/2: 143–88.

Ellis, N. 2003. 'Constructions, chunking, and connectionism' in C. Doughty and M. Long (eds.). *Handbook of Second Language Acquisition*. Malden, MA: Blackwell.

Ellis, N. 2005. 'At the interface: Dynamic interactions of explicit and implicit language knowledge'. *Studies in Second Language Acquisition* 27/2: 305–52.

Ellis, N. 2007. 'Dynamic systems and SLA: The wood and the trees'. *Bilingualism: Language and Cognition* 10: 23–25.

Ellis, N., F. Ferreira Jr., and J-Y. Ke. In preparation. 'Form, function, and frequency: Zipfian family construction profiles in SLA'.

Ellis, N. and D. Larsen-Freeman. 2006. 'Language emergence: Implications for applied linguistics. Introduction to the special issue'. *Applied Linguistics* 27/4: 558–89.

Ellis, R. 1985. 'Sources of variability in interlanguage'. *Applied Linguistics* 6/2: 118–31.

Ellis, R. and G. Barkhuizen. 2005. *Analysing Learner Language*. Oxford: Oxford University Press.

Elman, J. 1993. 'Learning and development in neural networks. The importance of starting small'. *Cognition* 48: 71–99.

Elman, J. 1995. 'Language as a dynamical system' in R. Port and T. van Gelder (eds.). *Mind as Motion: Explorations in the Dynamics of Cognition*. Cambridge, MA: The MIT Press.

Elman, J. 2003. 'Generalization from sparse input'. PDF of paper to appear in the Proceedings of the 38th Annual Meeting of the Chicago Linguistic Society.

Elman, J. 2005. 'Connectionist models of cognitive development: Where next?' *Trends in Cognitive Sciences* 9: 111–17.

Elman, J., E. Bates, M. Johnson, A. Karmiloff-Smith, D. Parisi, and K. Plunkett. 1996. *Rethinking Innateness: A Connectionist Perspective on Development*. Cambridge, MA: The MIT Press.

Evans, J. 2007. 'The emergence of language: A dynamical systems account' in E. Hoff and M. Shatz (eds.). *Handbook of Language Development*. Malden, MA: Blackwell.

Evans, V. and M. Green. 2006. *Introduction to Cognitive Linguistics*. Oxford: Blackwell.

Fairclough, N. 1989. *Language and Power*. London: Longman.

Fanselow, J. 1977. 'The treatment of error in oral work'. *Foreign Language Annals* 10/5: 583–93.

Fauconnier, G. and M. Turner. 1998. 'Conceptual integration networks'. *Cognitive Science* 22/2: 133–87.

Felix, S. 1981. 'The effect of formal instruction on second language acquisition'. *Language Learning* 31/1: 87–112.

Fenson, D., E. Bates, E. Reznick, J. Thal, and S. Pethick. 1994. 'Variability in early communicative development'. *Monographs of the Society for Research in Child Development* 59 (Serial No. 242).

Ferrer i Cancho, R. 2006. 'On the universality of Zipf's law for word frequencies' in P. Grzybek and R. Köhler (eds.). *Exact Methods in the Study of Language and Text. In Honor of Gabriel Altman*. Berlin: de Gruyter.

Ferrer i Cancho, R. and R. Solé. 2003. 'Least effort and the origins of scaling in human language'. *Proceedings of the National Academy of Sciences* 10: 788–91.

Firth, A. and J. Wagner. 1997. 'On discourse, communication, and (some) fundamental concepts in SLA research'. *The Modern Language Journal* 81/3: 285–300.

Fischer, K. and R. Bidell. 1998. 'Dynamic development of psychological structures in action and thought' in W. Damon and R. Bidell (eds.). *Dynamic Development of Psychological Structures in Action and Thought, Volume 1*. New York: John Wiley and Sons.

Fischer, K., Z. Yan, and J. Stewart. 2003. 'Adult cognitive development: Dynamics in the developmental web' in J. Valsiner and K. Connolly (eds.). *Handbook of Developmental Psychology*. London: Sage.

Fitch, W. T. 2007. 'An invisible hand'. *Nature* 449: 665–67.

Foster, P. and P. Skehan. 1999. 'The influence of planning and focus on planning on task-based performance'. *Language Teaching Research* 3: 215–47.

Gaddis, J. L. 2002. *The Landscape of History*. Oxford: Oxford University Press.

Gardner, R. and W. Lambert. 1972. *Attitudes and Motivation in Second Language Learning*. Rowley, MA: Newbury House.

Gass, S. 1997. *Input, Interaction, and the Development of Second Languages*. Mahwah, NJ: Lawrence Erlbaum and Associates.

Gass, S. 1998. 'Apples and oranges: Or, why apples are not orange and don't need to be'. *The Modern Language Journal* 82/1: 83–90.

Gass, S. and A. Mackey. 2006. 'Input, interaction and output in SLA' in J. Williams and B. Van Patten (eds.). *Theories in SLA*. Mahway, NJ: Lawrence Erlbaum Associates.

Gasser, M. 1990. 'Connectionism and universals of second language acquisition'. *Studies in Second Language Acquisition* 12/2: 179–99.

Gatbonton, E. 1978. 'Patterned phonetic variability in second language speech'. *Canadian Modern Language Review* 34: 335–47.

Gattegno, C. 1972. *Teaching Foreign Languages in Schools: The Silent Way*. New York: Educational Solutions.

Gazzaniga, M. and T. Heatherton. 2007. *Psychological Science. Mind, Brain, & Behavior*. 2nd edition. London: W. Norton and Co.

Gee, J. P. 1999. *An Introduction to Discourse Analysis*. London: Routledge.

Gell-Mann, M. 1994. *The Quark and the Jaguar: Adventures in the Simple and the Complex*. New York: W. H. Freeman and Company.

Gershkoff-Stowe, L. and E. Thelen. 2004. 'U-shaped changes in behavior: A dynamic systems perspective'. *Journal of Cognition and Development* 5/1: 11–36.

Gibbs, R. 2006. *Embodiment and Cognitive Science*. New York: Cambridge University Press.

Gilbert, N. and K. Troitzsch. 2005. *Simulation for the Social Scientist*. 2nd edition. Maidenhead: Open University Press.

Gilden, D. 2007. 'Fly moves. Insects buzz about in organized abandon'. Quoted in article. *Science News* 171: 309–10.

Givón, T. 1999. 'Generativity and variation: The notion "rule of grammar" revisited' in B. MacWhinney (ed.). *The Emergence of Language*. Mahwah, NJ: Lawrence Erlbaum Associates.

Gladwell, M. 2000. *The Tipping Point: How Little Things Can Make a Big Difference*. Boston, MA: Little Brown.

Gleick, J. 1987. *Chaos: Making a New Science*. New York: Penguin Books.

Gleitman, L., E. Newport, and H. Gleitman. 1984. 'The current state of the motherese hypothesis'. *Journal of Child Language* 11: 43–79.

Globus, G. 1995. *The Postmodern Brain*. Amsterdam/Philadelphia: John Benjamins.

Goffman, E. 1974. *Frame Analysis*. London: Harper and Row.

Goffman, E. 1981. *Forms of Talk*. Philadelphia, PA: University of Philadelphia Press.

Goldberg, A. 1995. *Constructions: A Construction Grammar Approach to Argument Structure*. Chicago, IL: University of Chicago Press.

Goldberg, A. 1999. 'The emergence of semantics of argument structure constructions' in B. MacWhinney (ed.). *The Emergence of Language*. Mahwah, NJ: Lawrence Erlbaum Associates.

Goldberg, A. 2003. 'Constructions: A new theoretical approach to language'. *Trends in Cognitive Sciences* 7/5: 219–23.

Goldberg, A. 2006. *Constructions at Work: The Nature of Generalization in Language*. Oxford: Oxford University Press.

Goldberg, A. and R. Jackendoff. 2004. 'The English resultative as a family of constructions'. *Language* 80/3: 532–68.

Goodwin, B. 1994. *How the Leopard Changed its Spots*. London: Phoenix Books.

Granott, N. and J. Parziale. 2002. *Microdevelopment: Transition Processes in Development and Learning*. Cambridge: Cambridge University Press.

Green, D. 1998. 'Mental control of the bilingual lexico-semantic system'. *Bilingualism: Language and Cognition* 1: 67–81.

Gregg, K. 1990. 'The variable competence model of second language acquisition, and why it isn't'. *Applied Linguistics* 11/4: 364–83.

Gregg, K. 2003. 'The state of emergentism in second language acquisition'. *Second Language Research* 19/2: 95–128.

Grice, H. 1975. 'Logic and conversation' in P. Cole and J. Morgan (eds.). *Syntax and Semantics*, Vol 3. New York: Academic Press.

Gries, S. T. and S. Wulff. 2005. 'Do foreign language learners also have constructions?' *Annual Review of Cognitive Linguistics* 3: 182–200.

Grosjean, F. and J. Miller. 1994. 'Going in and out of languages: An example of bilingual flexibility'. *Psychological Sciences* 5: 201–6.

Grossberg, S. 1976. 'Adaptive pattern classification and universal recoding: I. Parallel development and coding of neural feature detectors'. *Biological Cybernetics* 23: 121–34.

Gumperz, J. 1982. *Discourse Strategies*. Cambridge: Cambridge University Press.

Gumperz, J. 2001. 'Interactional Sociolinguistics: A Personal Perspective' in D. Schiffrin, D. Tannen, and H. Hamilton (eds.). *The Handbook of Discourse Analysis*. Oxford: Blackwell.

Haken, H. 1983. *Synergetics: An Introduction: Nonequilibrium Phase Transitions and Self-Organization in Physics, Chemistry, and Biology*. 3rd edition. New York: Springer-Verlag.

Hall, J. K. 2004. 'Language learning as an interactional achievement'. *The Modern Language Journal* 88/4: 607–12.

Halliday, M. A. K. 1973. *Explorations in the Functions of Language*. London: Edward Arnold.

Halliday, M. A. K. 1978. *Language as Social Semiotic: The Social Interpretation of Language and Meaning*. London: Edward Arnold.

Halliday, M. A. K. 1994. *An Introduction to Functional Grammar*. 2nd edition. London: Edward Arnold.

Halliday, M. A. K. and R. Hasan. 1989. *Language, Context and Text: A Social Semiotic Perspective*. Oxford: Oxford University Press.

Halliday, M. A. K. and Z. L. James. 1993. 'A quantitative study of polarity and primary tense in the English finite clause' in J. Sinclair, M. Hoey, and G. Fox (eds.). *Techniques of Description: Spoken and Written Discourse*. London: Routledge.

Harley B. and M. Swain. 1984. 'The interlanguage of immersion students and its implication for second language teaching' in A. Davies, C. Criper, and A. P. R. Howatt (eds.). *Interlanguage*. Edinburgh: Edinburgh University Press.

Harris, R. 1993. *The Linguistic Wars*. New York: Oxford University Press.

Harris, R. 1996. *Signs, Language and Communication*. London: Routledge.

Hatch, E. 1974. 'Second language learning—universals?' *Working Papers on Bilingualism* 3: 1–17.

Haugen, E. 1980. 'Introduction to symposium No. 4: Social factors in sound change'. *Proceedings of the Ninth International Congress of Phonetic Sciences 1979*, Volume III: 229–37. Copenhagen: University of Copenhagen.

Hauser, M., N. Chomsky, and W. T. Fitch. 2002. 'The faculty of language: What is it, who has it, and how did it evolve?' *Science* 298: 1569–79.

Hebb, D. O. 1949. *The Organization of Behaviour*. New York: John Wiley and Sons.

Herdina, P. and U. Jessner. 2002. *A Dynamic Model of Multilingualism*. Clevedon: Multilingual Matters.

Holland, J. 1995. *Hidden Order: How Adaptation Builds Complexity*. Reading, MA: Perseus Books.

Holland, J. 1998. *Emergence: From Chaos to Order*. New York: Oxford University Press.

Holliday, A. 1996. 'Developing a sociological imagination: Expanding ethnography in international English language education'. *Applied Linguistics* 17/2: 234–55.

Holliday, A. 2005. *The Struggle to Teach English as an International Language*. Oxford: Oxford University Press.

Hopper, P. 1988. 'Emergent grammar and the a priori grammar postulate' in D. Tannen (ed.). *Linguistics in Context: Connecting Observation and Understanding*. Norwood, NJ: Ablex Publishing Company.

Hopper, P. 1998. 'Emergent grammar' in M. Tomasello (ed.). *The New Psychology of Language*. Mahwah, NJ: Lawrence Erlbaum Associates.

Hopper, P. and S. Thompson. 1980. 'Transitivity in grammar and discourse'. *Language* 56/2: 251–99.

Hopper, P. and S. Thompson. 1984. 'The discourse basis for lexical categories in universal grammar'. *Language* 60/4: 703–52.

Hopper, P. and E. Traugott. 1993. *Grammaticalization*. Cambridge: Cambridge University Press.

Howatt, A. P. R. with H. G. Widdowson. 2004. *A History of English Language Teaching*. 2nd edition. Oxford: Oxford University Press.

Huebner, T. 1985. 'System and variability in interlanguage syntax'. *Language Learning* 35/2: 141–63.

Hull, D. 1982. 'The naked meme' in H. Plotkin (ed.). *Learning, Development and Culture*. London: Wiley.

Hulstijn, J. 2002. 'Towards a unified account of the representation, processing, and acquisition of second-language knowledge'. *Second Language Research* 18/3: 193–223.

Hyland, K. 2002. *Teaching and Researching Writing*. London: Longman.

Hymes, D. 1972. 'On communicative competence' in J. Pride and J. Holmes (eds.). *Sociolinguistics: Selected Readings*. Harmondsworth: Penguin Books.

Jacoby, S. and E. Ochs. 1995. 'Co-construction: An introduction'. *Research on Language and Social Interaction* 28/3: 171–83.

Jenkins, J. 2000. *The Phonology of English as an International Language*. Oxford: Oxford University Press.

Juarrero, A. 1999. *Dynamics in Action: Intentional Behavior as a Complex System*. Cambridge, MA: Harvard University Press.

Jurafsky, D., A. Bell, M. Gregory, and W. Raymond. 2001. 'Probabilistic relations between words: Evidence from reduction in lexical production' in J. Bybee and P. Hopper (eds.). *Frequency and the Emergence of Linguistic Structure*. Amsterdam/Philadelphia: John Benjamins.

Kauffman, S. 1993. *The Origins of Order: Self-organization and Selection in Evolution*. New York: Oxford University Press.

Kauffman, S. 1995. *At Home in the Universe: The Search for the Laws of Self-organization and Complexity*. London: Penguin Books.

Kay, P. and C. Fillmore. 1999. 'Grammatical constructions and linguistic generalizations: The what's X doing Y? construction'. *Language* 75/1: 1–34.

Ke, J. and J. Holland. 2006. 'Language origin from an emergentist perspective'. *Applied Linguistics* 27/4: 691–716.

Ke, J. and Y. Yao. Forthcoming. 'A study on language development from a network perspective'. *Journal of Quantitative Linguistics*. Also available in arXiv archive: http://arxiv.org/abs/cs.CL/0601005

Keller, R. 1985. 'Toward a theory of linguistic change' in T. Ballmer (ed.). *Linguistics Dynamics: Discourses, Procedures and Evolution*. Berlin: de Gruyter.

Kelso, J. A. S. 1995. *Dynamic Patterns*. Cambridge, MA: The MIT Press.

Kelso, J. A. S. 1999. *The Self-organization of Brain and Behavior*. Cambridge, MA: The MIT Press.

Kelso, J. A. S., K. Holt, P. Rubin, and P. Kugler. 1981. 'Patterns of human interlimb coordination emerge from the properties of non-linear limit cycle oscillatory processes: Theory and data'. *Journal of Motor Behavior* 13/4: 226–61.

Kemmis, S. 2001. 'Exploring the relevance of critical theory for action research: Emancipatory action research in the footsteps of Jurgen Habermas' in P. Reason and H. Bradbury (eds.). *Handbook of Action Research: Participative Inquiry and Practice*. London: Sage.

Kirby, S. 1998. *Language Evolution Without Natural Selection: From Vocabulary to Syntax in a Population of Learners*. Edinburgh: Language Evolution and Computation Research Unit, University of Edinburgh.

Klein, W. 1998. 'The contribution of second language acquisition research'. *Language Learning* 48/4: 527–50.

Koike, C. 2006. 'Ellipsis and body in talk-in-interaction'. Paper presented at the American Association for Applied Linguistics, Montreal, 17–20 June.

Kowal, M. and M. Swain. 1994. 'Using collaborative language production tasks to promote students' language awareness'. *Language Awareness* 3/2: 73–93.

Kozulin, A. 1990. *Vygotsky's Psychology*. London: Harvester Wheatsheaf.

Kramsch, C. (ed.). 2002. *Language Acquisition and Language Socialization*. London: Continuum.

Kramsch, C. 2006. 'Preview article: The multilingual subject'. *International Journal of Applied Linguistics* 16/1: 97–110.

Kramsch, C. 2007. 'Language ecology in practice: Implications for foreign language education'. Paper presented at the American Association for Applied Linguistics Conference, Costa Mesa, California, April.

Kress, G., C. Jewitt, J. Ogborn, and C. Tsatsarelis. 2001. *Multimodal Teaching and Learning: The Rhetorics of the Science Classroom*. London: Continuum.

Kristeva, J. 1986. 'Word, dialogue, and the novel' in T. Moi (ed.). *The Kristeva Reader*. New York: Columbia University.

Kroch, A. 1989. 'Reflexes of grammar in patterns of language change'. *Language Variation and Change* 1: 199–244.

Kuhn, T. 1970. *The Structure of Scientific Revolutions*. Chicago, IL: University of Chicago Press.

Labov, W. 1972. *Sociolinguistic Patterns*. Philadelphia, PA: University of Pennsylvania Press.

Lakoff, G. and M. Johnson. 1980. *Metaphors We Live By*. Chicago, IL: University of Chicago Press.

Lamb, M. 2004. 'Integrative motivation in a globalizing world'. *System* 32: 3–19.

Langacker, R. 1987. *Foundations of Cognitive Grammar: Vol. 1. Theoretical Prerequisites*. Stanford, CA: Stanford University Press.

Langacker, R. 1991. *Foundations of Cognitive Grammar: Vol. 2: Descriptive Applications*. Stanford, CA: Stanford University Press.

Lantolf, J. 2002. 'Comments' in C. Kramsch (ed.). *Language Acquisition and Language Socialization*. London: Continuum.

Lantolf, J. 2006a. 'Language emergence: Implications for applied linguistics—a sociocultural perspective'. *Applied Linguistics* 27/4: 717–28.

Lantolf, J. 2006b. 'Sociocultural theory and L2'. *Studies in Second Language Acquisition* 28/1: 67–109.

Lantolf, J. 2007. 'Sociocultural source of thinking and its relevance for second language acquisition'. *Bilingualism: Language and Cognition* 10/1: 31–3.

Lantolf, J. and A. Pavlenko. 1995. 'Sociocultural theory and second language acquisition'. *Annual Review of Applied Linguistics* 15: 108–24.

Lantolf, J. and M. Poehner. 2004. 'Dynamic assessment of L2 development: Managing the past into the future'. *Journal of Applied Linguistics* 1: 49–72.

Lantolf, J. and S. Thorne. 2006. *Sociocultural Theory and the Genesis of Second Language Development*. Oxford: Oxford University Press.

Larsen-Freeman, D. 1976. 'An explanation for the morpheme acquisition order of second language learners'. *Language Learning* 26/1: 125–34.

Larsen-Freeman, D. 1978. 'An ESL index of development'. *TESOL Quarterly* 12/4: 439–48.

Larsen-Freeman, D. 1985. 'State of the art on input in second language acquisition' in S. Gass and C. Madden (eds.). *Input in Second Language Acquisition*. Rowley, MA: Newbury House.

Larsen-Freeman, D. 1997. 'Chaos / complexity science and second language acquisition'. *Applied Linguistics* 18/2: 141–65.

Larsen-Freeman, D. 2000a. 'An attitude of inquiry'. *Journal of Imagination in Language Learning* 5: 10–15.

Larsen-Freeman, D. 2000b. *Techniques and Principles in Language Teaching*. 2nd edition. Oxford: Oxford University Press.

Larsen-Freeman, D. 2001. 'Individual cognitive/affective learner contributions and differential success in second language acquisition' in M. Breen (ed.). *Learner Contributions to Language Learning*. Harlow: Longman.

Larsen-Freeman, D. 2002a. 'Language acquisition and language use from a chaos/complexity theory perspective' in C. Kramsch (ed.). *Language Acquisition and Language Socialization*. London: Continuum.

Larsen-Freeman, D. 2002b. 'The grammar of choice' in E. Hinkel and S. Fotos (eds.). *New Perspectives on Grammar Teaching*. Mahwah, NJ: Lawrence Erlbaum Associates.

Larsen-Freeman, D. 2003. *Teaching Language: From Grammar to Grammaring*. Boston, MA: Thomson/Heinle.

Larsen-Freeman, D. 2004. 'CA for SLA? It all depends'. *The Modern Language Journal* 88: 603–7.

Larsen-Freeman, D. 2005. 'Second language acquisition and the issue of fossilization: There is no end, and there is no state' in Z-H. Han and T. Odlin (eds.). *Studies of Fossilization in Second Language Acquisition*. Clevedon: Multilingual Matters.

Larsen-Freeman, D. 2006a. 'Functional grammar: On the value and limitations of dependability, inference, and generalizability' in M. Chalhoub-Deville, C. Chapelle, and P. Duff (eds.). *Generalizability in Applied Linguistics: Multiple Research Perspectives*. Amsterdam: John Benjamins.

Larsen-Freeman, D. 2006b. 'The emergence of complexity, fluency, and accuracy in the oral and written production of five Chinese learners of English'. *Applied Linguistics* 27: 590–619.

Larsen-Freeman, D. 2007a. 'On the complementarity of chaos/complexity theory and dynamic systems theory in understanding the second language acquisition process'. *Bilingualism: Language and Cognition* 10/1: 35–7.

Larsen-Freeman, D. 2007b. 'Reflecting on the cognitive-social debate in second language acquisition'. *The Modern Language Journal* 91, Focus Issue: 773–87.

Larsen-Freeman, D. 2007c. 'A retrodictive approach to researched pedagogy'. Paper presented at a BAAL Seminar, University of Lancaster, July.

Larsen-Freeman, D. 2007d. 'Overcoming the inert knowledge problem'. Paper presented at the University of Pretoria, July.

Larsen-Freeman, D. and V. Strom. 1977. 'The construction of a second language acquisition index of development'. *Language Learning* 27: 123–34.

Laufer, B. 1991. 'The development of L2 lexis in the expression of the advanced learner'. *The Modern Language Journal* 75: 440–48.

Lave, J. and E. Wenger. 1991. *Situated Learning: Legitimate Peripheral Participation*. Cambridge: Cambridge University Press.

Leather, J. and J. van Dam. (eds.). 2003. *Ecology of Language Acquisition*. Dordrecht: Kluwer Academic Publishers.

Leclerc, J-J. 1990. *The Violence of Language*. London and New York: Routledge.

Lee, N. and J. Schumann. 2003. 'The evolution of language and of the symbolosphere as complex adaptive systems'. Paper presented at the American Association of Applied Linguistics Conference, Arlington, VA, March.

Lee, N. and J. Schumann. 2005. 'Neurobiological and evolutionary bases for child language acquisition abilities'. Paper presented at the 14th World Congress of Applied Linguistics, AILA 2005, Madison, Wisconsin, July.

Lemke, J. 2000a. 'Opening up closure: Semiotics across scales' in J. Chandler and
    G. van de Vijver (eds.). *Closure: Emergent Organizations and their Dynamics. Volume 901:*
    Annals of the New York Academy of Science. New York: New York Academy of Science
    Press.
Lemke, J. 2000b. 'Across the scales of time: artifacts, activities, and meanings in ecosocial
    systems'. *Mind, Culture and Activity* 7: 273–90.
Lemke, J. 2002. 'Language development and identity: Multiple timescales in the social ecology
    of learning' in C. Kramsch (ed.). *Language Acquisition and Language Socialization*. London:
    Continuum.
Lewin, R. 1992. *Complexity: Life on the Edge of Chaos*. New York: Macmillan.
Lewis, D. 1969. *Convention: A Philosophical Study*. Cambridge, MA: Harvard University
    Press.
Lewis, M. 1993. *The Lexical Approach*. Hove: Language Teaching Publications.
Lewontin, R. 1998. 'The evolution of cognition: Questions we will never answer' in
    D. Scarborough and S. Sternberg (eds.). *An Invitation to Cognitive Science, Volume 4:*
    Methods, Models, and Conceptual Issues. Cambridge, MA: The MIT Press.
Lewontin, R. 2000. *The Triple Helix: Gene, Organism, and Environment*. Cambridge, MA:
    Harvard University Press.
Lewontin, R. 2006. 'Gene, organism and environment'. Paper presented at the University of
    Michigan, Winter 2006 LSA Theme Semester: Explore Evolution.
Libet, B. 1985. 'Unconscious cerebral initiative and the role of conscious will in voluntary
    action'. *Behavioral and Brain Sciences* 8: 529–66.
Lieberman, E., J-B. Michel., J. Jackson, T. Tang, and M. Nowak. 2007. 'Quantifying the
    evolutionary dynamics of language'. *Nature* 449: 713–16.
Lightfoot, D. 1999. *The Development of Language, Acquisition, Change, and Evolution*.
    Malden, MA: Blackwell.
Linell, P. 1988. 'The impact of literacy on the conception of language: The case of linguistics' in
    R. Säljö (ed.). *The Written World*. Berlin: de Gruyter.
Linell, P. 1998. *Approaching Dialogue*. Amsterdam: John Benjamins.
Littlewood, W. 2007. 'Communicative and task-based language teaching in East Asian
    classrooms'. *Language Teaching* 40: 243–50.
Lobato, J. 2003. 'How design experiments can inform a rethinking of transfer and vice versa'.
    Educational Researcher 32: 17–20.
Logan, R. 2000. 'The extended mind: Understanding language and thought in terms of
    complexity and chaos theory'. *The Speech Communication Annual*, Volume XIV.
    New York: The New York State Communication Association.
Long, M. 1996. 'The role of the linguistic environment in second language acquisition' in
    W. Ritchie and T. Bhatia (eds.). *Handbook of Second Language Acquisition*. San Diego, CA:
    Academic.
Long, M. 1997. 'Construct validity in SLA research: A response to Firth and Wagner'. *The*
    Modern Language Journal 81/3: 318–23.
Long, M. 2003. 'Stabilization and fossilization in interlanguage development' in C. Doughty
    and M. Long (eds.). *Handbook of Second Language Acquisition*. Malden, MA: Blackwell.
Long, M. 2007. *Problems in SLA*. Mahwah, NJ: Lawrence Erlbaum Associates.
Long, M. and G. Crookes. 1993. 'Units of analysis in syllabus design—the case for task' in
    G. Crookes and S. Gass (eds.). *Tasks in a Pedagogical Context: Integrating Theory and*
    Practice. Clevedon: Multilingual Matters.
Lorenz, E. 1972. 'Predictability: Does the flap of a butterfly's wings in Brazil set off a tornado
    in Texas?' Paper presented at The American Association for the Advancement of Sciences,
    Washington, DC.
Loritz, D. 1999. *How the Brain Evolved Language*. Oxford: Oxford University Press.
Lyster, R. and L. Ranta. 1997. 'Corrective feedback and learner uptake'. *Studies in Second*
    Language Acquisition 19/1: 37–66.

Maasen, S. and P. Weingart. 2000. *Metaphors and the Dynamics of Knowledge*. London: Routledge.

MacWhinney, B. 1998. 'Models of the emergence of language'. *Annual Review of Psychology* 49: 199–227.

MacWhinney, B. (ed.). 1999. *The Emergence of Language*. Mahwah, NJ: Lawrence Erlbaum Associates.

MacWhinney, B. 2005. 'The emergence of linguistic form in time'. *Connection Science* 17: 119–211.

MacWhinney, B. 2006. 'Emergentism – Use often and with care'. *Applied Linguistics* 27/4: 729–40.

MacWhinney, B., S. Bird, C. Cieri, and C. Martell. 2004. 'TalkBank: Building on open unified multimodal database of communicative interaction'. *LREC 2004*. Lisbon: LREC.

Marchman, V. and E. Bates. 1994. 'Continuity in lexical and morphological development: A test of the critical mass hypothesis'. *Journal of Child Language* 21: 339–66.

Marchman, V. and D. Thal. 2005. 'Words and grammar' in M. Tomasello and D. Slobin (eds.). *Beyond Nature-Nurture: Essays in Honor of Elizabeth Bates*. Mahwah, NJ: Lawrence Erlbaum Associates.

Markee, N. and G. Kasper. (eds.) 2004. The special issue: Classroom talks. *The Modern Language Journal* 88/4: 491–500.

Markova, I. and K. Foppa (eds.). 1990. *The Dynamics of Dialogue*. London: Harvester Wheatsheaf.

Marocco, D., A. Cangelosi, and S. Nolfi. 2003. 'The emergence of communication in evolutionary robots'. *Philosophical Transactions of the Royal Society of London A* 361: 2397–2421.

Marr, D. 1982. *Vision: A Computational Investigation into the Human Representation and Processing of Visual Information*. New York: W. H. Freeman and Company.

Mason, J. 2002. *Qualitative Researching*. London: Sage.

Matthews, D., E. Lieven, A. Theakston, and M. Tomasello. 2005. 'The role of frequency in the acquisition of English word order'. *Cognitive Development* 20: 121–36.

Matthiessen, C. 2006. 'Educating for advanced foreign language capacities: Exploring the meaning-making resources of languages systemic-functionally' in H. Byrnes (ed.). *Advanced Language Learning: The Contribution of Halliday and Vygotsky*. London: Continuum.

Maturana, H. and F. Varela. 1972. *Autopoiesis and Cognition*. Boston, MA: Reidel.

Maturana, H. and F. Varela. 1987. *The Tree of Knowledge: The Biological Roots of Human Understanding*. Boston, MA: Shambala.

Mayberry, R. and E. Lock. 2003. 'Age constraints on first versus second language acquisition: Evidence for linguistic plasticity and epigenesis'. *Brain and Language* 87: 369–83.

McClelland, J. and J. Elman. 1986. 'The TRACE model of speech perception'. *Cognitive Psychology* 18: 1–86.

McLaughlin, B. 1990. 'Restructuring'. *Applied Linguistics* 11/2: 113–28.

McNamara, T. and C. Roever. 2006. *Language Testing: The Social Dimension*. Oxford: Blackwell.

McNeill, D. 1992. *Hand and Mind: What Gestures Reveal about Thought*. Chicago, IL: University of Chicago Press.

McWhorter, J. 2001. 'The world's simplest grammars are creole grammars'. *Language Typology* 5: 125–66.

Meadows, S. 1993. *The Child as Thinker*. London: Routledge.

Meara, P. 1997. 'Towards a new approach to modelling vocabulary acquisition' in N. Schmitt and M. McCarthy (eds.). *Vocabulary: Description, Acquisition and Pedagogy*. Cambridge: Cambridge University Press.

Meara, P. 2004. 'Modelling vocabulary loss'. *Applied Linguistics* 25/2: 137–55.

Meara, P. 2006. 'Emergent properties of multilingual lexicons'. *Applied Linguistics* 27/4: 620–44.

Mehan, H. 1979. *Learning Lessons: Social Organization in the Classroom*. Cambridge, MA: Harvard University Press.

Mellow, J. D. 2006. 'The emergence of second language syntax: A case study of the acquisition of relative clauses'. *Applied Linguistics* 27/4: 620–44.

Mellow, J. D. and K. Stanley. 2001. 'Alternative accounts of developmental patterns: Toward a functional-cognitive model of second language acquisition' in K. Smith and D. Nordquist (eds.). *Proceedings of the Third Annual High Desert Linguistics Society Conference*. Albuquerque, NM: High Desert Linguistics Society.

Menn, L. 1973. 'On the origin and growth of phonological and syntactic rules'. *Papers from the Ninth Regional Meeting of the Chicago Linguistic Society*: 378–85.

Mercer, N. 2004. 'Sociocultural discourse analysis: Analysing classroom talk as a social mode of thinking'. *Journal of Applied Linguistics* 1: 137–168.

Milroy, J. and L. Milroy. 1999. *Authority in Language*. 3rd edition. New York: Routledge.

Mitchell, R. 2000. 'Applied linguistics and evidence-based classroom practice: The case of foreign language grammar pedagogy'. *Applied Linguistics* 21/3: 281–303.

Mohanan, K. P. 1992. 'Emergence of complexity in phonological development' in C. Ferguson, L. Menn, and C. Stoel-Gammon (eds.). *Phonological Development*. Timonium, MD: York Press.

Mondada, L. and S. Pekarek Doehler. 2004. 'Second language acquisition as situated practice: Task accomplishment in the French second language classroom'. *The Modern Language Journal* 88/4: 501–18.

Morson, G. S. and C. Emerson. 1990. *Mikhail Bakhtin: Creation of a Prosaics*. Stanford, CA: Stanford University Press.

Muchisky, M., L. Gershkoff-Stowe, L. Cole, and E. Thelen. 1996. *The Epigenetic Landscape Revisited: A Dynamic Interpretation, Advances in Infancy Research*, Volume 10. Norwood, NJ: Ablex Publishing Company.

Mufwene, S. 2001. *The Ecology of Language Evolution*. Cambridge: Cambridge University Press.

Munakata, Y. and J. McClelland. 2003. 'Connectionist models of development'. *Developmental Science* 6: 413–29.

Myles, F. 2005. 'Interlanguage corpora and second language acquisition research'. *Second Language Research* 21: 373–91.

Nattinger, J. and J. DeCarrico. 1992. *Lexical Phrases and Language Teaching*. Oxford: Oxford University Press.

Negueruela, E., J. Lantolf, S. Jordan, and J. Gelabert. 2004. 'The "private function" of gesture in second language speaking activity: A study of motion verbs and gesturing in English and Spanish'. *International Journal of Applied Linguistics* 14: 113–47.

Nelson, R. 2007. 'The stability-plasticity dilemma and SLA'. Paper presented at American Association for Applied Linguistics Conference, Costa Mesa, California, April.

Nettle, D. 1999. *Linguistic Diversity*. Oxford: Oxford University Press.

Newman, D. 1990. 'Opportunities for research on the organizational impact of school computers'. *Educational Researcher* 19: 8–13.

Newport, E. 1999. 'Reduced input in the acquisition of signed languages' in M. DeGraff (ed.). *Language Creation and Change, Creolization, Diachrony, and Development*. Cambridge, MA: The MIT Press.

Nichol, L. (ed.). 2003. *The Essential David Bohm*. London and New York: Routledge.

Ninio, A. 2006. 'Syntactic development: Lessons from complexity theory'. Paper presented at the Eighth Annual Gregynog/Nant Gwrtheyrn Conference on Child Language, April.

Nishimura, T., A. Mikami, J. Suzuki, and T. Matsuzawa. 2003. 'Descent of the larynx in chimpanzee infants'. *Proceedings of the National Academy of Sciences*, USA. 100: 6930–33.

Noels, K., R. Clément, and L. Pelletier. 1999. 'Perceptions of teachers' communicative style and students' intrinsic and extrinsic motivation'. *The Modern Language Journal* 83/1: 23–34.

Norton, A. 1995. 'Dynamics: An introduction' in R. Port and T. van Gelder (eds.). *Mind as Motion: Explorations in the Dynamics of Cognition*. Cambridge, MA: The MIT Press.

Ochs, E. and L. Capps. 2001. *Living Narrative: Creating Lives in Everyday Storytelling*. Cambridge, MA: Harvard University Press.

O'Grady, W. 2003. 'The radical middle: Nativism without universal grammar' in C. Doughty and M. Long (eds.). *Handbook of Second Language Acquisition*. Malden, MA: Blackwell.

O'Grady, W. 2005. *Syntactic Carpentry: An Emergentist Approach to Syntax*. Mahwah, NJ: Lawrence Erlbaum Associates.

Ortega, L. and G. Iberri-Shea. 2005. 'Longitudinal research in second language acquisition: Recent trends and future directions'. *Annual Review of Applied Linguistics* 25: 26–46.

Ortony, A. 1975. 'Why metaphors are necessary and not just nice'. *Educational Review* 2: 45–53.

Osberg, D. 2007. 'Emergence: A complexity-based critical logic for education?' Paper presented at the Complex Criticality in Educational Research colloquium of the American Educational Research Association, Chicago, April.

O'Shannessey, C. 2007. 'Language variation and change in Northern Australia: The emergence of a new mixed language'. Paper presented at the Linguistics Colloquium Series, University of Michigan, February.

Oyama, S., P. Griffiths, and R. Gray (eds.). 2001. *Cycles of Contingency, Development Systems and Evolution*. Cambridge, MA: The MIT Press.

Pagel, M., Q. Atkinson, and A. Meade. 2007. 'Frequency of word-use predicts rates of lexical evolution throughout Indo-European history'. *Nature* 449: 771–21.

Pawley, A. and F. Syder. 1983. 'Two puzzles for linguistic theory: Nativelike selection and nativelike fluency' in J. Richards and R. Schmidt (eds.). *Language and Communication*. London: Longman.

Pennycook, A. 2003. 'Global Englishes, Rip Slyme, and performativity'. *Journal of Sociolinguistics* 7/4: 513–33.

Perdue, C. (ed.). 1993. *Adult Language Acquisition: Cross-linguistic Perspectives*. Cambridge: Cambridge University Press.

Piatelli-Palmerini, M. (ed.). 1980. *Language and Learning: The Debate between Jean Piaget and Noam Chomsky*. Cambridge, MA: Harvard University Press.

Pica, T. 1983. 'Adult acquisition of English as a second language under different conditions of exposure'. *Language Learning* 33/4: 465–97.

Pickering, M. and S. Garrod. 2004. 'Towards a mechanistic psychology of dialogue'. *Behavioral and Brain Sciences* 27: 169–226.

Pienemann, M. 1998. *Language Processing and Second Language Development*. Amsterdam/ Philadelphia: John Benjamins.

Pierrehumbert, J. 2001. 'Exemplar dynamics: Word frequency, lenition and contrast' in J. Bybee and P. Hopper (eds.). *Frequency and the Emergence of Linguistic Structure*. Amsterdam/Philadelphia: John Benjamins.

Pikovsky, A., M. Rosenblum, and J. Kurths. 2001. *Synchronization: A Universal Concept in Nonlinear Sciences*. Cambridge: Cambridge University Press.

Pinker, S. 1994. *The Language Instinct*. New York: Harper Perennial.

Pinker, S. and A. Prince. 1994. 'Regular and irregular morphology and the psychological status of rules of grammar' in S. Lima, R. Corrigan, and G. Iverson (eds.). *The Reality of Linguistic Rules*. Amsterdam/Philadelphia: John Benjamins.

Pinter, A. 2007. 'Some benefits of peer-peer interaction: 10-year-old children practising with a communication task'. *Language Teaching Research* 11: 189–208.

Plaza Pust, C. 2006. 'Universal grammar and dynamic systems theory'. Paper presented at the Language Learning Round Table on Dynamic Aspects of Language Development, American Association for Applied Linguistics Conference, Montreal, June.

Port, R. and T. van Gelder (eds.). 1995. *Mind as Motion: Explorations in the Dynamics of Cognition*. Cambridge, MA: The MIT Press.

Preston, D. 1996. 'Variationist perspectives on second language acquisition' in R. Bayley and
    D. Preston (eds.). *Second Language Acquisition and Linguistic Variation*. Philadelphia, PA:
    John Benjamins.

Prigogine, I. and I. Stengers. 1984. *Order out of Chaos*. New York: Bantam Books.

Prodomou, L. 2007. 'Is ELF a variety of English?' *English Today* 23: 47–53.

Purpura, J. 2006. 'Issues and challenges in measuring SLA'. Paper presented at the American
    Association for Applied Linguistics Conference, Montreal, June.

Ramanathan, V. and D. Atkinson. 1999. 'Ethnographic approaches and methods in L2 writing
    research: A critical guide and review'. *Applied Linguistics* 20/1: 44–70.

Rampton, B. 1995. *Crossing: Language and Ethnicity Among Adolescents*. Harlow: Longman.

Reder, S., K. Harris, and K. Setzler. 2003. 'The multimedia adult ESL learner corpus'.
    TESOL Quarterly 37/3: 546–57.

Reinking, D. and J. Watkins. 2000. 'A formative experiment investigating the use of multimedia
    book reviews to increase elementary students' independent reading'. *The Reading Research
    Quarterly* 35: 384–419.

Robins, R. H. 1967. *A Short History of Linguistics*. Bloomington, IN: Indiana University Press.

Robinson, B. and C. Mervis. 1998. 'Disentangling early language development: Modeling
    lexical and grammatical acquisition using an extension of case-study methodology'.
    Developmental Psychology 34: 363–75.

Robinson, P. 2001. *Cognition and Second Language Instruction*. Cambridge: Cambridge
    University Press.

Rogoff, B. 1990. *Apprenticeship in Thinking*. Oxford: Oxford University Press.

Rogoff, B. 1998. 'Cognition as collaborative process' in D. Kuhn and R. Seigler (eds.).
    Handbook of Child Psychology. 5th edition. Volume 2: Cognition, Perception, and
    Language. New York: John Wiley and Sons.

Rommetveit, R. 1979. 'On the architecture of intersubjectivity' in R. Rommetveit and
    R. Blakar (eds.). *Studies of Language, Thought and Verbal Communication*. London:
    Academic Press.

Rosch, E. and C. Mervis. 1975. 'Family resemblances: Studies in the internal structure of
    categories'. *Cognitive Psychology* 7: 573–605.

Rowe, M. B. 1986. 'Wait time: Slowing down may be a way of speeding up!' *Journal of Teacher
    Education* 37: 43–50.

Rumelhart, D. and J. McClelland. 1986. 'On learning the past tenses of English verbs' in
    J. McClelland, D. Rumelhart and the PDP Research Group (eds.). *Parallel Distributed
    Processing: Explorations in the Microstructure of Cognition. Volume 2: Psychological and
    Biological models*. Cambridge, MA: The MIT Press.

Rutherford, W. 1987. *Second Language Grammar: Learning and Teaching*. London: Longman.

Rutherford, W. and M. Thomas. 2001. 'The child language data exchange system'. *Second
    Language Research* 17: 195–212.

Sacks, H., E. Schegloff, and G. Jefferson. 1974. 'A simplest systematics for the organization of
    turn-taking for conversation'. *Language* 50/4: 696–735.

Saffran, J. R. 2003. 'Statistical language learning: Mechanisms and constraints'. *Current
    Directions in Psychological Science* 12: 110–14.

Saffran, J. R, R. N. Aslin, and E. L. Newport. 1996. 'Statistical learning by 8-month old infants'.
    Science 274: 1926–28.

Saltzman, E. 1995. 'Dynamics and coordinate systems in skilled sensorimotor activity'
    in R. Port and T. van Gelder (eds.). *Mind as Motion: Explorations in the Dynamics of
    Cognition*. Cambridge, MA: The MIT Press.

Sandler, W., I. Meir, C. Padden, and M. Aronoff. 2005. 'The emergence of a grammar in a new
    sign language'. *Proceedings of the National Academy of Science, USA*. 102: 2661–65.

Satterfield, T. 2001. 'Toward a sociogenetic solution: Examining language formation processes
    through SWARM modeling'. *Social Science Computer Review* 19: 281–95.

Saussure, F. 1916/[1959]. *Cours de Linguistique Générale*. C. Bally and A. Sechehaye (eds.) (translated in 1959 as *Course in General Linguistics*, W. Baskin, translator.) New York: Philosophical Library.

Schachter, J. and W. Rutherford. 1979. 'Discourse function and language transfer'. *Working Papers on Bilingualism* 19: 3–12.

Schegloff, E. 1987. 'Some sources of misunderstanding in talk-in-interaction'. *Linguistics* 25: 201–18.

Schegloff, E. 2001. 'Discourse as an interactional achievement III: The omnirelevance of action' in D. Schiffrin, D. Tannen, and H. Hamilton (eds.). *The Handbook of Discourse Analysis*. Oxford: Blackwell.

Schiffrin, D., D. Tannen, and H. Hamilton. 2001. 'Introduction' in D. Schiffrin, D. Tannen and H. Hamilton (eds.). *The Handbook of Discourse Analysis*. Oxford: Blackwell.

Schmidt, R. 1990. 'The role of consciousness in second language learning'. *Applied Linguistics* 11/2: 129–58.

Schmidt, R., C. Carello, and M. Turvey. 1990. 'Phase transitions and critical fluctuations in the visual coordination of rhythmic movements between people'. *Journal of Experimental Psychology: Human perception and performance* 16: 227–47.

Schumann, J. 1976. 'Second language acquisition research: Getting a more global look at the learner'. *Language Learning* Special Issue 4: 15–28.

Schumann, J. 1978. 'The relationship of pidiginization, creolization, and decreolization in second language acquisition'. *Language Learning* 28/2: 367–79.

Schumann, J., S. Crowell, N. Jones, S. Schuchert, and L. Wood. 2004. *The Neurobiology of Learning: Perspectives from Second Language Acquisition*. Mahwah, NJ: Lawrence Erlbaum Associates.

Schutte, A., J. Spencer, and G. Schöner. 2003. 'Testing dynamic field theory: Working memory for locations becomes more spatially precise over development'. *Child Development* 74: 1393–1417.

Sealey, A. and B. Carter. 2004. *Applied Linguistics as Social Science*. London: Continuum.

Searle, J. R. 1969. *Speech Acts*. Cambridge: Cambridge University Press.

Seedhouse, P. 2004. *The Interactional Architecture of the Language Classrooms: A Conversation Analysis Perspective*. Oxford: Blackwell.

Seidlhofer, B. 2001. 'Closing a conceptual gap: the case for a description of English as a lingua franca'. *International Journal of Applied Linguistics* 11: 133–58.

Seidlhofer, B. 2004. 'Research perspectives on teaching English as a Lingua Franca'. *Annual Review of Applied Linguistics* 24: 209–39.

Selinker, L. 1972. 'Interlanguage'. *International Review of Applied Linguistics* 10: 209–31.

Selinker, L. and U. Lakshmanan. 1992. 'Language transfer and fossilization: The "multiple effects principle"', in S. Gass and L. Selinker (eds.). *Language Transfer in Language Learning*. Rowley, MA: Newbury House

Senghas, A., S. Kita, and A. Ozyurek. 2004. 'Children creating core properties of language: Evidence from an emerging sign language in Nicaragua'. *Science* 305: 1779–82.

Sfard, A. 1998. 'On two metaphors for learning and the dangers of choosing just one'. *Educational Researcher* 27: 4–13.

Sharwood Smith, M. and J. Truscott. 2005. 'Stages or continua in second language acquisition: A MOGUL solution'. *Applied Linguistics* 26/2: 219–40.

Sidman, M. 1960. *Tactics of Scientific Research*. New York: Basic Books.

Sinclair, J. 1991. *Corpus, Concordance and Collocation*. Oxford: Oxford University Press.

Sinclair, J. and M. Coulthard. 1975. *Towards an Analysis of Discourse*. Oxford: Oxford University Press.

Skehan, P. 1998. *A Cognitive Approach to Language Learning*. Oxford: Oxford University Press.

Slobin, D. 1996. 'From "thought and language" to "thinking for speaking"' in J. Gumperz and S. Levinson (eds.). *Rethinking Linguistic Relativity*. New York: Cambridge University Press.

Slobin, D. 1997. 'The origins of grammaticizable notions: Beyond the individual mind' in D. Slobin (ed.). *The Crosslinguistic Study of Language Acquisition.* Volume 5. Mahwah, NJ: Lawrence Erlbaum Associates.

Smith, L. 2003. 'Learning to recognize objects'. *Psychological Science* 14: 245–50.

Smith, L. and L. Samuelson. 2003. 'Different is good: Connectionism and dynamic systems theory are complementary emergentist approaches to development'. *Developmental Science* 6: 434–39.

Smith, L. and E. Thelen (eds.). 1993. *A Dynamic Systems Approach to Development: Applications.* Cambridge, MA: The MIT Press.

Smolka, A., M. de Goes, and A. Pino. 1995. 'The constitution of the subject: A persistent question' in J. Wertsch, P. d. Rió, and A. Alvarez (eds.). *Sociocultural Studies of Mind.* New York: Cambridge University Press.

Snow, C. 1996. 'Change in child language and child linguists' in H. Coleman and L. J. Cameron (eds.). *Change and Language.* Clevedon: BAAL/Multilingual Matters.

Sokal, A. and J. Bricmont. 1998. *Intellectual Impostures.* London: Profile Books.

Spencer, J. and G. Schöner. 2003. 'Bridging the representational gap in the dynamic systems approach to development'. *Developmental Sciences* 6: 392–412.

Sperber, D. and D. Wilson. 1986. *Relevance.* Oxford: Blackwell.

Spiro, R., P. Feltovitch, R. Coulson, and D. Anderson. 1989. 'Multiple analogies for complex concepts: Antidotes for analogy-induced misconception in advanced knowledge acquisition' in S. Vosniadou and A. Ortony (eds.). *Similarity and Analogical Reasoning.* Cambridge: Cambridge University Press.

Spivey, M. 2007. *The Continuity of Mind.* Oxford: Oxford University Press.

Spolsky, B. 1989. *Conditions for Second Language Learning.* Oxford: Oxford University Press.

Stauble, A. and D. Larsen-Freeman. 1978. 'The use of variable rules in describing the interlanguage of second language learners'. *Workpapers in TESL*, UCLA, Vol. 12.

Steels, L. 1996. 'Emergent adaptive lexicons' in P. Maes, M. Mataric, J-A. Meyer, J. Pollack, and S.W. Wilson (eds.). *From Animals to Animats 4: Proceedings of the Fourth International Conference on Simulation of Adaptive Behavior.* Cambridge, MA: The MIT Press.

Steels, L. 2005. 'The emergence and evolution of linguistic structure: From lexical to grammatical communication systems'. *Connection Science* 17: 213–30.

Stefanowitsch, A. and S. Gries. 2003. 'Collostructions: Investigating the interaction of words and constructions.' *International Journal of Corpus Linguistics* 8: 209–43.

Stevick, E. 1996. *Memory, Meaning, and Method.* 2nd edition. Boston, MA: Heinle/Thomson.

Stewart, I. 1989. *Does God Play Dice?* London: Penguin Books.

Stewart, I. 1998. *Life's Other Secret.* London: Penguin Books.

Swain, M. and S. Lapkin. 1998. 'Interaction and second language learning in two adolescent French immersion students working together'. *The Modern Language Journal* 82/3: 320–37.

Swales, J. 1990. *Genre Analysis.* Cambridge: Cambridge University Press.

Tarone, E. 1982. 'Systematicity and attention in interlanguage'. *Language Learning* 32/1: 69–84.

Tarone, E. 1990. 'On variation in interlanguage: A response to Gregg'. *Applied Linguistics* 11/4: 392–400.

Tarone. E. and G-Q. Liu. 1995. 'Situational context, variation, and second language acquisition theory' in G. Cook and B. Seidlhofer (eds.). *Principle and Practice in Applied Linguistics.* Oxford: Oxford University Press.

Taylor, J. 1998. 'Syntactic constructions as prototype categories' in M. Tomasello (ed.). *The New Psychology of Language.* Mahwah, NJ: Lawrence Erlbaum Associates.

Taylor, J. 2004. 'The ecology of constructions' in G. Radden and K-U. Panther. (eds.). *Studies in Linguistic Motivation.* Berlin: de Gruyter.

Thelen, E. 1995. 'Time-scale dynamics and the development of an embodied cognition' in R. Port and T. van Gelder (eds.). *Mind as Motion: Explorations in the Dynamics of Cognition.* Cambridge, MA: The MIT Press.

Thelen, E. and E. Bates. 2003. 'Connectionism and dynamic systems: Are they really different?' *Developmental Science* 6: 378–91.

Thelen, E. and D. Corbetta. 2002. 'Microdevelopment and dynamic systems: Applications to infant motor development' in N. Granott and J. Parziale (eds.). *Microdevelopment*. Cambridge: Cambridge University Press.

Thelen, E., G. Schöner, C. Scheier, and L. Smith. 2001. 'The dynamics of embodiment: A field theory of infant perseverative reaching'. *Behavioral and Brain Sciences* 24: 1–86.

Thelen, E. and L. Smith. 1994. *A Dynamic Systems Approach to the Development of Cognition and Action*. Cambridge, MA: The MIT Press.

Thelen, E. and L. Smith. 1998. 'Dynamic systems theories' in W. Damon and R. Bidell (eds.). *Dynamic Development of Psychological Structures in Action and Thought*, Volume 1. New York: John Wiley and Sons.

Thom, R. 1972. *Stabilité Structurelle et Morphogenèse*. New York: Benjamin (also Paris: Intereditions, 1977).

Thom, R. 1983. *Mathematical Models of Morphogenesis*. Chichester, England: Ellis Horwood.

Thompson, E. and F. Varela. 2001. 'Radical embodiment: Neural dynamics and consciousness'. *Trends in Cognitive Science* 5: 418–25.

Thompson, G. and S. Hunston (eds.). 2006. *System and Corpus: Exploring Connections*. London: Equinox.

Thompson, S. and P. Hopper. 2001. 'Transitivity, clause and argument structure' in J. Bybee and P. Hopper (eds.). *Frequency and the Emergence of Linguistic Structure*. Amsterdam/Philadelphia: John Benjamins.

Tomasello, M. 1999. *The Cultural Origins of Human Cognition*. Cambridge, MA: Harvard University Press.

Tomasello, M. 2000. 'First steps toward a usage-based theory of language acquisition'. *Cognitive Linguistics* 11: 61–82.

Tomasello, M. 2003. *Constructing a Language*. Cambridge, MA: Harvard University Press.

Toolan, M. 1996. *Total Speech: An Integrational Approach to Language*. Durham, NC: Duke University Press.

Toolan, M. 2003. 'An integrational linguistic view' in J. Leather and J. van Dam (eds.). *Ecology of Language Acquisition*. Dordrecht: Kluwer Academic Publishers.

Trofimovich, P., E. Gatbonton, and N. Segalowitz. 2007. 'A dynamic look at L2 phonological learning'. *Studies in Second Language Acquisition* 29/3: 407–48.

Truscott, J. 1998. 'Instance theory and Universal Grammar in second language research'. *Second Language Research* 14: 257–91.

Tucker, M. and K. Hirsch-Pasek. 1993. 'Systems and language: Implications for acquisition' in L. Smith and E. Thelen (eds.). *A Dynamic Systems Approach to Development: Applications*. Cambridge, MA: The MIT Press.

Turner, F. 1997. 'Foreword' in R. Eve, S. Horsfall, and M. Lee (eds.). *Chaos, Complexity, and Sociology: Myths, Models, and Theories*. Thousand Oaks, CA: Sage.

Ushioda, E. 2007. 'A person-in-context relational view of emergent motivation, self and identity'. Paper presented at the American Association for Applied Linguistics Colloquium: Individual Differences, Language Identity and the L2 Self. Costa Mesa, California, April.

van Dijk, M. 2003. 'Child language cuts capers: Variability and ambiguity in early child development'. Unpublished Ph.D. thesis. University of Gröningen.

van Geert, P. 1991. 'A dynamic systems model of cognitive and language growth'. *Psychological Review* 98: 3–53.

van Geert, P. 1994. 'Vygotskyan dynamics of development'. *Human Development* 37: 346–65.

van Geert, P. 2003. 'Dynamic systems approaches and modeling of developmental processes' in J. Valsiner and K. Connolly (eds.). *Handbook of Developmental Psychology*. London: Sage.

van Geert, P. 2007. 'Dynamic systems in second language learning: Some general methodological reflections'. *Bilingualism: Language and Cognition* 10: 47–9.

van Geert, P. Forthcoming. 'The dynamic systems approach in the study of L1 and L2 acquisition: An introduction' in K. de Bot (ed.). Special issue of *The Modern Language Journal* on research in dynamic systems.

van Geert, P. and H. Steenbeek. 2005. 'Explaining "after" by "before": Basic aspects of a dynamic systems approach to the study of development'. *Developmental Review* 25: 408–42.

van Geert, P. and H. Steenbeek. In press. 'A complexity and dynamic systems approach to development assessment, modeling and research' in K. Fischer, A. Battro, and P. Léna (eds.). *The Educated Brain*. Cambridge: Cambridge University Press.

van Geert, P. and M. van Dijk. 2002. 'Focus on variability: New tools to study intra-individual variability in developmental data'. *Infant Behavior and Development* 25: 340–74.

van Gelder, T. and R. Port. 1995. 'It's about time: An overview of the dynamical approach to cognition' in R. Port and T. van Gelder (eds.). *Mind as Motion: Explorations in the Dynamics of Cognition*. Cambridge, MA: The MIT Press.

van Lier, L. 1988. *The Classroom and the Language Learner*. London: Longman.

van Lier, L. 1996. *Interaction in the Language Curriculum*. London: Longman.

van Lier, L. 2000. 'From input to affordances' in J. Lantolf (ed.). *Sociocultural Theory and Second Language Learning*. Oxford: Oxford University Press.

van Lier, L. 2004. *The Ecology and Semiotics of Language Learning: A Sociocultural Perspective*. Boston, MA: Kluwer.

Varela, F., E. Thompson, and E. Rosch. 1991. *The Embodied Mind: Cognitive Science and Human Experience*. Cambridge, MA: The MIT Press.

Verschueren, J. 1999. *Understanding Pragmatics*. London: Arnold.

von Bertalanffy, L. 1950. 'An outline for general systems theory'. *British Journal for the Philosophy of Science* 12/1: 134–65.

von Neumann, J. 1958. *The Computer and the Brain*. New Haven, CT: Yale University Press.

Vygotsky, L. S. 1962. *Thought and Language*. Cambridge, MA: The MIT Press.

Waddington, C. H. 1940. *Organisers and Genes*. Cambridge: Cambridge University Press.

Waldrop, M. 1992. *Complexity: The Emerging Science at the Edge of Order and Chaos*. New York: Simon and Schuster.

Wardhaugh, R. 1986. *An Introduction to Sociolinguistics*. New York: Basil Blackwell.

Watanabe, Y. and M. Swain. 2007. 'Effects of proficiency differences and patterns of pair interactions on second language learning: Collaborative dialogue between adult ESL learners'. *Language Teaching Research* 11: 121–42.

Wegirif, R. Forthcoming. *Dialogic, Education and Technology: Expanding the Space of Learning*. New York: Springer-Verlag.

Wegner, D. and T. Wheatley. 1999. 'Apparent mental causation: Sources of the experience of will'. *American Psychologist* 54: 480–92.

Weiner, J. 1995. *The Beak of the Finch: The Story of Evolution in our Time*. New York: Vintage Books.

Weinreich, U., W. Labov, and M. Herzog. 1968. 'Empirical foundations for a theory of language change' in W. P. Lehmann and Y. Malkeil (eds.). *Directions for Historical Linguistics: A Symposium*. Austin, TX: University of Texas Press.

Wertsch, J. 1998. *Mind as Action*. New York: Oxford University Press.

White, L. 2003. *Second Language Acquisition and Universal Grammar*. Cambridge: Cambridge University Press.

Whitehead, A. N. 1929. *The Aims of Education*. New York: Macmillan.

Widdowson, H. G. 1989. 'Knowledge of language and ability for use'. *Applied Linguistics* 10/2: 128–37.

Widdowson, H. G. 2003. *Defining Issues in English Language Teaching*. Oxford: Oxford University Press.

Wiener, N. 1948. *Cybernetics or Control and Communication in the Animal and the Machine*. New York: John Wiley and Sons.

Willett, J. B. 1994. 'Measuring change more effectively by modeling individual growth' in T. Husen and T. N. Postlethwaite (eds.). *The International Encyclopaedia of Education*. Oxford: Pergamon Press.

Willis, D. 1990. *The Lexical Syllabus*. London: Collins COBUILD.

Wilson, A. 2000. *Complex Spatial Systems*. Harlow: Pearson Education.

Winter, D. 1994. 'Sacred geometry.' A video produced by Crystal Hill, Eden, New York.

Wittgenstein, L. 1953/2001. *Philosophical Investigations*. Oxford: Blackwell.

Wolfe-Quintero, K., S. Inagaki, and H-Y. Kim. 1998. *Second Language Development in Writing: Measures of Fluency, Accuracy, and Complexity*. Honolulu, HI: University of Hawai'i Press.

Wray, A. 2002. *Formulaic Language and the Lexicon*. Cambridge: Cambridge University Press.

Yule, G. 1996. *Pragmatics*. Oxford: Oxford University Press.

Zee, E. 1999. 'Change and variation in the syllable-initial and syllable-final consonants in Hong Kong Cantonese'. *Journal of Chinese Linguistics* 27/1: 120–67.

Zipf, G. K. 1935. *The Psycho-biology of Language*. Boston, MA: Houghton Mifflin.

Zipf, G. K. 1949. *Human Behavior and the Principle of Least Effort: An Introduction to Human Ecology*. 1972 Facsimile of the 1949 edition: New York: Hafner Publishing Company.

Index